IN HITLER'S MUNICH

In Hitler's Munich

JEWS, THE REVOLUTION, AND THE RISE OF NAZISM

MICHAEL BRENNER

TRANSLATED BY
JEREMIAH RIEMER

PRINCETON UNIVERSITY PRESS

PRINCETON & OXFORD

Published by Princeton University Press
41 William Street, Princeton, New Jersey 08540
99 Banbury Road, Oxford OX2 6JX

press.princeton.edu

Library of Congress Cataloging-in-Publication Data

Names: Brenner, Michael, 1964– author. | Riemer, Jeremiah, 1952– translator.
Title: In Hitler's Munich : Jews, the revolution, and the rise of Nazism / Michael Brenner ; translated by Jeremiah Riemer.
Other titles: Der lange Schatten der Revolution. English | Jews, the revolution, and the rise of Nazism
Description: Princeton : Princeton University Press, [2022] | Original title "Der lange Schatten der Revolution: Juden und Antisemiten in Hitlers München, 1918–1923" published by Jüdischer Verlag im Suhrkamp Verlag, 2019—Publisher. | Includes bibliographical references and index.
Identifiers: LCCN 2021018403 (print) | LCCN 2021018404 (ebook) | ISBN 9780691191034 (hardback) | ISBN 9780691205410 (e-book)
Subjects: LCSH: Jews—Political activity—Germany—Munich—History—20th century. | Antisemitism—Germany—Munich—History—20th century | Munich (Germany)—History—20th century | National socialism—Germany Munich. | Germany—History—Revolution, 1918—Influence. | Soviet Union—History—Revolution, 1917–1921—Influence. | Eisner, Kurt, 1867–1919.
Classification: LCC DS134.36.M86 B738 2022 (print) | LCC DS134.36.M86 (ebook) | DDC 943/.364004924009042—dc23
LC record available at https://lccn.loc.gov/2021018403
LC ebook record available at https://lccn.loc.gov/2021018404

British Library Cataloging-in-Publication Data is available

Editorial: Priya Nelson, Thalia Leaf, and Barbara Shi
Production Editorial: Mark Bellis
Jacket Design: Karl Spurzem
Production: Danielle Amatucci
Publicity: Alyssa Sanford and Kathryn Stevens
Copyeditor: Cynthia Buck

Jacket Credit: Meeting of the NSDAP in the Bürgerbräukeller, Munich, ca. 1923 / German Federal Archives (Bundesarchiv)

This book has been composed in Arno

Printed on acid-free paper. ∞

Printed in the United States of America

10 9 8 7 6 5 4 3 2 1

To the memory of my mother Henny Brenner, 1924–2020

CONTENTS

WHEN I BEGAN writing this book about the period following the First
World War in Bavaria, I did not foresee that it would become relevant
to events happening in the United States of America one hundred years
later. Obviously, the numerous differences between interwar Germany
and the insurrection at the US Capitol on January 6, 2021, stand out
more starkly than the similarities. The instigators of the Beer Hall
Putsch in Munich did not support a president who had been voted out
of office. They did not gather in front of the nation's seat of power. Instead, they started their rally in a beer cellar in the Bavarian capital
where a young Adolf Hitler seized control after silencing the politicians
and the crowd assembled there with a pistol shot into the ceiling. But
despite these and other differences, Germany during the 1920s offers
crucial lessons for us today about how democracies become imperiled.[1]
History never repeats itself, but in this case it does rhyme. The German
example warns us that knocking down an insurrection does not mean
the fight for democracy has been won yet.

For a fuller understanding of the attack on Germany's still young
democracy, it is crucial to tell the story from its beginning. It is a multi-
layered story of Jewish revolutionaries, antisemitic conspiracy theories,
a frightened Jewish community, and the rise of the Nazi movement. It
is also the story of an unknown soldier returning from the First World
War who was without employment and in search of a mission. Adolf
Hitler would soon become not only the focus of the new extreme right-
wing forces in Weimar Germany but also the dominant political figure
in Munich. The political upstart had left such a strong imprint on the
Bavarian capital that in the summer of 1923 Germany's foremost

novelist, Munich resident Thomas Mann, called Munich "the city of Hitler."[2]

The failure of his Beer Hall Putsch a few months later would temporarily propel Hitler away from the public eye, but after a year in prison, where he wrote his programmatic *Mein Kampf*, he was back in action and relaunching his political career. Munich during the early 1920s had served him well as an ideal laboratory for his future role as Reich chancellor in Berlin starting in January 1933. By 1923, he had realized that antisemitism would facilitate and not impede the rise of his new political movement.

This book is not yet another study about Hitler. It is the first work to place at its center the people who would become the actual targets of his emerging movement: the Jewish revolutionaries in Munich and the local Jewish community. The Jews in Hitler's Munich of the early 1920s paid the price for the failed left-wing revolution and served as a foil for the right-wing revolution to come. They were the first victims on Hitler's long and twisted road to power.

IN HITLER'S MUNICH

1

A Change of Perspective

A very fine theme, the revolution and the Jews. Make sure to treat the
leading part the Jews have played in the upheaval.[1]

— GUSTAV LANDAUER TO MARTIN BUBER,
NOVEMBER 2, 1918

"The Whole Thing, an Unspeakable Jewish Tragedy"

February 26, 1919, marked a unique moment in the history of Germany
and its Jews. On this cold winter's day, a crowd of one hundred thousand assembled at Munich's Ostfriedhof cemetery to mourn Bavarian
prime minister Kurt Eisner, the first Jewish head of state in German
history. Eisner had toppled the Wittelsbach dynasty, which had reigned
in Bavaria for seven centuries. He and his socialist government had
ruled Bavaria for three months until he was assassinated by a right-wing
extremist. Another German Jew, Gustav Landauer, who would himself
assume a powerful position in one of two short-lived council republics
established in Munich in April 1919, delivered the eulogy for his friend
Eisner. Both had long since broken with the Jewish religion of their
ancestors, and yet both identified with the values of Jewish tradition as
they defined it. Standing before the casket of his murdered friend, Landauer told the crowd: "Kurt Eisner, the Jew, was a prophet because he
sympathized with the poor and downtrodden and saw the opportunity,
and the necessity, of putting an end to poverty and subjugation."[2]

Kurt Eisner the Jew. Usually only his enemies rubbed his nose in his Jewish background. His estate includes a huge file of letters with crude antisemitic insults. Landauer, like other revolutionaries, also became the target of antisemitic attacks and was gruesomely murdered when the socialist experiment was brought to an end by paramilitary forces in the first days of May 1919. Even among the Jews themselves, the Jewish background of many revolutionaries was a fiercely debated topic. The majority of Bavaria's Jews were decisively opposed to the revolution or sensed that, in the end, they would be the ones paying the price for the deeds of the Eisners and Landauers. The philosopher Martin Buber, a close friend of Landauer's and an admirer of Eisner, had visited Munich at Landauer's invitation in February 1919. He left Munich on the day Eisner was murdered and summarized his impressions of his visit to the city as follows: "As for Eisner, to be with him was to peer into the tormented passions of his divided Jewish soul; nemesis shone from his glittering surface; he was a marked man. Landauer, by dint of the greatest spiritual effort, was keeping up his faith in him and protected him—a shield-bearer terribly moving in his selflessness. The whole thing, an unspeakable Jewish tragedy."[3]

Not long before that, on December 2, 1918, Landauer was still urging Buber to write about these very aspects: "Dear Buber, A very fine theme, the revolution and the Jews. Make sure to treat the leading part the Jews have played in the upheaval."[4] To this day, Landauer's wish has not been fulfilled. While the connection between Jews and the Bavarian revolution has certainly been broached again and again, it has ultimately been relegated to a footnote in most historical accounts. Even in the flood of new publications occasioned by the centenary of the revolution, historians and journalists are reticent to point out that the most prominent actors in the revolution and the two council republics were of Jewish descent.[5] Biographies of the chief actors emphasize that their subjects had stopped viewing themselves as Jews.[6]

The reason for the reticence is obvious. As a rule, one skates on slippery ice when researching the Jews and their participation in socialism, communism, and revolutionary movements. The ice becomes very slippery indeed when dealing with a place that, so soon after the events of

FIGURE 1. Gustav Landauer in the middle of a crowd at Kurt Eisner's burial at Munich's Ostfriedhof cemetery. Süddeutsche Zeitung Photo.

the revolution, became the laboratory for Adolf Hitler and his National Socialist movement. After all, it was mainly the antisemites who highlighted the prominence of Jews in this revolution to justify their own anti-Jewish behavior.[7] In *Mein Kampf*, Hitler himself entitled the chapter about the period when he was active in Munich after November 1918, "Beginning of My Political Activity." He drew a direct line between what he called "the rule of the Jews" and his political awakening.[8]

In conservative circles the motif of a link between Jews and leftists served, if not as a justification, then certainly in many cases as an explanatory framework for antisemitism. Thus, Golo Mann, son of the writer Thomas Mann and himself a witness to the revolutionary events in the city as a high school pupil, referred explicitly to the Munich episode: "Not Jewry—there is no such thing—but individual people of Jewish extraction have, through their revolutionary experiments in politics in Central Europe, burdened themselves with serious blame. For example, there was the attempt to set up a council regime that was unquestionably made by Jews in the spring of 1919 in Munich, and that was indeed a criminal, horrible mischief that could not and would not end well." There were certainly "noble human beings," such as Gustav Landauer, among those revolutionaries, Golo Mann concluded. "Yet we as historians cannot ignore the radical-revolutionary impact of Jewry with a gesture of disavowal. It had serious consequences, it fed the view according to which Jewry was revolutionary, insurrectionary, and subversive in its totality or overwhelmingly."[9] An even sharper formulation of the same sentiment came immediately after the Second World War from the historian Friedrich Meinecke in his book *The German Catastrophe*: "Many Jews were among those who raised the chalice of opportunistic power to their lips far too quickly and greedily. They now appeared to all anti-Semites as the beneficiaries of the German defeat and revolution."[10]

For many contemporary witnesses as well as subsequent interpreters of these events, there was a clear causality: the conspicuous prominence of Jewish revolutionaries (most of whom, moreover, were not from Bavaria) prompted a reaction that created a space for antisemitic agitation to an unprecedented degree. Jewish contemporaries claimed to have recognized the link as much as antisemites did. From the vantage point of 1933, even revolutionaries referred to this connection, albeit from another perspective: On "the day my books were burned in Germany," Ernst Toller wrote in the preface to his autobiography *I Was a German*: "Before the current debacle in Germany can be properly understood, one must first know something of those happenings in 1918 and 1919 which I have recorded here."[11]

One fundamental principle of historical analysis is to reject predetermined thinking.[12] By no means did the events between 1918 and 1923 lead inevitably to the events of 1933. Yet even historians cannot simply omit their knowledge about what happened in 1933 and the years that followed. A history of the 1918–1919 revolution and the counterrevolution in Munich as it might have been written in 1930 would inevitably have produced different results than a history written after 1945, not because the course of historical events had been changed in any way retroactively, but rather because our viewpoint had shifted and other questions had been posed in the interim. Had Hitler not been appointed chancellor in 1933, the events taking place between 1918 and 1923 would certainly have remained a marginal episode in Germany history. Yet in seeking explanation for the central event in German history in the twentieth century, we must turn to the historical moment when Hitler developed the core of his subsequent worldview.

Historians agree that we have no record of antisemitic or anti-Communist views from Hitler before 1919. But opinions diverge on whether he went through an initially socialist phase in the first half of 1919 or was rejected by another party, and whether he was already interested in politics or still apolitical.[13] Anton Joachimsthaler was one of the first historians to draw attention to the importance of this phase for the formation of Hitler's worldview. He stated categorically: "The key to Hitler's entry into politics lies in this period of time in Munich, not in Vienna! The revolution and the reign of the councils that followed, events that profoundly shook the city of Munich and its people, triggered Hitler's hatred of everything foreign and international as well as of Bolshevism."[14] In Andreas Wirsching's view, the special climate of Bavaria in the summer of 1919 provided Hitler with a stage to rehearse a new role in his search for authenticity: "What he learned by rote, amplified, and intensified demagogically, and what he also ended up believing, was initially nothing more than the kind of völkisch-nationalist, anti-Bolshevik, and antisemitic propaganda that was ubiquitous in Bavaria and its army. . . . What turned Hitler first into the drummer and then the 'Führer' he became, then, was by no means an idea, a firmly established, granitic worldview. Rather, he found his stage and the role that fit in with this rather more by accident."[15] It is not the aim of this book to revisit once again the questions about Hitler's worldview and his role in the political events of the ensuing years, but rather to illuminate the stage on which the young Adolf Hitler tested out his new role.

We must be vigilant in recognizing that only knowledge about subsequent events allows us to assess Munich as a stage for Hitler and as the ideal laboratory for the growing National Socialist movement. To suggest that Hitler and other antisemites really needed Jewish revolutionaries in order to spread their ideology may be to encourage the argument that, in the end, the Jews themselves were to blame for their misfortune. Without a Leon Trotsky and a Rosa Luxemburg, without a Gustav Landauer and an Eugen Leviné, Hitler's antisemitic picture of the world would perhaps have lacked the image of the "Judeo-Bolshevik." But his worldview might have still included stereotypes of Jews as war profiteers, usurers, and capitalists, as Christ killers and unbelievers. Would these shifts in Hitler's worldview have made a difference in the astonishing success story of antisemitic movements? We can only speculate about the answer to this question.

Historians cannot act as if the Jewish revolutionaries, socialists, and anarchists never existed—as if their prominence during this brief moment of German history was not there for all to see, and as if they were denying their Jewishness—just because these arguments may have been used in the past and are revived in today's antisemitic propaganda. Let us try for a moment to turn the tables in our thinking about this: if subsequent history had turned out differently, we would have been able to regard this chapter as a success story for German Jews, as an episode of pride rather than of shame. Let us take a moment to imagine that Kurt Eisner's revolution took root in Bavaria, that the Weimar Republic survived, and that Walther Rathenau remained foreign minister instead of being murdered.[16] We would then write a history of successful German-Jewish emancipation in which the Jewish origins of some of Germany's leading politicians did not stand in the way of their political advancement, a story reflecting what actually happened in Italy and France. This was the very hope articulated by some Jewish contemporaries for a brief moment in November 1918. In their minds, the fact that Kurt Eisner became the first Jewish prime minister of a German state constituted proof of successful integration. Yet this perception was quickly overturned, and when Martin Buber spoke of a Jewish tragedy in February 1919, he echoed an opinion already shared by the larger Jewish public.

This book is not counterfactual history. It is also not another summary of these years, for which we have plenty of cogently presented studies.[17] Instead, this book rests on a change of perspective. It brings out those aspects of this story customarily left out of previous scholarship and places them more firmly in the context of Jewish history. From this perspective, too, the events that played out in Munich between 1918 and 1923 acquire more than merely local or regional significance. The questions pursued in the following chapters are: What was the relationship of the Jewish revolutionaries to their Jewishness, and how did it shape them? How did the larger society and the Jewish community react to what they did? How was the city of Munich, widely regarded as a cozy hometown only a short time before, transformed within a few years into enemy territory?

The book deliberately opens by quoting a letter to Martin Buber. On his visit to Munich in February 1919, the most influential German-Jewish philosopher of his generation, and of the entire twentieth century, saw firsthand the full scale of what only a few of his contemporaries recognized: the Jewish dimension of what was happening. Buber had met Eisner, and he was familiar with the literary work of the other Jewish revolutionaries: Erich Mühsam's poems, Ernst Toller's plays, and Gustav Landauer's theoretical writings and translations. In addition, Landauer had contributed several articles to Buber's journal *Der Jude*. Buber could foresee no good coming out of these Jewish intellectuals' decision to become central actors on Bavaria's political stage. When he called "the whole thing, an unspeakable Jewish tragedy," this self-consciously Zionist thinker had more in mind than just the intra-Jewish fissures and the murder of Eisner. He was also thinking of the invisible wall that had opened up between the Jewish revolutionaries and their Bavarian-Catholic surroundings. Buber knew this environment better than many of those taking part in the Munich revolution; after all, his wife, Paula Winkler, was from a Catholic family from Munich.[18]

Buber's role in the German-Jewish philosophy of his time perpetuated that of Hermann Cohen in the previous generation. Just as Buber influenced Landauer, Cohen had played an important role in shaping Kurt Eisner's thinking. Eisner himself characterized the neo-Kantian philosopher from the University of Marburg as the only person who exercised "intellectual influence on my innermost being."[19] To explore Eisner and Landauer without Cohen and Buber would be like reading Marx without Hegel.

Although the Jewish background of the Munich revolution's protagonists did not necessarily play a central role in their self-perception, it
figured in their complex personalities and reflections, and it was also
used by outsiders to reproach them. Even if they had dissolved their
formal ties to the Jewish religious community, their Jewish heritage was
by no means just a burdensome birth defect to them—in contrast, say,
to how Rosa Luxemburg or Leon Trotsky viewed their Jewishness. Previous historical research has largely overlooked this factor, because antisemites later latched onto the events of 1918–1919 so obsessively. If the
revolutionaries really regarded themselves as "Jews" and not just as having a "Jewish background," then antisemites might possibly have a legitimate argument, according to a line of argument already articulated
by a number of their Jewish contemporaries who sought to distance
themselves from the revolutionaries.[20]

So were they really Jews? In what is widely regarded as a classic contribution to our understanding of the modern Jewish experience, the
Trotsky biographer Isaac Deutscher has closely examined the figure of
the "non-Jewish Jew" and, in so doing, traced the tradition that emerged
in Judaism of the Jewish heretic. With a view toward Spinoza, Marx,
Heine, Luxemburg, and Trotsky, he wrote: "They were each in society
and yet not in it, of it and yet not of it. It was this that enabled them to
rise in thought above their societies, above their nations, above their
times and generations, and to strike out mentally into wide new hori-
zons and far into the future."[21] The same could be said of most of the
Munich revolutionaries. They were not part of the organized Jewish
community, and most of them did not have any kind of positive relationship with the Jewish religion or with religion in general. Yet, in contrast to Deutscher's non-Jewish Jews, some of them evinced an active
interest in their cultural Jewish heritage, as will be shown in the next
chapter. Like Sigmund Freud, they were "godless Jews"—Jews whose
Jewishness could not be unambiguously defined in terms like religion,
nation, or even race.[22] It was this very ambiguity that, as the sociologist
Zygmunt Bauman has observed, was one of the reasons why Jews ran
up against enormous resistance in the new international system of European states that emerged after the First World War, with its notion of

clear definitions of nations. Precisely because these Jews were not recognizable as the "others"—given the way they spoke and their general appearance—they came to be regarded as especially dangerous enemies in the eyes of their opponents.[23]

Historians, past and present, have speculated about why a relatively large number of Jews—Leon Trotsky, Lev Kamenev, and Grigory Zinoviev in St. Petersburg, Béla Kun in Budapest, and Rosa Luxemburg in Berlin—occupied leading roles in the revolutionary events of Europe during the period of upheaval between 1917 and 1920. They have found different answers to this question.[24] Some scholars fall back on the conditions of earlier Jewish life to explain the high level of Jewish participation in these revolutionary movements. In the Czarist Empire, where most Jews lived, they were systematically oppressed and could not actively participate in politics. Many discovered in socialism an opportunity to escape their own desperate situation. In Germany, even before that Jews could participate in politics since the establishment of legal equality in 1871, and they were represented in legislative bodies. Yet only in the left-liberal and leftist camps did they find what appeared to be full acceptance. For this reason, most Jewish deputies in the Reichstag before the First World War were Social Democrats, although the vast majority of Jewish voters voted for centrist bourgeois parties.[25]

Even earlier, to be sure, starting with Karl Marx (whose anti-Jewish statements were well known) and Ferdinand Lassalle, numerous pioneers of the labor movement had a Jewish background. The secularization of the Messianic tradition, so deeply rooted in the Jewish tradition, and the aspiration to justice associated with the biblical prophets, not only for Jews but also for other disadvantaged social groups, was an additional reason for the commitment of many Jews to revolutionary concerns.[26] To the historian Saul Friedländer it seems "that the activities of Jewish revolutionaries in Germany were based on an unquestionably naive, but very humane idealism—a sort of secular Messianism, as if the revolution could bring deliverance from all sufferings. Many also believed that the Jewish question would disappear with the victory of the revolution."[27] Gershom Scholem saw in anarchism—more than he did in Zionism—the realization of a Messianic utopia: "There is an anarchic element in the very nature of Messianic utopianism; the dissolution of old ties which lose their meaning in the new context of Messianic freedom."[28] With respect to the German-Jewish revolutionaries, one may also join George Mosse in invoking the transformation of the German-Jewish *Bildungsbürgertum*—the educated middle class—in the direction of a radical political universalism.[29] Moreover, solidarity with the international workers' movement offered the prospect of a homeland beyond the community of nations that often rejected Jews as rootless.[30] Finally, there was their willingness "to show solidarity with the stigmatized class of the proletariat, since as intellectuals they had suffered from the social stigma of their background."[31]

None of these motives should be glossed over. Yet we must be leery of looking for a single explanation that was decisive for all of the Jewish revolutionaries active in Munich and beyond. Whatever reasons propelled individuals to action, it is indisputable that neither before nor afterward in Germany had so many Jewish politicians stood in the public limelight as during the half year between November 1918 and May 1919. In Germany, the appearance of a Jewish prime minister and of Jewish cabinet ministers and people's commissars was especially conspicuous because, in contrast to other European countries like Italy and France, Jews had not been entrusted with any governmental responsibilities in the period prior to the First World War.[32] "Until November 1918 the German public had only known Jews as members of parliament and party functionaries, or as members of municipal councils. Now, suddenly, they were showing up in leading government posts, sitting at Bismarck's desk, determining the fate of the nation."[33] In 1919, however, contemporaries could not overlook what Rudolf Kayser, the literary historian, unequivocally articulated in the journal *Neue Jüdische Monatshefte*: "No matter how excessively this is exaggerated by antisemites or anxiously denied by the Jewish bourgeoisie: it is certain that that the Jewish share in the contemporary revolutionary movement is large; it is, at any rate, so large that it cannot be the product of any accident, but must have been dictated by an inherent tendency; it is a repercussion of the Jewish character in a modern-political direction."[34]

In Berlin too, during this time, Jewish politicians, such as Kurt Rosenfeld as head of the Justice Ministry and Hugo Simon as finance minister,
had governmental responsibilities, and in Paul Hirsch there was even a
Jewish prime minister in Prussia for a brief time. Yet in no city was the
participation of Jews in the revolutionary events as pronounced as in
Munich.[35] There great numbers of people of Jewish background stood
among the most prominent exponents of the revolution and the council
republics. In addition to Eisner, these included his private secretary,
Felix Fechenbach, and the finance minister, Edgar Jaffé (already baptized at a young age), as well as Landauer's comrades in arms in the First
Council Republic, Ernst Toller, Erich Mühsam, Otto Neurath, and Arnold Wadler. The mastermind of the Second Council Republic was the
Russian-born Communist Eugen Leviné. There were other Russian
Communists active in his circle, such as Towia Axelrod and Frida Rubiner. The only city that exhibits any parallels to Munich in this respect
and at this time is Budapest. István Déak wrote that "Jews held a near
monopoly on political power in Hungary during the 133 days of the
Soviet Republic [established] in [March] 1919."[36] And as in Munich,
Budapest's Jews became scapegoats for all the crimes of the revolutionary era.[37]

Jewish Revolutionaries Do Not a
Jewish Revolution Make

Yet the other side of the coin is often forgotten. Just as Jewish revolutionaries wanted to have nothing to do with the official Jewish community,
the great majority of the Jewish community's members distanced themselves from the revolution. Subsequently, the local Jews felt like direct
victims, since they became identified with the revolution without having a hand in the matter. Many of them turned directly to Eisner or other
actors in the council republic with the aim of convincing them to resign
or at least letting them know about their disapproval. Some Jewish activists even attempted to topple the council republic. Jewish newspapers
made it unmistakably clear that their readership did not wish to be identified with any radical political position. I argue that, in addition to the

antisemites, it was members of the Munich Jewish community who objected most strenuously to the involvement of prominent Jews in the revolution. They remembered well the saying from the Russian Revolution a year earlier about Leon Trotsky (whose real name was Bronstein): "The Trotskys make the revolution, and the Bronsteins pay the price."

The spectrum of protagonists who had a Jewish family background and were involved in the Munich events of 1918–1919 covers an extremely wide range. In the following chapters, we encounter figures whose personalities could not be more different. There are the well-known names, like Kurt Eisner, his secretary Felix Fechenbach, Gustav Landauer, Ernst Toller, and Erich Mühsam, who figured prominently on the public stage as much for their literary output as for their politics. Next to them stand the Communists of the Second Council Republic, Eugen Leviné and Towia Axelrod. We also meet two prominent attorneys at the time, Philipp Löwenfeld and Max Hirschberg, who, like many other Munich Jews, favored a moderate socialism and campaigned against "communist terror."[38]

After World War I, for the first time women appeared on the stage as political activists. Although they did not figure as prominently as their male counterparts in the Bavarian revolution, some of their biographies are highly illuminating. Kurt Eisner's early comrade in arms, the Polish-born Sarah Sonja Lerch-Rabinowitz, motivated workers (both men and women) to stage a strike in January 1918 at a munitions factory. Shortly afterward, she took her own life in the Stadelheim prison in Munich. Her sister, Rahel Lydia Rabinowitz, advocated equally radical views, though as a Zionist she argued that a Jew should not assume any public office in a German state. Then there was the physician Rahel Straus, who—also as a Zionist—did not regard Jews as aliens in Germany. Frida Rubiner, in turn, played an active role as a convinced Communist during the Second Council Republic.

We will discover Orthodox Jews like the Regensburg-based editor of the *Deutsche Israelitische Zeitung*, Rabbi Seligmann Meyer, who advocated voting for the conservative Bavarian People's Party; and Commercial Counselor Siegmund Fraenkel, the chairman of the Orthodox synagogue association Ohel Jakob, who wrote a public letter distancing himself from the Jewish members of the council government. A few years later, a gang of Nazi thugs beat him up on a Munich street.

Meanwhile, there were outside observers such as Victor Klemperer, who was lecturing as an adjunct professor at the University of Munich and reporting for the *Leipziger Neueste Nachrichten*. Although he converted to Protestantism in his early years, he described with growing alarm the antisemitism of the period—just as he would later become one of the most powerful chroniclers of Nazi rule.[39] For Gershom Scholem, still called Gerhard at the time, Munich was the way station (between 1919 and 1922) on his route "from Berlin to Jerusalem," and the place where he would write his doctorate on the Kabbalistic anthology *Sefer-ha-Bahir*. That launched him on his path to becoming the most important scholar of Jewish mysticism. In Munich he also forged friendly ties with the future Nobel Prize–winning novelist Shmuel Yosef Agnon, who arrived in the city from Leipzig in the middle of the revolutionary turmoil at the beginning of April 1919, sent there by his patron, Salman Schocken, to work on a children's book in Hebrew with the illustrator Tom (Martha) Freud, a niece of Sigmund Freud.

Finally, this book incorporates a discussion of individuals whose thoughts and actions may be at least partly explained by the ways in which they distanced themselves from their own Jewish background—an attitude characterized by the philosopher Theodor Lessing, in a much-discussed book from 1930, as "Jewish self-hatred."[40] This group includes Paul Nikolaus Cossmann, editor of the *Süddeutsche Monatshefte*; Cossmann was also the crucial mind behind the city's most important daily newspaper, the *Münchner Neueste Nachrichten*, and one of the chief disseminators of the "stab in the back" legend about Germany's defeat in the First World War. Cossmann had converted to Christianity, like the Hungarian-born Ignatz Trebitsch-Lincoln, who after his roles as a Canadian missionary to Jews, English member of Parliament, and German spy, showed up in Munich in the 1920s; there he made common cause with right-wing radicals to pull the strings behind a plot aiming to establish a reactionary Alpine republic. Last but not least, mention should also be made of Eisner's murderer, Count Anton von Arco auf Valley. He hoped his crime would win him approbation from the radical right-wing Thule Society, which had excluded him because of the Jewish background of his mother, Emmy von Oppenheim.

Many of these characters were in open conflict with each other. Erich Mühsam rejected the politics of Prime Minister Kurt Eisner as too moderate. During the Second Council Republic, the pacifist Ernst Toller skirmished vehemently with the Communist Eugen Leviné, who in turn accused Toller, Mühsam, and Landauer of "complete cluelessness."[41] Eisner came from the moderate wing of Social Democracy, and he joined the Independent Social Democrats (USPD) as his rejection of the war slowly grew. Landauer's worldview was shaped by the basic tenets of anarchism, and Leviné took his marching orders from the Communist Party. These conflicts extended far beyond differences of opinion. On Palm Sunday 1919, the Social Democratic lawyer Walter Löwenfeld and Franz Guttmann, a law student, attempted to topple the council republic. In 1922, Paul Nikolaus Cossmann (as plaintiff) and Felix Fechenbach (as defendant) were on opposite sides of a trial for high treason. Frequently the political fissure cut right through the middle of families. A cousin of Ernst Toller in 1919 fought as a lieutenant of the White Guard in the right-wing militia Freikorps Epp. Erich Mühsam's siblings were Zionists, and his cousin, the writer Paul Mühsam, sharply condemned the "mass terror of the Spartacus group." The brother of Max Süßheim, the Social Democratic Landtag (the Bavarian state parliament) representative from Nuremberg, was the conservative Orientalist and Munich university lecturer Karl Süßheim, who voted in 1919 for the center-right German People's Party (DVP).[42]

The antisemitic myth of a "Jewish revolution" is therefore just as absurd as the Jewish community's defensive assertion that all the Jewish revolutionaries were no longer really Jews. No political consensus prevailed among the Jewish revolutionaries, nor in the Jewish community as a whole. All that can be established is that there was lively participation of Jewish actors on all sides, for reasons that, as previously mentioned, were hardly secretive but instead were entirely comprehensible historically. For a brief historical moment, Jews were swept onto the political stage—a position that, in turn, supplied their adversaries with ammunition against them. For the right-wing nationalists seeking explanations for Germany's defeat in the world war, the downfall of the monarchy, the shame of war guilt, and the punitive measures imposed on the country, the military defeat and the failure of the old political ruling elite were not compatible with the sense of honor upheld in these circles. So they found scapegoats for the "stab in the back" legend, according to which Germany was not defeated by external armies but by the enemy within (where they were easiest to identify): among the Jews and the leftists. If these two groups overlapped, the target was especially large.

The Good Old Days?

The writer and later Nobel Prize laureate Thomas Mann was perhaps the most prominent early observer of the transformations sweeping his adopted city. Within a few short years, Munich changed from a center of "cheerful sensuality," "artistry," and "joie de vivre" to a city decried as a "hotbed of reaction, as the seat of all stubbornness and of the obstinate refusal to accept the will of the age," a city that could only be "described as a stupid city and, indeed, as the stupidest city of all." Before the war Munich had been the liberal city, Berlin the center of reaction: "Here one was artistic, there political-economic. Here one was democratic and there feudal-militaristic. Here one enjoyed a lively humanity, while the harsh air of the world city in the north could not do without a certain misanthropy." In 1926, while writing these sentences about Munich, Mann was already "watching in sorrow" as the city had "its healthy and lively blood poisoned by antisemitic nationalism."[43] Munich native Lion Feuchtwanger made this transformation the theme of his novel *Success*. It describes the special atmosphere of Munich in the early 1920s more vividly than any history book can. "In former times," Feuchtwanger writes, "the beautiful, comfortable, well-beloved city had attracted the best brains in the Empire. How was it that all these had left now, and that all the lazy and the vicious, who could not find a home in the Empire or anywhere else, rushed, as if magically drawn, to Munich?"[44] Berliners reading Thomas Mann or Lion Feuchtwanger might have been reminded that the *Vossische Zeitung* (the liberal newspaper "of record" from Berlin) had already noted this development in October 1923: "In Imperial Germany, Munich was democratic and the asylum for all those in the north with a reputation for revolutionary notoriety and who needed to get away from the intolerance of the north German police. Now Munich has again become a German asylum site. Only now it is for the exponents of that old Prussian Junker [aristocratic] rule, against which the Bavarians earlier could not have been more up in arms."[45]

To properly assess the events of the period following the war, it is indispensable to cast at least a quick glance back at the period before. The stereotypes are clear. The era of Prince Regent Luitpold was regarded as the Bavaria of "the good old days," the world war destroyed the old order, and the revolution as well as the two short-lived council republics laid the cornerstone for the ensuing reaction.

In the popular take on the prince regent's era, this idealized image has been maintained to the present day. For the Jews as well, the world seemed to have been in order in this period—at least at first glance. One need only envisage how the Orthodox Feuchtwanger clan, after visiting the synagogue on Saturday morning and enjoying a little midday snack, made its way in the afternoon to the *Hofbräuhaus* to drink coffee or beer at the family's regular reserved table. Needless to say, since carrying money was forbidden on the Sabbath, the family had its bill put on a tab, which they paid on a weekday. Not infrequently the breaking of the fast on Yom Kippur, the Day of Atonement, ended with a liter of beer in a festival tent at Oktoberfest.[46] The beer gardens seemed tailor-made for Orthodox Jews: they could bring in their own kosher food, and the beer brewed according to the Bavarian Purity Law (hops, water, and malt were the only permissible ingredients) conformed to the Jewish dietary laws.

Munich's Jews—who, with the exception of a few families, had long since discarded their strict orthodoxy—cultivated the same Bavarian dialect as their Christian neighbors. They loved the mountains and vacationed in the summer on Bavaria's lakes. They were loyal supporters of the Wittelsbach monarchy. Jewish textile firms like the Wallach Brothers, merchants who specialized in retailing and exhibiting traditional folk costumes, pioneered the dissemination of *lederhosen* and *dirndls*. Munich Jews headed the Löwenbräu brewery and the FC Bayern München soccer club. Some were bankers and department store owners, physicians and attorneys, society ladies hosting salons, and secretaries. Others were rag dealers and beggars, East European immigrant Jewish factory workers and artisans. They were royalists and revolutionaries, religious Jews and atheists. They pointed with pride to the central synagogue in the city center, a building that defined the silhouette of the city alongside the twin domes of the Frauenkirche, as shown on many postcards. In the presence of city dignitaries, it was dedicated on September 16, 1887, in a festive ceremony. From the outside it looked like a neo-Romanesque church. Services included organ music, a regular feature of reform-oriented communities, although it also represented an affront to Jewish religious laws for the Orthodox minority. Five years later, the latter erected the smaller but equally splendid Orthodox synagogue Ohel Jakob (Jacob's Tent). The synagogue buildings reflected Munich's steadily increasing Jewish population, which had grown from two thousand in 1867 to eleven thousand in 1910.[47]

The face of the Jewish community changed after the turn of century. If the Jews arriving in Bavaria's capital before then came above all from Franconian and Swabian rural communities, seeking work and upward mobility, now they were increasingly immigrants from Eastern Europe, especially from the part of Galicia that was a province of the Habsburg Empire, a region that many Jews and non-Jews in the West regarded as the epitome of cultural backwardness. The writer Karl Emil Franzos, who grew up there, derogatorily characterized it as "Half-Asia."[48] Before the outbreak of the war, about one-quarter of the community's members were "Ostjuden" who mostly settled in the neighborhood of Isarvorstadt and were not always welcomed with open arms by their Western Jewish co-religionists.

Very few of Munich's Jews wanted anything to do with the Zionist movement founded in 1897. This became abundantly clear when Theodor Herzl announced that he planned to hold the first Zionist Congress in the city along the Isar. The city's central location and many transportation links convinced him that it was the ideal location. He had already seen to it that the invitations were printed when Munich's

FIGURE 2. The central synagogue erected in 1887 shaped the cityscape of Munich until its demolition in 1938. Stadtarchiv München.

official Jewish community signaled him in no uncertain terms that he would have to find a different venue, since Munich's Jews, like the rest of their German coreligionists, had no intention of forsaking their homeland on the Isar, Danube, or Rhine for one by the banks of the Jordan. Thus it transpired that the Swiss city of Basel, not Munich, became the birthplace of political Zionism. In Munich a small local Zionist chapter, supported mostly by recently arrived East European Jews, was formed. As elsewhere in Germany, the aim of local Zionists was not so much to emigrate to Palestine themselves as to create a national home there for the much larger Jewish population of the Czarist Empire, who were plagued by pogroms and economically impoverished.[49]

Munich's Jewish community regarded itself as part of the city but also had numerous institutions of its own, from welfare organizations to student fraternities, from the Jewish Nurses' Home to the Jewish Women's League. The most important organization politically was the local affiliate of the Central Association of German Citizens of the Jewish Faith, which was committed to intervening everywhere it saw the legal equality of Jews, guaranteed on paper since the foundation of the modern

German Empire in 1871, under threat. Along the spectrum of political parties, most Jews in Munich, like Jews elsewhere in Germany, voted for the National Liberals and Progressives. They did not find a home in the parties on the right, with their open or thinly disguised antisemitism, nor, for most, did the Social Democrats, at the time still largely a class-based party, appeal to their economic interests.

Munich's reputation as Germany's cultural center had been increasingly challenged by Berlin since the turn of the century. Yet for now Munich remained the center of numerous cultural enterprises, from the artists of the Munich Secession to the satirists and cartoonists of the journal *Simplicissimus*, from the journal *Jugend* (which owed its name to its youthful new artistic style) to the trendsetting painters of the Blue Rider group. In those years Munich was home to the writers Heinrich and Thomas Mann, to Rainer Maria Rilke and Ludwig Thoma, Frank Wedekind, and Lion Feuchtwanger. The master painters Franz von Lenbach and Franz von Stuck resided here, while the master poet Stefan George presided over his literary circle. Cultural life mostly played out in the narrow quarters of the Schwabing district. One may imagine this space—a few square kilometers between the Café Stefanie, also known as the "Café Größenwahn" ("Café Megalomania"), and the Café Luitpold, between the Alter Simpl and the cabaret Elf Scharfrichter (the "Eleven Executioners")—as the capital of German-language culture and simultaneously as a mix of provincial Bavarian Gemütlichkeit, bohemia, and avant-garde.

But for both Munich's cultural society and its Jews, the good old days were hardly as rosy as often portrayed. In spite of Jews' legal equality in the Kingdom of Bavaria since 1861, anti-Jewish sentiment had never completely disappeared. When the word "antisemitism" was coined in Germany in 1879, it represented a new, pseudo-scientific variation on hatred of Jews. Racially based, antisemitism meant that a Jew could no longer escape by converting to Christianity. In 1891, the first openly antisemitic organization, the Deutsch-Sozialer Verein, was founded in Munich. The cartographer Ludwig Wenng edited the journal of the organization, the *Deutsches Volksblatt*, with a telling subtitle: *Bayrische antisemitische Zeitschrift für Stadt und Land* (Bavarian Antisemitic

Magazine for Town and Country). Later Wenng's organization was renamed the Antisemitic People's Party (Antisemitische Volkspartei). In
Munich, as in Bavaria as a whole, the antisemitic parties remained less
successful than they were in many other parts of Germany. They hardly
got more than 1 percent of the vote. But it became clear that antisemitism had the potential to appeal more widely when Hermann Ahlwardt,
an antisemite known nationwide, attracted an audience of five thousand
to a rally in 1895. A partial success was then scored by the party now
calling itself the Christlich-Soziale Vereinigung, modeled after the party
of Vienna's mayor Karl Lueger, when it struck an electoral alliance with
the Catholic Center Party and succeeded in sending an antisemitic candidate to Munich's city council in 1905.[50] The extent of antisemitic prej-
udice in the center of society was visible on the neo-Gothic facade of
the new city hall. The Jewish pair it depicted were outfitted the way a
broad public imagined Jews: the husband with a money bag, the wife
with a jewelry box. As the historian Andreas Heusler put it, antisemitism was "the common creed on which all of the völkisch-nationalist
groups, fraternities, and sects in fin de siècle Munich could agree."[51] In
addition, just before the end of the war Munich became the center of
pan-German agitation and, as Erich Mühsam asserted, had the reputation,
in free thinking and anarchist circles, of being the city with Germany's
most reactionary police.[52]

An epoch came to an end just prior to the outbreak of the First World
War. It was symbolized by the death of the Prince Regent Luitpold. This
popular ruler was succeeded by his son Ludwig III, who was reproached
by many for having himself crowned in 1913 even though the actual incumbent on the throne, his mentally ill cousin Otto, was still alive. In
December 1914, when municipal elections took place in Munich despite
the war, the Social Democrats were able to continue expanding their
first-place spot as the strongest party. A few months later, food was ra-
tioned because of supply problems and food stamps were introduced in
the city. For residents of Munich things got even worse: as of 1916, the
only beer to be had was watered down.[53] Around this time, a peace-
minded group began to gather at the Goldener Anker inn. It was from
this group, in which not only Kurt Eisner but also his associates Ernst

Toller and Sarah Sonja Lerch-Rabinowitz were active, that the strike movement at Munich and Nuremberg munitions factories emerged in January 1918.

The outbreak of the war and Kaiser Wilhelm's commitment to a *Burgfrieden*—the wartime political truce in which there would no longer be any differences among the parties and religious denominations—also introduced an end to social barriers, though only briefly. By 1916 at the latest, when the Prussian war minister ordered a census to see how many Jews were serving in the military, a measure that also affected the Bavarian army, the distinction was reintroduced.[54] In Bavaria there was also growing disillusionment as the war dragged on. Thus, at the general assembly of the Central Association of German Citizens of the Jewish Faith in February 1917, Munich rabbi Cossmann Werner warned: "We are heading toward hard times, let us not deceive ourselves about this. National chauvinism has come alive." After America's entry into the war, the Munich merchant even predicted pogroms against Munich's Jews.[55] The Munich branch of the right-wing German Fatherland Party (Deutsche Vaterlandspartei), founded in 1917, not only propagated annexationist war aims but also positioned itself as an antisemitic party and was among the forerunners of the ultranationalist and *völkisch* (right-wing nationalist and racist) movements of the immediate postwar period. Its membership included industrialists and bourgeois intellectuals, the popular writer Ludwig Thoma, the publisher Julius Lehmann, the composer Richard Wagner's widow Cosima Wagner, and the antisemitic philosopher Houston Stewart Chamberlain, as well as the man who would later found the German Workers' Party (Deutsche Arbeiterpartei, forerunner of the Nazi Party), Anton Drexler.[56]

The "Jewish Question" Moves to Center Stage

The antisemitic excesses of the period following the war would have been unthinkable if they had not been planted on fertile ground from the outset. Anti-Jewish resentments had struck deep roots going well back into the early modern era. They repeatedly pushed to the surface, especially at times of political upheaval, such as during the restoration of the old order accompanying the anti-Jewish riots of 1819 and during the failed revolution of 1848, when thousands of petitions from all over Bavaria arrived opposing the emancipation of Jews that was envisioned. By the turn of the century, these resentments mostly proliferated underground.[57] It is no accident that they resurfaced in 1918–1919, during another tumultuous period. Eisner and his comrades did not cause antisemitism; the events associated with them merely reactivated it.

But what had fundamentally changed now was the ubiquity of the "Jewish question." It would be worthwhile to investigate systematically how rarely the word "Jew" appeared in the press before the First World War and how frequently it occurred after the war. Starting in 1919, hardly a week went by without reporting about Jews as Communists or capitalists, draft dodgers or war profiteers—or articles featuring disclaimers of such reporting. There was talk about "foreign" or "alien elements," the customary code words for Jews, alongside terms like "profiteer," "trafficker," and "black marketeer." The right-wing press held the Jews responsible for losing the war, for the revolution, and for the *Schandfrieden* (the "ignoble" or "disgraceful" peace treaty) of Versailles. But in the centrist and leftist press, too, there was constant talk about Jews: in reporting on the revolutionaries and their bloody demise; in discussions of expulsions of East European Jews; in the accounts of the murder of a Jewish cabinet minister and a member of parliament being publicly challenged; and in reporting on the beating of a Jewish merchant on the street and graffiti scrawled on synagogues.

The tone of these articles varied, sometimes against the Jews and sometimes in favor of them. Yet the frequency of the Jewish theme cannot be overlooked. In the Munich of the early 1920s, the idea took shape that the "Jewish question"—regardless of what anyone understood this to mean—was of immense importance. It made no difference that the Jews made up less than 2 percent of Munich's population. The "Jewish question" had a presence in public perceptions in Munich long before it was apprehended in the same way in other parts of the German Reich.

Before Munich became the capital of the National Socialist movement, it had already become the capital of antisemitism in Germany. It laid claim to this title in the immediate postwar era thanks to many factors: the high concentration of antisemitic groups, from the Thule Society through the Freikorps to the National Socialist German Workers' Party (NSDAP); the radical antisemitic network of ethnically German emigrants from the Baltics surrounding the later Nazi ideologue Alfred Rosenberg and his dissemination of antisemitic concoctions from the Czarist Empire;[58] the antisemitic publishing house of Julius Lehmann and newspapers like the *Völkischer Beobachter* (originally, *Münchener Beobachter*), the *Miesbacher Anzeiger* published nearby, and the paper *Auf gut deutsch* (the name meant "In Plain German") published by Hitler's mentor Dietrich Eckart; and finally, the graffiti smeared on synagogues, the desecrations of cemeteries, and the brutal attacks on Jewish citizens. Munich became the capital of antisemitism above all by the circumstance that, during the years following the First World War, antisemitism had penetrated into the center of Bavarian politics as well as into its law enforcement forces, its legal system, and its mainstream media.

There was thus no public authority capable of defusing the explosive mix concocted in Munich following the First World War. On the contrary, in the Ordnungszelle (cell of order) he created, the Bavarian prime minister and later the state commissioner general, Gustav von Kahr, saw to it that this mixture would also actually detonate. In 1920 and 1923, just a few days after he had taken office as prime minister, Kahr planned the expulsion of Jews who were not German citizens. Leading figures in Munich's police headquarters, including the chief of police, Ernst Pöhner, and the head of the political division, Wilhelm Frick, openly manifested their antisemitism and were among the earliest Nazis in the party organization. While crimes committed by people on the left were punished severely, Bavarian judges praised crimes committed by people on the right as heroic and patriotic deeds and handed out mild sentences for them. As of 1920, the most important Munich newspapers had also steered into right-wing channels. As early as June 1923, as far as Thomas Mann was concerned, Munich had already become "the city of Hitler."[59]

Hitler's failed attempt to seize power on November 9, 1923, only appeared to mark the beginning of the end for the rise of an antisemitic movement in Germany. In spite of the failure of his putsch, the marginalization of the Jewish population had been successfully tested. Identifying the revolution as a Jewish undertaking, branding Jews as draft dodgers or shirkers or war profiteers, attempting twice to deport East European Jews, and committing extreme acts of violence during the night of November 8 and early morning of November 9, 1923—collectively, these actions sent a clear signal to Munich's Jews. While the city's population continued to grow, the number of Jewish residents declined significantly between 1910 and 1933, falling from eleven thousand to nine thousand. Some of the city's most famous Jews left Munich and Bavaria, and Jewish travelers were urged to avoid Bavaria. Nobody could have known at the time that this was only the prelude to a drama that would unfold anew ten and twenty years later when what Martin Buber had called the "unspeakable Jewish tragedy" would finally acquire a name.

2

Jewish Revolutionaries in a Catholic Land

Jews are the Jacobins of our age.[1]

—JAKOB WASSERMANN, *MY LIFE AS GERMAN AND JEW*

Hanukkah 5679 (November 1918)

It was the 25th of Kislev in the year 5679, or November 18, 1918, on the secular calendar. As was happening all over the world, Munich's Jews were gathering that evening in the company of their families to light the first Hanukkah candle. They would celebrate the miracle of Jerusalem, where, according to Jewish tradition, the Temple was rededicated by the Maccabees two millennia ago after having been desecrated by Hellenic rulers.

In 5679, Hanukkah had a special meaning. It was the first Jewish holiday after the end of World War I, into which hundreds of thousands of Jewish soldiers throughout Europe had been drawn, and many of whom did not return. The war had ended, the czar and the kaiser had been toppled, and new democratic states had arisen. In Germany, Jews wanted finally to achieve not only full equality before the law but also de facto equality in society; in Eastern Europe, they were fighting as a national minority for a far-reaching cultural and legal autonomy; and in

Palestine, the new British rulers even promised Jews their own national homeland.

For Bavarian Jews, this Hanukkah represented a unique situation. For three weeks already, the new Free State of Bavaria had been headed by a prime minister, Kurt Eisner, who was the first Jew ever to govern a German state. A new Hanukkah miracle? A modern Maccabee on the banks of the Isar River? By no means! Eisner himself, so far as we know, celebrated neither Hanukkah nor any other Jewish holiday. On the contrary, a month later he would join his companion Gustav Landauer in Krumbach, a small town seventy-five miles west of Munich, to spend the Christmas holiday with their families. Similarly, the writer Erich Mühsam, who insisted that he had proclaimed the republic before Eisner and who later became an important figure in the Bavarian Council Republic (Bairische Räterepublik) alongside Landauer, was busy founding the Association of Revolutionary Internationalists during the Hanukkah festival instead of lighting candles.

Eisner, Landauer, and Mühsam all came from Jewish families, like numerous other leaders of the Bavarian revolution and the two ensuing council republics, including Eisner's private secretary, Felix Fechenbach; his finance minister, Edgar Jaffé; his comrade in arms and later cofounder of the First Council Republic, Ernst Toller; the leading thinker of the Second Council Republic, Eugen Leviné; and his Communist comrade Towia Axelrod, to name just a few of the most important figures.[2] None of them celebrated Hanukkah, and yet they were certainly aware, especially as the Christmas season approached, of the fact that they would be regarded as strangers, or at best as outsiders, in Catholic Bavaria. In his poem "Holy Night," Erich Mühsam articulated this very sense of being an outsider in ironic verse.

> There once was born in Bethlehem
> a wee child from the tribe of Shem.
> And even if it's been a while
> since in the manger that child lay,
> its birth has made the people smile
> from then until the present day.

Minister and agrarian,
Bourgeois and proletarian,
They all rejoice, each Aryan,
At this same time and wherever they're able
The birth of Christ in that cow stable.
(Except the people for whom this was fate:
It's Hanukkah they'd rather celebrate.)[3]

This chapter looks at the role of the Jewish players on all sides of these revolutionary events from the very outsider perspective suggested by Mühsam. It examines the way they positioned themselves toward the Jewish community. By no means is it suggested here that they constituted a unified political group. On the contrary: there were Social Democrats, Communists, and anarchists among the Jewish revolutionaries, and they fought each other vehemently. Many of them were closer to their non-Jewish comrades than to their fellow (often nonpracticing) Jews. And let us not forget that there were also numerous prominent non-Jewish revolutionaries and that the majority of local Jews were opponents of the revolution. Nevertheless, the guiding questions of this chapter are: What was the relationship of the Jewish revolutionaries to Judaism and Jewishness? And what influence did their background have on their political activity?

"It Has to Be My Jewish Blood That Is Incensed"—Kurt Eisner

For many in Munich, the revolution came as a surprise. It seemed unimaginable that the first German republic would emerge in, of all places, largely agrarian Bavaria, a state whose conservative-clerical government also enjoyed good relations with the Social Democratic opposition.[4] On November 7, 1918, the king went for a quiet stroll in Munich's English Garden. As the conservative *Bayerischer Kurier* reported, a mass of demonstrators marched by the state parliament, just at the moment "in which [Interior] Minister v. Brettreich was unsuspectingly speaking about the supply of potatoes."[5] Most people in Munich certainly knew about the huge demonstration at the Theresienwiese, where about sixty thousand demonstrators had gathered, as they also were familiar with other demonstrations that had taken place days earlier. Yet here, at the very site where the beer mugs clinked during Oktoberfest, they had also heard the chairman of the Majority Social Democrats (SPD), Erhard Auer, calling for cautious political reforms. Auer issued this summons to moderation before sending his followers home after they had a chance to march through the city. He wanted evolution rather than revolution, and around midnight he had paid a visit to Friedrich von Brettreich, still the incumbent interior minister. In vain he urged Brettreich to try stopping the revolution by military means while there was still time to implement the promised coalition government that included his own Social Democrats. Auer would have been content with a constitutional monarchy with proportional representation while largely containing the right-wing forces dominating the aristocratic Chamber of Imperial Councilors.[6]

But Kurt Eisner, the chair of the Independent Social Democrats (USPD), who in 1917 had split from the majority SPD over the latter's support of the war, had not gone home that night along with his followers. He appreciated the meaning of the moment on that first anniversary of the Russian Revolution. His followers marched on to the barracks, where they were joined by a mass of soldiers. "The march had begun and was not to be checked," wrote one active participant, the writer Oskar Maria Graf. "There was no resistance. The police seemed to have vanished. Inquisitive faces gazed down upon us from the many open windows in the houses. At every point fresh bands joined us, and now some were armed. Most of the people laughed and chattered, as though they were going to a fair. From time to time I turned round and looked back. It seemed that the whole town was marching."[7]

Nor was there any resistance on the part of the old governing apparatus. Eisner's followers made their way unimpeded into the royal residence. The palace administrator, Jakob Willner, noted later: "When the most sovereign gentlemen had left the residence, I shut the windows in the Royal Palace, helped extinguish the lights, and after the officiant on duty and the footman, who had no further instructions, had left, I closed all the doors and made my way to the chapel court-yard."[8] To a great extent, the revolution in Munich unfolded in beer cellars. In the Mathäserbräu brewery, the Workers', Soldiers', and Farm-ers' Councils had formed, and it was here that Kurt Eisner, in his func-tion as their chairman, proclaimed the People's State of Bavaria on the evening of November 7. With the symbolism of these sites in mind, however, the formal assumption of power by the new government did not take place in a beer cellar but in the parliament building, where the old elected officials were still in session until six in the evening. That was where Eisner, around midnight, had himself declared in a long proclamation as minister-president (equivalent to prime minister or governor) of the new republic, now also designated as the Free State of Bavaria.[9]

The pacifist Eisner had achieved the unexpected and brought about a completely bloodless revolution. Bavaria, he wanted to show the world, could accomplish what had never succeeded anywhere else: carrying out a peaceful regime change. Many residents of Munich were sleeping as the events in the Mathäserbräu brewery and the parliament building followed in rapid succession. "Munich had gone to bed as the capital of the Kingdom of Bavaria, only to wake up as the capital of the Bavarian People's State," noted Josef Hofmiller, a conservative journal-ist and respected expert on French literature, on November 9, 1918, in his diary.[10] Similarly, the Munich attorney Max Hirschberg, looking back a half year later in July 1919, wrote for an American reading public: "The people of Munich went to bed as usual on November 7, railing at the thin war-beer, and awoke astonished on November 8 as citizens of the first German democratic republic."[11]

Hardly anyone overlooked the fact that on the morning of Novem-ber 8, 1918, a socialist Jewish journalist from Berlin was governing Cath-olic Bavaria from the very rooms that had constituted the power center of the house of Wittelsbach, the ruling dynasty for seven centuries. "Red has become the dominant color of the street scene. Red flags are flutter-ing from the tower of the cathedral and the city hall, red posters instruct the population that the new rulers have declared the Wittelsbach dy-nasty as deposed, the numerous military sentinels are wearing red

FIGURE 3. Cheering soldiers on the morning of November 8, 1918, welcoming the proclamation of the republic in front of the Mathäserbräu. Bayerische Staatsbibliothek München / Bildarchiv.

armbands, red flags and standards designate the military cars, and even the sentinels' horses are wearing read headdress."[12]

It is hardly any surprise that this turn of events was met with incomprehension and rejection among the Munich bourgeoisie, whose chronicler was Hofmiller: "Bavaria is not ripe for this entire development, nor will it ever be. . . . We are not made for a republic. Monarchical feeling resides in our blood for many hundreds of years. . . . The old Bavarian wants to have someone above him, with a crown on his head and not with a top hat; someone who has a uniform and not a tuxedo; who drives to Oktoberfest in a carriage drawn by six horses and not in an automobile. The ruling house and the people have grown together for 700 years; that cannot be shoved aside from one day to the next even by the most well-meaning slogans of some journalist."[13] On November 8, Liberal Landtag deputy Ernst Müller-Meiningen was still characterizing Kurt Eisner as a "comical street character," and the revolution as a "Carnival joke."[14]

It would be hard to pin down what mattered more to Bavarians: that the new ruler was a *Preiß* (a Prussian) or a *Jud* (a Jew). That neither of these attributes mattered much to Eisner was of little interest to the public. What counted as far as Bavarians were concerned was articulated by the historian Sterling Fishman: "The full bearded Eisner spoke like a Prussian, sounded like a socialist, and looked like a Jew."[15] In his unpublished memoirs, the man who would later become Bavaria's prime minister and state commissioner, Gustav von Kahr, lamented that the Bavarian people "was letting itself be enticed and terrorized by the Prussian Jew and his clan and Prussian sailors who have descended upon the state."[16] It was of little help to Eisner that not only could he count on support from intellectuals and soldiers, but that he also marched side by side with the popular blind peasant leader Ludwig Gandorfer and, after Gandorfer's fatal car accident on November 10, 1918, with his brother Karl, and that he had included the Bavarian Peasants' League in his government.

The Romance language and literature scholar Victor Klemperer was then reporting out of Munich for the *Leipziger Neueste Nachrichten*. The rabbi's son and convert to Protestantism who would later become known for his meticulously kept diary of survival during the Third Reich depicted the enthusiasm for Eisner of the Munich population supporting the revolution. And Klemperer could not hide his own amazement: "Once again, this was truly a Bavarian people's assembly, quite obviously made up of workers, tradesmen, shopkeepers—and Eisner had been the editor of *Vorwärts* in Berlin, he was a 'Prussian and a Jew' (synonyms to many Bavarians). Where had this Munich enthusiasm come from? What kind of man was the prime minister?" It is from Klemperer that we have one of the most apt characterizations of Eisner as a human being:

A delicate, tiny, frail, stooped little man. His balding head is of unimposing size, his dirty gray hair hangs to the nape of his neck, his heavy, cloudy gray eyes peer through spectacles. There is nothing brilliant, nothing venerable, nothing heroic about his entire appearance. He is a mediocre, spent man that I peg as being at least 65, although he is still in his very early fifties. He does not look especially Jewish, but he is certainly not Germanic like his opponent Levien, or Bavarian like his devotee Unterleitner. And in the way that he subsequently jokes around on the podium (he does not stay behind the lectern), he actually does remind me of caricatures of Jewish journalists. . . . [A]nd this columnist had toppled the Bavarian throne and was now the ruler of Bavaria, and his rapt audience—I had to keep reminding myself of this—was not a heap of literary "intellectual workers," but literally the people of Munich.[17]

As ringleader of the 1918 January strike, which had succeeded in mobilizing more than ten thousand workers at ammunition factories in Munich alone and landing Eisner in jail through October 1918, this chairman of the Bavarian USPD, until then only known in narrow circles, made a name for himself among the workers of Munich. Like no other person, he represented the pacifist wing of this antiwar protest party, which had split off from the SPD a year earlier. Now, in November 1918, only recently released from prison, Eisner wanted to redeem the promise of those rights due the common people. He pledged an eight-hour day for workers and suffrage for women, and he quickly put into practice both promises. Who cared, his followers argued, where he was born and to what religious community his parents had belonged? Eisner did not give a fig for Prussia. On the contrary, Prussian ideals and Prussia's power-obsessed comportment were partly responsible, in his view, for the German Reich instigating the war. Lujo Brentano, one of the most important economists of his time and the man Eisner persuaded to assume chairmanship of the newly created Council of Intellectual Workers, described Eisner as "a Prussian Jew who was filled with unbounded hatred of Prussia."[18] To pit himself against the Prussian state, the epitome of Prussian militarism, remained one of Eisner's most urgent wishes during his brief administration.

By contrast, he bore no feelings of hatred for his Jewish background, which had not always been especially important to him but was also not something he denied. In Berlin his family belonged to the largely assimilated Jewish bourgeoisie. There was a certain irony to the fact that the future pacifist Eisner was born in 1867 as, of all people, the son of a

FIGURE 4. Bavarian Minister-President Kurt Eisner. bpk / Bayerische
Staatsbibliothek München / Archiv Heinrich Hoffmann.

"purveyor to the court of military insignias and orders" in Berlin. Emanuel Eisner's business was located on the main boulevard, Unter den
Linden, and the family lived modestly but prosperously. Kurt Eisner's
grandfather came from the Bohemian town of Husinec, birthplace of
the church reformer Jan Hus. On his mother's side, Eisner was descended from a Berlin family named Lewenstein. Eisner's mother died
a few days after her son had become Bavarian prime minister. Like her

husband barely twenty years before, she was interred in the Jewish cemetery in Berlin—Weißensee.[19]

Practicing religion was irrelevant as far as Eisner was concerned, yet all his life he acknowledged being a part of the Jewish community. Thus, the entry about religious affiliation in his diploma from the Askanisches Gymnasium read: "Jewish religion."[20] His certificate of admission to the Bavarian member state from 1908 described him as someone of the "Mosaic persuasion,"[21] and his entry in the marriage registrar from the registry office in Munich from May 1917 still listed him as belonging to the "Jewish religion." It was not until his death certificate was issued that he was described as "non-denominational" (*freireligiös*).[22]

After Eisner had spent eight semesters studying philosophy and German literature in Berlin, during which time he was partly supported by the Association to Aid Jewish Students (Hilfsverband für jüdische Studierende), he pursued a career as a journalist.[23] Initially he worked in the dispatch office of the *Berliner Herold*, then at the editorial staff of the *Frankfurter Zeitung*, until he was finally lured to Marburg by the future Social Democratic Reichstag deputy Paul Bader, the founder and editor of the *General-Anzeiger für Marburg und Umgegend* (later the *Hessische Landeszeitung*). As editor of the Social Democratic paper, one of his principal tasks was to take up the fight against the antisemitic librarian and "peasant king" Otto Böckel. In 1887, Böckel had won the seat for the Marburg-Kirchhain electoral district as the candidate of the Antisemitic People's Party he had founded, thus entering the Reichstag as its first declared antisemite. In spite of Bader's tireless campaigning against him, Böckel was elected to parliament without challenge three more times. His populist campaign against "Jews and Junkers [Aristocrats]" was extremely popular, especially among the rural population.[24]

At first it was the ever-recurring clash over antisemitism that kept Eisner holding on to his Judaism. During his time in Marburg, he wrote about the growing variety of antisemitic parties: "For every Jew there is approximately one antisemitic faction. The religious, aesthetic, socially conscious antisemitism, every kind has its different exponents. Under this family umbrella you will find the most antithetical people gathered together, starting with the antisemites who cannot forgive the Jew for having crucified Christ to those who view Israel as a misfortune for world history because it brought forth Christ."[25] And in another article he complained that Jews had to suffer as the convenient scapegoats for all manner of grievances, so that complex relationships could be explained in the simplest manner: "There is no need to rack one's brains over political and social problems; for the antisemitic cell theory teaches: Omnia ex judaeo [everything is the Jews' fault], and the puzzle of the world is thereby smoothed out, solved."[26]

Fighting antisemitism remained a lifelong matter of importance to Eisner. Like other socialists, he assumed that antisemitism would, as a matter of course, disappear in a socialist world order. Yet so long as it still existed, he would not turn his back on the Jewish community. One of his daughters later recalled how he answered the question about his sense of belonging to the Jewish community: "When he was asked why, under these circumstances, he didn't leave the Jewish community, he said that he would not abandon a community that was persecuted and despised."[27]

Especially important in relationship to Eisner's attitude toward Judaism was his friendship with Hermann Cohen, the famous neo-Kantian philosopher who taught at the University of Marburg and was one of the few Jews appointed to a university chair during the late nineteenth century while simultaneously maintaining his identity as a Jew. Cohen, who had studied at the Jewish Theological Seminary in Breslau and was regarded as the leading German-Jewish philosopher of his time, became the most formative personality in Eisner's life. On the occasion of Cohen's seventieth birthday, Eisner wrote: "Before him I had never encountered anyone who might have gained power over me. Later, when I went other ways from time to time, I certainly found the occasional person to whom I felt bound in reverence. . . . But intellectual influence on my innermost being was something only one person ever gained: Hermann Cohen, a maker of men."[28] Eisner dedicated a handwritten note on the same occasion to "the only man who gained intellectual power over me."[29]

Hermann Cohen's reaction to the success of political antisemitism also made a big impression on Eisner. What triggered Cohen's defense of Judaism was Heinrich von Treitschke's antisemitic essay in the 1879 *Preußische Jahrbücher* in which the Berlin historian attacked the "pants-peddling youths" from Eastern Europe and also coined the phrase later picked up by the National Socialists: "The Jews are our misfortune."[30] Otto Böckel's antisemitic activities right in front of Cohen's door strengthened the Marburg scholar's need for a clear declaration of his commitment to a German-Jewish symbiosis. As Eisner recalled, the most distressing experience in Cohen's life was "the onset of the antisemitic movement," to which the Marburg philosopher responded by "solemnly and loudly profess[ing] his Judaism."[31] One way Cohen did so was to prepare a legal opinion defending the Talmud against antisemitic attacks in a sensational trial in 1888.[32]

Cohen's work *Religion der Vernunft aus den Quellen des Judentums* (*Religion of Reason: Out of the Sources of Judaism*) had not yet been published during the time Eisner was working in the Hessian provinces. Yet the ideas developed in that book were already present, and Eisner was well aware of Cohen's linking of biblical prophecy with Kantian ethics and his sympathy for a kind of Messianism interpreted in socialist terms.[33] Under Cohen's influence, Eisner also attempted to draw connections between Kantianism and Marxism. Martin Buber wrote that Eisner and his comrade in arms Gustav Landauer were both "governed by this tendency, which is ultimately rooted in the religious. The earth should be renewed, the kingdom of God is coming."[34] Eisner himself would certainly not have located the driving forces behind his political ideals in the religious realm. Thus, in 1908, in a lecture called "Religion of Socialism," he criticized the attempt at locating answers to issues of the day in an inherited past: "The religion of socialism, with its sense of power and affirmation of existence, has forever overcome the despair of the vale of tears, the hopelessness of earthly fate."[35]

In spite of his criticism, Eisner maintained a lifelong respect for the power of religions and especially of the biblical prophetic books. The way Eisner characterized Cohen, whom he greatly admired, was similar to how Eisner himself was often described in years to come and after his death: "The spirit of the old prophets merged with classical German philosophy and art, where he in turn detected features of socialism."[36]

And what he wrote about Cohen's relationship to Judaism may not be as far removed from his own as it is often depicted by historians: "He loved Judaism (in its world-historical purity) because it knew no spiritual estate reserving knowledge for itself; . . . because it primarily serves the this-worldly. For Cohen the Jewish Messiah is the moral humanity of the historical future."[37]

Cohen reciprocated Eisner's friendship. When, on the occasion of his sixtieth birthday, he received a painting of his hometown of Coswig from Eisner and his wife, he wrote the pair a letter full of gratitude from Silvaplana in Switzerland, telling the Eisners that the painting would "always be at the top" of his gifts. It is also apparent from the letter that the two certainly had an intensive exchange about Judaism and Zionism, as Cohen wrote: "Although I have raved about Judaism much more than you would have liked, you have nonetheless recognized my love for my German homeland, for my little hometown as the living root of my being, and thus your gift [has] for me a symbolic importance of sympathetic recognition for my German-Jewish feeling of humanity."[38]

Eisner's biographer Bernhard Grau is correct in his assessment of "how little Eisner's Judaism has taken shape in the biographies we have of him so far." In his own meticulously researched biography, however, Grau comes to the same conclusion as Eisner's other biographers: "One can briefly summarize Eisner's attitude by saying that he no longer understood himself as a Jew and also no longer behaved as such."[39] In an older study, Franz Schade had written: "As for the rest, Eisner himself never feels as if he is a Jew; he never attends synagogue."[40] Yet one can also define belonging to Judaism more broadly than synagogue attendance and identification with a religious community.[41] Recall Isaac Deutscher's definition of the "non-Jewish Jew" alluded to in the introduction, or the words of the convinced atheist Sigmund Freud, who articulated his sense of distance from Judaism yet simultaneously insisted on deliberately remaining part of this community. What connected him to Judaism, Freud said, was neither religion nor "national pride," which he always despised. Rather, "plenty of other things remained . . . to make the attraction of Jewry and Jews irresistible [including] many obscure emotional forces which were the more powerful the less they could be expressed in words as well as a clear consciousness of an inner identity, the safe privacy of a common mental construction."[42]

For Eisner, too, religion and "national pride" had no positive meaning, and yet he kept his connection to Judaism as a community. It may have been the "common mental construction" of which Freud spoke that compelled Eisner—even though both of his marriages were to non-Jewish women—to turn in critical situations to intellectual and political comrades who came from Jewish families. Hermann Cohen was his spiritual mentor, Gustav Landauer was the person closest to him intellectually among the revolutionaries, and his private secretary Felix Fechenbach was his closest confidant during his time as Bavarian prime minister.

Even if Kurt Eisner had wanted to forget his Jewish background, it would have been impossible for him to do so. The more he was in the public limelight, the more he was perceived by those around him as a Jew. He embarked on this path as a public figure in the years following his time in Marburg, when, after a career full of ups and downs as editor of socialist newspapers like the *Vorwärts* and the *Fränkische Tagespost*, he became a political activist himself. Initially closer to the moderate wing of Social Democracy, the pacifist convictions that took shape during the war drew him toward the newly founded Independent Social Democratic Party (USPD), which he joined in 1917. He became its most important representative in Munich, where, at the beginning of 1918, he organized a strike of ammunition workers. For that he had to go to jail. (Twenty years earlier, he had already served a sentence for lèse-majesté.) The Jewish background of some of the party's cofounders and activists certainly played a role in the way they were perceived from the outside. Notes from the police reports made this clear: they explicitly recorded which of the members were Jews.[43]

A few weeks before November 1918, nobody would have thought it possible that this opposition politician relatively unknown outside his immediate circle would be toppling the Wittelsbach dynasty that had ruled Bavaria for over seven centuries. Eisner's meteoric rise looks even more astonishing in light of how precarious his private life was in the years preceding it. Thus, in January 1916 he started a letter to his future father-in-law with the following words: "It seems as if everything is now conspiring against me. And this time it is becoming deadly serious." At stake here was a considerable sum that Eisner was supposed to repay the party and for which he could not raise the money. Even his father-in-law initially refused to advance the money. As his second wife, Else, later remarked, the still unmarried couple was determined to commit suicide if they were expelled from the party.[44]

In private letters to Else, Eisner sometimes alluded to his Jewish background. Thus, during the terrible quarrels over the separation from his first wife, he wrote: "It must be my Jewish blood that is outraged against the suffering of children who demand paternal care."[45] From Berlin he sent her, not without a touch of self-irony, a card from the German-Israelite Community Federation with a portrait of a bearded Jew by Rembrandt and the caption: "A learned Jew."[46]

Above all, Eisner's Jewish background was repeatedly rubbed in his face by his political opponents during the few months of his tenure as Bavaria's prime minister, as the next chapter will show in greater detail. Thus, the rumor that the Bavarian prime minister hailed from Galicia and that his real name was Salomon Kosmanowsky or Koschinsky or maybe Karowskarek lasted long beyond his death.[47] In reality, he was born in Berlin, lived in Bavaria since 1907 as editor-in-chief of Nuremberg's *Fränkische Tagespost*, and resided since 1910 in the Munich suburb of Großhadern as a freelancer and Landtag reporter for the *Münchner Post*.

If one were to believe the antisemite Rudolf Glauer, alias von Sebottendorff, Eisner did not evade his Jewish background even during the speeches he gave as Bavarian prime minister. Thus, at an event in the Upper Bavarian town of Bad Aibling (where Sebottendorff planned to kidnap him), he was supposed to have said that he was a "Jew, belonging to that unfortunate people that lived for millennia in slavery, that was not allowed to do any work, and that was hated. For that very reason

Jews were always in favor of true freedom, true equality, because they had suffered such indescribable ignominy and such total misfortune firsthand."[48]

Regardless of where Eisner stood on his Jewish background, during his brief governing tenure he was constantly forced to struggle with the doubt it cast on his authority. Thus, only four days after the revolution, Munich's Archbishop Michael Faulhaber explained in his diary why the people would not follow Eisner: "It is not the same whether the people look up to a king with trust and a sense of religious obligation or whether they say: What does this Jew have to do with us?"[49] Faulhaber was thus alluding to a public mood that extended widely throughout clerical circles. The archbishop of Bamberg, Jakobus Hauck, took a similar tone writing to Faulhaber: "It would be ignominious for the Church if a pastor were to be appointed by a revolutionary government headed by a Jew. The Catholic people, I believe, would never forgive its bishops giving way in this regard; instead, they would interpret this as weakness, if not as something worse."[50]

The Social Democratic Munich attorney Max Hirschberg recalled in a similar manner the lack of recognition of Eisner's authority by Catholic Bavaria's citizens and farmers: "Kurt Eisner was thus a tragic figure with a light touch of Don Quixote about him. A Berlin Jew who, in addition, was 'only' a journalist, was seen by the established Bavarian society of peasants and the petit bourgeois as a 'rogue,' while the well-nourished Erhard Auer was regarded as one of their own."[51] And his colleague, the attorney Philipp Löwenfeld, confirmed that the chair of the Majority Social Democrats, Erhard Auer, was the hope of the bourgeois camp, while Eisner was viewed as the purported Bolshevik. "The fact that the revolutionary prime minister was—thank God—a Jew contributed substantially to his odiousness in broad circles of the bourgeoisie."[52]

This view was also transmitted through political channels abroad, as a report from the Austrian general consulate in Munich to the Foreign Ministry in Vienna confirms. After first stating unequivocally that Eisner was a Jew, it goes on to say: "Marx and Lasalle were his gospel. He is an aesthete of the purest kind, pacifist, opponent of the death penalty.

He abhors violence and blood. A fantastic political child, cowardly in essence, dependent on the moment and the mood, obstinate, radical." Here, too, his Social Democratic antagonist, Interior Minister Auer, is presented as the opposite of Eisner: distinguished by honorable convictions, Auer is equal to the duties of his office and acquainted with Bavaria and its needs.[53] Admittedly, both were socialists, yet one was a foreign Jew and the other a native Catholic. During the period of upheaval, the Social Democrat Auer himself also applied anti-Jewish stereotypes to his prime minister, as when he talked about how "Jewish money" was going to be at work helping his rival Eisner, or how the Independent Social Democrats and the Jews certainly knew how to exploit a possible trial against Eisner for their own purposes.[54]

But one thing was clear to Eisner's followers and opponents: the man who had been a blank page for many in Munich up until the end of the war was at the center of the political action within just a few days. The journalist Sebastian Haffner assessed the Munich revolution, very much in contrast to the one in Berlin, as a "one-man show . . . under the direction of Kurt Eisner and with Kurt Eisner in all the leading roles: He was at the same time the Otto Wels and the Liebknecht, the Emil Barth and the Scheidemann, in a certain sense even the Ebert of the Munich Revolution, inasmuch as he was the only one to know exactly what he wanted and how to bring it about."[55] And elsewhere Haffner attested that Eisner's "management of the Bavarian Revolution . . . deserves the epithet 'masterly,'" since "Eisner was the only man in Germany who had enough shrewd insight to grasp what the German revolution was aiming at and ably assist its birth."[56]

In fact, not only did the revolution proceed bloodlessly, but the economic situation had become relatively stable compared with the rest of Germany, and in contrast to the picture later drawn of absolute chaos. In its annual report, one of the major banks in the state, the Bayerische Hypotheken- und Wechselbank, reported that, in the weeks following the events of November 1918, but especially in the months of January and February, capital from all over Germany was flowing into Bavaria, since account holders saw "in overwhelmingly agricultural Bavaria a secure haven against the billowing storm."[57]

In many respects, Kurt Eisner's revolution offered more continuity than change. This was especially true as it affected the staffing of the state apparatus. Key positions in the legal system, police, and many other fields remained untouched. The majority of cabinet ministers in the "People's State" belonged to the moderate Majority Social Democrats. Eisner appointed his old rival, Erhard Auer, as interior minister, and he reappointed Heinrich Ritter von Frauendorfer, a proven public servant from the monarchy, to his old office as minister of transportation. Wilhelm Ritter von Borscht, who was close to the Catholic Center Party, stayed on as mayor of Munich. Eisner brought together intellectuals in the newly created Council of Intellectual Workers. Here, too, he did not grant the leading roles to people with radical views. The chair was given to the respected economist Lujo Brentano, who harbored major reservations about Eisner and his revolution.[58]

And yet Eisner's political project was bound to fail. His ideals, in spite of all the compromises he entered into, were too far from reality, his ideas were supported by only a small part of the population, and his notions of how parliamentary democracy might be combined with a radical council system of popular representation were too diffuse. Eisner was convinced that the revolution he was leading could take a different path from all previous revolutions. At a celebration of the revolution, he proclaimed in an impressive speech delivered at Munich's National Theater: "We want to give the world an example of how, finally, there is a revolution, perhaps the first revolution in world history, that unites the idea, the ideal, and the reality."[59]

One of these ideals was the new role of women in society. "Of this party it has to be said that it took equality of the sexes seriously. Everywhere young ladies are involved," wrote Isolde Kurz in the Wiener *Neue Freie Presse*.[60] As early as the January 1918 strike of the ammunition workers, there was a woman, in the person of Sonja Lerch-Rabinowitz (of whom much more will be said later in another context), standing at Eisner's side. On Eisner's orders, the Ministry for Social Welfare had a department for women's rights, which introduced trade unions for women, did press work, and dealt with the consequences for women of massive layoffs following the war.[61] There was now certainly a stronger representation of women's voices than before the war. Yet even after the revolution, they were not penetrating into leadership positions. Traditional gender roles were still too strongly embedded in the mindscape of most revolutionaries. As a modern scholar has observed, "Nowhere was there any equal participation of women in the politics of the Bavarian revolution."[62] It was above all actors operating outside the party apparatus, like Gustav Landauer, Erich Mühsam, and Ernst Toller, who voiced their support for breaking away from old gender roles. Toller also criticized the dilatory acceptance of these demands by the grass roots of the party: "It makes the workers uncomfortable when their wives get serious about fulfilling socialist demands."[63]

Among the Jewish participants in the revolution, Nannette "Nettie" Katzenstein held public speeches and joined the writers Karl Wolfskehl, Alfred Wolfenstein, and Rainer Maria Rilke in founding the Council of Intellectual Workers in the home of Edgar Jaffé.[64] The pacifists and women's rights activists Anita Augspurg and Lida Gustava Heymann had close ties to Kurt Eisner and were repeatedly but incorrectly portrayed in the antisemitic press as Jewish women.[65] As one of eight women, Augspurg was also a member of the Provisional National Council. She failed to be elected to the Bavarian Landtag in January 1919, as did Heymann as a candidate to the German National Assembly for the USPD.[66] Both candidates' failures were attributable not least to the fact that, as activists, they did not succeed in mobilizing women voters for the parties that had advocated voting rights for women and women's rights in general. In the first elections to the Bavarian Landtag, women revealed a strong attachment to the traditional values of the Catholic Church and voted in much higher numbers than men for the conservative Bavarian People's Party (supported by 49 percent of women compared to 33 percent of men). The female share of votes for the Majority and Independent Social Democrats was correspondingly lower. Only 1 percent of Bavarian women opted for Eisner's USPD.[67]

The gynecologist Rahel Straus was the first woman to study medicine at the University of Heidelberg and the first licensed female physician in Munich ever to have studied at a German university. She was one of the very few women to have an academic training, a working life, and a family, as well as roles in both the Workers' Council and the Council of Intellectual Workers. Straus was married to the attorney Elias Straus, who chaired the association of Munich Zionists. As a convinced feminist, Rahel Straus fought against the ban on abortions; as a Zionist, she advocated for the development of Palestine; as the daughter of an Orthodox rabbi, she remained observant about Jewish religious laws; and as a political reformer, she welcomed the downfall of the monarchy and the idealistic goals of the revolution's first phase.

Perhaps because of her varied experience, she was struck, more than was the case for most of her male colleagues, by what was Jewish about the revolution's most important actors. She later wrote about the opening session of the Workers' Council: "Eisner opened the meeting. He spoke well, but like a Jewish journalist. There were more who spoke, but apart from Auer, who had Jewish relatives by marriage, only Jews." Straus called Gustav Landauer, like her a native of Karlsruhe, "with his broad gray havelock, with his fine facial features, spiritual look, passionate, with long, well groomed artists' hands," a "Christ figure." With some disquiet, she noted that Landauer, as a Jewish revolutionary, was calling for churches to be transformed into sites for popular culture, and the comments of Erich Mühsam, whom she described as "wild, fantastic, with reddish hair and beard . . . full of passionate hate against everything that exists, against everything bourgeois," also made her uneasy. "Then Toller spoke. I remember thinking of him as young and sympathetic. But, all in all, I had the feeling (and I said this at the time, this is not something reconstructed after the fact): his speech would have been possible at the opening of a Zionist congress, but at the opening of the Workers' Council for the Free State of Bavaria it was impossible."[68]

Straus wrote down these observations long after the failure of the Eisner government. Yet they were a most apt characterization of Eisner's dilemma. It would soon emerge that Eisner lacked popular support. He was a revolutionary for a transition period, and his days as Bavarian prime minister were numbered. In the Landtag elections of January 12, which he had scheduled against resistance from the radical ideologues advocating a council system, the USPD's vote total amounted to 2.5 percent, yielding just three seats in the new Landtag. Eisner

FIGURE 5. Rahel Straus, the first female physician licensed in Munich, a Zionist, and a member of the Workers' Council, pictured here as a student (1905). Call number Rahel Straus Collection: AR 1454, Leo Baeck Institute New York.

remained in office as prime minister for another month and used this time to attempt to implement his most important goals as far as possible. One of his main goals for domestic German politics, in addition to embedding the councils in the political system of Bavaria, was the struggle for a nationwide federalist system of states not dominated by

Prussia. He tried in vain to build an alliance of the southern German states in support of this objective.[69]

But Eisner was also the Bavarian foreign minister, an office that was especially important to him. He was convinced that he could avert damage to Germany's and Bavaria's foreign policy by going on the offense about the question of war guilt and arguing that the new Germany needed to position itself decisively against the policy of the old Imperial regime in order to avoid harsh sanctions. Only if one could demonstrate Germany's complete renewal, he believed, could the worst sanctions be prevented. On the basis of this conviction, he had documents published, in an abbreviated and apparently also incorrect format, that suggested German war guilt, and he also advanced this line of argument at the conference of the Socialist International convened in Bern between February 3 and 10. At home these views earned him the reputation of a traitor along with death threats from nationalists, who were already stirred up against him.

When Eisner spoke about the conference in Bern on February 13 at a public meeting in Munich, students distributed leaflets that ended with these words from Friedrich Schiller's drama *Wilhelm Tell*: "Make haste, governor, your time has run out."[70] Eisner interpreted this, as did his friends, as a summons to murder. Only shortly before, on January 15, the Spartacists Karl Liebknecht and Rosa Luxemburg had been killed in Berlin. Attacks on Eisner also now increased, including a failed putsch attempt against him on February 19, led by the sailor Konrad Lotter. Eisner had his resignation speech in his jacket pocket on February 21 when he took the short footpath from the Foreign Ministry to the parliament building. He refused to accept the advice of his friends and take an alternative route to avoid danger, since "one cannot permanently evade a murder attempt, and one can only shoot me dead one time, after all."[71] Shortly after leaving the ministry, he was shot by a young man who waylaid him in a building entrance.

His assassin was Count Anton von Arco auf Valley, who had jotted down his motives on a piece of paper before the murder: "Eisner aims for anarchy, he is a Bolshevik, he is a Jew, he's not a German, he doesn't feel German, he is undermining every kind of German feeling, he is a

Trauer-Blatt

zum Tode des Gründers der Republik, des Minister-Präsidenten Kurt Eisner.

Die Ermordung Kurt Eisners durch Leutn. Graf Arco vor dem Ministerium

am Freitag, den 21. Februar 1919.

† Kurt Eisners letzter Gang! †

Text siehe Seite 2.

FIGURE 6. Death notice on the assassination of Kurt Eisner reconstructing the sequence of events. F.Mon. 231, Münchner Stadtbibliothek / Monacensia.

traitor to his country. The entire people is screaming for liberation. So!! My reason: I hate Bolshevism, I love my Bavarian people, I am a loyal monarchist, a good Catholic. Above all, I respect Bavaria's honor. Therefore a cheer for the monarchy, a cheer for [Crown Prince] Rupprecht!" The day before, he had mentioned to the chambermaid at his boarding-house: "Tomorrow I am going to shoot Eisner. . . . Eisner is a Bolshevik and a Jew."[72]

Ironically, it seems that at least one motive behind Arco's deed was his obsession with his own partially Jewish background. He wanted to join the right-wing extremist Thule Society but was not admitted because of his mother's Jewish descent (her maiden name was Emmy von Oppenheim). Thus, the founder of the Thule Society, Rudolf von Sebottendorff, wrote: "Count Anton Arco auf Valley had Jewish blood in his veins on the side of his mother (née Oppenheim), he is a Yid [Jüdling], and was therefore admitted neither by the Thule Society nor by the Militant League [the Kampfbund that was the predecessor to the Thule Society]. He wanted to show that even a half-Jew can execute a task."[73] Since Sebottendorff's own attempt to kidnap Eisner had failed, there certainly resonates in his assessment of Arco's deed a certain trace of jealousy that, of all people, a "Yid" managed to carry out what the genuine Aryan had not succeeded in doing. And so he considered Arco's deed misdirected: "Arco's insane deed toppled all plans. This deed gave Eisner, who was already half finished, the halo of a martyr."[74]

Arco's partly Jewish background was already known shortly after the assassination. The writer Ricarda Huch experienced this day close up and noted immediately afterwards: "He is supposed to belong to an old Bavarian aristocratic family; he is supposed to be a Jew; others maintained that his father was a genuine Count Arco, his mother a rich Jew. According to all the reports he was still very young, of slight build, and very odd."[75]

The right-wing extremist press did not quite know how it should deal with the fact that the deed actually planned from their own camp had now been executed by a "non-Aryan." In the extreme right-wing *Münchener Beobachter* (which would later be renamed the *Völkischer Beobachter* and become the official organ of the NSDAP), the story read like this: "It is more than a cruel joke of world history that Kurt Eisner, who founded and laid down Jewish domination, had to fall at the hand of a half-Jew. . . . All who know Anton Arco are in agreement that his stupidity was so great that one could break into walls with it."[76]

The Oppenheim family, from which Arco was descended on his mother's side, had long since exchanged its Judaism for Christianity and positioned itself clearly on the political right. Three months before the assassination, Arco's uncle, the banker Simon Alfred von Oppenheim, wrote his nephew: "It is outrageous that a land like Bavaria can be led on the leash or terrorized by a fool like Kurt Eisner, just as it is that the Bavarian people could be treated this way by the workers of Munich."[77] Even after the assassination, the Cologne banker praised "poor Tony" as a "heroic son." As late as 1935, the archaeologist and diplomat Max von Oppenheim could still write how proud he was that his family had done so much for Germany, and he cited as the first example his great-nephew, "who is rightly celebrated as Bavaria's savior."[78] Two of Anton's cousins, Friedrich Carl and Waldemar von Oppenheim, distinguished themselves during the Weimar Republic by their right-wing nationalist convictions. Even by the beginning of the 1930s, they were members of the right-wing nationalist Stahlhelm, the paramilitary group close to the German National People's Party.[79]

Arco, described by Sebastian Haffner as "a half-Jewish Nazi" (although he was neither "half-Jewish" nor a Nazi), was initially sentenced to death, but by the day after the trial his sentence had already been commuted to life in prison and would eventually be reduced to a lesser sentence.[80] While he was in detention pending trial, he encountered inmates who had been on the other side of the political divide during the revolution. Among them was Erich Mühsam, who depicted Arco this way: "Yesterday during my stroll with Toller I had the opportunity to see Eisner's killer face to face. He was led across the courtyard, his head still heavily wrapped. My God! What a young kid! Rosy-cheeked, with a baby's mouth, smoking a cigarette, friendly in a childish way, with open blue eyes, still not a trace of any beard, scrutinizing me with curiosity, that was how the historic personality of Count Arco-Valley presented himself to me. Is this what murderers look like?"[81]

If Eisner was controversial during his short time in office and only able to get a small number of votes, the people of Munich showed solidarity with him in death. Initially the city fell into a state of shock: "The bells in all the towers began to ring, the streetcars all at once stopped running, here and there somebody stuck a red flag with a black ribbon out of a window, and a heavy, uncertain stillness began. All the people were walking into town with faces looking distraught," recalled the writer Oskar Maria Graf. As he approached the site of the murder, "hundreds of people were pressing in a silent circle around the traces of Eisner's blood, now covered over with shavings. Hardly anyone spoke a word; women, and even men, were crying softly. Several soldiers stepped into the centre and erected a pyramid of rifles. One of them had big tears running down his sunburnt cheeks. 'Our own Eisner! Our one and only Eisner!' a woman wailed in a loud voice, and now the sobs were heard more plainly."[82]

Munich's Jewish community, which had a skeptical attitude toward Eisner as a politician, showed solidarity toward Eisner as a murder victim. The brief obituary in the Zionist-oriented Munich newspaper *Das Jüdische Echo* deserves to be quoted in full:

Kurt Eisner has fallen victim to a murderer's hand. His temporal existence and work did not belong to his people, and yet he was flesh of the flesh and spirit of the spirit of his people. He was indifferent to the cause of the Jewish people; his cause was indifferent to many of us. Now, since the shroud of the temporal has fallen, only the eternally human remains to be appreciated. His eternally human was the eternally Jewish. Fulfilling the highest commandment of Jewish morality was his life, which was a life for others. In him there lived the moral challenge of an Amos and the will to redemption of the Galilean [i.e. Jesus]. Those for whom he fought reprimanded him as alien to their people and their land. In death may he be brought back to his people from whom he was estranged. "Beloved be each human being, who is made in the image" is Judaism's first commandment. He fulfilled it. "You shall be holy, for I am holy" is Judaism's final commandment. He lived the life of a saint and died the death of a saint. He was very proud to be a Jew, he said to the blasphemers of the Jewish name. The Jewish people is also proud of this its lost son. Proclaim the renown of this people, whose lost sons are good enough to redeem the world.[83]

Eisner's funeral ceremony was the occasion for a final grand demonstration of solidarity with the murdered prime minister. A funeral procession of hundreds of thousands of citizens from all over Bavaria, stretching for several miles, marched peacefully through Munich. At some historical distance, Sebastian Haffner issued this assessment: "Vast numbers of country people poured into the city to join it, and the Bavarian mountaineers with their chamois-tufts and leather shorts marched seriously and solemnly behind the coffin of this Berlin Jew who had, they felt, understood them so well."[84] Oskar Maria Graf, who took part in the funeral ceremony, was impressed: "The Eastern Cemetery was so full that there was nothing to be seen but heads and banners. Gustav Landauer made a funeral speech, but nobody heard him, though many were there to honour the dead. It really seemed, when the final shout: Long live the revolution! re-echoed, as if the earth was crying aloud."[85]

It was a situation still unimaginable just weeks before in a Germany where no Jew had been able to hold any government office. Here was the Jewish revolutionary, Gustav Landauer, looking like a prophet with his long beard, standing at the grave of his Jewish friend, the prime minister, speaking the words: "Kurt Eisner, the Jew, was a prophet."[86] Hermann Cohen had died the year before. During the war, much had happened to separate the two friends. Cohen's enthusiasm for the war and his attempts to reconcile Germanness and Judaism (*Deutschtum und Judentum*) philosophically stood in stark contrast to Eisner's (and Landauer's) pacifism and opposition to nationalism. Yet Landauer's invocation of the biblical prophets was something Cohen would certainly have accepted in a spirit of benevolence.

After his death, Eisner, who had reaped little praise as a politician while he lived, acquired in many leftist circles the very status of a martyr that the right-wing extremists had feared. In the days following the assassination, Thomas Mann's mother-in-law, Hedwig Pringsheim, herself no Eisner fan, wrote to the journalist Maximilian Harden:

> You say that you do not completely understand what was going on with us. Eisner [you say] could certainly not have taken root in *Bajuwarien* [a humorous term for Bavaria]. But maybe more so than people believed. While the lads in the high schools were staging dances of joy upon the report of his assassination and the students at the university were cheering, the workers of all parties were pouring out of the factories as one man onto the Theresienwiese. On the day of his burial—which transpired, against all expectation, in absolute calm—all the palaces of the higher nobility, on orders, hoisted black mourning flags at half mast, and all the church bells were ringing five days long, as happens *only* and exclusively for governing kings, ringing out midday from 12 to 1: for the Jew Kurt Eisner. The pious are having a rest. Well, I can't blame them.[87]

Ricarda Huch, who spent a "fun-filled" evening with her daughter on the day after Eisner's murder, listened in on a neighbor reporting about the soldiers who were guarding the portrait of Eisner on the site of the assassination. They told about how they "beat up everyone who did not raise his hat in front of the picture; and, further, how people dipped cloths in Eisner's blood and carried them home as a relic. 'In brief, *meshuga* is trump,' said my daughter."[88]

In the Majority Social Democrats' newspaper the *Münchner Post*, which had adopted a thoroughly critical stance toward the Independent Social Democrat Eisner during his lifetime, there now appeared announcements like this: "New! Kurt Eisner. Best photos with Kurt Eisner's signature. Valuable for every liberal-minded person." Also: "Party comrades! In a few days we are publishing the most exclusive wall decoration for the home of every revolutionary: Kurt Eisner at his writing desk (similar to Bebel). An art print . . . price only 1.60 marks."[89] In a memorial address for Eisner on March 16 in the Odeon concert hall, the writer Heinrich Mann (Thomas Mann's older, more leftist brother) commemorated the "first truly spiritual human being at the head of a

German state" with these words: "The hundred days of the Eisner government brought forth more ideas, more joys of reason, more animation of the spirits, than that of fifty years before."[90]

By no means was Eisner the only Jewish actor during the political upheaval in Munich. His private secretary Felix Fechenbach, whom we will meet again in a later chapter, came from an Orthodox Jewish family and had completed an apprenticeship as a shoe salesman in Würzburg before, as a trade union functionary, he came in contact with Kurt Eisner.[91] Working very closely with Eisner, he soon advanced to become a confidant and political comrade in arms who gave political speeches on his own and was also nominated as a candidate near the top of the USPD list for elections to the German National Assembly. During the decisive revolutionary events at the Theresienwiese on November 7, it was "that movingly awkward, simple Felix Fechenbach . . . [who] swept us all along," according to Oskar Maria Graf, who was there in the front ranks.[92] Everywhere Eisner appeared, Fechenbach, just twenty-four years old, was not far away. Thus, he was right next to Eisner on the prime minister's last walk to the parliament and helped overpower the murderer.

Even as a Social Democrat, and in spite of his criticism of Orthodox Judaism, Fechenbach did not turn away completely from the Jewish religion. As a soldier during the war, he reported back to his parents that he took part in prayer services and was even called to read from the Torah. He sent them New Year's greetings on Rosh Hashanah and told them that he was given leave and visited the synagogue on Jewish holidays.[93]

It is noteworthy that Eisner's two other secretaries also came from Jewish families: Sophie Breitenbach, whose brother Josef was active in the Provisional Central Workers' Council, performed courier services for the Eisner government's messages to Switzerland, and later became a well-known photographer;[94] and the Posen native Ernst Joske, who had joined the photographer Germaine Krull, also born in Posen, shortly before the end of the war in contemplating an assassination attempt on the kaiser. The Breitenbach siblings belonged to that group of

FIGURE 7. Kurt Eisner with his wife Else and Felix Fechenbach (wearing the coat with a fur collar) at the Council demonstration on February 16, 1919. Bayerische Staatsbibliothek München / Bildarchiv.

young Social Democrats in Munich who, along with Felix Fechenbach, had organized open discussions in the Goldener Anker restaurant at which Kurt Eisner, Erich Mühsam, Ernst Toller, and Oskar Maria Graf also appeared.[95]

The finance minister in Eisner's cabinet was the economist Edgar Jaffé, a professor at Munich's Commercial College and a student and close friend of the sociologist Max Weber. Jaffé was linked to Max Weber not only through professional and private friendships but also through their relationship to the same woman: Jaffé's wife, Else von Richthofen. Jaffé was related by marriage to D. H. Lawrence, whose wife was Else's sister Frieda and who cultivated close ties to the Jaffés. The Jaffé house was a social center in the life of Munich's bohemia before the First World War.

Although Jaffé had already been baptized as a Protestant at age fifteen, he was still usually perceived as a Jew.[96] Thus, the attorney Philipp Löwenfeld wrote:

I knew this impeccable and sensitive Jewish scholar well enough over the years, in order to regret most deeply his decision to make himself available as a minister of the revolution in clerical-Catholic Bavaria. It was clear to me that he would have to fail at the task assigned him. He was by his very nature everything other than a revolutionary. I had no doubt about his brilliant expertise in the field of government finances. But I also knew the hard-nosed Bavarian finance bureaucracy, whose chief superior officer he was supposed to become by his decision, all the gentlemen who were privy councilors and undersecretaries and enforcement officers, down to the tax office superintendent. I knew that Jaffé, in his boundless modesty and kindness, would never be able to assert himself against these offspring of the old student corps and fraternities who would see him as nothing more than an impudent Jewish intruder.[97]

Jaffé's "brilliant expertise" was also beyond dispute among neutral observers from abroad, as was the competence of most members of Eisner's cabinet. Thus, on November 14, 1918, the clergyman and close confidant of President Wilson in Europe, George D. Herron, reported enthusiastically to the US State Department: "The members of the new Bavarian Ministry are the best that Germany has to offer. The new republic is practically constituted by the faculty of the University of Munich. Each Minister is a man of the highest personal value and has steadfastly stood against German militarism both before and since the war. Some of these men, especially such as Professor Jaffe and Professor Foerster, are personal friends of long standing." Herron was reacting to the Eisner government's request for support from Washington against the harsh peace terms, a request that Herron emphatically recommended accommodating: "If we do not find some method of encouraging this inner changed Germany we may find ourselves in the paradoxical and even horrible position of being obliged to support the very classes that brought on the war, the junkers [aristocrats] and the industrial magnates."[98]

How different this was from the assessment that the Austrian general consulate in Munich sent to the Foreign Ministry in Vienna: "Finance

FIGURE 8. Finance Minister Edgar Jaffé. Bayerische Staatsbibliothek
München / Bildarchiv.

Minister Jaffe, Jew, university professor for economics, socialist, but not
a Bolshevik, impractical, theoretician, vain, but honest, insecure, and
easily influenced. No match for his office." And further: "Eisner, Jaffe,
and Unterleitner are radicals, behind him only the most despicable and
not very numerous bawlers stand. They are alien to the people, do not
know the country, and would be otherwise unfit for work. The other
ministers are supported by the capable and organized working class;

they have the sympathies of the liberal bourgeoisie and also of those extending well into the other bourgeois parties." There is a clear tendency here to juxtapose the two members of the government with Jewish ancestry (for the author of this report it hardly mattered that Jaffé had been baptized as a child) as well Eisner's close associate Hans Unterleitner (in October 1919 he would marry Eisner's daughter Ilse from his first marriage) against the competent "authentically" Bavarian cabinet colleagues. The dispatch goes on to say in the same tone: "The Munich Workers', Soldiers', and Farmers' Council consists of the scum of the earth, of these who were simply right out in front on the night of the revolution, among them mostly non-Bavarians, sailors who had come by special train to initiate the putsch, lots of Jews of a youthful age."[99]

"My Judaism . . . Lives in Everything That I Start and That I Am"—Gustav Landauer

A special role among the revolution's Jewish actors was assumed by Eisner's close confidant Gustav Landauer, who became a member of the Provisional National Council and had friendly ties to Eisner for years. During the period of political upheaval, the two men were especially close. Because he was taken ill by influenza on November 7, 1918, Landauer was tied to his sickbed in the Swabian town of Krumbach, the hometown of his wife, who had only recently died. Yet he was counting on Eisner needing his help. On November 22, he asked his old friend for some assurance: "Would it be possible for me to tell my daughters something specific already because of the move [to Munich]?"[100] As soon as there was a slight improvement in his health, he rushed to Munich and was immediately active in the political events.

Among all the revolutionaries connected with the revolution, Landauer is the one for whom Jewish spirituality had the greatest meaning. His parents belonged to that class of assimilated bourgeois Jews against whom their children often rebelled.[101] Landauer described his own search for a deeper meaning as a reaction, often mixed with his sense of the romantic, against the "cramping barriers of Philistinism" at his parental home in Karlsruhe.[102] He also saw these "cramping barriers" as imposed by all official representatives of religion. Thus, he once said that "a rabbi cannot be in possessions of true religion; otherwise, he would not be the cleric of an existing religion."[103] His idols from Jewish history were "heretics" like Jesus and Spinoza.[104]

A decisive factor in Landauer's relationship to Judaism was his close relationship with the philosopher and Zionist Martin Buber. Buber was to Landauer what Hermann Cohen was to Eisner: a mentor on matters both Jewish and way beyond. The two met for the first time in 1899 in the Neue Gemeinschaft (New Community) founded by the brothers Heinrich and Julius Hart. What initially drew them together was their common interest in Christian mystics. Landauer was then writing about Meister Eckhart, and Buber about Jakob Böhme. They were both searching for a romantically defined *Urgemeinschaft* (original community) believed to have been lost. Both shared the critique of the theory of evolutionary progress and longed instead for some combination of German Romanticism and Jewish Messianism. When Buber published his *Tales of Rabbi Nachman* (1906) and then two years later *The Legend of the Baal-Schem* (1908) (as these Hasidic masters were interpreted by Buber), Landauer was one of his many enthusiastic readers. Landauer also published an extensive review of *The Legend* in which he elucidated his own relationship to Judaism: Judaism, for him, was no mere "external accident," but rather an "inalienable inner trait."[105] Here is where Landauer's deliberate debate with Judaism began. He became a part of that wave of enthusiasm among young German Jews that Gershom Scholem once ironically described as "buberty" (*Bubertät*).[106]

His second wife, Hedwig, whose father was the cantor for the small Swabian Jewish community of Krumbach and who had grown up in a traditional Jewish manner, may also have contributed to Landauer's newly awakened interest in Jewish culture.[107] Gustav and Hedwig Landauer, however, neither belonged to a Jewish congregation nor were practicing Jews. Their daughter Brigitte Hausberger, born in 1906, recalled that the family had a big Christmas tree at home and that she was the only one among the Jewish children in her school in Berlin who celebrated Christmas and Easter. Her parents designated her as "non-demoninational."[108] At the beginning of 1918, the Landauers moved from Berlin to Krumbach, where they had previously spent long periods of time at regular intervals. After Landauer's death, the Jewish community of Krumbach let the world know that, although the Landauers had been "born as Jews," they nonetheless did not have "any kind of relationship to Judaism," had lived "like heathens," and had entered "neither a church nor a synagogue."[109]

Yet, although he stood outside the organized Jewish community, throughout his lifetime Gustav Landauer felt a deep attachment to the values of the biblical prophets and a sense of belonging to a persecuted minority who, in his eyes, were in a better position to understand and relate to certain historical developments because of their own experience. In what was certainly his most popular book, *Aufruf zum Sozialismus* (translated half a century later as *For Socialism*), he made it clear why he thought Jews and other outsiders had a special calling to make history, a vocation that "is not attended to . . . in the high times of upheaval by the philistines and contemporaries, but by the lonely, the isolated, those who are isolated precisely because nation [*Volk*] and community are as if at home [to them], as if they have fled to them and with them."[110] In this spirit, he wrote that "the prophetic books of the Jews are more important for true knowledge of Jews living yesterday, today, and tomorrow than all momentary experiences with brittle lives."[111]

Landauer's closest friends were Jews who, in very different ways, were also struggling with their Jewish heritage. Thus, the three people he described as the "very closest to me intellectually and personally" were the linguist Fritz Mauthner, the philosopher Constantin Brunner, and Martin Buber.[112] He also stood alongside them in a dialogue about his own conception of Judaism. To Brunner he explained that "I have not the slightest disposition to forget even for a day the joy I take in my Judaism."[113] When Mauthner wrote him on October 20, 1913, that "I feel only like a German; though I know that my brain somehow has a duct that is called Jewish," Landauer replied that this was "about how you, in the way you call this duct Jewish, are not merely talking about a feature that belongs to you individually, but about one that you have in common with a number of people. And what kind of value I attach to this community deriving from a common history, that is not something only logic decides for me. For my own part, I do not find so much in the commonalities going back for millennia that I would want to dispense with them, especially since I have no grounds to do so. . . . It has much more to do with a feeling that accompanies a reality."[114]

In the years before and during the First World War, Landauer published numerous articles in Jewish periodicals like *Selbstwehr*, *Die Freistatt*, and Buber's literary magazine *Der Jude*. He gave speeches before Zionist groups and opened the Jüdisches Volksheim (Jewish People's Home)—a settlement house in Berlin where penniless East European immigrants and German Jews could meet—with a lecture on the subject of Judaism and socialism. Before the Zionist university group Bar Kochba in Prague, he explained what was special about Jewish nationality. Landauer's concern was always about connecting Judaism with its environment—and with socialist values. His universalistic conception of Jewish Messianism is also expressed in this lecture, published under the telling title "Are These Heretical Thoughts?" There he writes: "Like a wild cry across the world and like a barely whispering voice in our innermost being, an irrefutable voice tells us that the Jew can only be redeemed at the same time as humanity and that it is one and the same: to await the Messiah in dispersion and banishment and to be the Messiah of the nations."[115]

Like many of his generation's Jewish rebels, Landauer rejected the self-satisfied, bourgeois, religiously reformed German Judaism of his parents' generation, which he contrasted with a lively and spiritual East European Judaism. In Martin Buber's journal *Der Jude*, which became a mouthpiece for the veneration of East European Jews among German-speaking Jews, he wrote: "The Jew . . . who repeatedly interrupts his common everyday life in order . . . to devote himself to what is uppermost, who brings into his business year the customs of ritual and, on the High Holy Days, bending low before the Eternal, for that very reason stands at a higher level than his brother in the Western metropolis, painted over with a varnish of education, who in place of religiosity of any kind has only . . . novels to read, theatrical fashion, and gossip about art."[116]

Landauer was simultaneously a Jew and a German. He also showed sympathy for the Zionist project. Thus, in a letter he wrote to Fritz

Mauthner in 1906, he characterized the Zionist periodical *Ost und West* as "the organ of the Young Zionists who do not emphasize denominational matters, but instead profess their Judaism for reasons that are national and individual and, on these grounds as well as for reasons of social welfare, want to promote Jewish colonization. I find this sympathetic."[117]

Yet he was unable to give himself away to the Zionist cause:

> It may be that the mother tongue for someone of the descendants sprung from my loins will be Hebrew; this does not move me; my language and that of my children is German. My Judaism is something I detect in my gestures, in my facial expression, my posture, my looks, and so these signs give me certainty that it lives in everything that I start and that I am. But much more—to the extent that there is anything more—than Chamisso the Frenchman was a German poet, am I, who is a Jew, a German. German Jew or Russian Jew—I find these expressions distorted, just like Jewish German or Russian. I don't know of any dependent or adjectival relationship there; the strokes of fate I take and I am as they are, my Germanness and my Jewishness do not harm each other and do a lot for the sake of each other. Like two brothers, a first-born and a Benjamin, not of the same kind but loved in equal measure by one mother, and how these two brothers live in unity with each other, where they come in contact with each other, and also where each goes his own way, that is how I experience this strange and familiar coexistence as something exquisite, and in this relationship I know neither what is primary and what is secondary.[118]

And in light of the dispersion of Jews across the entire world, Landauer—like the revisionist Social Democrat Eduard Bernstein—regarded the Jews as the ideal mediators between the nations.[119] In contrast to other "nations, which have demarcated themselves as states, [and] have neighbors outside who are their foes; our nation has neighbors in its own breast. . . . Should this not be a sign of the vocation that Judaism has to fulfill to humanity and in humanity?"[120]

During the war, the relationship between Landauer and Buber was subjected to a crucial test. When Buber, writing in the foreword to the first issue of his new journal *Der Jude*, discerned in the war experience something positive for the emergence of a new feeling of community, Landauer distanced himself from his friend, whom he now took to calling "war Buber" (*Kriegsbuber*).[121] Landauer replied to Buber in the words of a pacifist: "A pity for the Jewish blood, yes indeed; a pity for every drop of blood that is spilled in this war; a pity for every human soul; a pity, too, that you have gone astray in this war."[122] Their relationship to Zionism constituted another difference. Landauer told Buber a few months after the Balfour Declaration, in which the British government for the first time favored "the establishment in Palestine of a national home for the Jewish people," that the events in and around Palestine were of only marginal interest to him, while socialism was much more important: "The real event that is important and perhaps decisive for Jews is only the liberation of Russia. What happens in and around Palestine now and in the near future can only be a matter of maneuver confined to the area of the political angle of vision, and not much more is likely to come of it than of the Prince of Wied's Albanian kingdom. . . . For the present, I am pleased—in spite of everything—that Bronstein is not a professor at Jaffa University, but Trotsky in Russia."[123]

Yet the friendship between Landauer and Buber recovered once the war was over. From Munich, Landauer reported to Buber about the accomplishments of the revolution and especially of Eisner: "Collaboration with him goes splendidly. You will have gathered from his proclamations how 'anarchistic' his democracy is."[124] In the periodical he edited, Buber himself would have this to say about the revolution: "And thus the ideal whose fruit is the revolution finds its limits—but not its conclusion—in the institutions it brings forth. . . . A new socialism that continues and implements the old one is preparing itself in the creative spirits of the age—not least of all in the Jewish ones. Perhaps only now the creative period of the socialist ideal is truly beginning."[125]

More than any other of the active participants, Landauer also recognized a Jewish dimension to the revolution. In this light he wrote to Buber on December 2, 1918: "The revolution in Munich, for instance, where no one had thought of organizing on a wider scale before, was prepared by seven persons: at the head Kurt Eisner, who had thought out the procedure in prison; two ardent young Jews were his best and tireless helpers; one ally was a well-to-do Bavarian farmer who had been blind for seven years; the other three were young workers."[126] It is not entirely clear whom Landauer had in mind when he mentioned the "two ardent young Jews." It seems obvious that one was Fechenbach, and the other one could have been Ernst Toller.

He told the Provisional National Council at least once, on December 18, 1918, how sure he felt about belonging both to the Jewish and the German people: "We are the ones who know ourselves best. In the same way that we Jews, if you will permit me to say this, are truly the only legitimate and the best of all antisemites, that is, those who can recognize and articulate best of all and most profoundly all the damage inflicted on our national body because we have grown together with this nation, just so are we Germans obligated to articulate unsparingly what we observe not just from the outside somehow, the way a foreigner could, but rather what burns deep in our heart, where we feel."[127]

Kurt Eisner and his family spent the Christmas holidays with Landauer and his daughters in Krumbach, as the latter reported in a letter to Auguste Hauschner (the Prague-born Jewish novelist who hosted an important salon for artists in Berlin): "Kurt Eisner, with wife and children, spent Christmas eve with us here. . . . The first lighted tree since 1913, the first festival of peace!"[128] What Landauer could not have known: for both Jewish intellectuals, who had now become politicians, this was also going to be their last Christmas.

Zionist intellectuals saw in Landauer a potential ally in their cause. The writer Arnold Zweig, then living in Starnberg, very close to Munich, wrote to Buber: "It would be fortunate if one could transplant Landauer from German into Jewish politics. He faces a tragedy if he persists in this way, for he will only disturb and unsettle, but hardly accelerate, the rhythm of German events."[129] Yet Buber did not end up drawing Landauer into Jewish politics; instead, it was Landauer who first familiarized Buber with Bavarian politics. At Landauer's invitation, Buber traveled to Munich for a week in order to form his own impression of the revolution's consequences. He left the city on the very day in February, the 21st, when Eisner was murdered. Shortly thereafter,

Landauer confided to Buber his feelings for Eisner, the news of whose death reached Landauer on the first anniversary of his wife's death: "I was painfully fond of this man in life; now the pains are gone; I absorbed him into the love and loyalty that called me to my children on the morning of his death."[130]

The biblical prophets were often present when Landauer named the models for the revolution, and so they were again at the funeral speech for Eisner. This was something of which his contemporaries were also aware; they often likened Landauer himself to a prophet. This image—certainly also influenced by Landauer's physical appearance, with his long beard, longish hair falling over the back of his neck, and imposing body size, draped in a long dark cape—was one that cropped up in the way Fritz Mauthner, Martin Buber, Margarete Susman, and others wrote about him.[131] Moreover, Landauer was convinced that the revolution would bring forth a new kind of religion, a religion of life and love.[132] He was aware, of course, that he and Eisner had both come into the center from the fringe. Landauer regarded this development, in which marginal forces become central, as part of the prophetic vocation: the masses had been seized by "the spirit of the utopians, visionaries, and idealists who have been ridiculed, the spirit of those who have always stood in the corner, who were always isolated in their party, outside every party; regardless of where they stood, they were the lonely ones, and suddenly, when the time was ripe, this had become Prophetic Reality."[133]

The Eisner-Landauer relationship had a brief epilogue. Landauer had taken up quarters in Eisner's house in the Munich neighborhood of Großhadern. The widower Gustav Landauer and the widow Else Eisner got to be so close that, only a few weeks after Eisner's murder, they decided to become a couple. Thus, we find among the papers of Eisner's widow a handwritten note starting out with words "To our friends" and continuing: "in this wild time, in which the tempo is so turbulent, we two have found ourselves quietly and steadfastly in love and want to be a couple so long as life lasts."[134]

Even after Eisner's assassination, and just a few weeks before his life came to a violent end, Landauer was corresponding with Martin Buber and the young Zionist (and later president of the World Jewish Congress)

FIGURE 9. Gustav Landauer, portrait by Hitler's later personal photographer
Heinrich Hoffmann. Bayerische Staatsbibliothek München / Bildarchiv.

Nachum Goldmann about his participation in a conference of Jewish socialists scheduled to convene in Munich, at which discussions about the
kibbutz idea and other Zionist ideals were planned. Landauer agreed to
participate: "I believe the conference can be fruitful."[135] But before that
could happen, more important events intervened.

On April 7, after prolonged hesitation and against the resistance of
the Communists, writers with anarchist inclinations—with Ernst
Toller, Erich Mühsam, and Gustav Landauer in the lead—proclaimed

the Council Republic of Bavaria (Räterepublik Baiern). It was Landauer's forty-ninth birthday, and he was at the peak of his political career. In this First Council Republic, he had become the people's commissar for public education, instruction, science, and arts. The writer Isolde Kurz noted a year later: "In the bookstores all you saw was socialist and communist literature; the most widely read author during those days was Gustav Landauer."[136] The day the council republic was founded—also Gustav Landauer's birthday—was spontaneously declared a national holiday. As Kurz described the public response, Munich's population took note of all this with indifference: "We also got a national holiday, so in droves the people of Munich went for a walk in the warm glow on dry sidewalks, here and there studying one of the new government's gigantic posters without a wince, at most someone would just sigh 'That's something!' and then continue strolling on in peace. . . . It was like a ball falling into a woolen sack. Nobody answered, either to approve or contradict. The soul of the crowd seemed entirely absent." For many, she continued, the council republic was nothing more than a "substitute for Carnival."[137]

Just a week later, the First Council Republic collapsed. The Communists, who only one week earlier had nothing but scorn and derision for the Landauer-Toller-Mühsam regime, now seized power following the failed Palm Sunday Putsch of the Republican Guard, backed by the Hoffmann government that had fled to Bamberg. Under the leadership of the Russian-Jewish journalist Eugen Leviné, the Russian-born ethnic German Max Levien (frequently and falsely labeled a Jew because of his name), and the Munich-born city commandant and Red Army leader Rudolf Egelhofer, a second and significantly more radical council republic emerged as of April 13. Gustav Landauer could no longer identify with its politics and submitted his resignation from all of his political positions.[138]

When "White" troops, who were made up of Freikorps members and Reichswehr (national army) soldiers, crushed this Second Council Republic in Munich on May 1 and 2, Landauer's fate was initially uncertain. Worried that he would become a target of the right-wing troops despite his disassociation from the radical Communist regime, his friends rushed to save his life. Martin Buber called for the creation of a committee that would publicly advocate for Landauer. His initiative met with approval from Fritz Mauthner: "I assume that we are completely in agreement on the matter: Saving, if possible, the valuable and so lovely person of G.L., without approving any particular politics. . . . We cannot protect him from himself, and he would also reject that. . . . Very sad that it is exactly the idealism of his circle—not to mention some Russians I find suspicious—that is allowing a new wave of antisemitism to take storm over Germany. The rage in Bavaria is alarming."[139]

These efforts to assist came too late. On May 1, sitting at the desk of Kurt Eisner, Gustav Landauer was arrested by right-wing Freikorps members and brutally murdered the next day in the Stadelheim prison in Munich.[140] In his last letter to Fritz Mauthner, on April 7, 1919, less than a month before his murder, he had written: "If I'm allowed a few weeks of time, then I hope to accomplish something; but it is easily possible that it will only be a few days, and then it was all a dream."[141]

Just as after Kurt Eisner's assassination, the Zionist paper *Das Jüdische Echo* again published a moving obituary: "Gustav Landauer did not enter into any relationship with local Jewish circles and Jewish politics. . . . Yet there is evidence from Landauer's earlier works of the serious humane feeling and inner sympathy with which he approached the problems of Judaism." The article in *Das Jüdische Echo* called it a sacred duty to honor his memory. As a sign of its solidarity, the newspaper reprinted Landauer's essay on East and West European Jews.[142] Despite their political differences, Martin Buber kept faith with his friend after death and posthumously dedicated the seventh of his "Speeches on Judaism" to Landauer with the title: "The Holy Path: A Word to the Jews and to the Gentiles."

"I Will Demonstrate Once More That I Am Someone from the Old Testament!"—Erich Mühsam

"That I am a Jew is something I view neither as an advantage nor as a defect; it is simply part of my essence like my red beard, my bodily weight, or my inclinations and interests," Erich Mühsam wrote in reply to a letter from the Orthodox merchant (and commercial councilor) Siegmund Fraenkel, who had accused Mühsam and his comrades of committing treason against the Jewish community by proclaiming the council republic.[143] Like Eisner and Landauer, Mühsam had also cut himself loose from Judaism as a religious community yet never questioned that he belonged to the Jewish community as such. The poem mentioned at the beginning of this chapter, "Holy Night," may be an indicator of his cultural attachment, even as an anarchist (and later, for a short time, as a Communist), to Judaism.[144]

He was born in 1878 in Berlin, yet his family soon moved to North German Lübeck, where his father Siegfried operated a pharmacy and held office for twenty-eight years as a member of the city parliament. There are extremely contradictory assessments of Siegfried Mühsam's Judaism. As Erich's cousin Paul Mühsam later reported, while Siegfried Mühsam was acquainted with Jewish traditions from his own home, "personally he was completely assimilated and took pains to make sure that nothing distinguished him from his Christian fellow-citizens."[145] By contrast, the historian Ingaburgh Klatt writes: "Siegfried Seligmann Mühsam remained a lifelong Orthodox Jew . . . and he clung to traditional Jewish rituals and values."[146] The truth likely lies in between. The diary entries of eleven-year-old Erich about a vacation in Sylt (a wealthy seaside island resort on the North Sea) clearly indicate that the family did not keep kosher and that Siegfried Mühsam could not have been characterized as strictly Orthodox.[147] Nor was he "completely assimilated." Otherwise he would hardly have let himself be nominated as a candidate for the board of the Lübeck Jewish Community, and a few years later for its council of elders.[148]

But above all, Siegfried Mühsam, whose brother was a rabbi in the Austrian city of Graz and whose sister was married to a rabbi, could never have been so utterly assimilated given his authorship of two books depicting Jewish community life in a small town around 1850. These publications—so strongly peppered with Yiddish expressions that a special glossary had to be added to the two volumes—were quite clearly meant for a Jewish reading public. Even the title, *Die Killeberger: Nach der Natur aufgenommen von Onkel Siegfried* (The Killebergers: Recorded from Real Life by Uncle Siegfried), can only be understood if one knows that *Kille* was the word German Jews used for *Kehillah* or "Jewish community" (from the Hebrew word for "assembly" or "gathering").[149] The publication went through three printings, with an impressive sixty thousand copies, and its success even inspired "Uncle" Siegfried Mühsam (his full name was aired only when the third edition came out) to produce a sequel with the title *Neu-Killeberg*.[150]

As witty and sensitive as Siegfried Mühsam may have shown himself to be in his literary work, he was just as humorless and authoritarian in his parenting. When Erich's teacher complained about the pupil's lack of diligence, the father noted in the boy's class register: "There will be no lack of severity on my part."[151] He also made sure that his offspring got to feel some bodily thrashing. Erich Mühsam felt repelled both by the bourgeois narrowness of his parental home and by the Wilhelmine values propagated at his school. Owing to "socialist machinations," he was expelled from his high school shortly before graduation. Since his socialist activities kept him from getting his graduation certificate (which would have entitled him to move on to a university), he instead completed an apprenticeship (reluctantly, but at his father's insistence) as a pharmacist. After a short period as a pharmacist's assistant in Blomberg and then Berlin, he embarked on his career as a writer. Many years later, in a lengthy diary entry on the occasion of his father's seventy-second birthday, Erich Mühsam described his father's uncaring brutality: "Whenever I ask myself what I should thank him for, nothing really comes to my mind, apart from the fact that he created me."[152]

Yet Mühsam could not let go of the relationship with his father. Shortly before his father's death, he noted in his diary: "Years ago I once dreamed that I had my father subjected to a medical examination. An entire commission of physicians undertook the task. In an adjoining room I awaited the results. When the commission entered, its spokesman, a white-bearded scholar, announced: 'The meticulous examination of your father has shown that he is the eternal Jew.'—I am starting to believe in prophetic dreams."[153] At his father's burial, the main note he struck was abhorrence of religious rituals: "What I found dreadful after the coffin was lowered was the religious ceremony in the consecration hall, where Hans and I, believe it or not, had to take off our shoes and run back and forth." Finally, he learned that he would be disinherited of everything except the compulsory share required by German inheritance law unless he should become a pharmacist, "marry a Jewish-born (very funny!) Jewish woman, or get to be 60 years old."[154] While his father was still alive, he had many non-Jewish girlfriends, but he had also fallen in love with Jenny Brünn, a young woman from a wealthy Jewish family. It gave him a certain degree of satisfaction that this relationship would gratify his parents, but here, too, it was religious ritual that acted as the greatest deterrent to a marriage. Since her parents rejected the match, he wrote with some relief: "We are now spared the revolting concession of a religious wedding."[155]

Nevertheless, it would not be until 1926 that Mühsam would officially leave the organized Jewish community as a religious denomination. It cannot be determined with any certainty whether he had remained loyal to the Jewish community until then out of consideration for his family background, because he identified with a persecuted community, or for the pragmatic reason that he did not want to be disinherited.[156] Like Landauer, Erich Mühsam was part of a generation that frequently rebelled against their fathers' bourgeois values. Often Judaism also played a role in this rebellion, as when Jewish practice consisted only in superficial ritual whose meaning was no longer recognized or had become a joke, as Franz Kafka depicts in his "Letter to Father."[157] This conflict often led the next generation to try radical solutions, such as Zionism, on the one hand, or communism, on the other. One famous example of this intergenerational dynamic is the Scholem family from Berlin. It produced both Gershom (Gerhard), a Zionist activist, scholar of Jewish mysticism, and later professor at the Hebrew University of Jerusalem, and his brother Werner, who became a Communist member of the Reichstag.[158] A third brother, Reinhold Scholem, as a member of the German National People's Party, was a German Nationalist. In November 1919, Reinhold wrote a birthday greeting to Gerhard, then studying in Munich, in which he expressed his joy about how "the German idea is still alive and had not been drowned in the torrent of phrases from the coffee house literati. Now that the days of the council government are over, it is in Munich of all places that the highlight of the Independent [Social Democrats] and similar riff-raff seems to have disappeared. . . . The Russian and Bavarian Jews have also given us a bad reputation there."[159]

The situation was similar in the Mühsam family. While Siegfried Mühsam rejected socialism and Zionism, his son Erich took the path of an anarchist and later Communist, and his other children, Hans and Charlotte, embraced Zionism. Like her father, Charlotte Landau-Mühsam was a representative on Lübeck's city council, which she entered as a candidate of the liberal German Democratic Party (DDP) and where she also championed women's rights. In 1933, she joined her husband in emigrating to Palestine. Toward the end of the First World War, another writer in the family, Erich's cousin Paul Mühsam, was just as dismissive as the rest of his family in his assessment of the revolutionary events in Germany. In his diary entry for November 11, 1918, he warned about the chaos of the Spartacus Group, which wanted to bring about "mass terror." On December 31, he expressed his fear that the Spartacus Group, whose goal was "chaos and anarchy," was continuing to run rampant. Like the rest of his family, Paul Mühsam adopted a skeptical attitude toward his cousin Erich.[160]

Yet there was one experience shared by all the Mühsams of Erich's generation: the continued social ostracism of Jews and the encounter with antisemitism. In her memoirs, Erich Mühsam's sister Charlotte described the kinds of social barriers that continued to separate Jews from Christians in Lübeck in spite of the family's social community involvement: "Because of the strict separation between Jews and Christians in Lübeck, we associated almost exclusively with Jewish families."[161] She also depicted what antisemitism was like in her childhood years. In school it was said of her brother Hans, for example, that he "smelled of garlic," an old anti-Jewish trope.[162]

For Erich Mühsam, too, the encounter with antisemitism was important, even though in his case it meant looking at the Czarist Empire, where persecution of the Jews was at the time more tangible than in the German Empire. As was the case with Kurt Eisner and other socialists, antisemitism also reinforced his sense of identifying as a Jew. In *Kain*, the "journal for humanity" that he founded in April 1911 and most of whose articles were composed almost exclusively by him, he repeatedly devoted coverage to attacks against Judaism, as in the article "Ritual Murder" from 1913.

In this article, he takes the side of Mendel Beilis, the superintendent of a brick factory put on trial in Kiev after being charged with murdering a Christian child. It enraged Mühsam that the medieval fiction of blood libel had resurfaced in this case, and he left no doubt that in this situation even the most secular Jews had to show solidarity with Jewish victims:

> If you will forgive me for saying so: the Beilis trial is indeed a matter for international Jewry, since the dreadful accusation affects every Jew. And the trial would also be of concern to international Christendom if there were even the smallest hint of truth in the accusation. Whoever has Jewish blood flowing through one's veins knows that this is not the case, knows this with the same absolute certainty as the accused and his accusers. That is why it is the duty of all of us who are Jews to remind ourselves at a moment like this of our Jewish heritage and to demand that the matter against which Beilis has to defend himself is raised against all of us. In this moment there cannot be any orthodox and liberal Jews, no baptized and ex-Jews, no European and Asian Jews. In this moment I know that I am in solidarity with every Galician horse trader, just as Spinoza or Heinrich Heine would have known solidarity with him.[163]

This solidarity with the Jewish community distinguished Mühsam, and most of the Munich Jewish revolutionaries, fundamentally from other socialists with a Jewish background, such as Rosa Luxemburg, who, alerted to "Jewish distress" and the "special pangs of Jews" in Russia by her friend Mathilde Wurm, said dismissively: "I feel . . . just as close to the poor victims of the rubber plantations in Putomayo, the Negroes in Africa." She had no "special corner in [my] heart for the ghetto."[164]

Mühsam did not share this repudiation of any kind of collective ties to the Jewish community. In an article from 1908 about Maximilian Harden, a Jewish convert to Christianity, he expressed his conviction

FIGURE 10. The first edition of
Erich Mühsam's journal *Kain* (1911).
Süddeutsche Zeitung Photo.

that one could not just break away from the Jewish community. Here,
it should be noted, he was certainly using the concept of "race" in the
colloquial manner that was common at the time, not in some "scientific" sense:

> The thought of trying to solve a racial problem by having one race
> absorbed into another strikes me as absurd. . . . Harden is completely
> overlooking the immense value of the Jewish race as a leaven in the
> different nationalities and cultures. He underestimates the skill with
> which the Jews have preserved their race in spite of all the instances
> of harassment, and he fails to appreciate the driving principle, the
> aesthetic incentive that resides in the preservation of such valuable
> races as those of the Jews and the gypsies. That is why Zionism, es-
> pecially the kind of cultural Zionism recommended by Martin Buber,
> seems far more appropriate to me than Harden's ideas of amalgama-
> tion, even if I certainly see hardly any promise in the kind of Zionism
> that is now the custom of the country, with its [schemes for] found-
> ing a state.[165]

For Mühsam, who kept his distance from any kind of religious activity, there was even a certain pride in the way he spoke about the heritage

of the Old Testament: "All those who would have me atone for having convictions—for this is what it all comes down to—they should all regret this! Wait, you dogs! I will demonstrate once more that I am someone from the Old Testament!"[166] Just as with Eisner and Landauer, the prophetic ideal also shows up in the case of Mühsam. He, too, was a prophetic figure to many, if only because of his external appearance. And he, too, shared Eisner's and Landauer's sense of absolute justice, saw himself as a pacifist, and thunderously declared his political opinions in public. Between the lines there also resonated a goodly portion of pride about belonging to those "from the Old Testament"—just as in the Christmas poem quoted at the beginning of this chapter, in which he acknowledges with a certain note of irony that he, unlike those celebrating Christmas, belongs to the people of Jesus.

Erich Mühsam's relationship to Judaism, like his political worldview, was shaped decisively by Gustav Landauer, the man to whom he "owed the most intellectually."[167] Like Martin Buber, Mühsam was somebody Landauer also became acquainted with in the circle of the New Community established by the Hart brothers in Berlin. Mühsam read Landauer's essay "Through Separation to Community" five to six times and immediately recognized its author as "a great thinker and human being."[168] Landauer and Mühsam—like Buber—shared the circle's enthusiasm for a romantic-oriented, anti-urban ideal of society. They participated actively in two different ventures aimed at creating agricultural settlements—an experiment that failed in both cases even though it did serve as one (though certainly not the main) inspiration for the socialist Zionists who established the kibbutz way of life in Palestine. Both Landauer and Mühsam were publishers of anarchist-oriented journals.

In a letter to Hedwig Mauthner, Landauer articulated a belief very similar to Mühsam's conviction that ethnic communities are not so easy to dissolve: "I don't know anything about races; just about realities, and since humankind is not some kind of porridge, not even a fruit salad, but rather a garden, it will certainly remain the case that the same bark does not grow on all trees." Five days later, he wrote to her husband Fritz: "As far as humankind is concerned, as your wife maintains, the idea that we all are of one humankind will be able to do as little damage to all the differentiated nations and other natural-societal-historical communities as the fact that we are all mammals is capable of exterminating humankind."[169] This was a very clear rejection of Mauthner's abandonment of his Judaism and of every other attempt at negating the belonging to one's own community.

Residing in Munich since 1908, Mühsam participated in the artistic life of the city and kept in close touch with Frank Wedekind and the theater and cabaret scene there.[170] He was frequently viewed as the personification of the bohemian world and took a certain pride in acknowledging himself as a bohemian. In April 1918, arrested for violating the ban on political activity, Mühsam served his sentence in the town of Traunstein and was not released until October 31. A week later he was already in the thick of the revolutionary events. He himself boasted that he was the first person to have proclaimed the republic in Germany, although there is no proof of this. In a letter from December 1, 1918, he wrote: "I believe I have a special claim to be heard. For on November 7 toward a quarter to 6 in the afternoon I was the first person in Germany to publicly proclaim the deposition of the dynasties and the establishment of a free Bavarian council republic. The demonstration that Eisner and Auer had convened on the Theresienwiese started out very boringly, although there were enormous masses taking part in it. Only a few soldiers with red flags were splendidly lively." Most people, according to Mühsam, were rejecting any kind of action, so he made his way to the army barracks. "My wife had herself lifted onto a military auto on which a number of soldiers were waving a red flag. Yet I also crawled up there and gave a speech to the soldiers congregating there and to the public in which I called for revolution and proclaimed the republic. Now the revolution was suddenly there. I was declared its leader." Mühsam claimed that Eisner "proclaimed at half past eleven at night the same thing that I had proclaimed 6 hours earlier."[171]

Mühsam was part of the revolution from the outset, yet in a certain way he always played a kind of outsider role. He thought that Eisner was proceeding too cautiously. Although he did replace the monarchy with a republic, Eisner left the old elites untouched. Mühsam wanted a more radical change. On November 30, 1918, he founded the Union of

FIGURE 11. Erich Mühsam. Sueddeutsche Zeitung.

Revolutionary Internationalists, which called for a more substantial revolution in the structures of the state. On April 7, 1919, when the First Council Republic was proclaimed, Mühsam was convinced that his moment had come. Although he did not receive the appointment as foreign minister he had sought, he played an active role in the politics of the new rulers. A week later, he was among the prisoners of the failed putsch of the Majority Social Democrats on April 13, which probably saved his life. For just a few weeks later, when Gustav Landauer and other revolutionaries were murdered, Mühsam happened to be in custody in the detention center at the former Ebrach abbey in Upper Franconia. He was then transferred to the prison in Niederschönenfeld (another former cloister, somewhat closer to Munich, where several other supporters of the council republic charged with high treason were confined). He was finally released on December 20, 1924—ironically, on the same day Adolf Hitler left the Landsberg prison after a much shorter and more comfortable internment.

"But Am I Not . . . a Member of That People That for Millennia Has Been Persecuted, Harried, Martyrized and Slain?"—Ernst Toller

On April 8, 1918, one day after the first Munich Council Republic was proclaimed, the teacher Ernst Niekisch resigned as the chair of the Revolutionary Central Committee of the Workers', Farmers', and Soldiers' Councils. His successor was Ernst Toller. This meant that the person now heading the People's State of Bavaria (Volksstaat Baiern) was a twenty-five-year-old student whose livelihood was basically maintained by financial contributions from his mother. Like Eisner, Mühsam, and Landauer, Toller was regarded as one of the "literati," and like them he was also a "newcomer" to Bavaria and the son of Jewish parents. Yet Toller belonged to a younger generation that was different from his fellow literati, and he came from the border region between Germany and Poland, where East European Jews intersected with West European Jewry.

Toller was born in 1893 in Samotschin (Szamocin) in what was then the Prussian province of Posen. His father was a grain wholesaler and the only Jewish representative in the small town's municipal assembly. Ernst Toller said very little about his Judaism during the revolution in Munich.[172] But in his moving autobiography from 1933, *I Was a German*, he looked back and reflected extensively on his childhood living among Jews, Poles, and Germans in what, by the time he wrote this book, had once again become the Polish province of Posen. All these groups' positions were sharply defined, and from the perspective of 1933, they all seemed infinitely wide apart: "Against the Poles, Jews and Germans showed a united front. The Jews looked upon themselves as the pioneers of German culture. . . . [O]n the Kaiser's birthday the Jews sat at the same table as the Reserve officers, the War League, and the Home Defense Corps, and drank beer and schnapps and raised their glasses to the Kaiser's health."[173] As a child, Toller was repeatedly exposed to antisemitism, as when the rumor of a Jewish ritual murder surfaced in the West Prussian town of Konitz: "On the street the children shout: 'Jew, hep, hep!' . . . In Konitz the Jews have slaughtered a Christian boy and used his blood to make matzos." Or when he went into the room of his Polish friend Stanislaus, who had internalized the anti-Jewish prejudices of Toller's Christian neighbors, and secretly prayed to the crucifix hanging there: "Please, dear Savior, forgive me for letting the Jews kill you dead."[174]

Toller went to war enthusiastically. As soon as the war broke out, he returned to Germany from Grenoble, where he was a university student, and volunteered while he was in Munich, still on his way back home. In May 1916, after thirteen months of harrowing experiences on the front in France, he suffered a complete breakdown and was admitted to a military hospital. He began to write, established contacts with Munich writers, met Rainer Maria Rilke, and was invited to visit Thomas Mann in his home.

In September 1917, he accepted the invitation of the publisher Eugen Diederichs to attend a conference at Lauenstein Castle in Thuringia. Among the many intellectuals he met there was Max Weber, to whom he would remain especially close. Yet in this dry cerebral climate, Toller's thirst for action stood out in contrast to the purely theoretical discussions at this secluded intellectual retreat. In his memoir, he summed up his disappointment at all the grand rhetoric accompanied by inaction. "There had been nothing but words, words, words." His closeness to Max Weber was one reason he enrolled as a student at the University of Heidelberg for the winter semester of 1917. The dissertation topic he was given by his supervisor, the economist Eberhard Gothein, was a rather intriguing choice for a budding Jewish revolutionary. According to Toller's own account, the subject was "Pig-breeding in East Prussia."[175] One of the consequences of Toller's participation in the Lauenstein conference was his decision to found the Young Germans' Cultural and Political Union "to shake up the students" and combat power politics and militarism. Their demands included abolishing the death penalty, the separation of church and state, lowering the voting age, and fighting poverty. Gustav Landauer's call for socialism had the same decisive influence on Toller as it did on Mühsam. In their exchange of letters from the end of 1917, Toller showed himself to be a "pupil quick and eager to learn" from Landauer. Later he visited him at Landauer's home in the Swabian town of Krumbach.[176]

Under the influence of Landauer, Toller returned to Munich in January 1918. In weekly discussions, he met up with Landauer along with Kurt Eisner, Erich Mühsam, Felix Fechenbach, Hans Unterleitner, and Edgar Jaffé, the group that would later become the hard core of the revolutionary leadership.[177] Toller made a special impression on Oskar Maria Graf, another regular participating in the meetings of the Independent Socialists at the Goldener Anker: "Ernst Toller, who had fled from Heidelberg, was making a fiery speech against the war. Fervent, ecstatic, with fierce gesticulations and face convulsed with passion, he poured out his feelings. He shivered like a man in fever and foamed at the mouth. He seemed to me all blackness. . . . Everybody was swept off their feet. A few women wept or became frenzied."[178]

Shortly after his return to Munich, Toller participated, though only briefly, in the strike of ammunition workers organized by Eisner. Like the latter, he was arrested. In jail, he completed the drama he had begun writing in 1917, *Transfiguration* ("Die Wandlung"). In that play he describes his protagonist Friedrich's transformation from a soldier with war fever to a pacifist. Toller's own experience as a Jewish outsider is also reflected in the character of Friedrich. In the drama's opening scene, the protagonist, looking at the Christmas trees "in the windows of the houses across the street," proclaims: "I, . . . [an] outcast, struggle between one shore and the next, far from the old and farther from the new. A nasty hybrid. . . . No—I'll no longer drag around this weariness. What are they to me—my people? Their blood is in my veins, but what is that to me? It is to you over there I belong—to you. A simple creature, ready to prove himself." Responding to his mother's question about where he has been all day, he answers: "Wandering, Mother. Wandering—as usual . . . I've told you—wandering. . . . Like him, Ahasuerus. . . . Yes, it is him I seek, my great brother, Ahasuerus, the eternal wanderer, the homeless one. . . . They have homes, over there, homes of their own to which they belong. Over there they are at one with themselves and with their homes. . . . They can laugh, over there, and live with joy in their hearts."[179] When, at the end, he is confronted by his mother with the charge that he has become estranged from his people and his family back home, Friedrich replies: "I am nearer to them than ever I was before."[180]

Most likely owing to the intervention of his mother, who was unwilling to admit that her son might be guilty of treason, Toller was transferred to a psychiatric clinic led by Professor Emil Kraepelin, one of the most prominent psychiatrists of his generation and founder of the German Research Institute for Psychiatry. Kraepelin was a staunch German nationalist and certainly amenable to antisemitic prejudices. In his memoirs, Toller described the psychiatrist as a national chauvinist who bellowed at his patients and laid the blame on pacifists like Toller for the German army's failure to conquer Paris. Immediately after the council republic in Bavaria was put down, Kraepelin published "On the Truth about the Revolution," an article in the *Süddeutsche Monatshefte* in which he attempted to demonstrate connections between psychiatric disorders and the revolutionaries. In the article he also insinuated that Jews—and those he had in mind would certainly have included his former patient Toller—suffered from a psychopathic predisposition: "This is also the context for the substantial involvement of the Jewish race in these revolutions. The frequency of a psychopathic predisposition in this group could have contributed to this, even if it is most certainly their aptitude for corrosive criticism, their linguistic and theatrical talent, as well as their tenacity and ambitiousness that come into question here."[181] From his personal notes we know that Kraepelin advocated "purposeful racial breeding" and, in this context, actively opposed "Jewish domination" in public life. While Germans cared above all about "inner fulfillment," Jews were superficial creatures who craved success and only had "external advantages" in mind.[182] Later, foreign observers would express the same kind of derogatory sentiments about Toller, as in an assessment written up by the British secret service.[183]

After Toller was released in the autumn of 1918, he first made his way to Berlin and then to visit his mother in Landsberg an der Warthe (the Pomeranian town 150 kilometers west of his birthplace in Posen, today known by its Polish name Gorzów Wielkopolski). Like Landauer, Toller was also in bed with a cold on November 7, 1918, so that, under his mother's care, he missed the outbreak of the revolution in Munich. A few days later, however, he headed for Munich, where, as the vice-chair of the Executive Council of the Bavarian Workers', Farmers', and Soldiers' Councils, he immediately played a critical role in the revolutionary events of November 1918. But the decisive moment in his political career was the proclamation of the Council Republic in April 1919. This eruption flushed the young student all the way to the top of the revolutionary geyser.[184]

In addition to Toller, Landauer, and Mühsam, there were a number of other prominent Jewish actors in the short-lived First Council Republic. They included, as president of the Central Economic Office, the eminent economist Otto Neurath, who had a position as lecturer with Max Weber in Heidelberg and was director of the German War Economy Museum in Leipzig; and the people's commissioner for housing, the jurist Arnold Wadler from Cracow. Both of these men were original minds who would present the world with creative ideas long after their involvement in revolutionary politics. After his release from prison, Neurath returned home to Austria, where he became a pioneer in museum education and made a name for himself as the inventor of the Viennese method of pictorial statistics. In Bavaria he had fostered a plan to construct a moneyless economy. Wadler was given an excessively high eight-year sentence, despite his nonviolent behavior, after the fall of the council republic and the failure of his plans to end the housing shortage. He was convinced that there was a primal community of all the world's languages, and he pursued this idea in his scholarly writings after his release from prison.

Women were now also close to the reins of power. This elicited indignation from some commentators. The papal nuncio, and later Pope Pius XII, complained about the "horde of young women not looking very confidence-inspiring" who had now "ensconced" themselves in the Wittelsbach Palace. One woman the future pope found especially repugnant was a Russian Jew; identifying her as the lover of Max Levien, he reported that "she commands like a mistress."[185] In reality, almost all power remained in the hands of men during both of the council republics. One of the few exceptions was the Communist Frida Rubiner. During the Second Council Republic, she was a member of the Transportation Commission and Propaganda Committee, editor of the newspaper *Rote Fahne* (*Red Flag*), and, under the name "Comrade Friedjung," gave a lecture on "Bolshevism and Democracy."[186] The Lithuanian-born tailor had enrolled as a student in Zurich before the war and earned a doctorate in physics. In Switzerland, she had become acquainted with Lenin and was among the founders of the German Communist Party (KPD) in 1918. She first arrived in Munich after the proclamation of the Second Council Republic but was arrested after its suppression and sentenced to a year and nine months in prison for the key role she had played in the revolution.[187] One of Toller's closest friends from his time as a student in Heidelberg was Nelly Auerbach, who was also an active participant in the revolutionary events in Munich, working in the office of the press department.[188]

Toller was one of the few actors who continuously played an important role in three periods: during Eisner's tenure in office (as chair of the Bavarian USPD, a role in which he continued after Eisner's death), in the First Council Republic (as chair of the Central Committee and thus as its most important political figure de facto), and in the Second Council Republic. In the Communist council government, however, his influence waned decisively from the very outset. It was the pacifist Toller, of all people, who was now degraded to the post of city commandant for Munich, commanding just one section of the revolutionary army. Yet even in this function he rejected any use of violence against civilians and attempted to prevent the incident later described

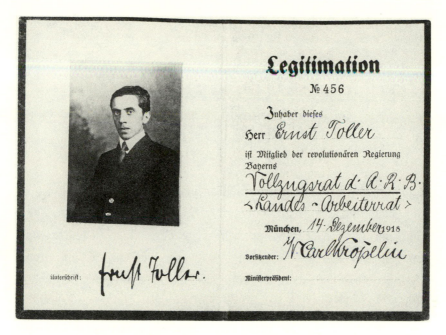

FIGURE 12. Identification card as member of the revolutionary government for Ernst Toller. Stadtarchiv München.

as a "hostage murder"—the killing of prisoners held by the council republic in a secondary school, the Luitpold Gymnasium.[189]

By no means did Toller ignore the antisemitism widespread among the opponents of the revolution, which had escalated along with the appearance of numerous Jewish protagonists prominent in the two council republics. The situation had become so serious that the Provisional Revolutionary Executive Council, only in power for a very short time, felt obliged to issue a proclamation signed by Toller and addressed "To the Citizens of the Council Republic." In this appeal, he protested against the leaflets "that are attempting, in the most disgraceful and criminal manner, to incite the passions of the masses against the Jews. At the same time, bourgeois provocateurs are inciting against Jews on the streets."[190] As a child living in Munich at the time, Fritz Rosenthal (who later achieved some prominence as a philosopher of religion in Jerusalem under his Hebrew name Schalom Ben-Chorin)

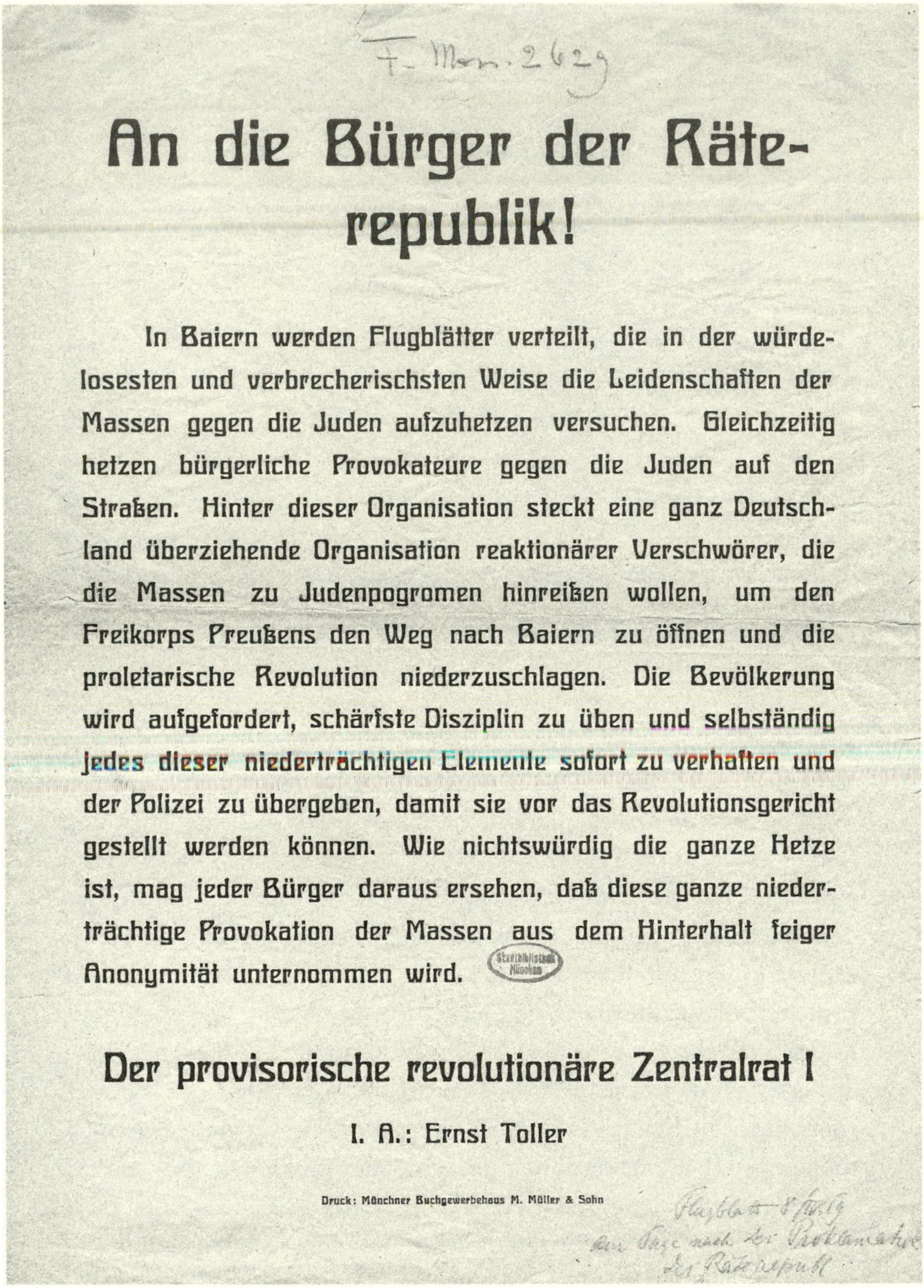

An die Bürger der Räte-republik!

In Baiern werden Flugblätter verteilt, die in der würde-losesten und verbrecherischsten Weise die Leidenschaften der Massen gegen die Juden aufzuhetzen versuchen. Gleichzeitig hetzen bürgerliche Provokateure gegen die Juden auf den Straßen. Hinter dieser Organisation steckt eine ganz Deutschland überziehende Organisation reaktionärer Verschwörer, die die Massen zu Judenpogromen hinreißen wollen, um den Freikorps Preußens den Weg nach Baiern zu öffnen und die proletarische Revolution niederzuschlagen. Die Bevölkerung wird aufgefordert, schärfste Disziplin zu üben und selbständig jedes dieser niederträchtigen Elemente sofort zu verhaften und der Polizei zu übergeben, damit sie vor das Revolutionsgericht gestellt werden können. Wie nichtswürdig die ganze Hetze ist, mag jeder Bürger daraus ersehen, daß diese ganze niederträchtige Provokation der Massen aus dem Hinterhalt feiger Anonymität unternommen wird.

Der provisorische revolutionäre Zentralrat I

I. A.: Ernst Toller

Druck: Münchner Buchgewerbehaus M. Müller & Sohn

FIGURE 13. Leaflet against antisemitism signed by Ernst Toller. F.Mon. 2626, Münchner Stadtbibliothek / Monacensia.

furnished this leaflet with the comment: "In this manifesto Toller had the courage to oppose openly the antisemitic incitement that was already being stirred up into pogroms in 1919. . . . Toller did not suspect that his signature to this proclamation must have had less of an impact than one of the Bavarian revolutionaries with a name like Kohlschmid, Wimmer, or Mehrer."[191]

Like Landauer, Toller also became a victim of the vengeful new rulers who overthrew the revolution. But after the fall of the council republic—whose leadership he had left in the end in a dispute—he did manage to stay secluded for several weeks in different hideouts. The wanted man was not discovered until June 4, 1919, a delay that undoubtedly saved his life. In the trial at the special tribunal following his arrest, he was sentenced to five years in prison. Even his political opponents acknowledged that Toller had attempted to prevent acts of violence during the council republic. His advocates included Max Weber, Thomas Mann, and Ricarda Huch.[192]

In his 1933 autobiography, Toller reflects on his "life as German and Jew" (to pick up on the title of the novelist Jakob Wassermann's own autobiographical work). His remarks on the subject were triggered by an antisemitic incident during an organized disruption of his play *Hinkemann* at the Dresden State Theater. As a man in one of the boxes collapsed as a result of the excitement and suffered a heart attack, one of the disrupters bent over him, "coolly studied him, saw the arched nose, and turning to his companions said: 'It's only a Jew!'" This prompted Toller to think back on his youth and the humiliations he experienced when others identified him as a Jew. As Wassermann did in his autobiographical reflections, Toller asked himself why he always had to prove that he was a German, that he loved the German landscape and language as part of his only homeland. But, he added, could he not simultaneously be a Jew? "Am I not . . . a member of that people that for millennia has been persecuted, harried, martyrized and slain; whose prophets had called the world to righteousness, had exalted the wretched and the oppressed, then and for all time. . . . I had denied my own mother, and I was ashamed. . . . How much of me was German, how much Jewish? I could not have said." Finally, he arrived at the frequently quoted insight about what summed up his very essence, the facts "that a Jewish mother had borne me, that Germany had nourished me, that Europe had formed me, that my home was the earth, and the world my fatherland."[193]

"Jewish Is How My Head Thinks, Russian How My Heart Feels"—Eugen Leviné

In his testimony before a special tribunal in Munich, Eugen Leviné, who had helped determine the fortunes of the city for three weeks in April 1919, was on record saying: "My father died when I was three years old, so the only upbringing I had was from my mother. My mother was a Russian, but she had a German education. I attended the German gymnasium in Petersburg. At age fourteen I came to Germany. At first I moved with my mother to Wiesbaden, where I attended gymnasium, then I went to gymnasium in Heidelberg, and later to the university there."[194] He went on to describe how he became a member of the Russian Social Revolutionary Party in 1903, took part in the revolution of 1905, was frequently jailed in Russia, returned to Germany in 1908, and earned a doctorate in political economy at Heidelberg University in 1914.

He also did not deny his Jewish background. "I am well aware that I am a Russian by descent, I am a Jew, not a Bavarian. How could I presume to take on the post that is the equivalent of a prime minister. In order to understand this, you have to put yourself in the position of the working class; our ideal is the German council republic of the future that will later be absorbed into the international council republic."[195]

Even if he had not pointed this out himself, the fact that he was a Jew kept being introduced into the trial record by others. This happened, for example, when his chauffeur, Anton Nothelfer, was asked if he had worked for Leviné. Yes, Nothelfer answered, he was forced to do this, and he continued to relate how an acquaintance had asked him "if I am driving for the Jew pig Levien-Nissen [sic], which I answered in the affirmative."[196] Or when Munich's military command headquarters wrote this description for a wanted poster: "Leviné-Niessen ca. 35–36 years old, 178–180 cm. tall, thin, Jewish type, speaks conspicuously through

FIGURE 14. Eugen Leviné, leading figure of the Second Council Republic in Bavaria. Bayerische Staatsbibliothek München / Bildarchiv.

the nose, black, usually uncombed hair, pale face, light complexion, big nose with noticeably protruding bones through which this nose appears bent." Another wanted poster contains almost identical wording, though without the remark "Jewish type," which someone at the police had obviously edited out.[197]

Eugen Leviné-Nissen was the "Jewish Bolshevik" that antisemites could not have done a better job inventing. He came from Russia. He was regarded as an agent of the Moscow Communists, and his outward appearance conformed to anti-Jewish stereotypes. Before he became a citizen of Baden in 1913, he had already obtained Italian citizenship via his father's contacts there. He embodied cosmopolitan and internationalist ideals. From time to time this brought him into conflict with his own party comrades. Thus, at an Easter 1919 meeting of factory committees, he had to defend himself against the charge that the Finance Commission, staffed by Prussians and Russians, was too international. Leviné had this response to that argument: "[O]ne of the comrades said: You are all foreigners and do not need to take any responsibility. We, comrades, all of us take the international point of view."[198]

Leviné himself was not typical of Jews who had grown up in the Czarist Empire. He was born in 1883 in St. Petersburg into a prosperous bourgeois family, and his native language was German; even as a boy, he accompanied his mother on trips to Germany. During his studies in Heidelberg, he wrote the following poem, which was found among his personal papers after his death:

> The anxious question: and what now?
> Jewish is how my head thinks, Russian how my heart feels,
> My songs sound in German,
> a (fantastic) joke,
> Of the fate that has hurled me back and forth![199]

Like Toller, Leviné also processed his childhood experiences with antisemitism in literary form, although they were not published during his lifetime. In a prose fragment only recently published, he depicted the experiences of a protagonist he named Jeremias Goldberg, who is insulted in school by the son of an aristocratic marshal as a "dirty Jewish hack." When he slaps the maligner in response, he and not the antisemitic schoolmate is punished by the principal, for whom all Jews are "an unruly gang."[200]

As a Communist, he had turned away from Judaism as a religion very early in his life, although he seemed to have at least a rudimentary command of Yiddish, and when in need he would invoke his Jewish background. One such emergency is depicted by his wife, Rosa Meyer-Leviné.

As he was traveling to Moscow for the inaugural meeting of the Communist International, he found himself detained in Kovno (Kaunas). As Meyer-Leviné later recounted, he thought of the Jewish community as a safe place to go underground: "He needed help but had no associates. His brain worked feverishly. Jews! They were the only people from whom to expect a certain solidarity. He knocked at the first likely door. 'Jews,' he said in Yiddish. 'You would not inform [*mosser zayn*] on a Jew.'" [201] His attempt at going underground succeeded.

After a brief stopover in Berlin, where he had found a position on the staff of the Soviet embassy, the leadership of the German Communist Party sent him to Munich at the beginning of March 1919. There he was to assume the editorship of the party newspaper *Rote Fahne*. Rosa Meyer-Leviné described her husband's new workplace as a place full of hope for the fulfillment of revolutionary ideas: "Famous for its easygoing, highly inflammable population, with a good sprinkling of artists and cranks, Munich was more susceptible than any other large center to experiments and revolutionary ideas." Yet she also recalls the antisemitism of that time, which was also not entirely absent from the ranks of comrades from the various socialist parties. On April 4 and 5, as Leviné was explaining to Social Democrats and the Peasants' League that the Communists would not be participating in a council republic at that time, the Hoffmann government's minister for military affairs, the Social Democrat Ernst Schneppenhorst, responded by shouting (in Rosa Meyer-Leviné's account), "Punch the Jew on the jaw!"[202]

That the Jewish participants in the revolution all agreed with one another is, of course, a myth cultivated by antisemites. Leviné, after several successful speaking appearances at mass meetings in the industrial Ruhr region, had already been a delegate at the German Congress of Workers' and Soldiers' Councils in Berlin and was enthusiastic about Communist ideals. But he had little patience for the council-based "pseudo-council republic that a group of bourgeois ideologues, confused Majority Socialists, independents, and anarchists had spawned as a premature miscarriage." He accused Toller, Mühsam, Landauer, and their comrades of "complete cluelessness." All they had done was deliver pretty speeches, and their only achievement was proclaiming a national holiday.[203] Leviné increasingly distanced himself above all from Toller, who continued to play a role in the Second Council Republic. He called on his colleagues to "put [Toller] in his place." Toller had entered into negotiations with the White Guard without authorization: "This action is outrageous. . . . If Toller had done this in the Kaiser's army, he would have been court-martialed for high treason."[204] Leviné's close comrade Towia Axelrod agreed and called Toller an "unreliable and dubious personality."[205]

Toller's opinion of Leviné was just as negative. On April 21, while he still held office in the Council Republic, Toller told a meeting that Leviné controlled only a small clique, not the proletariat. In the statement he gave on his resignation on April 26, 1919, Toller went even further: "I view the current government as a calamity for the working people of Bavaria. To me, the leading men represent a danger to the council idea. Incapable of constructing anything, no matter how slight, they are engaged in senseless destruction."[206] Erich Mühsam, who had little direct contact with Leviné, had a very similar attitude: "In the Central Council we exchanged a couple of words just a few times and shook hands politely. The part he played in the events in Munich was not a good one. His doggedness prevented the unification of the proletariat."[207]

By May 2, the council adventure was finished. The White Guard troops had conquered the city. What followed was a wave of terror that took a fatal toll of over a thousand victims. Leviné had to go underground. Perhaps he was cherishing the same hope that had kept him alive a half year earlier in Kaunas when he had found a way to keep himself hidden by a Jewish family. But he knew only too well that in Munich many Jews would have immediately handed him over to the police. He was able to fall back on a network of mostly Jewish friends with socialist convictions, including the physician Erich Katzenstein and his wife Nettie Katzenstein-Sutro (a sister-in-law of the attorney Max Hirschberg). It was the same group where Ernst Toller found shelter.[208] It is also noteworthy that the conservative economist Arthur Salz, part of the same milieu around the Stefan George Circle as his brother-in-law, the historian Ernst Kantorowicz, was prepared to assist Leviné in finding a hideout. Kantorowicz, moreover, was part of the White

Guard that was active in bringing about the collapse of the council republic.[209]

Leviné's colleague on the Action Committee of the Works and Soldiers' Councils (*Betriebs- und Soldatenräte*), Towia Axelrod, was also in flight. As the former director of the press office for the Moscow Council of People's Commissars—which Lenin had tasked with the creation of a foreign press office and the establishment of the Communist newspaper *Rote Fahne*—he was regarded by many as Moscow's official representative in Munich. His July 27 directive to confiscate valuables from bank safe deposit boxes had also caused unease and conflict within the council government. A few days later, he had crossed the border into Austria, using the identity card of Friedrich Pollock, who (like his later colleague at Frankfurt's Institute for Social Research, Max Horkheimer) had been spending his time experiencing the revolution in Munich.[210] After Axelrod had been discovered and arrested in Tyrol, he was sentenced to fifteen years in prison. But in Munich the effort to save these prisoners was in full swing. Horkheimer found an attorney for Axelrod, while the photographer Germaine Krull headed for Budapest in order to get the Hungarian government to exert pressure and have Axelrod released.[211] As early as 1920, he and Karl Radek, imprisoned in Berlin, were exchanged for five German hostages held in Russia and sent to Moscow.

Leviné had a less favorable fate in store. On May 13, he was discovered in the home of Salz's friend Botho Schmidt. After the summary court-martial to which he was subjected, the death penalty awaited him. The role played by his Judaism among the participants in what transpired is made clear in the memoirs of Philipp Löwenfeld, who was initially asked to be Leviné's defense attorney. Löwenfeld rejected the offer, since he expected the death penalty for his potential client and was convinced that "it would be said, without a doubt, by many people that this sentence could have been avoided if Leviné had not been defended by a Jew. Leviné's affiliation with Judaism had already elicited so much damage in public opinion and provided so much space for antisemitic agitation that my reservations seemed absolutely necessary."[212]

Löwenfeld later regretted his reservations. Admittedly, he was right about the sentence. On June 3, 1919, Leviné was sentenced to death and shot two days later. He was thirty-six years old and left behind his wife and a two-year-old son. In the minutes of the court, the abbreviation "israel." (for "Israelite") was used to indicate his religious affiliation.[213] His burial took place at the New Israelite Cemetery in Munich. Rabbi Leo Baerwald, who had a reputation for being rather conservative and monarchist, gave a brief address.[214] Thus, of all people, it was the most radical of the Jewish revolutionaries who ended up being buried in a Jewish cemetery, while Eisner and Landauer, the murdered revolutionaries influenced by a more anarchist and pacifist socialism inflected by Jewish prophetic teachings, found their (provisional) resting place in the municipal Ostfriedhof and the cemetery in Schwabing.

Even after Leviné's death, the public announcement of his Jewish affiliation led to a conflict with the Central Association of German Citizens of the Jewish Faith (Centralverein deutscher Staatsbürger jüdischen Glaubens). The issue was whether the Jewish affiliation of a revolutionary condemned to death as a criminal should be publicized, or whether this might be interpreted in some antisemitic way. The news agency Süddeutsche Correspondenz-Bureau (Correspondenz Hoffmann) had referred to Leviné's Jewish affiliation in a dispatch, which led the Centralverein to compose a letter of complaint by way of the state commissioner for Southern Bavaria. The agency defended itself in the following words: "[I]n reporting the denomination of Leviné we were not thinking in the slightest of giving offense. Besides, it is quite explicable that our reporter, even without having given any special thought to this, would emphasize the denomination of the accused, since during the trial the defendant himself placed special emphasis on his Jewish faith. We regret that we have given offense among the German citizens of the Jewish faith in this way, but we must quite vehemently protest against the charge of having stirred up agitation against Jews."[215]

"Foreign Bolshevik Agents"—Jews in the Fight against the Council Republic

Many young Jews felt an urgent need to reorient themselves in the light of the revolutionary conditions surrounding them. But that this search for a change of direction did not always yield unambiguous answers is shown by a letter that the young Leo Löwenthal wrote to his parents on June 17, 1920. Löwenthal, along with Friedrich Pollock and Max Hork-heimer, later became one of the pillars of the Frankfurt Institute for Social Research. Like his future colleagues, he was in Munich when he wrote home: "Eisner is dead, Gustav Landauer, and now Max Weber as well. . . . Two Jews and the third one a great philo-Semite. Jews as intel-lectuals, as revolutionaries, as pioneers, all of them murdered! If it is our calling on earth to be pioneers, heralds of a new spirit, pathbreakers through revolution, the thought occurs as to whether our task would be fulfilled more beautifully and more fruitfully if we could unite into a close community." These reflections led Löwenthal to ponder the ques-tion as to whether Zionism (among whose adherents he mistakenly included Landauer) might not provide the answer. Yet, initially at least, he did not regard himself as a Zionist. His ruminations expose the kind of identity conflict plaguing a young German Jew with socialist convic-tions: "If I am to serve the idea of humanity—as a socialist—then this has to be more so, or even altogether so, by when I'm acting from out of the community of people who share my blood and my history; or is it the case that I am integrated into a community of history with the Ger-man spirit? I'm only asking; I don't have the answer."[216]

Nor did the Munich Jewish writer Lion Feuchtwanger find a clear answer to the question posed by Löwenthal. Feuchtwanger had not yet achieved the degree of fame of his Weimar-era years, but he had already celebrated some early success. At a young age, he had turned away from his family's Orthodox religiosity and come to sympathize with socialist ideas. Nowhere does his name show up in the politically turbulent months between November 1918 and April 1919. He refused to collabo-rate with the Council of Intellectual Workers. As his biographer An-dreas Heusler writes, Feuchtwanger had certainly "seen through the flimsy quality of revolutionary euphoria quite early and feared the pa-thetic failure of the council experiment, purchased at such a high cost in blood."[217] Already then, he may have been thinking of the words he would put into the mouth of the writer Tüverlin in his novel *Success*: "Karl Marx once opined that since philosophers had explained the world, the next step was to change it. But for my part I think the only way of changing the world is to explain it. If you explain it plausibly enough, then you change it quietly by the operation of reason. It's only the men who can't explain it plausibly who try to change it by force."[218] In his drama *Thomas Wendt*, however, Feuchtwanger would give the revolution a literary rendition. Quite likely, Ernst Toller served as the model for that play's protagonist.

By contrast with the uncertainty of Löwenthal and Feuchtwanger, there were clear answers from those Jews in Munich who rejected the revolutionary experiment from the outset or were even fighting against it. Among the Jewish skeptics of the revolution was the attorney Max Friedländer. In November 1918, he was a cofounder and first chairman of the Bavarian Bar Association, yet he kept his distance from the Eisner government. Of Eisner he later wrote: "[He was] a literary bohemian, not a politician . . . a quixotic journalist with long hair, who gave the most radical speeches but was constantly oscillating back and forth between democracy and Bolshevism."[219] Friedländer distanced himself from the major players in the council republic and emphasized that "none of the Jews involved had anything at all to do with Judaism or represented Jewish interests." He himself was involved in the Civil Defense Guard (the Einwohnerwehr, or citizens'militia) but left it after the Kapp Putsch made it clear to him that a majority of its members welcomed that right-wing extremist coup attempt.[220]

Both in contemporary accounts and in retrospective reports, Jewish observers noted that the chroniclers of the revolution were always forgetting to mention that the majority of Jews, even the politically active among them, hardly identified with radical socialism or the ideology of the council-style republics. Looking back, the Munich native Werner Cahnmann, who later taught sociology at several US colleges, wrote: "The council republic was represented as 'Jewish' from the outset. . . . On the other hand, the much more characteristic involvement of Jews on the other side was hardly ever mentioned."[221] The same view was quite clearly articulated by Immanuel Birnbaum, a cofounder of the student union Allgemeiner Studentenausschuss (AStA) in Munich at the time who would later become (after World War II) deputy editor-in-chief of Munich's newspaper of record, the *Süddeutsche Zeitung*: "Among Jewish intellectuals . . . most were clearly on the frontlines against the council republic adventure."[222] This group included the jurist Fritz Stern and the economist Carl Landauer, who were in open opposition to the council regime. Carl Landauer, together with some trade union leaders and Social Democratic Party functionaries, actively opposed the council republic and tried "to avert what finally turned out to be such a bloody 'political *Fasching*' [Bavarian for 'carnival' or 'Mardi Gras']." In the years to come, Landauer would become a close confidant of Erhard Auer, Eisner's Social Democratic archenemy.[223]

On Palm Sunday, the law students Franz Guttmann and Walter Löwenfeld even attempted to topple the council republic. We have evidence of their committed yet amateurish modus operandi from a note sent to the State Commissariat for Southern Bavaria.[224] At the last minute, Löwenfeld was able to find refuge in Neu-Ulm, a town about 150 kilometers west of Munich. From there he continued his fight, even in the face of massive resistance, for the government established by the Landtag in mid-March and led by the Majority Social Democrat Heinrich Hoffmann: "In the meetings of the Workers', Peasants', and Soldiers' Councils, L. represents the view of the Hoffmann government; against the council government; upon leaving he was threatened by soldiers with being arrested or shot."[225]

Walter's brother was the respected attorney Philipp Löwenfeld, whom Gustav Landauer would gladly have seen as commissioner of justice in the council republic. Like his brother, however, Philipp backed the moderate Hoffmann government in remote Bamberg. On the eve of the First Council Republic's proclamation, he gave a fiery speech against the council system, whose advocates were "foreign Bolshevik agents up to ninety percent."[226] He also claimed—at least in hindsight—to have seen the antisemitic consequences coming: "In addition to the political madness that the establishment of such a combination meant, one could easily picture what kind of mass antisemitic impact the announcement of these facts was bound to have in an overwhelmingly agrarian Catholic land."[227]

Outside Munich, too, Jews were involved in defeating the council republic during its reign. Dr. Julian Marcuse, the director of the sanatorium in Ebenhausen where Eisner had Towia Axelrod detained under "house arrest," conveyed news from Social Democratic circles in Munich to the Hoffmann government residing in Bamberg. Adolf Braun, editor-in-chief of the *Fränkische Tagespost* and later a Social Democratic Reichstag deputy, "was then running counter-propaganda against the council adventure and saw to it that Central Franconia was not dragged into this dreadful state of affairs." From Munich, the student Immanuel Birnbaum wrote sketches about the council republic for the Nuremberg newspaper in order to highlight the "political immaturity of the leaders of this improvisation."[228]

Yet it was by no means only in the left-liberal camp where Jewish opponents of the council republic were to be found. In his research on Hitler and the early Nazi Party, Thomas Weber argued that the percentage of people in the Freikorps with Jewish ancestry roughly corresponded to their percentage in the overall population. This nationalist paramilitary force included such prominent members as the later historian Ernst Kantorowicz and close relatives of the revolutionaries, such as one of Ernst Toller's cousins. Some of them even belonged to distinctively right-wing groups, like the Freikorps Oberland.[229]

In spite of the occasional dig against Jews made by some of its members and press outlets, the Bavarian People's Party (Bayerische Volkspartei, or BVP), which was the Munich-based branch of the Catholic Center Party, enjoyed the confidence of a part of local Orthodox Jewry. For instance, Hans Lamm, who became president of the Munich Jewish Community in the 1970s, described his father as a loyal BVP voter.[230] One factor contributing to Orthodox Jewish support for this Catholic party was its opposition to the abolition of denominational schools. One of Bavaria's few Jewish newspapers, the *Deutsche Israelitische Zeitung*, was published in Regensburg by the city's Orthodox rabbi Seligmann Meyer, along with the popular supplement *Die Laubhütte*, a family magazine that used the German word for *sukkah*. During the elections to the Landtag in January 1919, the paper called openly for Jewish voters to support the BVP.

The wide range of political identification among Munich's Jews was discernible among the leading representatives of the community during the 1920s. Both the longtime chair of the Munich Jewish Community,

Higher Regional Court justice Alfred Neumeyer, and his vice chairman, Elias Straus, who chaired Munich's Zionist organization, supported the German Democratic Party. Other prominent Munich Jews represented that center-left party and the Social Democrats in the city council. Toward the end of the Republic, the BVP also picked up in popularity among non-Orthodox Jewish voters as the liberal political camp deteriorated to the point of insignificance and the Social Democrats lost the confidence of the Jewish population after they voted in the Bavarian parliament for a Nazi Party initiative to ban kosher slaughter.[231]

The picture of Jewish public opinion is unambiguous. The dominant attitude was a clear disassociation from the Jewish actors in the revolution and and the two council republics. To place this disassociation in context, it is first necessary to cast a glance at the city's rapidly spreading anti-Jewish mood. As early as 1921, the Franconian-Jewish writer Jakob Wassermann wrote in his autobiographical book *My Life as German and Jew*, summarizing the public mood, it could not be denied that, "whenever a preemptory demand or a clean sweep is made, whenever the idea of governmental metamorphosis is to be translated into action with frenzied zeal, Jews have been and still are the leaders." Yet they did not assume this role with any sinister intent, and certainly not even as Jews: "True, if fairness were to be expected it would have to be conceded that these Jews, almost without exception, were inspired by honest conviction, that, Utopian Idealists, they felt they were bringing salvation to the world. It would have to be conceded that in their activity lies a consistency which, though it may perhaps be absurd and criminal, may, on the other hand, be prophetic of the distant future: the transplanting from the religious into the social field of the messianic ideal derived from Judaism. . . . It would also have to be conceded that Jews are equally often the preservers and guardians of tradition, though thoroughly versed in the law and observant of the commandments. But fairness cannot be expected. Nor is fairness their [the antisemites'] design. Their design is hate, and hate smolders on. It makes no distinctions as to persons or achievements, it inquires after no meaning or aim. It constitutes its own meaning and aim. It is German hate."[232]

3

A Pogrom Atmosphere
in Munich

It is only Jewish Socialists and Communists who are not forgiven;
these are drowned in the soup and cut up small with the roast.[1]

—FRANZ KAFKA, MAY 1920

Passover 5679 (April 1919)

In the Hebrew calendar year 5679, Passover fell in the third week of
April 1919 according to the Gregorian calendar. All over the world Jews
transported themselves back spiritually into the biblical era of the Exodus from Egypt. At the beginning of the festival, as they did every year,
families conducted a Seder, ate matzo, drank the symbolic four glasses
of wine, and recounted the story of liberation from Egyptian servitude.
As the holiday started, Munich's Jews, for whom abstaining from their
beloved beer for a whole week must surely have been just as hard as
doing without bread and pasta, were just experiencing another revolution in their hometown. And as had already been the case less than a
year earlier under Kurt Eisner, Jewish revolutionaries were once again
taking center stage in the two council republics. At first it was Ernst
Toller, Erich Mühsam, Gustav Landauer, Arnold Wadler, and Otto

98

Neurath. Later came Eugen Leviné and Towia Axelrod. As always for the Seder meal, the physician Rahel Straus and her husband Eli, regarded as the leading Zionist in the city along the Isar, had assembled a large group in their house. This time the invitees included a special guest: the young Galician-born writer Shmuel Yosef Agnon, who had just made a name for himself with his Hebrew stories (and would receive the Nobel Prize half a century later), had settled in Munich after a lengthy stay in Palestine with interim stops in Leipzig and Berlin. "It was an exciting Seder evening," Rahel Straus later recalled.[2]

Yet there was no real joy setting in among most of Munich's Jews, as the mathematician Adolf Abraham Fraenkel recalled looking back. Half a year earlier, he had returned to his hometown along the Isar, taken off his soldier's uniform, and founded the local branch of the Mizrachi, an Orthodox Zionist association. His family belonged to the minority of Munich's Jews who remained loyal to Orthodox Judaism even in the twentieth century. They prayed at the Ohel Jakob synagogue in the Herzog-Rudolf-Straße. They were no less bourgeois or less attached to their Bavarian homeland than the Liberal Jews who met for services in the grand synagogue in the Herzog Max-Straße.

Adolf Abraham Fraenkel, who would later work in Marburg, Kiel, and Jerusalem as a mathematics professor (one of the pioneers of set theory), loved lakes and mountains and was an active member of the Alpine Club for as long as this hiking group still tolerated Jews in its ranks. In April 1919, his greatest anxiety was about the Jewish middle class in his hometown, among whom his father had a leading role: "The Passover festival took place under increasing terror and worries about my father, who, as a religious Jew and representative of the mercantile community, was being attacked from both the left and right."[3] Commercial counselor Siegmund Fraenkel was the chairman of the Orthodox synagogue association Ohel Jakob and vice chair of the Munich Chamber of Commerce. He was a known quantity in Munich's bourgeois and civic circles, and many of Munich's Jews shared his conservative stance. Yet in contrast to them, he did not shy away from public statements.

Thus, "on April 6, 1919, the eve of the Passover festival 5679," he addressed an open letter "to Messrs. Erich Mühsam, Dr. Wadler, Dr. Otto Neurath, Ernst Toller, and Gustav Landauer." He addressed them

> not as a frightened capitalist worried about his property and possessions, but rather because I acknowledge, with pride and out of inner religious conviction, my membership in that community of faith to which you or your parents once belonged. In all the difficult weeks so full of suffering gone by, we Munich Jews have remained silent about how you and other alien [*landfremd*] fantasts and dreamers ignorant of the Bavarian national character are exploiting the bitter distress and psychic depression of our people in order to recruit believers for your plans, perhaps well-intentioned but fateful and contrary to human nature, for an economic and social order. We remained silent because we feared damaging our community of faith if we shook you off in public and because we hoped from day to day that the sense of responsibility for the religious community from which you or your parents derived would sooner or later awaken in you and make you conscious of the kind of chaos, destruction, and devastation the path you have chosen must lead to.

But now, since thousands of antisemitic leaflets were being handed out in the streets of Munich, it had become clear what kind of danger "threatens Jewry itself when the great mass of Munich's working people associate the solemn teachings and dogmas of the Jewish religion ideologically with the Bolshevik and Communist false doctrines that you have been preaching for weeks to the masses worn down and confused by four and half years of war."

In the elder Fraenkel's Orthodox rendering, the kind of socialism authentic to Judaism and based on biblical principles had nothing in common with the ideals espoused by the Munich revolutionaries: "My Jewish sense of solidarity admonishes me to make you aware of all this in your own interest. . . . I am further admonished by an inner voice to protect my community of faith from the odium that traditional Judaism has anything to do with the destructive tendencies of ambitious revolutionary politicians." The appearance of these revolutionaries, according

to Fraenkel, was only creating new antisemitism. Hence, "Bavaria's in-
digenous Jewry shouts out, by way of me, to Bavaria's population: Our
hands are clean of the horrors of chaos and of the misery and suffering
that your politics must needs conjure up over Bavaria's future development. You alone and only you bear full responsibility for this."[4]

Siegmund Fraenkel wanted to show a broad public that Munich's
Jews had nothing to do with those revolutionaries who had shaped the
political landscape of Bavaria and especially of Munich over the past
several months. On the morning of April 7, he made his way to the editorial offices of Munich's biggest newspaper, the *Münchner Neueste
Nachrichten*, in order to hand over the letter personally. But there he
encountered the first members of the Red Guard, whose socialist commanders would at this time be determining the fate of the council republic then taking shape. Under the circumstances, Fraenkel was unable
to deliver his letter. His son later deemed this a fortunate, even life-
saving turn of events. Speaking of his father and his letter, he wrote:
"Fortunately for him, it was not published at that time, since he might
have otherwise shared the same fate as the hostages, who were murdered in the Luitpold Gymnasium in Munich in late April, after several
Jewish leaders, particularly Landauer, resigned from the leadership."[5]

While Siegmund Fraenkel's voice thus remained unheard for the
time being, the Jewish revolutionaries to whom it was addressed remained for a few weeks in the limelight of the city's political events and
became well known well beyond Munich. For many years both the revolution and the two short-lived council republics of April 1919 would be
associated with "the Jews." Hardly anyone was interested in knowing
that Fraenkel represented a much larger share of the Jewish community
than Landauer, Toller, and Mühsam.

One and a half years after the elder Fraenkel wrote his public letter,
it was finally printed in the *Münchner Neueste Nachrichten*.[6] And one
of those to whom it was addressed made an immediate reply. Erich
Mühsam wrote from his prison cell in Ansbach: "I am a Jew and will
remain a Jew for as long as I live, have never denied my Judaism, and
have not even left the religious Jewish community (since that would not
make me cease to be a Jew, and I am completely indifferent as to

whatever rubric I am registered under in the civil records of any given state). That I am a Jew is something I view neither as an advantage nor as a defect; it is simply part of my essence like my red beard, my bodily weight, or my inclinations and interests."

Mühsam accused the commercial counselor of misrepresenting Judaism and betraying its core ideas: "I do not see how belonging to Jewry is a commitment to lack of character." He is astonished to see the word "alien" (*landfremd*), borrowed from the vocabulary of right-wing radicals, hurled against him as well. After all, like most of the other addressees of Fraenkel's letter, Mühsam was from Germany. So why should he and his comrades be regarded as alien? And Mühsam vehemently contested Fraenkel's orthodox interpretation of Judaism, juxtaposing it against the putatively socialist basic principle of the Hebrew Bible.

In conclusion, Mühsam emphasized that antisemitism hardly needed any Jewish revolutionaries to exist. There were entirely different reasons for why it thrived after the socialist experiment in Munich was suppressed. If the revolution had been victorious, antisemitism would also have disappeared. But as it happened "the swastika has almost been elevated to the status of a cockade for respectability. You can see how antisemitism, even without us five Jews that you have fished out of ten thousand, finds enough material in order to ply its murky dealings. But I am of the view that it does bring more honor to Judaism when it is associated with idealists and martyrs like Rosa Luxemburg, Leo Jogiches, Gustav Landauer, or Eugen Leviné than when the antisemites busy collecting materials have to confine their daily denunciations to Jewish usurers and racketeers. This was what I would have had the defender of Judaism say against his degenerate sons."[7]

Here there was a clash of opinions that, in spite of their differences, both invoked Jewish traditions: on the one hand, the orthodox representative of the organized Jewish community argued for the need to protect that community from growing antisemitism; on the other hand, the heretic viewed himself and his socialist and anarchist comrades in arms as Judaism's modern prophets. Both invoked prophetic traditions. And neither man could shut his eyes to the fact that political change was being identified in the larger community with the rise of Jewish

politicians to prominent positions. Both Fraenkel's and Mühsam's contemporaries were well aware of this state of affairs as early as the first few
days of the upheaval.

"We Don't Want Any Bavarian Trotsky"—
The Mood Shifts

On the morning after the revolution, November 8, 1918, sixteen-year-old
Werner Cahnmann accompanied his father on a journey through the
city in order to find out how the royal residence of the Wittelsbach dynasty had been transformed overnight into the capital of a people's state.
At this time Cahnmann, whose family belonged to the city's Jewish
bourgeoisie, was still a monarchist by conviction, yet this attitude would
soon change under the impact of these initial postwar experiences.
Father and son rambled through the streets of the new republic in a
spirit of curiosity. A whiff of the extraordinary hung in the air, an atmosphere that also tempted them to address strangers on the street. As
they encountered another curious onlooker, Cahnmann reported later,
his father turned to him and asked: "'What do you have to say about the
situation?' The answer was 'The Jew's sitting on top.' At once it was clear
to me where I needed to stand. I knew that Jewish destiny was bound
up with the destiny of the Republic. This tie could be recognized earlier
and more clearly in Munich than in any other site. In Munich hostility
toward Jews, a time-honored topic, had become a political tool with
unusual explosive power."[8] That was how Werner Cahnmann recalled
the experience of his first few hours in the new republic.

A similar experience was described by the young Oskar Maria Graf,
who traveled in Munich's revolutionary circles: "One night I was passing
Stachus [a major square in Munich]. A lean creature darted at me, hastily thrust a leaflet into my hand, and ran on quickly into the gloom.
I stepped under a lamp and looked at the rag. These words were printed
on it, and no more: 'The Jew interposes, Germans, reflect!'"[9]

For Max Weber, the sociologist who had recently started teaching in
Munich, what these unidentified people on the street were expressing
awkwardly served as a warning, which he had already articulated a few

days before the old regime had collapsed. In a letter from November 15, 1918, to Else Jaffé, the wife of the new finance minister who had been involved in an affair with Weber, he wrote that her husband would certainly know how to handle his new job properly: "Only, for the time being, I still don't have any trust that this will last. Separatism is raising its head, and it is going to embellish itself with antisemitism."[10]

Another prominent resident of Munich was Thomas Mann, whose father-in-law, the mathematician Alfred Pringsheim, was one of the few Jewish professors at the University of Munich. Mann had an extremely complex relationship with Jews and Judaism.[11] Observations that can be regarded as antisemitic show up above all in his early works, like the novella *The Blood of the Walsungs*, as well in the remarks he made during the revolutionary period. More than once in his diary entries from that time, Mann expressed his disgust about the prominent role of Jews and the "big-city piss elegance of the Jew-boy" leading to a "Jew regiment." As early as November 8, 1918, he asked in his diary: "Both Munich and Bavaria governed by Jewish scribblers. How long will the city put up with that?" A few days later, he was planning, in case of an attack on him, to say the following: "Listen, I am neither a Jew, nor a war profiteer, nor anything else that is bad." And this was Mann's comment on his experience of Eisner on November 17 at the celebration of the revolution in the National Theater, where Bruno Walter was conducting Beethoven's Leonore Overture: "Tasteless Eisner, little long-bearded Jewish man, delivering his address in front of the big curtain instead of from his box. One had to admit that Goethe would turn over in his grave."[12] His mother-in-law, Hedwig Pringsheim, also feared being associated with the unpleasant "fellow members of the race" (*Rassegenossen*—a racial variation on *Glaubensgenossen*, the polite German word for "coreligionists"). A few weeks after the monarchy was toppled, she wrote to the journalist Maximilian Harden: "Over time things are becoming dreadful for me with the fellow members of my privy councilor's race,[13] spreading out to make themselves at home and acting self-important, this is really upsetting, and there will be consequences. They all have such repulsive names, the ones making themselves at home here, and not a single one of them is a Bavarian."[14]

No sooner had Eisner taken office than the antisemites went on the offensive. On November 9, Rudolf von Sebottendorff gave a speech before the Thule Society in which he warned: "Since yesterday we have experienced the collapse of everything that was familiar, dear, and valuable to use. In place of our consanguineous princes, it is now our mortal enemy who rules: Judah. . . . Now we need to speak about the German Reich, now we need to say that the Jew is our mortal enemy, and as of today we will act."[15]

From the very first day Eisner took office, the Bavarian prime minister had to deal with a campaign of defamation that extended well beyond the narrow circles of the Thule Society and of dedicated antisemites. He was widely described as an East European Jew from Galicia whose real name was sometimes given as Kosmanowsky, then as Koschinsky, or perhaps as Karowskarek. It was by no means only the radical antisemites who participated in this campaign. The Catholic newspaper *Bayerischer Kurier* circulated the rumor as well, as did the high-circulation (and, for the moment, still liberal) paper *Münchner Neueste Nachrichten*. Liberal politicians participated in the rumormongering in the same way as Catholic clergy all the way up to the papal nuncio.

The liberal politician who would later become Bavarian justice minister, Ernst Müller Meiningen from the recently formed German Democratic Party, took the same line when he asserted at a public meeting: "We won't let ourselves be governed by a Galician from Berlin." In his memoirs, he defended himself against being branded a "crass antisemite" because of this one remark. He had, after all, always stood up for the Jews (by his own account): "In a single day, twenty years fighting on behalf of equality for Jews was forgotten!"[16] Yet even these memoirs bristle with allusions to Eisner's alleged origins. One passage, for example, reads: "Up to and including the noodle soup he ate, up to the smallest Galician virgin who surrounded him, everything that the 'great man' did was usually not told, even in part, but really not at all, to the wide-eyed public." Another time he claimed that Eisner was surrounding himself in the Foreign Ministry with "Galician office people."[17] And repeatedly he notes with astonishment that Bavaria even let itself be given over to the "Galician from Berlin," whom he accused of having undermined the morale of the population while the war was still going on and then, after the war ended, of putting peace-loving Germany in a false light "with refined craftiness."[18] It was "really a veritable miracle that the Berliner and Jewish press man could even get the Southern Bavarian peasants behind him." He talked about the aversion "against 'Jews and tricksters,' by whom on the other hand one let oneself be completely led, since they were the ones who were intellectually superior." And, finally, he placed the blame for the revival of antisemitism on the Jewish revolutionaries themselves. "The deeply entrenched antisemitic feature that is undoubtedly characteristic of our southern German workers, for all their radicalism, and in spite of Mühsam and Toller, in spite of Landauer and the other revolutionary heroes, reared up mentally against the rule of 'the Berlin Jew.'"[19]

In his unpublished memoirs, the conservative politician who would later become Bavarian prime minister and state commissioner general, Gustav Ritter von Kahr, repeatedly drew attention to Eisner's Jewish—and presumably East European—origins. At one point Kahr described him as an "*Ostjude*" (East European Jew), but later he crossed out the prefix *Ost-*. Another time he wrote that an "overexcited fanatical Berlin Jew" must have been "of East European descent, it was said."[20] With regard to the "sly Jew" Eisner, then, Kahr avails himself in his memoirs of nearly every antisemitic stereotype.[21]

The envoy to Bavaria from the state of Württemberg, Moser von Filseck, issued a report from Munich saying that Eisner had already acquired numerous enemies just a month after the revolution, something the emissary ascribed to antisemitic motives: "He is simply not trusted, and his ancestry raises reservations."[22] Foreign diplomats also spread the rumor about Eisner's Galician ancestry. In December 1918, as the Austrian consul general in Munich prepared a characterization of the new members of the Bavarian government for the Foreign Ministry back in Vienna, the dispatch began with these words: "The Prime Minister Kurt Eisner is a Jew. He was born in Berlin; his parents came from the east and were still going by their Polish-Galician name."[23]

The Catholic newspaper *Bayerischer Kurier*, the antisemitic *Miesbacher Anzeiger*, and the right-wing extremist *Münchener Beobachter* (which would later become the Nazi Party's *Völkischer Beobachter*) out-bid each other in slandering Eisner. These defamations were also grate-fully picked up by newspapers outside Bavaria, such as the conservative *Kreuzzeitung*.[24] This gave the oldest German-Jewish newspaper, the *Allgemeine Zeitung des Judentums*, cause to worry, with some justifica-tion, that antisemitism had penetrated far into moderate political cir-cles: "As in Prussia, in Bavaria too the most outrageous accusations are being raised against the 'Jew' Eisner." In the same issue it went on to say: "The origins of Bavarian Prime Minister Kurt Eisner are being used by reactionary forces reaching well into the ranks of the old progressive parties as a welcome opportunity for antisemitic jostling. The 'Bayer-ischer Kurier' is engaged in furious agitation against Jews and is talking about the Polish-Jewish-Prussian House of Eisner that has now taken the reins into its hands in Bavaria."[25]

The slanders had become so widespread in the Bavarian press that, on December 6, 1918, Eisner summoned the editor-in-chief of the *Bayer-ischer Kurier* to his office in order to complain about the dissemination of the "Koschinsky rumor."[26] Only a few days earlier he was still trying to use humor as a way of countering the doubts about his name. In a speech before the Bavarian Soldiers' Council on November 30, he said: "I don't even have a name any more; it is said, or some lunatic has put about the rumor, I don't know who, that I have a much lovelier first name, not something short like Kurt, I'm supposedly called Salomon. (Cheers!) They are forcing me to publish my biography sometime soon, and you will get the shock of your life when you find out what this Sa-lomon Kosmanowsky, or whatever he's called, really is. (Cheers!)"[27]

All this time, however, contemporaries were well aware, if they were at all interested in knowing this, that the Galician background falsely attributed to Eisner rested on lies. The Romance language and literature scholar Victor Klemperer, who was another journalist chronicling those days in Munich, wrote in a piece for the *Leipziger Neueste Nachrichten* at the beginning of February 1919: "It is truly unnecessary to ascribe Galicianness [*Galiziertum*] to the Prime Minister and raise doubts about his German name. He himself has confessed to being a 'Prussian' [*Preiß*] and even a Berliner."[28]

Eisner had been living apart from his first wife since 1908. In 1917, because of his marriage to the philosophy student and Social Democrat Else Belli, whose two daughters Freia and Ruth he intended to recognize "as his own," he had produced the documents needed to acquire Bavarian citizenship. His denominational affiliation to the "Israelite" community was mentioned therein.[29] Moreover, there was also clear documentation that his birth name was Eisner and his birthplace was Berlin.[30] It is hardly any wonder that National Socialist history-writing nonetheless fell back on this lie.[31] But it is surprising that, even after 1945, the legend of Eisner as Kosmanowski continued to be spread by the head of the Bavarian State Chancellery, Karl Schwend, and the distinguished conservative historian Gerhard Ritter.[32]

In the attacks against Eisner, the issue was not just his allegedly East European Jewish background. Other anti-Jewish stereotypes also surfaced. Needless to say, the image of the rich Jew could not fail to be among them. Here, too, the stereotype was not restricted to völkisch circles.[33] It belonged both to the clerical-Catholic repertoire of anti-Eisner rhetoric and to the political left. The Reverend Hermann Sturm, owner of the right-wing conservative newspaper *Bayerisches Vaterland*, spread the rumor of an alliance of rich Jews to Archbishop Faulhaber: "Gigantic sums of money are available, donated by big capitalists and Jews, who in this way have the movement in their hands."[34] During the period of upheaval, Eisner's Social Democratic interior minister and political opponent Erhard Auer also availed himself of antisemitic stereotypes, as when he talked about how "Jewish money" was at work helping his rival Eisner, or how the Independent Social Democrats and the Jews really knew how to exploit a possible trial against Eisner for their own purposes.[35] In addition, he told about how "the racial question is being mentioned" among grassroots Social Democrats. And he articulated the claim that the Jews had ducked military service. According to reports in the press, the Majority Social Democrat Schöneck complained before an assembly of working-class Christians in Munich on November 12 that Eisner was a Jew: "In a Christian state like Bavaria, no Jew could be at the head; we don't want any Bavarian Trotsky."[36]

The first Jewish politician to serve as the head of a German state became the target of all manner of anti-Jewish prejudices. To many outsiders peering in, this Social Democrat residing in the petty bourgeois suburb of Großhadern was a Prussian Rothschild and Bavarian Trotsky all rolled into one. The Bavarian citizen who had grown up in Berlin was branded by his opponents as a Galician or, as if this was not sufficient, an Eastern Galician. The established journalist was characterized as a destitute bohemian. To this mixture could be added any rumor that anyone cared to spread—and this could be held not only against Eisner but against Jews on the whole. Along these lines, Josef Hofmiller noted in his diary that Eisner had "his race's trait of not feeling offended by any kind of rejection, but rather, if he has been escorted out through the front door, of sticking his head back in at the back door."[37]

One of the most depressing archival finds in connection with the revolution in Munich is a bundle of two thick files containing hundreds of antisemitic hate letters against Eisner, many of them laced with incitements to violence. They include a postcard addressed to the "Hebrew Residence," as well as a letter to the "King of the Jews" that says: "Control yourself, or disappear to the country where you belong, to Palestine! The broad masses of the German people will eradicate you, something one person can accomplish!" A member of the "Association for Self-Help" writes: "You're no German, but rather a tolerated alien." And a letter writer who called himself a Social Democrat rants: "[W]e demand a National Assembly and not some common Jew gang dictatorship. . . . The Jew gang has already taken a large share of stolen money abroad, and the families are living in splendor and joyously in the Switzerland." The letters are teeming with expressions like "Jew pig," "dirty Jew, " and "uncircumcised scum Jew." Eisner is called a "little dirty Jewish Polish schnorrer" and a "Russian Jew trickster." The tenor of the letters is that Eisner is "after all, a Jew, not a German." Or as another letter writer formulates it: "Your fatherland is not our German Reich; rather, it lies in Poland, Galicia, or Palestine, where the dirty Jews all come from and also belong." Sometimes Eisner is called Koschinsky, at other times Kosmanowski, and then again "Salomon Kruschnovsky, Jew from Galicia." One postcard contains a picture of Eisner with his eyes punched out.[38]

During the three months or so that Eisner was in office, the tone of these letters became increasingly inflammatory, and the threats they contained were increasingly aimed not just at Eisner but at the "fellow members of his race." The senders—some were anonymous, and others identified themselves—were demanding that "Jews like this must now be hunted" or that there be a "quick death for these executioners of Christianity."[39] Jews were not appropriate as heads of state, the letters said. They were merely tolerated aliens and should be sent to Palestine, or, as some simply said, "a Galician Jew should not rule over Germans." This letter writer tells Eisner that he will be "shot at the first opportunity" if he does not give up his office within four days. He did not even think it was necessary to send his letter anonymously.[40] Another contemporary writing from Zurich, referring to the pogroms raging in Eastern Europe, says that the policies pursued by Eisner and members of his tribe were responsible for Jews being killed in Poland and that, should "many innocent people also come to harm in the German Reich, we would chiefly have the fellow members of your race to thank for that."[41] An observer who describes himself as artistically talented draws Eisner's likeness on a self-made wanted poster with a reward on his head. Another one lists a catalog of abuses in order to repeat the mantra that "the Jews" were responsible for all of it.[42]

Even after Eisner was murdered, the tirades of hatred did not diminish. One day after the assassination, Josef Hofmiller noted in his diary: "Eisner's very behavior provoked his violent removal." Hofmiller's students registered Eisner's death with cheers.[43] And in its obituary, the *Kreuzzeitung* characterized the Bavarian prime minister as "one of the nastiest representatives of Jewry who have played such a characteristic role in the history of the last several months."[44]

In one of the first attempts at a historical account of the revolution and council republic in the conservative *Süddeutsche Monatshefte*, Paul Busching, an economist and professor for housing construction at Munich's Technische Hochschule, repeatedly characterized Eisner and his companions by referring to their Judaism: "The little Jewish journalist,

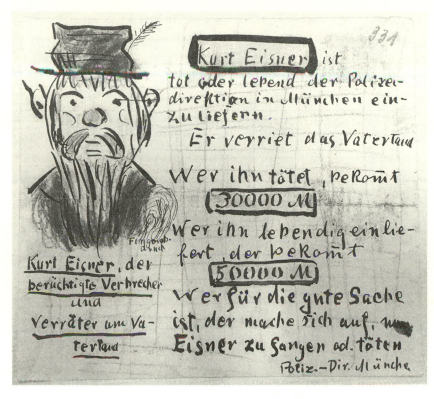

FIGURE 15. One of many antisemitic letters sent to Kurt Eisner during his time in office as Bavarian prime minister. This leaflet in the form of a "wanted dead or alive" poster for the "traitor" Eisner says: "30,000 Marks to the person who kills him." NY 4060/82–84, p. 331, Bundesarchiv.

who had never been taken seriously in his own party, made himself—to the unanimous applause of the workers, including those immediately elevated to the status of 'intellectual workers'—prime minister of an old, important German state and took up his dangerous office, initially accompanied only by some Jewish literati from Berlin."[45] It was hardly surprising that it was "the Russian Jews in the Wittelsbacher Palais" who were playing a decisive role in the events to follow "with fiery calls inciting the people." They were the ones who had blindingly dazzled the people: "Certainly, under Jewish influence the intellectuals concluded their special pact with the council republic and had joyfully become proletarians for the time being."[46]

In their contemporary writings about the first Bavarian prime minister during the 1920s, the established historians at the University of Munich also did not neglect to trot out Eisner's Jewish origins as a negative feature. This was especially clear in the case of Michael Doeberl, who held the chair for Bavarian history. In his 1920 publication *Sozialismus, soziale Revolution, sozialer Volksstaat* (Socialism, Social Revolution, Social Welfare People's State), which included the first comprehensive depiction of the revolution and is generally characterized by a moderate attitude toward the Majority Social Democrats, he had very little that was flattering to say about Eisner. The "representative of international Jewry with his 'international airs' was anything but a German statesman, the East European Jew who immigrated here via Berlin anything but the appointed leader of the Bavarian people." He incorrectly associated Eisner with Russian Bolshevism. But in contrast to his description of Lenin, as a masculine "man of will," the image Doeberl painted of Eisner was as someone weak and "feminine"—a common antisemitic stereotype in the early twentieth century associating Jews and women. It was clear which group Doeberl had in mind when, alluding to anti-Jewish notions, he discussed how this was the moment of revenge for "the Bavarian government having tolerated for so many years such a massive influx of corrosive elements who were foreign not only by tribe but by nationality and who knew how to abuse certain weaknesses of the Bavarian national character with their superior dialectic." By way of characterizing Eisner, Doeberl's royalist colleague Max Buchner spoke disparagingly of the "abysmal vanity of this Berlin Jewish journalist."[47]

For the otherwise moderate-minded Doeberl, the issue was obviously not just Eisner as an individual. Rather, what bothered him was the penetration of socialism, something he regarded as thoroughly Jewish. This he made clear in his characterization of Karl Marx, in whom he encountered features "that recur among the other leading personalities of his tribe and denomination: a strictly rational-intellectual talent, ruthless logic, corrosive criticism, a sharp eye out for the downsides of life and of human nature, burning ambition for public activity . . .

without any real piety toward that which is holy to the majority in a Christian body politic. A product as much of race as of forced education!" For Doeberl, because of these two personalities' common Jewish heritage, there was a direct line from Marx to Eisner, whose views he explained solely on that basis, adding that their views provided them with "the only escape route open to them for getting out of the uniformity surrounding their life circumstances."[48]

Rarely, too, did the conservative Munich press fail to point out the Jewish background of the revolutionaries, especially when there was something negative to report. Thus, in its coverage of a prosecution for embezzling files from the Eisner government by his former private secretaries, the *Bayerische Kurier* began by listing the defendants this way: "The 26 year-old Israelite merchant Felix Fechenbach from Mergentheim, now in Chemnitz, the 24 year-old Israelite private student Ernst Joske . . ."[49] And the general secretary of the Bavarian Peasants' League wrote in the association's paper, *Das Bayerische Vaterland*, that "the Jews Eisner and Fechenbach are perpetrating a monstrous crime on the German people." Further down, antisemitic language is used to describe Fechenbach: "Eisner is dead, but the Jew Fechenbach is still running around on his flat feet somewhere in the world. . . . The whole cause of Eisner and Fechenbach was paid labor in the interest of the enemy alliance, and for the Jew Fechenbach there is no gallows anywhere in Germany high enough to atone for this guilty deed."[50] In the estimation of the Prussian envoy in Munich, this was an antisemitic newspaper, and he reported to the Foreign Ministry in Berlin: "The manner in which the 'Vaterland' discusses conditions in a north[ern Germany] purportedly governed only by Jews, tricksters, and Bolsheviks overshoots the mark so much that it can only have a repulsive effect on the impartial reader. Unfortunately, though, this little and nondescript paper does have a certain influence."[51]

The *Völkischer Beobachter* expressed itself even more clearly on the anniversary of the revolution. This paper was ready with one brief explanation for all the evils supposedly caused by Kurt Eisner—the answer to the questions raised about why Eisner was prepared to commit his allegedly disgraceful deeds: "Four words supply the answer to all the above questions: 'He was a Jew.'"[52] When a street was about to be named after Eisner in the Swabian town of Göggingen, the newspaper that was later to become the party organ of the National Socialists was appalled: "And whoever believes that one should immortalize this racially alien and foreign Jewish-Bolshevik tramp (he was once called Salomon Kosmanowsky), of him one can only assume that he has lost his eye for the concerns of our people and our homeland. . . . Such people, like the like-minded members of their race and belief, deserve to be deported to Palestine."[53]

Even if the Jewish activists participating in the revolution and council republic were far from professing any faith, outsiders were constantly referring to their purported Jewish religious affiliation. In his autobiography, Ernst Toller, for example, describes his interrogation by the public prosecutor Lieberich following his arrest: "'What is your religion?' 'I have none.' He turned to a stenographer: 'Put down "Jew, non-professing".'"[54] Erich Mühsam, who most likely hesitated to leave the Jewish community formally for fear of losing the paternal share of his inheritance,[55] made this diary entry about his interrogation: "When it came to recording my personal details, I refused to answer the question about religion but then declared when I saw that this was regarded as impermissible: If I were not a Jew, I would insist on refusing to answer."[56] Was Mühsam possibly thinking at this moment about a poem he had composed over a decade earlier and that began this way?

The Interrogation:
Your name? the director asked me
I gave my name
Born?
Yes!
When?
I named the date
Religion?
None of your concern.
So, then write: Mosaic!—The official wrote . . .[57]

In his autobiography *From Berlin to Jerusalem*, Gershom Scholem recounted what he had said to his brother, the Communist politician and future Reichstag deputy Werner Scholem, when he accompanied Werner to a speaking appearance during the revolutionary events in Halle: "'Don't fool yourself,' I told him 'they'll applaud your speech and probably they'll elect you a deputy at the next election . . . but behind your back nothing will change.' I heard one of the workers say to his colleagues: 'The Jew [not 'our comrade'] makes a nice speech."[58]

Antisemitism was hardly aimed exclusively at the revolutionaries, and it was not restricted to Munich. Everyone was talking about pogroms, especially after the murder of several Jews in the Polish city of Kielce on November 11, 1918, along with subsequent anti-Jewish acts of violence throughout Eastern Europe. News of this violence was already haunting Germany in November. Thus, on November 29 the *Allgemeine Zeitung des Judentums* reported: "Instead of what is certainly their very strong participation in government helping to improve the lot of Jews, it seems only to have worsened it. Something like a pogrom atmosphere, of the kind we have not seen in Germany for centuries, prevails in Berlin and elsewhere. One notices this in conversations, one detects it above all in assaults and leaflets."[59] In Görlitz, the writer Paul Mühsam, Erich's more bourgeois-minded cousin, made this entry to his diary on New Year's Eve: "It is dreadful how antisemitism is raising its head, since once again the Jews have to serve as a whipping boy. It is on them that the Pan-Germans and militarists are trying to shift responsibility for their serious blood guilt, in order to distract attention from themselves. The people are being stirred up with the basest lies, and in Berlin they are expecting bloody pogroms. A self-defense corps has already formed. This is what the Germany of today looks like."[60]

But nowhere was the pogrom atmosphere more pronounced than in Munich, the city where Jewish politicians were also most conspicuously present. As early as November 16, 1918, Thomas Mann was writing in his diary about a "pogrom atmosphere in Munich."[61] And a young Austrian soldier who would soon rise from obscurity to become the leader of Germany's emerging right-wing movement wrote a few years later in his manifesto *Mein Kampf*, composed during his internment at the

Im neuen Deutschland

Mephisto, Ahasver und +++ Adonai —
Nennt Eisner, und ihr habt sie alle drei.

Kurt Eisner
weiland bayerischer Ministerpräsident.

Daß Mühsam, dieser seelenvolle Mann,
Noch heut in Ebrach sitzt — versteh's, wer kann!

Erich Mühsam
„Volksbeauftragter" der Münchener Räterepublik.

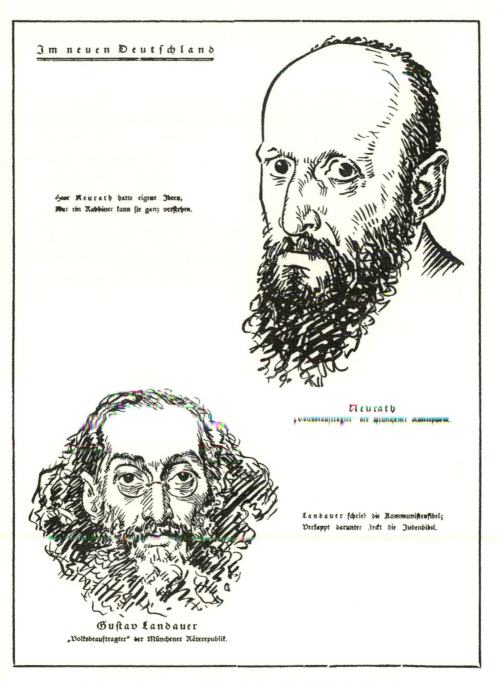

FIGURE 16A AND 16B. Antisemitic caricatures of Kurt Eisner, Erich Mühsam,
Otto Neurath, and Gustav Landauer from the newspaper *Auf gut deutsch* (1920),
published by Dietrich Eckart (pp. 20 and 24).

Landsberg prison: "In the winter of 1918–1919 a kind of antisemitism began slowly to take root. Later on the National Socialist Movement presented the Jewish problem in a new light. Taking the question beyond the restricted circles of the upper classes and small bourgeoisie we succeeded in transforming it into the driving motive of a great popular movement."[62]

Living conditions were not essentially improving two months into the Eisner government; unrest was spreading throughout the city, and more and more vigiliante groups were forming alongside the Spartacists. At the same time, antisemitism began to have wider repercussions. "The first antisemitic leaflets made their appearance. They were chiefly to be seen in small dairies and greengrocers' shops, or were pasted on the walls by stealth. Penny dreadful legends were spread about Eisner's origins and his supposed wealth," reports Oskar Maria Graf in his memoir.[63] And elsewhere he writes: "'Bloodhounds! Mass murderers! Traitors!' rang out on all sides 'Down with them' Down with them!' roared a thousand voices in all the streets. People slowly lost faith in Eisner and grew more embittered. The papers lied and incited to violence. The censorship had been abolished. Any story might be told. The wildest rumors found credence and intensified the agitation."[64]

What was decisive was not the exploitation of antisemitism for political purposes, or its intentional deployment as a political weapon by extremist elements of society. The critical point was that, in Munich as of November 1918, the very public involvement of Jews served as a pretext for pushing the so-called Jewish question into the very heart of the political discourse for the first time. The question had moved center stage to such a degree that even moderate elements of society could no longer evade it. It was not only antisemites and Jews who took part in the debate about the "Jewish character" of the revolution and council republic as early as the winter of 1918–1919. So, too, did liberal and national-minded writers, the papal nuncio and the archbishop, and Austrian and American diplomats, as did the press affiliated with the Catholic Center Party and the Social Democrats. Regardless of where one stood on the Jews, they seemed ubiquitous.

"A Government of Jehovah's Wrath"—The Attitude
of the Catholic Church

Protestants in Bavaria during the 1920s were close to 30 percent of the population, and in Munich the figure was nearly 15 percent. With Gustav von Kahr, the state even had a Protestant prime minister. Yet the state of Bavaria and the city of Munich saw themselves as intensely Catholic. In politics the dominant force was the Bavarian People's Party, a branch of the Catholic Center Party. In Munich, the envoy of the pope and the archbishop of Munich and Freising were accorded a special status. The papal nuncio in Munich was Eugenio Pacelli, who would later become pope as Pius XII. According to the church historian Hubert Wolf, he was not free from believing in a "Jewish-Bolshevik global conspiracy"[65] Pacelli, too, made use of the lie about Eisner's supposed East European origins: in his view, Eisner was the embodiment of the revolution, since he was an atheist, radical socialist, implacable propagandist, bosom buddy of Russian nihilists, and, to top it all off, a Galician Jew. Eisner was ultimately the symbol, program, and soul of the revolution that imperiled religious, political, and social life in Bavaria, Pacelli wrote in one of his routine reports to the Vatican.[66] A few days later he repeated his conviction: "Especially controversial, however, is the person of the Foreign Minister Kurt Eisner, a Galican Jew who was repeatedly sentenced to prison sentences for political crimes."[67]

After Pacelli had temporarily escaped the turmoil of the revolution in Munich, the job of managing the correspondence from Munich to the Vatican was taken over by his closest employee, the church auditor, Lorenzo Schioppa. His view of Eisner hardly differed from that of his superior. Even before the revolution in Bavaria, Schioppa had made utterances about a Jewish global conspiracy with regard to the Russian Revolution. The Russian Revolution, according to Schioppa, was "mainly the work of Jews" and was "based on the idea of a Jewish world government."[68] On November 28, Schioppa reported that the *Germania* (the national newspaper of the Catholic Center Party) was quite right to question who Eisner, this man so presumptuous as to

FIGURE 17. The papal nuncio, Eugenio Pacelli. Bayerische Staatsbibliothek München / Bildarchiv.

give himself the title of a Bavarian prime minister, really was. He claimed that hiding under a German name was a Jew of Eastern Galician origin who had assumed the manners of a grand seigneur as representative of the proletariat.[69] And shortly later, on December 6, he was writing to the Vatican: "The Munich Workers' and Soldiers' Council is made up of the dregs of the population, of lots of non-Bavarians from the navy, Jews, natives who have long been rebelling against the nobility and the clergy, and hardly of citizens and soldiers who were actually at the front."[70]

This attitude of the Vatican's representatives was shared by the city's most important Catholic dignitary, Archbishop Michael Faulhaber. In his unpublished autobiography, written during the Second World War, Faulhaber also expressed the widespread view that Eisner came from Galicia: "How was it possible that a people whose royalism was so proverbial would swerve into the republican camp and let its king go into banishment on the reputation of a foreign Galician writer, overnight without a shot and not shedding even a drop of heroic blood?"[71]

Frequently historians have pointed to seeming contradictions or complexities in Faulhaber's relationship to Judaism, since his statements that should be assessed as anti-Jewish can be contrasted with reports that he placed a protective hand over the Jewish community when it was brutally attacked from the outside. In this case he seems to have hewed to a clear line that was certainly not unusual for a conservative representative of the Church. He stood in the tradition of a clerical-conservative anti-Judaism, shared its prejudices against Eastern European Jews, and often equated Judaism with socialism. At the same time, however, he rejected the kind of modern antisemitism that was based on racism and the violence associated with it. Buttressing his theological anti-Judaism was his political conviction that a socialist government was anticlerical and needed to be decisively fought, and that the political influence of Jewish representatives had to be curtailed.

As discussed in the previous chapter, Faulhaber had already seen the authority of a government run by a Jewish prime minister seriously questioned by the people. He himself avoided meeting with representatives of the "people's state" and advised the papal nuncio to withdraw to Switzerland temporarily so that he would not have to come into contact with Eisner. In his New Year's Eve sermon for 1918, Faulhaber characterized the new rulers as a "government of Jehovah's wrath," which gave both contemporaries and later analysts plenty of material for different interpretations.[72]

Only a few weeks after the Eisner government came to power, antisemitism had reached such an ominous level that the Munich rabbi,

Leo Baerwald, felt obliged to pay a call on Archbishop Faulhaber, on December 7, 1918. The two clerics knew each other from their time as military chaplains in the First World War. Baerwald disassociated himself from Eisner and the fellow members of his government who were Jewish. The rabbi asked the archbishop to speak up "for the protection of the persecuted Jews" and to take a stance against antisemitic reporting in the press, especially in the Catholic newspapers. Faulhaber's laconic diary entry read: "A nicely worded speech about speaking up for the protection of the persecuted Jews. The Jews in the government no longer belonged to them. Everyone is living in fear, especially because [the much maligned department store owner] Isidor Bach was incidentally one. The Jew is hard-working, sober, 'even more intelligent through preoccupation with the Talmud.' . . . I disapprove of all programs [sic] but cannot make any promise that I will speak up against the Kurier and the Morgenblatt [newspapers]."[73] Faulhaber made clear he would not make any public statement about the attacks against the Jews.

One year later, a committee of Catholics expressed its concern that, "throughout the Fatherland, hatred of Jews is being zealously stirred up" in a manner that "threatens to destroy completely the reputation of German culture." When the committee asked the archbishop for a public statement in opposition to antisemitism, Faulhaber preferred to remain silent again.[74]

By contrast, Faulhaber had no trouble finding very blunt words against the Eisner government to put in his pastoral letter on February 2, 1919. For him, the abolition of clerical school supervision and obligatory religious instruction were more grievous "than Herod's Massacre of the Innocents." There was a special twist to his characterization of the government as a "government hostile to Christ," given that it was headed by a Jewish prime minister. After all, at a time of mounting death threats against Eisner and other cabinet members, the reference to Herod's demise in the Gospels could only help to cultivate many an already preexisting aggression: "'For they are dead that sought the life of the child' (Matthew 2:20), and before History's Throne of Judgment, Herod had the curse of a child murderer placed upon him."[75]

FIGURE 18. Archbishop (and, as of 1921, Cardinal) Michael Faulhaber.
Bayerische Staatsbibliothek München / Bildarchiv.

Faulhaber privately condemned the murder of Eisner, not least
because of the even greater political uncertainty that came in the wake
of the assassination. He confided this only to his diary: "This is very
bad, Bavaria was on the way to calm, and God only knows what is now
in store."[76] But any tribute to the murdered prime minister, of the kind
usually forthcoming from the Church for high-ranking political dignitaries, was out of the question for Faulhaber. He rejected both flying
flags at half-mast and the ringing of church bells, in order "to evade any
inquiry about funeral services."[77] While Faulhaber avoided any contact
with Eisner, he later received a visit from his murderer, Count Arco. In
1925, the assassin, only recently released from prison, personally presented the archbishop with his book *From Five Years of Imprisonment*,
dedicated to the leader of the Catholic Center Party in Bavaria, Georg
Heim.[78]

Faulhaber reacted indignantly to Gustav Landauer's funeral oration, in which Landauer compared Kurt Eisner to Jesus and Jan Hus, the Bohemian religious reformer burned at the stake for heresy. After all, Faulhaber remarked, the Jew Landauer was a "part of that force that had crucified Jesus, but not of Jesus himself."[79] In the short period when the council government was in power, Faulhaber's view of the initiators of the revolution became even clearer as as he invoked the liturgical language of the Church's Good Friday intercession to describe the "perfidious Jews" in an attribution that struck him as particularly relevant: "[W]hile the Jewish revol[ution] continues to ponder destroying the Church, let us pray: Oremus et pro perfidis Judaeis."[80]

The historian Antonia Leugers accurately summarizes Faulhaber's attitude toward Judaism when she writes: "All the anti-Judaic stereotypes can be find in Faulhaber: Christ-killer; stubbornness, blindness in spite of the 'proofs' of Jesus's 'miracles'; self-curse: 'his blood be upon us and our children' (Matthew 27:25); substitution thesis: Old Covenant replaced by the Church; rejection theory: rejection of the Jews, destruction of the Jerusalem Temple in 70 A.D.; dispersion of the Jews; disinheritance theory: the new people of God are Christians, Church appointed by Jesus, only through mercy is conversion of the Jews possible; Good Friday intercession 'for the faithless Jews.'"[81] During a visit to Palestine in 1898, Faulhaber himself had already documented this attitude in his autobiographical notes when he spoke about the "curse of God that lies upon this land since the crucifixion of Christ." He continued: "Since then the former Chosen People has wandered across the earth without peace or rest, and over and over again the punishment is fulfilled that challenged its fathers with the word: 'His blood be upon us and our children.'"[82]

Faulhaber's diary also conveys an impression of the anti-Jewish mood that was widely prevalent in Catholic circles. Less than a week after the revolution, Faulhaber was approached by a Father Blume, who expressed the opinion that the red flag belonged better on top of the synagogue than on the tower of the Frauenkirche (the Church of Our Lady, a signature structure in Munich's skyline).[83] The revolution of 1918 and the council republic were both legitimating the open display of a

Catholic antisemitism in other parts of Bavaria as well. The dean of the Regensburg Cathedral, Franz X. Kiefl, saw the Jews as the basic evil and cause of the upheaval. The revolution was Jewish, whereas the monarchy embodied "the Christian ideal of the state." The point was put more clearly in his book *Die Staatsphilosophie der katholischen Kirche* (The Political Philosophy of the Catholic Church): "Just as the intellectual forces of subversion never grew out of the people themselves in any of the modern revolutions, but were rather grafted onto the peoples from outside the nation, so it was in Germany: To be sure, the German revolution emanated from Hegel, the architect of modern constitutional law; but Hegel's philosophy itself was merely the collective repository of the new Occidental intellectual culture, and furthermore the founders of scientific socialism, which re-forged the dialectic into an intellectual weapon for the revolution, were not of the German tribe, but rather Jews."[84] It is clear with whom the sympathies of the Regensburg dean lay when he went on to talk about Eisner's murderer, Arco: "Selfless, pure idealism, of the kind that flared up in the midst of our collapse and decline in the shape of our young national hero Count Arco, can only ignite new life in our people."[85] This book was brought out by the Manz publishing house in Regensburg, which published an entire series with similar content.

Already by the end of 1918, the discussion about antisemitism taking place in Catholic circles had become public. The organ of separatist political Catholicism in Bavaria, the newspaper *Das Bayerische Vaterland*, repeatedly provoked attacks against Jews and Judaism. In response, the Zionist-oriented paper *Das Jüdische Echo* demanded that the Bavarian People's Party (BVP), as the Catholic Center Party was called in Bavaria, clarify its relationship with Jews. Thereupon the Catholic party published a December 31 letter from its general secretariat that read: "The 'Bavarian People's Party' is completely free of any kind of antisemitism. . . . If antisemitic tendencies are ascribed to the 'Bavarian People's Party' because of misunderstood statements in the party press, it should be pointed out that these attacks are not directed against our Jewish fellow-citizens in their totality, but are occasioned by the unjustified and all too forceful protrusion of certain Jewish personalities in the current government of the Bavarian and German people, as well as by acts of economic exploitation that individual Jews allowed to do wrong against our people in our Fatherland's most difficult time."[86] After the BVP had a pamphlet distributed in which it said that the Bolsheviks were "mostly men of Jewish descent and therefore [!] without national feeling," the charge of antisemitism resurfaced again in the Jewish press.[87] In another electoral poster from the BVP ahead of the elections in January 1919, Jewry and trafficking were mentioned in a single breath. Whoever "does not want that we become completely and solely governed by Berlin Jewry" was urged to vote for the party of Bavarian Catholicism.[88]

By no means were Jewish readers the only ones to discern antisemitic tendencies in the Catholic press. The envoy from the state of Württemberg in Munich, Moser von Filseck, took a skeptical view of the anti-Jewish reporting in the Catholic press: "Their attempts to draw the more religious Jews to their side are not very well received after the attacks in the Center press against the prominent Jewish element in the current government have cast suspicion of antisemitism on the party."[89]

After the First Council Republic was declared, the *Bayerischer Kurier* was forced to print a proclamation from the Revolutionary Central Council in the Council Republic of Bavaria stating: "We have solid proof that the anonymous pamphlets massively distributed in which agitation against Jews is shamelessly promoted, and whose outcome could be and is intended to be that there will be serious acts of violence against the Jewish population, have been sent here from Northern Germany with the deliberate intention of eliciting bloody clashes and conditions in the capital of Bavaria of the kind that have taken place in Berlin through the fault of the government there."[90] The clear intention of this opponent of the antisemites was to make them look just as "foreign" as the revolutionaries were portrayed by their enemies.

The proclamation of the two council republics exacerbated the anti-Jewish atmosphere not only in the Catholic press but also inside the Church and among its dignitaries. After the papal nuncio, just a few months earlier, had insinuated that Kurt Eisner, the Jew from Berlin, had

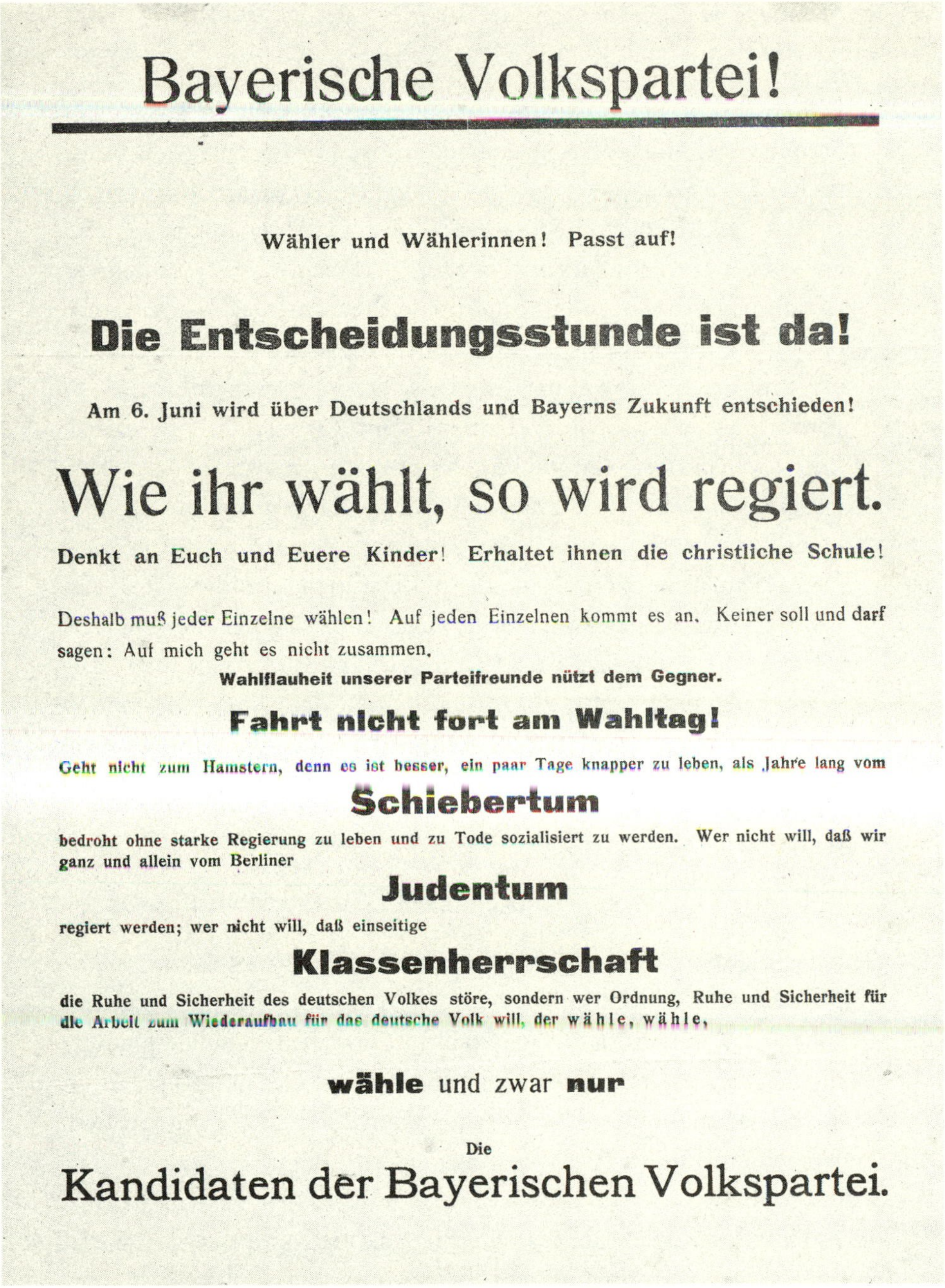

Bayerische Volkspartei!

Wähler und Wählerinnen! Passt auf!

Die Entscheidungsstunde ist da!

Am 6. Juni wird über Deutschlands und Bayerns Zukunft entschieden!

Wie ihr wählt, so wird regiert.

Denkt an Euch und Euere Kinder! Erhaltet ihnen die christliche Schule!

Deshalb muß jeder Einzelne wählen! Auf jeden Einzelnen kommt es an. Keiner soll und darf sagen: Auf mich geht es nicht zusammen.

Wahlflauheit unserer Parteifreunde nützt dem Gegner.

Fahrt nicht fort am Wahltag!

Geht nicht zum Hamstern, denn es ist besser, ein paar Tage knapper zu leben, als Jahre lang vom

Schiebertum

bedroht ohne starke Regierung zu leben und zu Tode sozialisiert zu werden. Wer nicht will, daß wir ganz und allein vom Berliner

Judentum

regiert werden; wer nicht will, daß einseitige

Klassenherrschaft

die Ruhe und Sicherheit des deutschen Volkes störe, sondern wer Ordnung, Ruhe und Sicherheit für die Arbeit zum Wiederaufbau für das deutsche Volk will, der wähle, wähle,

wähle und zwar **nur**

Die

Kandidaten der Bayerischen Volkspartei.

FIGURE 19. Election poster of the Bavarian People's Party with antisemitic content.
Münchner Stadtbibliothek / Monacensia.

an (Eastern) Galician background, he now branded the Russian-born ethnic German Max Levien as a Jew:

> Levien and his general staff—or, if you prefer, with the Council of People's Deputies—has ensconced himself in the former Wittelsbacher Palais. The spectacle now offered by the palace is indescribable. Absolute chaos, nauseating filth, uninterrupted coming and going by armed soldiers and workers, the crude words and curses resounding there make a true hell out of the former favorite residence of the kings of Bavaria. An army of employees that come and go, transmit orders, spread news reports, and among them a horde of young women whose looks hardly inspire confidence, Jews like all the people in the other official positions, with provocative facial expressions and equivocal smiles. At the top of this group of women is Levien's lover: a young Russian, Jewess, divorced, and put in command as mistress-arbiter. And the nunciature has unfortunately had to bow before this person in order to obtain a pass permit! Levien is a young lad, also a Russian and a Jew, of about thirty or thirty-five years. Pale, dirty, with expressionless eyes, a raw voice and loutish tone: a really repulsive type, although with an intelligent and sly facial expression.[91]

"To the Gallows"—Radicalization in Word and Deed

Thomas Mann was a seismograph for the changing mood among Munich's bourgeoisie after the First World War, a shifting temper characterized in part by growing radicalization of anti-Jewish sentiment, especially in the days after the suppression of the Second Council Republic in May 1919. Within hours after the council adventure had been crushed, he wrote in his diary: "We also spoke of that type of Russian Jew, the leader of the world revolutionary movement, an explosive mixture of Jewish intellectual radicalism and Slavic Christian enthusiasm. A world which retains any instinct of self-preservation must act against this sort of people with all the energy that can be mobilized and with the swiftness of martial law."[92]

FIGURE 20. Election poster of the German National People's Party with antisemitic caricatures. BArch Plak 002-004-111, graphic designer: Otto v. Kursell, Bundesarchiv.

This verbal radicalization is also clearly evident in the case of another bourgeois chronicler, the conservative teacher Josef Hofmiller. In February 1919, he quoted a line from the *Vaticanum Lehninense* (a medieval manuscript from a Cistercian abbey in Brandenburg that combines a historical chronicle with prophecy): "Israel infandum scelus audet morte piandum" (Israel dares to commit an unspeakable outrage, which must be atoned by death). In his notes on April 8, he included an allusion to rich Jews as those profiting from the events in Munich: "Here and there an anti-Jewish atmosphere makes its presence felt. I have kept two leaflets of this kind. One hears that Jews, who were owners of houses or had mortgages on them, had already, some considerable time ago, transferred their property and their rights to American coreligionists." And shortly before the suppression of the council republic he reported rumors that the Jewish middle class would prevent a strike necessary for the putdown of the revolution out of self-interest (and no doubt also out of unconscious sympathy with their "purring mishpocha," as he called "our current rulers"): "It is said that the citizens' strike could not be carried out because of the Jews. The Jewish attorneys, who are quite numerous, would promptly make themselves available as judges and administrative officials. But, above all, the Jewish physicians wouldn't join in; ostensibly for humanitarian reasons, but in reality in order to take over the practice of their non-Jewish colleagues. Who can check up on these rumors?"[93]

In his reporting and diary entries, the scholar Victor Klemperer depicted the antisemitic atmosphere among his colleagues. He told the wife of the German Nationalist historian Paul Fritz Joachimsen—who, like Klemperer, was a Jew who had converted to Protestantism—that he "had not at all agreed with Eisner's politics, but the murder committed by Count Arco had brought about much greater confusion than Eisner ever could have. At that point, Frau Joachimsen went into hysterics. 'How dare you call the count a murderer!' she screeched. 'How dare you blame him for our dire circumstances! He sacrificed himself for us, he roused us, he liberated us from the Galician, I revere him like a savior, I wish I could staunch his wounds, I'm not worthy of unlacing his shoes!' and she ran out of the room sobbing."[94]

And a bit later he noted: "So the agitation—which, I should say in advance, is still in a state of torpor, still generally a calm before the storm—gradually swelled. It expressed itself neither beautifully nor cleverly, but *antisemitically*. And it thus gave the tyrannical government the opportunity to make liberal gestures; the posters from the Central Council warn against the *persecution of the Jews*. In truth, the Jews have it no better than the Prussians here; they share the fate of being blamed for everything, and depending on the situation they are either the capitalists or the Bolshevists." And when passengers from an automobile on Odeonsplatz distributed leaflets for the revolution, "there was a bellowing chorus of 'Jews, Jewish pigs!'"[95] Klemperer summed up the situation as follows:

And once the bourgeoisie began to realize that the council republican game they had watched half apathetically, half-sullenly to that point could actually mean something worse for them than just a wild, car-nivalistic performance, how did they demonstrate their awakening to resistance? Through spontaneous anti-Semitism. "Jewish pigs!" ranted individuals in front of the posters on the walls, "Jewish pigs!" roared the occasional small chorus, and flyers appeared blaming the Jews entirely for the Council Republic, for the revolution itself, for inciting the war, for its disastrous outcome. The only difference be-tween the flyers and the speeches in the streets was that the flyers held the Jews alone responsible for everything, while in common bourgeois parlance Jews were mentioned alongside Prussians—and in such close alliance that Jew and Prussian often sounded like syn-onyms for the same principle of evil.[96]

Even the revolutionaries themselves were not entirely immune to anti-semitic stereotypes. The revolutionary schoolteacher Ernst Niekisch became chair of the Central Council of the Republic of Bavaria after Eisner was murdered, and during the 1920s he tried to develop ties be-tween Social Democratic and National Socialist thinking (an attempted synthesis that came to be known as National Bolshevism). In writing about Otto Neurath's economic policy, he spoke about "its Jewish im-pudence," and he characterized Ernst Toller as a "Jew rascal."[97] Niekisch also reported about the resistance inside the Workers' and Soldiers' Councils to naming Landauer as commissioner for enlightenment and public instruction: "The speaker for the Peasants' League intimated: Landauer was no Bavarian, he was one of the literati, he was a Jew. Would that really be acceptable to the Bavarian people? The Catholic Church was a power in Bavaria: would it accept Landauer? There were many who were impressed by these arguments. Then Mühsam made a passionate plea for Landauer, he heaped burning coals on the head of his friend. . . . It was reactionary to take offense at the 'foreign' literati and Jews."[98]

In his memoirs, Germany's Social Democratic Reichswehr minister, Gustav Noske, whose military strike would end the council republic and who was called a "bloodhound" by his opponents, denounced the "East European Jewish" influence in the German labor movement and distin-guished this influence from the attitude of the German working class.

Of the radicals he wrote: "[T]he East [European] Jewish 'Marxists' had a special proclivity for forming socialism into a dogma. . . . They hatched a secret science that has always been incomprehensible to the German workers."[99] The rhetoric of the Social Democrats also became more radical during the council republic. A diary entry by the journalist Josef Karl, one of the Majority Social Democrats, in April 1919 showed that he had little trust in "the vagabond and mostly Jewish-anarchist rabble-rousers." And he asked himself: "How long will foreign Jewish riffraff that cannot survive anywhere stay in power?"[100] Karl talked of the "Judas' work" that was accomplished "by these people" and the "hair-splitting" of a Eugen Leviné, characterized Arnold Wadler as a "Galician Jew," and labeled an entry on Towia Axelrod "A Russian Jew Bav. Finance Commissar."[101]

The temporary Social Democratic minister for military affairs in the Hoffmann government, Ernst Schneppenhorst, reacted to attacks coming from Eugen Leviné with a caustic remark castigating the "Jew boys, foreign elements, and failed academics."[102] In a dispute with the attorney Philipp Löwenfeld, who had accused Schneppenhorst of making the council republic possible in the first place through his wavering attitude, the Social Democratic newspaper from Bamberg, *Der Freistaat*, defended Schneppenhorst against the "great Jewish spell" with a turn of phrase alluding to Yiddish expressions: it was important not to be misled by all "the gedibber and geserres" (chatter and whining). Löwenfeld called this the first instance known to him in which a Social Democratic Party newspaper tried to fight the truth by arousing antisemitic instincts.[103]

A November 1919 memorandum from the Munich Police Authority about the leaders of the council republics claimed that the April revolution had been the "work of personalities . . . who were foreign to the national character and national essence." The police found it striking that the great majority of the leading revolutionaries ("especially from the radical and most radical tendency") were Jews, and that "within this category," most were "of predominantly Northern German and East European Jewish descent." The broad masses were becoming mistrustful: hence there were "movements" forming "in the people, that deserve attention as a reaction of mass feeling, especially from the standpoint of public order, which also has to consider the protection of those native Jewish sections of the people who in their totality are thoroughly opposed to the doings of these foreign members of their race."[104] Even Felix Fechenbach, who had grown up in Bavarian Würzburg, was briefly turned into a foreigner in the pages of *Bayerisches Vaterland*. The paper had Fechenbach actually coming from Palestine, and it characterized him as "Eisner's aide-de-camp on duty, Fechenbach from Samaria."[105]

In 1920, the historian Michael Doeberl wrote that the revolution was the revenge for the Bavarian government "having tolerated" such a "massive influx of corrosive elements who were foreign not only by tribe but by nationality and who knew how to abuse certain weaknesses of the Bavarian national character with their superior dialectic."[106]

After the council republic was put down, the authorities found that they had to work harder to deal with the impending danger of antisemitic pogroms. In June 1919, the state commissioner for Southern Bavaria informed the legitimate government, which had fled to North Bavarian Bamberg during the rule of the coucil republic, about the "excessive antisemitic agitation" of the extreme right-wing *Münchener Beobachter* and called for the paper to be banned: "Given the unusual excitability and receptivity of large parts of the public to provocative news at the moment, it strikes me as dangerous to look on passively at this pan-German newspaper. I ask the government to consider a publication ban for the *Münchener Beobachter*."[107] Despite appeals like this, we have no evidence of any sweeping measures being taken against antisemitism.

When antisemites instigated public clashes, they could usually rely on support from the police. That was the case in December 1919, when the premiere of Frank Wedekind's play *Castle Wetterstein* was accompanied by loud protests. Not only were there catcalls like "whorehouse" and "bordello," but also "pack of Jewish pigs." As the historian Peter Jelavich notes, a theater show this "un-German" just had to be the work of a "Jewish pack," even if Wedekind was not Jewish. The right-wing scene placed the Jews in their sights. The first five performances could still take place, yet during the sixth performance about fifty students and officers attacked all the theater patrons who supposedly looked Jewish. After two additional performances, the police, instead of stopping the riots, ordered that the play be discontinued. The flimsy excuse offered was that they were only trying to prevent a pogrom against Jews. The police reports themselves, however, were full of anti-semitic stereotypes, as when one of the complaints was described as coming from a "Jewess of the pronounced Asiatic type."[108]

One fixture of the Munich press that has not been followed closely by researchers provides a very good way of tracking the rapid change in mood between November 1918 and the summer of 1919 beyond what we hear from intellectuals and the political elite. The *Münchener Stadtanzeiger*, which captioned itself the "non-partisan weekly for the protection of Bavarianness" (*Parteiloses Wochenblatt für Schutz des Bayerntums*), was a petit bourgeois paper that did not rely on intellectual articles or reporting on world politics. Instead, it discussed Munich's coffeehouses, complained about rising beer prices accompanied by a lower quality of beer, and claimed to speak "from the mouth of the people." Local politics also played an important part in the coverage of the *Münchener Stadtanzeiger*. Although originally not noticeably antisemitic, over the course of 1919 the paper became radically hostile to Jews.

The paper's reporting about the upheaval in November 1918 was skeptical but not entirely negative. "Overnight the kindly citizens of the Bavarian state are supposed to be transformed into republicans. It will still take a lot of time to make this credible and seem comprehensible. . . . Kurt Eisner calls himself the bold entrepreneur who has taken the plunge into this daring enterprise."[109] The new government was still viewed at a distance, with a wait-and-see attitude. It is striking that Eisner was never characterized as prime minister but always simply called Kurt Eisner. Unlike his Bavarian-Catholic cabinet colleagues, Eisner was not written up by the *Stadtanzeiger* in the colloquial style that put the family name first, as the paper did with his state minister of social welfare: "Unterleitner, Hans."

By the end of the year, there was increased indignation toward those accused of having caused Germany's defeat and the economic distress of the postwar period by acting egotistically and in a way damaging to the community. The text under the unambiguous heading "To the gallows" was somewhat more roundabout: "The guilty parties for Germany's economic collapse are those who through their crass, criminal egoism, usury, hording foodstuffs and other goods, and shady dealings of all kinds have betrayed and sold out our own fatherland." Readers could quickly piece together which population group was being pilloried here, since the only person named is the Jewish department store owner Isidor Bach. "Usurers" and "shady dealers" were often clearly recognizable code words for "Jews." The question of what should happen with them was answered with immediate clarity: "an introduction of the death penalty for all these shameless elements who through usury for the most essential things of life are stealing and plundering in a manner that cries out to the heavens."[110]

In January 1919, the paper began to speak an anti-Jewish language that was less roundabout: "From Junker [aristocratic] rule we've fallen into Jewish rule. This outcome of the revolution seems like scorn. . . . Hopefully the German people will prove its political maturity at the National Assembly [election] in the near future and elect fellow members of our tribe as its representatives of the people in order to prove that it is capable of governing itself and that it has no need of borrowing from strangers."[111]

Yet, alongside the antisemitic reporting, some more positive tones were still occasionally struck by the *Stadtanzeiger*. After the murder of Eisner, the paper praised the Bavarian prime minister: "What the proletariat has lost with Kurt Eisner can never be replaced again," while Eisner's murderer, Count Arco, came in for severe condemnation: "With his supposed great deed the murderer has committed a crime that can prove fatal for the entire land."[112]

As church bells were ringing throughout the land during Eisner's burial, antisemitic polemics blended in with resistance from clerical circles, especially in small towns and villages.[113] With the beginning of the council republic, the paper now launched a frontal assault against the "Jewish foreign agents and popular agitators" who needed to be "rendered harmless as soon as they appear."[114] Starting in May 1919, then, the *Stadtanzeiger* was openly advertising for the Deutsche Bürgervereinigung

(German Citizens' Association) founded by Dietrich Eckart, the antisemite and later "party poet" for the National Socialists:

> The new Citizens' Association gives a certain sort of human being an upset stomach. Namely, those from the tribe of Israel, who see in this Citizens' Association a new foe. Whether correctly remains to be seen. It would be desirable, because the Jews are more to blame for our current political situation than is generally accepted, as anybody must admit who has open eyes and a clear understanding of things. Unscrupulous leaders like Lewien, Levinés [sic], Axelrod etc. have deliberately stirred up the workers, but not against the Jews, or against the only real danger of big capital, but against the citizenry and the middle class.... These dirty popular agitators, who only use the workers as a means to an end and usually consist of venal foreign agents for sale, are only pursuing a tactic of diverting the working class's attention from big capital.[115]

The radicalization of antisemitism can be tracked from one issue to the next. In August 1919, the *Stadtanzeiger*, referring to East European Jews living in Munich, talked about a "plague of Jews." Here the paper was using the same comparison of Jews with vermin that would later prove so popular among the National Socialists:

> Our poor Munich is so Jewified [*verjudet*] that it won't be long before we can't keep going on like this. The matter has gradually grown into a plague. But one doesn't need to believe, for example, that it is the poor, undernourished Jews from all over the world who are having a rendezvous in Munich; rather, these are entirely so-called overstuffed specimens, since the Jew is not so dumb as to starve from patriotism, he leaves that to the dumb goyim whom he is overcharging and swindling and whom he treats in a downright impertinent and pushy way. The plague of Jews has never emerged so clearly as right now, and if it keeps up like this, then under the Hoffmann government it will reach the point that we will have to emigrate if we want to be left alone by the Jews. It is only in positions of authority that this danger is overlooked, since wherever the Jew has established a foothold, he can't be removed any more. It's the same as with bugs.[116]

In subsequent issues, there were open calls to boycott Jewish businesses. In the meantime, the *Stadtanzeiger* had to face stiff competition in the city from the high-circulation *Völkischer Beoachter*, which had emerged out of the *Münchener Beobachter* in August 1919 and had adopted this radical language from the start. Not without a certain degree of involuntary irony, the *Stadtanzeiger*, a paper now fighting for survival, suspected that Jewish financiers were backing the *Beobachter*.[117]

In the wider press landscape of Munich, the *Stadtanzeiger* was a rather insignificant local paper. Yet this one newspaper mirrored the views of a large part of the lower-middle class in the city. In contrast to the major newspapers, it did not have to pay the same attention to owners' interests or attempts at political influence. The *Stadtanzeiger* spoke without mincing words, and this language changed drastically over the course of the year 1919.

"The Trotskys Make the Revolution, and the Bronsteins Pay the Price"—Jewish Reactions

Aside from the antisemites, hardly anyone had such strong aversions to the involvement of Jewish revolutionaries as Munich's Jews. They knew all too well that they were going to be held responsible for what the Jewish revolutionaries did, in line with a popular saying following the Russian Revolution about Trotsky, who was born Lev Davidovich Bronstein: "The Trotskys make the revolution, and the Bronsteins pay the price." Or as one Jewish newspaper put it in the midst of all the turmoil of the Bavarian revolution: "It's the old story, that the very men who stand out the furthest from Judaism are the ones constantly cited as crown witnesses against us."[118]

Thus, Minister of Justice Ernst Müller-Meiningen was not entirely wrong when he claimed: "The heavy involvement of Jewry in the revolution cannot be denied; it is also quite natural given the historical development and the literary and rhetorical agility of Jewry. It is equally self-evident that this introduced an extraordinarily strong antisemitic trait into the German people. Almost all of Munich's 'Greats' were Jews. . . . Nobody suffered more from this than the honorable, respectable Jewish community that had made the same sacrifices in blood and property during the war and that properly lamented the dangerous and unjust generalizations of accusations against dishonest and subversive elements."[119]

Munich's Jews were part of the city. Not only the so-called assimilated Jews—those who attended synagogue (if at all) three times a year and for whom Judaism had become only a sign of their origins—but also the Zionists and Orthodox Jews regarded themselves as citizens of Munich, as Bavarians, and as Germans, often in that order. A description of the Feuchtwanger family by a relative from Berlin comes to mind: "In Munich I had extensive family, the Feuchtwanger clan, which was mostly Orthodox. Not only were its members culturally German; they were downright Bavarian (*Bajuwaren*). One need only have heard prayers pronounced in Hebrew with an Upper Bavarian accent to know how much they were this way. . . . One would go to the beer cellars, where one could bring one's dinner along, one clambered up the mountains, knew the museums like one's own home, and it was 'our Munich,' in which even the Jew from Berlin was regarded as a foreigner."[120] Visiting the Hofbräuhaus was as self-evident as attending synagogue, and naturally practiced with the same enthusiasm as mountain-climbing and swimming in Lake Starnberg.

From the same family we know that there were also sometimes linguistic barriers to overcome. Thus, Lion Feuchtwanger's brother Martin described their father as follows: "My father spoke Munichese. He did not say 'Halte deinen Mund' [Shut your mouth], but: 'Halt die Goschen' [Bavarian dialect for 'Shut your gob']. When it came to asking what was for dinner, he didn't say 'Was gibt's heute Schönes zu speisen?' [What lovely dinner is there for us today?] but rather 'Was hammer denn heit zum essen?' [So wadda we got to eat t'day?]. And the exact same kind of Munichese was spoken by all the people in this house."[121]

At the beginning of the revolution, some Jews were still voicing hope that this new politically active role for Jews would finally grant them complete emancipation. The rather unpolitical *Israelitisches Familienblatt* from Hamburg stated: "If Jews are now occupying offices like this in numbers way above the percentage of the Jewish population in

Germany . . . we see in this circumstance nothing more than a serious charge against the old, decaying government just toppled, which had no idea of how to accept what was good. . . . Today the principle applies: *la recherche de la confession est interdite,* and it should remain this way."[122] (This classically French secularist statement—meaning "it is forbidden to ask about the religion anyone professes"—was a favorite quote of German liberals and often attributed to Bismarck.) The *Allgemeine Zeitung des Judentums* struck a similar tone in reporting from Berlin: "This much can already be said at the moment, that the involvement of so many Jews in the new regime completely rules out any restriction on Jews, any slight to their rights; the new era in whose dawn we now stand must, if we are not entirely deceived, bring our community its long-sought complete equality."[123] The newspaper warned individual young Jews involved in the Workers' and Soldiers' Councils to act cautiously, however, since the principle of not asking about a person's profession of faith did not entirely apply to Jewish politicians after all: "It is certainly understandable that those unaccustomed to ruling act unruly and cocky in the new role that has befallen them; but they should and must be and remain mindful of their exposed position. They need to consider that—by highhanded methods, by an imperious manner, by every unruly and imperious word—they are not only almost provoking rebelliousness, but that by way of every impropriety they are endangering the community from which they come, and that they are inflaming and amplifying a hostile disposition against Jewry."[124]

A significantly more optimistic outlook was expressed by an intellectual monthly founded during the First World War, the *Neue Jüdische Monatshefte.* Initially, its editorial asserted that—like it or not—there was nothing that could be done about the fact that Jews played a proportionally large part in the revolutionary events: "For the whole of Jewry, the German revolution represents an event of great historical consequence. Above all it has a downright revolutionary impact with regard to the position of German Jewry in government and politics. Today one may say without exaggeration that it is the revolution that has first brought Jews true equality. . . . In the new and free Germany Jews will also be able to occupy a different, sympathetic, and friendly position."[125] The Zionist *Jüdische Rundschau* took the same line when it expressed the hope "that the revolution . . . will also revolutionize Jewish life."[126]

Yet from the very start these voices remained in the minority. The same issue of the *Allgemeine Zeitung des Judentums* that saw Jewish involvement in government as a sign of equality for Jews also expressed a warning that the "high percentage of Jews' participation in the new government will make a bad impression on those left behind politically. . . . [T]hese people . . . will now, it is to be feared, transfer their aversion to the revolution that has taken place onto the Jews; they will be reinforced in the false view that the whole revolution was made by the Jews."[127] A week later the paper was already full of disappointment: "Instead of this certainly very heavy involvement in government improving the situation of the Jews in general, it seems to have only made it worse. Something like a pogrom atmosphere, which we haven't known in Germany for centuries, is prevailing in Berlin and elsewhere. One notices this in conversations, one senses it above all in posters and leaflets."[128]

As early as November 1918, there were already calls among Jews to take weapons into their own hands and defend themselves. A Jewish self-defense force had already formed since, as the *Allgemeine Zeitung des Judentums* put it, "As in Prussia, in Bavaria as well the most outrageous accusations are being charged against the 'Jew' Eisner."[129] One headlined letter from I. Herzberg in Bromberg exhorted readers: "So defend yourselves, German Jews! Present yourselves for battle! But form closed ranks, let nothing divide you! Just be Jews without regard for status or party, the same way the adversary also knows only Jews, indiscriminately."[130]

Another bellwether of Jewish anxiety was the official publication issued by the Central Association of German Citizens of the Jewish Faith (the Centralverein). The Centralverein's journal *Im deutschen Reich* (the monthly's title means "In the German Empire") feared what the impact of such a suddenly prominent role for Jews in Germany's political life might be: "The Jews are to blame for everything! Wherever and whenever something might happen that displeases some Germans, the Jews are behind it. And since, according to what antisemites everywhere demand, there should only be one percent of Jews in every occupation, with the exception, naturally, of public offices, which should not be occupied by even a single Jew, what Jewish Germans are to blame for is obvious and, for a change, even provable with numbers. The revolution is alleged to be one made by Jews." To be sure, there were people of Jewish descent among the revolutionaries, the journal continued, yet these people "hardly had anything or barely anything to do with the Jewish community." Even Kurt Eisner, according to the author of this piece, had already left the Jewish community.[131]

In Berlin's Jewish papers, too, Munich now figured more prominently, with more frequent coverage. In the *Allgemeine Zeitung des Judentums* there was detailed reporting on the antisemitic tendencies of the *Bayerischer Kurier*, the paper close to the Bavarian People's Party. This journal had printed an antisemitic article about Jews now supposedly heading all of Germany's governments that culminated in the adage: "'Tis all in vain when you look around / There's no longer any Christian to be found (Vergebens spähest Du umher / Du findest keinen Christen mehr). . . . Who are the true vanquishers of Germany? Is it the French, the English, the Americans? No. Of all of them, nobody rules so absolutely in Germany's 'free states' as Jewry. The granting of equality in 1848 had made room in 1871 for the supremacy and then in 1918 for the dictatorship of the Jewish people in Germany."[132] Shortly thereafter, the *Bayerischer Kurier* was reporting that Bavaria gave cause for concern that there was a danger of pogroms against Christians and not against Jews: "The Jewish gents who currently have power in Germany should not, however, deceive themselves: Pressure creates counter-pressure! If they proclaim terror against the majority of the population in order to maintain themselves in power under all circumstances, and to establish the Zionist empire in Germany and not in Palestine, sooner or later this is bound to trigger counteractions." The pogrom atmosphere was a product only "of Germany's current Jewish power wielders"[133]

And in Munich itself, this is what the Zionist *Das Jüdische Echo* had to say: "One should not confuse moods with opinions. But one can take moods into account without revealing his opinions. 'There are too many Jews in the government, both in the Reich and in Bavaria,' that is the general mood. If Jews are competent and can be of use to the general public, then they have the same rights as non-Jews; that would include the right to be at the head of government. That is our opinion. But if the general mood is fighting these leaders, who were not elevated by a broad-based and legally justified selection to become that which the revolution has made out of them, then they are perhaps not acting wisely when they remain in a leadership office." The Jewish public at large, the Zionist paper continued, had nothing to do with these politicians, just as these revolutionaries had cut themselves off from organized Jewry. "One should therefore address one's complaints to the correct address: not to German Jewry, but to the political parties in charge."[134]

The more time that went by, and the clearer anti-Jewish reactions to the revolution became, the more vehemently the Jewish community disassociated itself from the new rulers with whom it had become identified. The letter by Siegmund Fraenkel quoted at the beginning of this chapter is perhaps the most forceful expression of this sentiment, yet it is hardly the only prominent example of this kind. Schalom Ben-Chorin, the writer and scholar who grew up in Munich as Fritz Rosenthal, commented: "Especially affected were the Jews in the state capital, who as a bourgeois-conservative group looked with horror on the part played in the revolutionary upheaval by their co-religionists (who had long since ceased to be co-religionists any longer)." Ben-Chorin wrote in retrospect that when Eisner "was offered the honor of prime minister of the Bavarian government, a delegation of the Jewish Community led by Rabbi Dr. Baerwald implored him not to accept this office."[135] This scene most likely did not occur exactly this way, but there certainly may have been a request of this kind made by the community leadership and its rabbi, who had a reputation as a monarchist. More reliable is an entry from the diary of the Orientalist Karl Süßheim. There he writes about the visit of a delegation from the Jewish Women's League to Minister Unterleitner, who warned them that a pogrom was in the air. Süßheim himself would become a witness to the antisemitic machinations of students during the council republic. He noted in his diary: "Munich's Jews quite clearly are afraid of pogroms. Because Eisner is a Jew by birth, one part of Munich's population has turned against him and against the Jews in general."[136]

There could be no doubt about this. The majority of Munich's Jews rejected Eisner and the revolution. Most of them belonged to the bourgeois segments of society, and just like the Christian members of their class, they were attached to the monarchy and its values. The Jewish community's lack of support was also criticized by Eisner's non-Jewish followers. Thus, the Social Democratic newspaper *Die Neue Zeit* wrote shortly after Eisner's murder that the Jewish community had perceived him as an "apostate": "In general the local Jews were always opponents of Kurt Eisner's heavily exposed position, and they were hardly comfortable with it being one of their own who made the revolution and held the reins of the Reich in their hands."[137] There were also individual Jews who approached Eisner directly. Max Dreyfus Schwarz wrote "on behalf of several Jews from Landau [in Bavarian Palatinate]" to express his concerns about growing antisemitism in the press and asking Eisner to make every effort at "stopping, if possible, these kinds of attacks."[138] A Jew from Gerolzhofen (in Lower Franconia, northwestern Bavaria) complained: "You are making all Jews, your co-religionists, unhappy. . . . We Jews in Bavaria were content, after all." But Eisner and his "Jewish comrades" were driving "all of Jewry into ruin!" For now "the charge is being brought against us everywhere: The Jew bears the blame for every misfortune."[139]

The same kinds of fears were behind an initiative undertaken three years later when several prominent Jews urged Walther Rathenau to curb his political ambitions. When Rathenau was offered the post of foreign minister, he received a visit from Albert Einstein and the chair of the Zionist Association for Germany, Kurt Blumenfeld. Worried about both Rathenau's fate and that of German Jews, they spoke with him for five hours in a failed attempt to dissuade him from assuming the office.[140] Kurt Eisner had, of course, rejected interventions of this kind, but he did take time (even in the midst of all the revolutionary turmoil) to answer in detail one of the Jewish spokespersons, Commercial Counselor J. Mayer, who called on him to withdraw out of fear that there would be reprisals against the Jewish community:

Dear Sir! The views you hold have emerged from the conscious or unconscious anxiety of Jews who, although they are not ready to risk their lives for a revolutionary cause, do worry that their precious lives could suffer if the failure of revolutionary uprisings results in popular discontent being deflected against them. I am not the PM of Bavaria because it gives me pleasure; I will bless the day on which I no longer hold this office; but I am the creator and representative of these most wonderful of all freedom movements, and this makes it my duty to hold out as a living symbol. . . . I have bigger concerns than showing even momentary consideration for such 'questions of tact' [such as showing consideration for one's religious background] from a time gone by and overcome. No offense intended, signed Kurt Eisner.[141]

A brochure for the defense against antisemitism published by the Centralverein conveyed Eisner's view with similar wording: "If today there is still a distinction drawn between Jewish and non-Jewish and it is claimed that there are Jewish special interests, then I say that the entire revolution was in vain."[142] In the same brochure, the managing director of the Centralverein, Ludwig Holländer, gave this answer to an inquiry from the chair of the Citizens' Council of Metropolitan Berlin, Consul S. Marx, "regarding the conspicuous number of Jewish elements in the leadership of the Communist Party":

An explicit disassociation from Bolshevism strikes it [the Centralverein] as just as undignified as if one were to demand of the People's Association for Catholic Germany or the Protestant League a disassociation from this movement. The Centralverein has declared often enough that German Jews refuse to tolerate being confused in any way with Bolshevik elements, regardless of whether they are Jews or non-Jews. Jewish teaching condemns efforts hostile to the state in the strongest terms. Jewish life has a structure that tends to be rather more conservative than subversive, as everyone knows who has had even the slightest insight into Jewish families. If, over the last few years, a number of Russian and German Jews (mostly eccentric literati) have distinguished themselves in the movement, there is little Jewry can do about this, since the gentlemen in question have mostly long since left the Jewish community.[143]

To be sure, the Centralverein's newspaper, *Im deutschen Reich*, was anything but enthusiastic about Eisner (according to an unsigned article in the paper headlined "The Jew as Minister-President"). Yet, like all Jews, Eisner had not only all the duties of a citizen but also all the rights. And these included the exercise of political office. After all, the paper argued in rare agreement with the Zionist *Das Jüdische Echo* (whose language it adopted), the interests of Jewish Germans were identical with those of other Germans, because German Jews "live and have roots in the German people" for "incalculable generations."[144] And the chair of the Centralverein, the attorney Eugen Fuchs, thought it futile to lecture the Jewish revolutionaries about their politics: "It would be meaningless to preach to individual co-religionists who have been in the Social Democratic movement for years that they should now exercise restraint and steer clear of activities in public life for the sake of popular antisemitic trends. For us it would amount to antisemitic politics and adopting an antiquated standpoint if we should advise Jews to put aside their political convictions."[145]

Yet as the council republic brought a rise in both political radicalization and antisemitism, the local Munich branch of the Centralverein felt obligated to address a "public reply" "to all Christian fellow Germans." (The conservative term they used to address their fellow citizens was *Volksgenossen*—literally, "national comrades"—which would later become part of the National Socialist vocabulary.) The pamphlet issued by the local group countered the widespread antisemitic lies according to which all Bolshevik leaders were Jews, the Rothschilds were dictating the fate of Europe, German Jews had dodged the military draft, and Jews were war profiteers: "Once already, the combination of the political struggle with agitation against Jews has led to a bloody outburst and cost the life of the leader of the first revolution, Kurt Eisner, who openly affirmed his Jewish background. Today even his most vehement opponents at the time realize that he selflessly and wholesomely strived after the ideal he deemed correct. A worker who lets himself be lured into Jew-hatred defiles Kurt Eisner's reputation. German Christian fellow citizens (Volksgenossen)! Close your ear to the agitation against Jews operating in the darkness of anonymity, a hate campaign that does not and cannot serve the people's welfare but only, clandestinely, reactionary aims!"[146]

Actions like this, however, did not always generate the desired outcome. The journalist Josef Karl took note of the pamphlet and recorded in his diary: "The Association of Jewish Citizens proposes declarations against the accusations raised in pamphlets that designate the Jews as the real driving forces behind the revolution."[147] His antisemitism, however, was barely dimmed as a result, only as little toned down as the antisemitism of the *Münchener Stadtanzeiger* discussed at length earlier. In July 1919, the *Stadtanzeiger* reported, under a headline alluding mockingly to the Yiddish expression "Waih geschrien" (Screaming oy vey): "As a matter of principle, we are hardly Jew-eaters, but a certain kind of Jew that even gets on the nerves of his own co-religionists is a type we would gladly see disappear from public life. In particular, one needs to make sure that the Jew is not always there where there is something to be snatched and where there is no danger to his physical well-being. . . . If the Jews tone down their impudence a bit and do more to restrain their harmful influence, then one will also leave them in peace. But the Jew only wants to dish it out; if he has to take it, then he screams."[148]

And in November 1918, when Munich's Jewish community complained to the police about malicious tirades against its members, the paper commented this way: "If the Jews—toward whom (by the way) there is currently justified malcontent throughout Bavaria, and even all over Germany—had not made themselves so conspicuously dangerous to the public over the last several years, nobody would be so incensed. But nobody has dealt so shamelessly with our people as the Jew. . . . There is no more unscrupulous creature than the Jew. To achieve his aims, any means is good enough for him. He walks over bodies. . . . The Jews are like the eggs of bugs that suck dry everyone they set upon. The aversion to everything called a Jew is only too justified. And if war is declared on them, this is more than justified. Out with the Jews from Germany. To where they belong."[149]

In the memoirs of Jews who used to live in Munich, a recurring theme is fear of anti-Jewish backlash to the prominence of Jewish politicians. Given that these documents were often written years or decades later, they often construed in hindsight a direct link to the events of 1933. From the perspective of the longtime cantor of Munich's main synagogue, Emanuel Kirschner, the fateful political calamity was already under way at the end of the First World War. In 1935, he summarized it this way: "Instinctively, we Jews experienced . . . the political activity of Jewish leaders like Gustav Landauer, Levien, Leviné, Muehsam, Toller, and Waldler [*sic*], as much as they may have had the best intentions for the country and the people, as a great misfortune whose consequences could not be foreseen."[150] And the Jewish physician and Zionist Rahel Straus noted a few years later: "Even then we found it horrifying how many Jews were suddenly sitting on ministerial posts. . . . But it was certainly worst of all in Munich; here there were not only many Jews among the leaders, but even more among the staff employees that one met in the government building. It was understandable that so many Jews were in the vanguard; they were the 'intellectuals.' But it was a misfortune and the beginning of the Jewish catastrophe, whose dreadful end we are still experiencing. And it is not as if we first learned of this today; we already knew it and articulated it at the time."[151] Above all, Straus understood instinctively that those actions that Jewish actors undertook against Bavaria's Catholic traditions would have bad consequences. Thus, she criticized efforts to turn churches into cultural sites and the order to ring church bells at Eisner's burial and other occasions during the council republic: "We felt that this was bound to have consequences."[152]

In their memoirs, Jews from Munich who became émigrés emphasized that the prominence of Jewish politicians made them feel ill at ease. Alfred Neumeyer, then a recent secondary school graduate and later to become a renowned art historian (and not to be confused with his uncle, the president of the Munich and Bavarian Jewish Community), reflected: "At that time the seed of antisemitism was sown, and we citizens of the Jewish faith, untouched by the social Messianism of these noble and amateurish dreamers, look at the new popular leaders with apprehension and aversion."[153] Neumeyer, who had signed up for a brigade of volunteers to defeat Communist rule, left the paramilitary group after the failed right-wing Kapp Putsch. "The growing antisemitism among these troops, stirred up by the rise of the Hitler movement, the ever clearer unwillingness to support the democratic Republic, and finally the successful suppression of the Communist uprisings, which were what provided the occasion for my joining, all this gave me the feeling of no longer being in the right place."[154]

Alfred Wachsmann, who grew up in suburban Solln, described his family's house being singled out for a search after the city had been captured by the Freikorps in May 1919. "Of course, no reason was offered, and only much later did I realize that the only house search in Solln was meant for the Jewish newcomers." He and his brother would take a suburban train to school in Munich every morning and were subjected to antisemitic attacks from other schoolchildren "who, as the sons of their fathers, were still trying to win the war against us retroactively." At school they were usually met by teachers he characterized as "monarchist-reactionary antisemites." For Wachsmann and his brother, "it was made clear to us that we did not belong."[155] The retrospective impressions of Friedrich Bilski, then a medical student in Munich, expressed the attitude of many Jewish observers: "The so-called revolution [that] was led by amateurish literati had only given the name to what looked like a big mess."[156]

Yet, in light of these numerous testimonials, we should not forget how wide the range of views was inside the Jewish community. A Jewish Social Democrat like the lawyer Philipp Löwenfeld detested any kind of currying favor with the right-wing parties and came to the defense of Eisner against his coreligionists' attacks. Eisner, according to Löwenfeld, was a thorn in the side of Jewish capitalists. He accused them of believing that "the first duty of Eisner as a Jew was not to stand out and not to promote themselves . . . since in their ghetto mentality they viewed blandness as a more fundamental public duty for Jewish citizens than idealism, a sense of sacrifice, and loyalty to one's convictions. They still have not learned that antisemites . . . will not be grateful to them . . . for the slightest expression of supposed restraint." Antisemites did not need any reasons for their antisemitism. In certain Jewish circles at the time, it was believed that it was possible "to practice self-defense by seeking to cozy up as closely as possible to the enemies of democracy and Jewry."[157]

On the other side of the political spectrum, some Orthodox Jews were especially keen to disassociate themselves from Eisner and the other Jewish revolutionaries. The *Jüdische Monatshefte* set an example when it warned Jews to exercise restraint: "It befits the tradition of our Fathers in such a time for Jews to maintain the utmost restraint. It is not up to them to use the overthrow [of the old powers] in order to attain the power and governing position that the old regime had denied them."[158] In an additional article with the title "The First Jew to Head a Non-Jewish State," the Orthodox monthly agreed that Jews did have the same right as Christians to advance in politics, yet they should bear in mind that, while they might have reason on their side, psychology was not necessarily with them. "As psychologists we should all know that the world has not yet come so far as to regard the claim of a Jew to real legal equality as anything other than Jewish insolence." They also knew immediately whom to hold responsible for the malady now looming over the country. It was "German citizens of Jewish unbelief." As the Orthodox claimed, the model for a Jew in public service should not be the assimilated Jew Kurt Eisner, but instead the biblical patriarch Joseph, who was appointed statesman under the Egyptian pharaoh without having to abandon his Judaism.[159]

In the Bavarian provinces, the *Deutsche Israelitische Zeitung*, edited by Rabbi Seligmann Meyer from Regensburg, spoke for the interests of Orthodox Jews, especially with the paper's popular supplement *Die Laubhütte* ("Sukkah" in German). This publication was openly committed to the monarchy. Shortly before the collapse of the Wittelsbach dynasty, the paper commented: "Bavarian Jews are thoroughly monarchist."[160] And shortly thereafter, when the Free State of Bavaria had already been proclaimed, the paper had this to say: "But we devout Jews see Ludwig III departing with a tear of sorrow and send him, as to a dear friend, ... the holy words of the old Jewish Priestly Blessing."[161]

This Orthodox Jewish newspaper was in full agreement with the *Berliner Tageblatt* when that liberal paper noted that it was a matter of complete indifference what the religion of the Bavarian prime minister was, "if he would only pursue a smart policy, fruitful for the German people as a whole. Unfortunately, Eisner, who is distinguished as a literary figure, is not pursuing any such policy. And the confusion that his literati imagination has stirred is unbearable for Christians, Jews, and atheists, and for all who have the well-being of the country dear to heart." The Bavarian people, the newspaper from Regensburg commented, would certainly elect a qualified Jewish candidate to his office, but Bavarians were not dealing with politicians in the current government who had been legitimated by elections.[162] As antisemitic attacks against Jews piled up, the paper went so far as to maintain that these persons could no longer be characterized as Jews.[163]

The headline "Too Many Jews at the Top" could equally well have come from an antisemitic publication, yet it was displayed above an article in this Orthodox Jewish newspaper. Its assessment was unambiguous. For Jewish politicians to crop up at the head of a state was "quite certainly not a blessing for Jewry overall." For in the end the entire Jewish community would have to pay for those Jewish politicians' sins: "If non-Jews are attacked, then it is Konrad, Huber, and Hinterleitner. But when Jews are attacked, then it is not Simon or Levi; instead, it is *the Jews* all and sundry." The Orthodox rabbi Seligmann Meyer rejected both Social Democrats and Zionists, as well as all efforts "that place any international understanding higher ... than thinking of the greatness and restoration of our parochial Bavarian homeland and thus of Germany's greatness."[164]

As political conditions radicalized further, the paper disassociated itself even more clearly from the radical Jewish politicians: "For us here in Germany, only a few 'Jews' are among the 'Independents' and "Spartacists,' and among the Bavarian Jews certainly not a single solitary one!"[165] During the council republic, too, Orthodox Jews were far from impressed by the Jewish revolutionaries now at the head of the state: "[In] Bavaria, where unfortunately a number of Jewish-sounding names are loudly ruling the roost, ... [one] overlooks the fact ... that these men got there not via Judaism, but on pathways contrary to Judaism; today they are [inflicting] immeasurably great suffering on the fellow members of their tribe. ... Judaism as a whole rejects Bolshevism as the greatest danger ... with the most severe decisiveness. If, nevertheless, a couple of men are engaged in leading positions in this movement, then this only began long after they had already cut all mental ties to Judaism."[166]

On the occasion of the elections in January 1919, the newspaper published an editorial headlined, "Why the Religious Jew Must Vote for the Bavarian People's Party." The rabbi from Regensburg was perfectly aware of the objection that there was antisemitism inside this Bavarian branch of the Catholic Center Party. Yet he regarded antisemitism as a matter of individual statements that "are disapproved of and abominated by the [party's] leaders. . . . We need to keep in mind the greater goal of the Bavarian People's Party." And for Meyer and many other Orthodox Jews, this greater goal overshadowed all objections: the BVP and Orthodox Jews both strongly opposed separating religion and state and instead insisted on the state funding public denominational schools. Ahead of the first elections to the Bavarian parliament, the *Deutsche Israelitische Zeitung* put the point bluntly:

> Whether Christian or Jew,
> A believer like you
> We hope you'll come along:
> The BVP's where you belong.
>
> Jude oder Christ,
> Wer gottesgläubig ist,
> Komme herbei
> Zur Bayerischen Volkspartei.

This kind of fraternization with the BVP was noticed and rejected by the Social Democratic press in Bavaria. Its main paper, the *Münchener Post*, reported with outrage about Jewish voters picking the antisemitic-leaning party at the elections in January 1919; the paper said these voters had embraced the motto "Only the dumbest cows pick their own butcher." In Regensburg, the paper noted, Rabbi Meyer even delivered a sermon in which he openly called for congregants to vote for the BVP. It went on to point out that the Social Democrats were the only party actively fighting antisemitism and reported: "A Jewish fellow citizen writes us: The times have taught us so much that one really should not be surprised at anything—yet that voters from Jewish circles have flocked to the Bavarian People's Party (read: the [Catholic] Center [Party]) is something one should not have thought possible. It was Center party papers like the *Bayerischer Kurier* that, immediately after the revolution broke out and up until shortly before the onset of electoral agitation, continued to propagate bloodthirsty antisemitism and foment pogroms, and then suddenly heap flattery in the most despicable manner, like Nicolas II in his manifesto, 'To my dear Jews,' the very ones previously despised and persecuted by them. And numerous Jews have let themselves be duped by these wolves in sheep's clothing."[167]

Especially as viewed from Berlin, this new alliance between Orthodox Jews and the BVP looked extremely disconcerting. The *Allgemeine Zeitung des Judentums* scoffed at what it headlined "A New Aguda in Bavaria." Agudath Israel ("Agudath" being the compound form of "Aguda" or "Union") was the political organization representing Orthodox Jewry, created only a few years earlier. The Berlin newspaper quoted the fourth point of the BVP electoral platform: "'On all questions, the Bavarian People's Party is grounded in the Christian worldview.'" What exactly was a Christian worldview? How did it comport with the fact, the Jewish paper asks, "that the leading men and newspapers of the Bavarian People's Party" conducted propaganda "in their partisan onslaught against those of Jewish origins in the government of the Bavarian people's state, and in particular against Kurt Eisner"? Noting that, "[i]n truth, in all of Germany there will have been no citizen feeling the agony of decision so seriously and so deeply as the devout Israelite in Bavaria," the paper asserted that the overwhelming majority of Bavarian Jews, including the Orthodox, would be voting against the BVP and its antisemitism, with the exception of Rabbi Meyer and his followers.[168]

Some Jews even chose journals tainted with antisemitism to voice their concerns. The organ of the Bavarian People's Party, the conservative *Bayerischer Kurier*, was always happy to pick up Jewish crown witnesses against Eisner and his comrades. This included the tiny splinter group of German Nationalist Jews on the conservative side of the political spectrum who were eager to disassociate themselves from East European Jews within the Jewish community. Thus, the *Bayerischer*

Kurier quoted a Dr. Breslauer, who had scolded the Bavarian prime minister in a conservative Jewish publication: "The offense committed by Kurt Eisner in general and against Bavaria in particular is a hundred-weight more grave compared to how it weighs against all those benefits that can be ascribed to earlier, current, and future Jewish cabinet ministers. His memory is burdened by the charge of treason."[169]

Certainly the most controversial statement by a self-appointed spokeswoman for Bavarian Jewry was made by a young Zionist named Rahel Lydia Rabinowitz, in the mouthpiece of the Catholic Bavarian People's Party. No other article triggered such a fierce discussion in the Jewish public. Not only was the place of its publication peculiar, but so was the biographical background of the author. Even if she had not appeared in public before, her family was well known in various circles. She was the daughter of the Russian-Jewish scholar Saul Pinchas Rabinowitz, recognized widely in Jewish circles by his Hebrew acronym Shefer. He was among the earliest Zionists, even before Theodor Herzl and the foundation of the Hovevei Zion (Lovers of Zion). Among his major works was the translation into Hebrew of the most popular work of Jewish history, the multivolume history of the Jews written by Heinrich Graetz. Rahel's brother was Samuel Jacob Rabinowitz, who was involved in the Jewish labor movement and founded the Jewish Workers' Library in Zurich in 1887.

In Munich, Rahel's sister, Sarah Sonja Lerch-Rabinowitz, was the best-known member of her family. She was initially active on behalf of the Jewish Labor Union—the Bund—and then, after moving to Germany, in support of the Social Democratic Party. As one of the first women enrolled at the University of Gießen, she received her doctorate with a dissertation entitled "On the Development of the Labor Movement in Russia through the Great Revolution of 1905." After marrying the French literature scholar Eugen Lerch, she was among the activists (mentioned in chapter 2) who joined Kurt Eisner in organizing the strike of ammunition workers in January 1918. As one of the ringleaders of the strike, Sarah Sonja Lerch-Rabinowitz was arrested and sentenced to jail.[170] Shortly before the arrest, her husband had publicly come out against his wife's activities and—no doubt also out of consideration for his career as a civil servant—filed for divorce. The Munich press was full of sardonic reporting about this. Completely disgusted by the publicity, Kurt Eisner wrote: "The German public seems to have taken no umbrage at this business; they obviously found it to be a matter of course. What is more, she was a little Russian Jewess and he a man who was German to the core, even if a scholar of French literature."[171] Lerch-Rabinowitz was ruined. Ernst Toller, for whom she served as the model for his protagonist Irene L. in the drama *Man and the Masses*, told of the despair that overtook her at the Stadelheim detention center: "There she cried aloud day and night, and her cries echoed through the cells and the corridors and froze the blood of prisoners and warders alike."[172] On March 30, 1918, she hanged herself in her jail cell. As the *Münchner Neueste Nachrichten* reported, arbitration for her divorce was scheduled for the following day. On May 1, 1918, Sarah Lerch was buried at the Neuer Israelitischer Friedhof in Munich. Rabbi Cossmann Werner delivered the "words of religious consolation" and intimated that she had taken her life at a moment of spiritual confusion.[173] While still at the cemetery, the anarchist Josef Sontheimer was arrested after his retort to the rabbi; he had claimed that she died for the cause of the revolution.[174]

In contrast to her brother and sister, Rahel Lydia Rabinowitz had no connection to socialism and was an ardent Zionist in a category all her own. Victor Klemperer, the chronicler of that time and a close colleague of Eugen Lerch, got to know "the rabid Rabinowitz," as he called her, in Munich in 1919 and was astonished at the close resemblance between the two sisters: "In March the poor Sonja had been resurrected—barely changed on the outside, very much changed on the inside—in the form of her older sister. . . . With her hard eyes and her all-too confident manner, I found Lydia Rabinowitz rather unlikeable from the outset." This may also have had to do with how she treated Klemperer, a convert to Protestantism. "She refused my hand, stared at me stonily and said loudly enough for everyone around us to hear: 'I've heard you're playing the Protestant. I don't associate with converted Jews.' And then she turned her back on me." Klemperer reported that she boasted about having tried a dozen professions, in addition to various courses of study. She was a divorced woman with a ten-year-old son in Switzerland.[175]

FIGURE 21. The faculty of arts and sciences at the University of Gießen during a summer retreat in June 1909; Sonja Rabinowitz is the only female student amid 113 men. Christian Zimmer, Gießen, 1909.

This, then, was the woman who was raising the hackles of Munich's Jews with two articles in the *Bayerischer Kurier*. In the first place, she asserted that German Jews were not Germans but "neutral" strangers whom the German people were incapable of understanding. And then she characterized Kurt Eisner as a stranger who would never be accepted by the Germans. For that reason, and for that reason alone, he had also acknowledged Germany's war guilt.[176]

It was not just the assimilated Jews who were upset about the arguments that Rabinowitz was advancing. Even the Orthodox journal *Die Laubhütte* reacted excitedly: "The difference between the Bavarians of the Jewish faith and the rest of the Bavarians is only of a religious, not of a political nature. The Israelite religion does not demand anything that in any way contradicts a German disposition. In line with the overwhelming majority of Bavarian Jews we declare: Bavarian Jews are Bavarian by conviction, will, and feeling. Whoever infringes on this feeling infringes on what is sacred."[177] The Zionist paper *Das Jüdische Echo*, too, expressed outrage about an attitude that did not fit in with German

Zionism: "It is profoundly humiliating that there is a Jewess who betrays her people with these kinds of contortions and defamations—and that a paper that should be standing for the dignity of the Bavarian Center Party is unscrupulous enough to print this shoddy effort without even making sure if the author is mentally healthy enough, if she is someone who has the right to come forward as a Jew, if any kind of Jewish group stands behind her."[178] While defending German Jews against Rabinowitz, the Zionist paper also alludes to its readers' preference for caution: "We, too, wish that Jews today would hold back from leading government positions." The paper regarded this as "a requirement dictated by tact for German citizens of Jewish nationality."[179]

An attack like this on the "rabid Rabinowitz" was not without consequences. The *Bayerischer Kurier* promptly published a reply by Rahel Lydia Rabinowitz, who struck back with an even bigger counterpunch. Eisner, like all Jews, was a stranger in Germany, she wrote. She compared German Jews with Italians or Russians who lived in Germany. They ought to be represented in proportion to their share of the population, but they should never be at the head of a Christian nation. This was followed by sweeping blows against fellow Zionists and the Orthodox, whom she accused of simply hiding their real views. Many of the terms she used were adopted straight from an antisemitic vocabulary.[180] And, once again, this reply sent *Das Jüdische Echo* into a rage. Addressing Rahel Lydia Rabinowitz, the paper now wrote: "We Jews will not and cannot 'shake off' Herr Eisner; for as Jews we have absolutely nothing to do with him."[181]

The article caused something of a stir and apparently also came to the attention of Adolf Hitler. Two decades later, he claimed to have a vague memory of it. In 1942, as the deportation of Europe's Jews to the extermination camps got under way, the Führer told his guests in his headquarters: "In 1919 [*sic*] a Jewess wrote in the *Bayerischer Kurier*: What Eisner is doing now will be passed on to us Jews!" Hitler added, undoubtedly with reference to the systematic murder of the Jews then in progress: "This is a rare case of clear-sighted foresight."[182]

4

The Hotbed of Reaction

Mei' Ruah möcht' i hamm und a Revalution,
A Ordnung muaß sei und a Judenpogrom,
A Diktator g'hört hera und glei' davo'g'haut:
Mir zoagen's Enk scho', wia ma Deutschland aufbaut!

[Gimme me peace and quiet and a rev-a-lu-tion,
There's gotta be some order—and a Jew pogrom,
We need a dictator so we can send him packing now:
Germany gets built that way, we're gonna show you how!]

—*SIMPLICISSIMUS*, DECEMBER 3, 1923

Rosh Hashanah 5681 (September 1920)

The Jewish New Year, Rosh Hashanah, initiates a time of internal reflection that culminates ten days later in the Day of Atonement, Yom Kippur. In the Jewish calendar, Rosh Hashanah always occurs on the first day of Tishri, which in 1920 was celebrated on September 13. Even many of those among Munich's Jews who did not make a practice of following their religion's commandments during the rest of the year closed their businesses on Rosh Hashanah or took the day off, celebrated the holiday with family, and prayed in the city's synagogues, which were decorated in white. In Munich, as the Jewish year 5681 got under way, things did not bode well for this holiest season on the Hebrew calendar.

Looking back at the year gone by, Siegmund Fraenkel wrote: "We have lived through sad moons, and sorrowful days are what our oppressed people had to taste in 5680. This year is engraved in bloody letters in the history of the Jewish people."[1] By this he was primarily referring to the bloody pogroms against Jews in Eastern Europe. Yet his roving gaze also took in events taking place at the doorsteps of Munich's Jewish homes. There was a new sign adorning numerous posters in the city, a symbol previously known chiefly from the Indian subcontinent but now showing up in dark black twisted lines against a blood-red background: the swastika. In Adolf Hitler there was also a new name defining an emboldened antisemitism, and an organization that had recently been formed as just a local group, the National Socialist German Workers' Party, or Nazi Party (NSDAP), had taken center stage in the intensified agitation against Jews.

Hardly had the Jewish New Year's festival and Day of Atonement, with all the occasion's hopes for a better future, gotten under way than Rabbi Leo Baerwald entered the lion's den. Accompanied by five Jewish escorts, he attended an NSDAP rally in which the Jewish religion and especially the Talmud were maligned. The rabbi was not allowed to get in so much as a word; instead, his remarks were drowned out by shouting. His escorts were mishandled with rubber truncheons and thrown down the stairs.[2] Just a few days later, the well-known sex researcher Magnus Hirschfeld, in Munich on a lecture tour, was also beaten unconscious on the street by truncheon blows. He had, according to a contemporary report, "been warned not to travel to Munich, where, more than in any other place in the German Reich, reactionary elements are up to their mischief." As reported in the *Jahrbuch für sexuelle Zwischenstufen* (Yearbook for Intermediate Sexual Types), the attacks were certainly targeted against this advocate for a "freer conception of sexuality," but they were "largely a product of antisemitic agitation." While the Munich public prosecutor's office very quickly called off a belatedly launched trial against the instigators of the attack, it also launched an investigation against the victim of the assault, on the charge of disseminating indecent literature.[3] The Jewish year 5681 got off to a start that promised rather little hope for improvement.

FIGURE 22. *Simplicissimus*, December 3, 1923, poster (including the four-line verse at the beginning of chapter 4). Herzogin Anna Amalia Bibliothek Weimar.

"The Movement . . . Needed a Site That Would Become an Example"—Hitler's Laboratory

The period following the suppression of the council republic in May 1919 permanently changed the lives of Munich's Jews and sent a clear warning signal to the rest of the Jewish population in Germany. On May 2, 1919, the short-lived specter of Bavaria's Communist council republic had evaporated. What would happen next was the long-lived horror of reaction. Bavaria would become the self-declared "cell of order" for the entire German Reich, and its capital city would lose its liberal, cosmopolitan character. Beginning in the 1920s, Munich developed into the capital of antisemitism in Germany, and it was from here that Germany embarked on the path to its National Socialist dictatorship.

It was already dawning on some contemporaries, immediately after they experienced the chaos of the council republic and the ensuing White Terror of 1919, that the face of Munich had radically changed. No longer would the city be showing its once hospitable and cosmopolitan face to the rest of the world. In June 1919, the poet Rainer Maria Rilke packed his bags, left Munich, and headed for Switzerland. Before leaving the city, he had prophesied to a friend that "from now on innocent Munich may continue to be a bad and uneasy spot."[4] For, as he also wrote, "[t]he rule of the councils has shattered into a million little splinters, and it will be impossible to remove it everywhere." Moreover, "[b]itterness has increased enormously in all its many hiding places and will sooner or later become active again."[5] Hence, "one hears and sees nothing but departures; many of the most permanent residents are giving up their houses, here and there great moving vans spend the night before their gates."[6] In the summer of 1919, the writer Isolde Kurz contributed an article to a newspaper in which she wrote: "One can say that, in the bloody adventure of the council republic and its aftermath, the old and easygoing Munich zest for life came to an end."[7]

From the retrospective view of Rahel Straus, who was writing in her memoir under the impact of what happened after 1933, vexation and bitterness had now cast a dark shadow over the lives of Munich's Jews:

Life fell back into its normal bed, and yet it was not the same as before, and it would never remain so. There had always been antisemitism, varying in volume and aggressiveness. Now the mood was generally against the Jews. One had experienced unrest in which Jews—far too many Jews, and for the malicious-minded *only* Jews—were at the top. Seeping through from Russia there were reports about atrocious revolutionary events that had transformed the Czarist Empire into a Bolshevik state. And again there were Jews, far too many Jews, among the leaders. In Hungary there was the coup that had set in under the Jew Bela Kuhn [*sic*]. No wonder that Jews, subversives, Communists, and terrorists were seen at work in all of this. It was overlooked, perhaps out of ignorance, perhaps out of ill will, that the majority of Jews were capitalistically oriented and very orderly citizens for whom the Communist revolution was a greater specter than for Germany's workers and petit bourgeois.[8]

The memoirs of Max Friedländer, which the former chairman of the Bavarian Bar Association composed as an émigré in England, were also affected by his awareness of events that happened only later, toward the end of the Weimar Republic. Yet what Friedländer wrote sounds similar to what contemporaries were writing at the time:

In Munich especially, the Eisner era, the council republic, and the start of Hitler's agitation had all created a way of thinking that was called patriotic but in reality was nothing more than intellectual one-sidedness and narrow-mindedness in the extreme and, in the end, led to all the havoc from which the world and the German people are now suffering. Regrettably, there were some Jews at the forefront of the radical movements in Bavaria. But instead of telling ourselves that there were at least as many Christians participating, and that, to the extent that international adventurers and agents were active among them, naturally a larger percentage of these were Jews; that none of the Jews in question had anything to do with Judaism or were representing Jewish interests . . . and instead of reflecting on the social causes of all these more or less foolish and, in part, childish undertakings, one became obsessed with an antisemitism ever on the rise, one draped a little patriotic cloak around it. . . . The men and women whose way of thinking I have in mind here were no political hotheads, no extremists, or even people who, like the National Socialists, had a will to injustice. Instead, they were more or less upright and educated average citizens, civil servants, lawyers, merchants etc., former democrats and, what is more, the kind of people who regarded themselves as democrats, parliamentarians like Herr Müller (Meiningen) [Friedländer is referring to the German Democratic Party politician and Bavarian minister of justice Ernst Müller-Meiningen], who could not emphasize his liberalism enough etc.[9]

Rahel Straus and Max Friedländer knew whereof they spoke. As early as 1919, there already existed in Munich an extensive network of rightwing extremist and antisemitic organizations. The Thule Society, which had its headquarters in the luxury Hotel Vier Jahreszeiten (Four Seasons), and the German (later German Nationalist) Defense and Defiance Federation, which was founded in 1919 under the auspices of the Pan-German League, occupied prominent positions in this network. Antisemitic ideas were disseminated by newspapers like the *Münchener Beobachter* (which, as of August 1919, was renamed the *Völkischer Beobachter* and would soon become the official Nazi Party publication) and Dietrich Eckart's publication *Auf gut deutsch*. The Freikorps and home guard paramilitary units of the Civil Defense Guards (the different divisions of the Einwohnerwehr) often placed themselves at the disposal of the right-wing extremists. Munich had "become the reactionary antipole to the national capital Berlin."[10]

In this kind of atmosphere, Hitler had it easy. Munich became Hitler's city owing to an environment that was extremely favorable to him and his movement. In the years following the war and revolution, the city's political leadership, its police, its legal system, and its press all collaborated to usher in a radical transformation of the once-liberal city into a "hotbed of reaction" and "the seat of all stubbornness and of the obstinate refusal to accept the will of the age" (Thomas Mann) and to prepare a fertile ground for the growth of the National Socialist movement.[11]

After the council republic had been brutally suppressed with the backing of troops and the Freikorps from outside Bavaria, the democratically legitimated government led by the Social Democrat Johannes Hoffmann that had fled 150 miles north to Bamberg was unable to prevent the bloodshed of the so-called White Terror. Between 670 and 1,200 people (according to different estimates) were killed in the days following the breakdown of Communist rule. This was a number far greater than the death toll inflicted by the two council republics taken together.[12] What is more, Hoffmann's postrevolutionary rule proved to be no more than an unstable transitional phase. His government was toppled in March 1920 following the unsuccessful attempt to overthrow the democratic government in Berlin (the so-called Kapp Putsch). Contributing to its fall were the joint efforts of reactionary forces—including the leader of the Civil Defense Guards, the forester Georg Escherich; the commander of the Reichswehr in Bavaria, General Arnold Ritter von Möhl; and the leadership of the Munich police, which had already embarked on a staunchly right-wing course by 1919. In Bavaria, the left would never recover from the shock following the revolution of 1918–1919.

On March 16, 1920, Gustav von Kahr, who was the chief district administrator of Upper Bavaria and in favor of restoring the monarchy, was elected prime minister with the assistance of the Bavarian People's Party—the state's strongest parliamentary force—by a majority of one.[13] His goal was to set up Bavaria as a "cell of order."[14] Like Eisner, Kahr was also not part of Bavaria's Catholic majority. But a Protestant prime minister—in contrast to a Jewish one—did not provoke the same flood of outrage. His cabinet was the first in the Weimar Republic not to include Social Democrats, who had been setting the tone for German politics since the outbreak of the revolution. Kahr, an administrative official who was nominally above the partisan fray but had joined the BVP in 1920, was himself removed from power in September 1921 and replaced by a series of governments that promoted into office several conservative civil servants to the post of prime minister. The first was Hugo Graf von und zu Lerchenfeld, followed by the BVP legislator and former royal cultural minister Eugen Ritter von Knilling. Then, in September 1923, Kahr returned to office as a state commissioner general with extensive powers alongside Prime Minister Knilling for another half year in which the two conservatives were to shape the fortunes of Bavaria as a team. "Bavaria, Cell of Order," was, in the words of one historian, "hardly to be understood as a defense of the political order envisioned in the new constitutions of Bavaria and [Weimar] Germany. It was rather a reactionary defense against all those developments that could have pushed Bavaria further away from the old order of the pre-war era."[15]

Philipp Löwenfeld, the Jewish attorney and Social Democrat from Munich, looked back on developments in Bavaria at the time and summarized the situation pointedly: "Because of the way the council republic was suppressed and, following that, the way the council putsch was liquidated in the courts, Bavaria turned into that completely reactionary 'cell of order' whose organizing principles rested on applying the rule of force, deterioration of the legal system, arbitrary use of power, fear, and denunciation. In brief, [Bavaria rested on] on that 'order' that—in its aftermath, and by means of ongoing constitutional breaches, extra-judicial killings, legal scandals, and secret organizations—established Bavaria's tragic reputation in the civilized world as that of the major precursor to Hitler's barbarianism."[16]

From the other side of the political spectrum, the conservative BVP politician Karl Schwend (who would later head the Bavarian State Chancellery in the early 1950s) conceded that those years witnessed the establishment of "Kahr-Bavaria as a mix of conservative-Bavarian forces, conservative-North German influences, counterrevolutionary nationalist efforts, and emerging fascist currents."[17] In his own, more leftist portrait of that very same "Kahr-Bavaria" period, the writer Lion Feuchtwanger—availing himself of a novelist's poetic license—bestowed many features of the man who lent his name to that era on the fictional character Franz Flaucher. Flaucher, always seen with his dachshund, was depicted as a small-minded bureaucrat eager to push the goals of the völkisch politician Rupert Kutzner (alias Adolf Hitler).[18]

Kahr's aim was to use the "cell of order" in Bavaria as a platform from which to launch Germany's "recuperation." To this end, and funded by heavy industry, he promoted a postwar version of the policy known in Germany since the 1890s as *Sammlungspolitik* the concentration of nationalistic, conservative, and bourgeois forces. Kahr hardly kept it a secret that Jews did not fit into his scheme. To be sure, he was not a "rowdy antisemite" of the kind found among the National Socialists or other extremist groups. Yet it was no accident that some of his first official acts, both as prime minister in 1920 and as state commissioner general in 1923, included targeted expulsions of East European Jewish immigrants. These acts were accompanied by the anti-Jewish rhetoric typical of the era, replete with familiar images of Jews as war profiteers, usurers, and racketeers. Such actions were not unique in Germany nor elsewhere in Europe. Rather, they were part of a larger campaign against Jewish refugees from Eastern Europe.[19]

In his memoirs Philipp Löwenfeld articulated a very clear view of Kahr: "The Kahr dictatorship was especially disgraced by the way it behaved against Jews. Many people today have again forgotten, and there are even many more who never knew this in the first place, how the first active measures that were openly antisemitic emanated not from the Hitler movement but from the 'statesman' Kahr, who in this way achieved nothing else if not stealing Hitler's thunder with this nasty trick as well. Kahr did not dare, however, to go anywhere near the general mass of Jews living in Bavaria. As a miserable coward by nature, he sought out, like Hitler, the most defenseless among the Jews as victims of his despotism."[20]

Publicly, Kahr only went after East European Jews, but his negative attitude toward Jews and Judaism emerged clearly in his unpublished memoirs.[21] It seems as if this offspring of Protestant civil servants had already come under the influence of traditional anti-Jewish stereotypes brought home to him by the family cook at their house in the Central Franconian town of Gunzenhausen, a stronghold of antisemitism long before 1933: "Sometimes, in the stories told by old Anna, Jewish customs and the legend about Jews coveting the blood of Christian children also played a role. We boys therefore viewed the synagogue with very suspicious eyes. . . . Thus, even in elementary school I already had a strong aversion to certain depictions and thought processes in the Old Testament. The way the Jewish people idly speculated on Jehovah's help, especially when it came to military adventures, the way they were attuned to riskless acquisition, their spirit of haggling, of the kind we children even in Gunzenhausen got to know here and there among the Jews, was repugnant to me."[22]

A strong hostility to Jews suffuses Kahr's memoirs, which he wrote between 1925 and 1928. He still had some reservations about publishing the sentence "It is time that the war ends, for otherwise the German people's ethos will be Jewified [*verjudet*]," and he later crossed it out.[23] On the other hand, he kept his warning "that the German people is in the process of disrobing its cloak of honor, taking the pearl diadem inherited from its fathers off its crown, and bartering it away to foreign mercantile Jews."[24] Like many conservative politicians in Bavaria, Kahr was also convinced that the fateful November revolution and the months of "socialist chaos" that followed were essentially the Jews' fault. Misfortune fell over Bavaria when the "obstinate masses . . . preferred to let itself be led into total ruin by unscrupulous, international people and foreign Jews."[25] This resulted in "the saddest chapter of Bavarian history, the history that a Berlin Jew with a horde of foreign bandits had forced on the Bavarian people and—more's the pity, dear God!—could force on them."[26]

In September 1922, on the occasion of the six hundredth anniversary of the Battle of Ampfing, Kahr listened attentively (and apparently with complete approval) to "the wonderful sermon preached by the Capuchin father Casimir Braun. . . . He characterized the November Revolution of 1918 as perjury and Judas treachery. . . . He recalled that, after he was victorious in battle, Ludwig the Bavarian had raised a special Jewish tax to compensate the wounded and war widows and orphans. The same must now be done for the starving poor and for the orphaned. It must now be demanded of the Revolution's Judas traitors that they give back the assets they stole from our princes."[27] As so often in history, Jews were identified here too with Judas the traitor.

In a diary entry while he was visiting Berlin, Kahr expressed with special clarity his aversion to the "Jewish spirit" of the city: "In this city, subverted by the worst kind of Jewish spirit and immersed in shameless avarice and profiteering, thoughts about the honor of the people cannot flourish." And in another entry prior to his Berlin trip he wrote: "It always takes a toll on me, having to overcome visits to this nasty city with its Jewish materialism."[28]

Kahr was hardly the only leading Bavarian politician of that era shaped by antisemitism. Prime Minister Knilling also admitted to an anti-Jewish attitude, at least behind closed doors. One of the most revealing depictions of this came from Robert Murphy, the acting US consul in Munich at the time. In December 1923, he reported to the State Department: "The present Bavarian Premier has stated to me very frankly that he is decidedly anti-Jewish and considers the Jewish element in Germany responsible for much of the German misfortune and economic distress since the war."[29]

Quite early on, the postrevolutionary Justice Ministry fell into the hands of those politicians who were on the extreme right. During his first term in office, Kahr entrusted Christian Roth, an outspoken German Nationalist, with this office. Under Roth's aegis, no obstacles were placed in the way of the National Socialists, and in 1924 he himself entered the Bavarian Landtag as a delegate for the extreme right-wing Völkisch Bloc, while his son Theodor made a mark for himself in anti-Jewish riots and kidnappings on the night of Hitler's Beer Hall Putsch.[30] Franz Gürtner, at the time Bavaria's minister of justice, was another German Nationalist who encouraged Hitler's rise. Hitler would later show his gratitude and, until Gürtner's death in 1941, retain him as Reich minister of justice in the Nazi government's cabinet.[31]

The character of the Bavarian justice minister Otto Klenk in Feuchtwanger's novel *Success* combines elements of both Roth and Gürtner. In contrast to Flaucher (alias Kahr), Klenk joins the movement of the mechanic Kutzner (Hitler), whom he privately disdains. To Feuchtwanger the writer, it was clear that for all of them the Jews could never quite belong to Bavaria even if they had lived there for centuries, as had the Feuchtwanger family. The character of the Jewish attorney and Social Democratic Landtag deputy Siegbert Geyer provides Flaucher with an opportunity to illustrate how the Jews could never be part of the Bavarian national soul, "for those were sentiments which could only be entertained by people who were rooted in the soil." Yet Geyer understood only too well how his Jewishness was used to exclude him from the company of other Bavarians who otherwise had little in common: "And suddenly Dr. Geyer felt himself peculiarly isolated. . . . [T]he reactionary Minister, the reactionary author, and the two members of the Opposition" were all being treated as if they belonged together, "in spite of their political antipathies, as four sons of the Bavarian plateau, leaving the Jewish lawyer a disturbing and hostile alien among them."[32]

Even more than in its civilian branches, the Munich government's military power was in the hands of the extreme right during the early 1920s. A major player in the effort to topple the Hoffmann government in March 1920 was Franz Ritter von Epp. As a Freikorps leader the year before, he was one of those responsible for suppressing the council republic in Bavaria at the behest of Reichswehr minister Gustav Noske. Epp's Freikorps unit included such leading National Socialists of the future as Ernst Röhm, Hans Frank, Rudolf Heß, and the brothers Rudolf and Otto Strasser. As head of the Reichswehr's Rifle Brigade, Epp also exercised influence over the powerful home guard paramilitary units. His subsequent career was entirely at the service of Hitler. Elected to the Reichstag in 1928 for the first time for the NSDAP, Epp became Reich governor (*Reichsstatthalter*) for Bavaria in 1933.

As early as the middle of 1919, a circle of persons within the Munich police force had been able to place themselves at the top and make a decisive contribution to Hitler's rise. Since the beginning of May 1919, the chief of police was the appellate court judge Ernst Pöhner, until then director of the Stadelheim prison. Pöhner made no secret of his aversion to Jews as well as to socialists and the republic in general. In August 1921, at the time of major food demonstrations in Munich, he thought it was possible for "some Jews to be hanged because of the intolerable inflation."[33] The powerful Pöhner appointed Wilhelm Frick, who would become Reich interior minister when Hitler came to power in 1933, as head of the Munich police force's political department.[34] Pöhner sympathized openly with the National Socialist movement as soon as it was taking shape, granted shelter in Munich to right-wing extremist offenders being sought in other German states, and provided them—including the murderer of the Center Party politician Matthias Erzberger—with fake documents. At the time of the putsch attempt on November 8, 1923, he was part of Hitler's inner circle. Pöhner and Frick acted jointly in dismissing petitions from the Central Association of German Citizens of the Jewish Faith calling for a ban on NSDAP posters owing to their inflammatory rhetoric, as when they mentioned the "peace treaty of Versailles forced on all of us by the only ones responsible for this war, Jewish-international stock exchange capital." The reason given by the two for their dismissal of the Jewish organization's complaint was that "broad circles of population" thought about the peace treaty in much the same way.[35]

Hitler's rapid political rise in postwar Munich has been described so often that there is no need to repeat it here in detail. There is widespread agreement in recent scholarship that the decisive phase of Hitler's political formation took place in the second half of 1919.[36] On November 21, 1918, he returned to Munich as a soldier following the war. Hitler's attitude toward the new People's State of Bavaria under Kurt Eisner and toward the council republics is interpreted differently by historians. We know for certain that he was elected ombudsman of the "demobilization battalion" in February 1919 and then, in April 1919, appointed as councilor in the auxiliary battalion of the Munich council republic's Soldiers' Councils—facts that he later insisted on keeping secret for obvious reasons. It is questionable, however, whether these activities tell us anything about his political views at the time. Whether he can be recognized on contemporary film recordings as one of those attending Eisner's funeral is another question that, so far, cannot be definitely answered.[37] For obvious reasons, he later disassociated himself from the "Jew rule" (*Judenherrschaft*) of Bavaria's council republic. And he put the stamp of Jewishness on the entire revolution, as in this statement in *Mein Kampf*: "While the Bavarians were cursing the Prussians, the Jew organized the revolution and smashed Prussia and Bavaria at once."[38]

Yet, based on the existing sources, we can only speculate on what Hitler's political ideas really were (if he even had any) in the first half of 1919.[39] By the summer of 1919, an important role was undoubtedly played by his deputation as an informer who was being schooled in anti-Bolshevik courses. Thus, during the third "Education and Speaker Course" in July 1919, he listened to lectures by historian Karl Alexander von Müller and engineer Gottfried Feder, whose inclinations were not only anti-Communist but also anti-Jewish. Shortly afterwards, Hitler also had the opportunity to test his speaking talents for the first time.[40] We know for certain that by the second half of 1919 he had adopted right-wing extremist and antisemitic ideas and begun to express them openly for the first time. Both the general antisemitic mood in Bavaria after the suppression of the council republic and the pronounced and very specific hatred of Jews in military circles at that time had a decisive influence on him.[41]

On September 12, 1919, Hitler attended his first meeting of the German Workers' Party (Deutsche Arbeiterpartei, DAP), which had been founded on January 5, 1919, by Anton Drexler and Karl Harrer.[42] Hitler's first stated position on antisemitism stems from that same period, against the background of a widespread pogrom atmosphere. What gave rise to Hitler's statement was an article written by Bavaria's Social Democratic interior minister, Fritz Endres. While Endres himself echoed numerous stereotypes against East European Jews, he did reject three of the chief accusations hurled against Jews, namely that "they had shirked war service, exploited the people by profiteering, and 'made' the revolution."[43] In the wake of the discussion triggered by Endres's essay, Karl Mayr, the head of the "Education Department" in Reichswehr Group Commando 4, received an inquiry from Private Adolf Gemlich about the position being taken by the Majority Social Democrats on the kind of antisemitism that was now everywhere in sight.[44] Mayr instructed Hitler, who was assigned to his department, to reply to this letter.

In Hitler's first known written statement on the topic of antisemitism, from September 16, 1919, he went into the difference between an emotional antisemitism and a rational antisemitism: "Antisemitism as a political movement may not and cannot be defined by emotional impulses, but by recognition of the facts. . . . An antisemitism based on purely emotional grounds will find its ultimate expression in the form of programs [sic]. An antisemitism based on reason, however, must lead to systematic legal combating and elimination of the privileges of the Jews. . . . But the ultimate objective must be the irrevocable removal of the Jews in general."[45] A month later, Hitler joined the right-wing German Workers Party and, until he was released from the army on March 31, 1920, turned from being a soldier to becoming an agitator and propagandist for antisemitic and right-wing extremist positions. He was coauthor of the new program for the party, now calling itself the National Socialist German Workers' Party (Nationalsozialistische Deutsche Arbeiterpartei, NSDAP), and as of July 1921 he was deciding the fate of the party with quasi-dictatorial powers. But above all, it was his rhetorical talent that transformed a marginal political faction within a short time into a movement that became omnipresent, at first in Munich and then throughout Germany. From his first speech until November 8, 1923, Hitler gave 188 talks at party meetings, 132 of them in Munich. The theme of antisemitism often played a role in these talks—for example, in his speech entitled "Why Are We Antisemites?," delivered before an audience of two thousand in the ballroom of the Löwenbräukeller.[46]

In Munich, beginning in the early 1920s, Hitler was already surrounding himself with those confidants who would remain loyal to him as he continued his rise to power. These included the man who would later become his deputy, Rudolf Heß; the party ideologist Alfred Rosenberg; the SA leader Ernst Röhm (in whose paramilitary league Reichskriegs-flagge the young student Heinrich Himmler was involved); and the attorney and later governor-general of occupied Poland, Hans Frank. As early as the period before November 1923, this circle also included the future Reich marshall Hermann Göring. Some of the people from this early circle of Nazis in Munich would be reunited barely a quarter-century later as defendants at Nuremberg in the Major War Criminals' Trials. Support from General Erich Ludendorff, the "silent dictator" of the Supreme Army Command, who had been living in Munich since

FIGURE 23. NSDAP meeting at the Bürgerbräukeller, c. 1923. BArch Bild 146-1978-004-11A, photographer: Heinrich Hoffmann, Bundesarchiv.

1920, lent Hitler respect in conservative and monarchist circles. Gradually, many doors and sources of funding also started to open up for Hitler, who now climbed out of the dusty orbit of beer cellars into the circles of Munich high society. The houses of the Hanfstängls, Bruckmanns, and Bechsteins were soon open to him.[47]

Munich was not only the breeding ground for Hitler's rise. In his own view, it was unthinkable that any other city could compete with Munich for the status it was awarded in 1935 as "capital of the movement."[48] In January 1922, Hitler made this clear at the first nationwide NSDAP members' meeting in Munich: "The movement must initially concentrate on one place. . . . It needs to let one city become a model for the rest of the movement: this could only be Munich. . . . Munich had to become the model, the school, but also a granite pedestal." On the same occasion, he let there be no doubt that the main initial goal was "to break the power of Jewry" in one city, and this could only be done in Munich.[49] At the meeting of the Saxon NSDAP on June 12, 1925, Hitler then proclaimed that Munich had become a holy site for the party: "Rome—Mecca—Moscow! Each of the three places embodies a worldview. Let us stick with the city that witnessed the first blood sacrifices of our movement: it must become the Moscow of our movement!"[50]

"The Ostjuden Danger"—The First Expulsions of Jews

About one-fourth of Munich's Jews came from Eastern Europe. Some of them had already arrived before the turn of the century. Others had been recruited as laborers during the First World War. Still others arrived as refugees toward the end of the war, when the civil war in Ukraine, Belarus, and Poland hit the Jewish communities caught between White Terror and Red Terror especially hard. The pogroms from this period, with about one hundred thousand fatalities, exceeded by far the level of anti-Jewish violence from the days of the Czarist Empire.[51]

In Munich, as in most other German cities, the Ostjuden struggled to be integrated into Germany's established Jewish communities. ("Ostjuden" was the term applied by Germans to Jews from Eastern Europe, but it was soon internalized by the very people it designated.) With the new era, a small revolution was also in the offing inside the Jewish communities. The Ostjuden sensed the possibility of no longer needing to accept their status as second-class members. Owing to fierce protests from oppositional Zionists, the liberal majority worked its way through to a reform of the rules governing elections within the Munich Jewish Community (Israelitische Kultusgemeinde). The old census-based suffrage was replaced by a voting rule based on general proportional representation, and women would now also have the franchise in this new system. But it would still take several years before the reforms granting the right to vote and be elected went into effect for foreign members of the community, most of whom were East European Jews.[52] The Ostjuden found allies among the Zionists and Orthodox for their struggle, which all three groups waged under the banner of the Jewish People's

Party. Its main goal was to transform the predominantly religious con-
gregations into "people's communities," not only to provide for the
community's religious needs but also to pay more attention to members' social welfare and their educational system. One of the movement's demands, to open a Jewish elementary school of their own for
the numerous Jewish children from East European families, was put
into practice in 1924. To this was added a nursery school, a youth and
welfare office, and a Jewish youth center and adult education courses.
At community elections in 1921, it emerged that about two-thirds of
the voters favored the Liberals, while the Jewish People's Party (JVP)
got about one-third of the vote.[53] Because the opposition participated
in its leadership, Munich's Jewish community was spared the kind of
grueling internal political conflict that had taken hold of many other
communities—as in Berlin and especially in Saxony. Much the same
can be said about the larger Association of Bavarian Israelite Communities, founded in 1920. These consensual politics had a lot to do with
Alfred Neumeyer, who, as chair of both the association (representing
Jewish communities throughout Bavaria) and the Munich Jewish community, was the dominant figure in Bavaria's organized Jewish life between the wars. A judge on Bavaria's higher court, he was concerned
about reconciling the different factions. But an additional factor contributing to this extraordinary truce was certainly the rise of antisemitism with which citizens of Munich and Bavarian Jews were confronted
in the years following the First World War.[54] Yet another factor was the
early effort to organize among East European Jews in Munich.

On November 19, 1918, the General Committee of East European Jews
(Gesamtausschuß der Ostjuden) was founded to counter a rise in defamations against them, among other reasons.[55] Starting with their first
major meeting on December 16, 1918, it became clear that the new organization was able to mobilize large masses of people. In one mass meeting
of "East European Jews against Defamation and Deprivation of Rights,"
a crowd of one thousand showed up at the Hotel Bayerischer Hof to
protest against an article published in the *Münchner Neueste Nachrichten*
on December 7, 1918, in which the author attributed a "movement directed against property and order" to "Jews who immigrated from the

east over the last several years." The chairman of the General Committee, Jakob Reich, explained that part of the blame for these kinds of attacks making generalizations about Jews rested with the leadership of the Munich Jewish Community. East European Jews made up one-fourth of the community and were the major share of those who were religiously active, yet they were systematically kept at arm's length from the organization's business.[56]

The Ostjuden's loyalty was called into question most of all after the council republic in Bavaria had been overthrown. Immediately after this political reversal, East European Jews were held responsible for what the council republic had done, even if almost all of them had been either vehemently opposed to this political experiment or indifferent toward it. On May 21, 1919, City Commandant Major Hans Ritter von Seißer issued a "residency ban for foreigners": "Foreign nationals who have taken up residence in Munich after August 1, 1914 and former foreign nationals who after this time acquired Bavarian citizenship or citizenship from another German state and moved to Munich are prohibited from residing in Munich without special permission from the City Commandant's Headquarters."[57]

This "residency ban for foreigners" chiefly affected Jews from Galicia, as the attorney Dr. Leopold Ambrunn, speaking on behalf of the General Committee of East European Jews, explained in a petition submitted to Munich's police headquarters. Most of these Jews, according to Ambrunn, "have established ways of making a livelihood with the help of relatives, they were not a burden to anyone [this remark was underlined in blue and a question mark added to it by a police official, possibly Pöhner], and pay their taxes on time." Returning to their home countries had been made impossible for these East European Jews, according to Ambrunn, because German troops had proclaimed as they invaded these countries that they were arriving as the Jews' liberators, and the Jews had taken the Germans at their word. If they were now to follow the decree issued by the city commandant and return, they would be regarded as traitors, and that would "amount to nothing other than delivering these persons immediately to a certain death." Ambrunn continues: "For all those who are actually familiar with these conditions, it is clear that, of all the above-mentioned persons who immigrated to Munich, not a single one has anything in common with Spartacist or Communist elements."[58]

Very soon, internal conflicts over how to deal with these unwelcome immigrants from the East became apparent. Police chief Pöhner proved to be a rabble-rouser even inside völkisch circles. During a discussion that took place in the Bavarian Interior Ministry in June 1919, he contradicted something said by Captain Christian Roth, who at the time headed the legal division of the City Commandant's Headquarters and would later became Bavarian minister of justice. Although Roth, too, was hardly a friend of the Jews, he was at least willing to give Ambrunn's argument a partial hearing: "During the war a bunch of Polish Jews came here because pogroms were taking place in their homeland. We really need to let these people stay here. We'll deport all the ones who are a danger to security, then all the active Communists, meaning also the ones who may not have been sentenced but who have fallen short objectively, and in addition those foreigners who are depriving our native workers of bread."

Pöhner, by contrast, advocated a more energetic approach to expulsions. His choice of words speaks for itself: "But our will is frequently hindered by the higher authorities Mere expulsions aren't enough, these people will come back; instead, these people deserve to be interned in Landsberg, Plassenburg etc. Most of them intellectuals, academic riffraff."[59] The Munich Police Authority lodged complaints about "incomprehensible leniency" when it came to the expulsion of East European Jews. The City Commandant's Headquarters in particular had "not cracked down with the kind of energy required." City Commandant Seißer was not going far enough for Pöhner. Seißer, in turn, defended himself by saying that one "should not be guided by petty, and especially denominational, points of view. The so-called Ostjuden, who for the most part immigrated as refugees from their war-ravaged homes as early as 1915, are, with very few isolated exceptions, indifferent to politics."[60]

Repeatedly, however, the Police Authority, led by its chief, President Pöhner, underscored the department's uncompromising attitude. Pöhner's choice of words made it clear that the issue for him was not how individual fates might be viewed, but the kinds of measures to be taken as a matter of principle. A few months later, Pöhner reacted firmly when the only Jewish newspaper published in Munich, *Das Jüdische Echo*, seeking to give the editorship to an East European Jew without a residence permit in Bavaria, Dr. Israel Taubes, applied for a residency permit on his behalf. The editorship, Pöhner insisted, could also be assumed by one of Taubes's coreligionists already residing in Munich. Furthermore, the police chief could not see why this newspaper had to be published in Munich of all places, since it could just as easily be "done in Vienna or Zurich." Pöhner suspected something quite different was going on here, namely the

> buildup of Munich's East European Jewish colony into a central headquarters of East European Jewry for Germany as a whole. . . . This feeler Dr. Taubes put out to the leading domestic and foreign Jewish newspapers is apparently only meant to serve this one aim of racial policy and lay the groundwork propagandistically for East European Jews continuing to immigrate and establish themselves in Germany (or rather predominantly in Bavaria and Munich). The Police Authority regards it as its duty to point out the great danger that a continued strengthening of East European Jewry means economically and politically for Germany. The Ostjuden are and remain a harmful foreign body in the German people that does not serve the general public but only their private and racial goals and that, in pursuit of this goal, will shy away from nothing, not even from the continued existence of the state if it strikes them as expedient, as the events during this year's council rule have shown, where it was primarily Jewish elements who were the carriers of Bolshevik ideas. . . . We should especially point out further that the population of Munich, which is already very irritated against Jewry, will not likely just accept an additional increase and strengthening of East European Jewry in Munich, and it could therefore very easily come to disturbances and riots against the Jews, the consequences of which could not be foreseen today. On the aforementioned grounds, therefore, the Police Authority cannot accede to the request of Dr. Taubes.[61]

The argument that deporting or rejecting Jews trying to move in was justified for their own protection or in order to prevent pogroms against the native Jewish population was a pretext in Pöhner's war against the Ostjuden, but it was an argument that repeatedly fell on sympathetic ears.[62] The main point was to deport as many East European Jews as possible. That this did not succeed in the end is owed to resistance inside the government and to the protests of Jewish organizations.

In May 1919—the time scheduled to deport those East European Jews who had made themselves "politically bothersome," were allegedly violating "the ground rules of trade and commerce," or could be replaced "by the native unemployed who were available" for work—the chairman of the General Committee of East European Jews, Jakob Reich, drafted a compromise proposal. According to Reich's proposal, all persons for whom no radical political activity or unfair trade practices could be proven would be permitted to stay—and in cases where an expulsion could be justified, time would be granted to prepare for departure. In addition, the situation facing those people scheduled for expulsion would be taken into consideration: during the war some of them had still been viewed as allies in the fight against the Russians, and some had been recruited as munitions workers in Germany. Moreover, they were now being sent back to a region where, in all the postwar turmoil, the worst anti-Jewish pogroms were raging, costing tens of thousands in Jewish fatalities.[63]

Reich disassociated himself clearly from the few East European Jews who had been politically active during the Bavarian Council Republic. Thus, in June 1919, he wrote to Prime Minister President Hoffmann in Bamberg: "Because of the prominence of a few persons of East European Jewish origin (Levini [sic], Axelrod, Wadler) in the political struggle, the widespread error has emerged making it seem as if the Ostjuden in Munich were, in general or to a large extent, *Spartacists*. This view proves erroneous upon immediate examination of the circumstances. . . . To the greatest possible extent we are dealing with *bourgeois* elements whose economic interests alone would have to make them opponents of Bolshevism. Moreover, the Ostjuden living in Munich, the whole lot of them, are completely removed from the political struggle." Reich

emphasized further that he had told Wadler, even before the First Council Republic was proclaimed, that it was not any business of the naturalized East European Jews "to be waging the battles of the Bavarian
people." Following the proclamation of the Communist council republic in Bavaria, Reich sought out Towia Axelrod and, in the name of
Munich's East European Jews, disassociated himself from the regime,
since "we Ostjuden" have "no fellowship of any kind with Axelrod and his
friends and with the Bolshevik movement." Axelrod, however, banned
any such declaration as a counterrevolutionary act. By the spring of 1919,
Reich was now appealing to the Hoffmann government to prevent a
return of the roughly four hundred East European Jews affected by the
expulsion effort to the pogrom zones in Galicia, since "this would most
gravely endanger the lives of the deportees." Moreover, the Ostjuden
were the only group of foreigners singled out for the residency ban.[64]

On June 18, 1919, Reich met with representatives of the police, the
Interior Ministry, and the City Commandant's Headquarters to prevent
the expulsion of about four hundred people affected by the order.[65] He
received a receptive hearing from representatives of the Bavarian government led by the Social Democrats, but in Munich Pöhner refused to
ease up. Pöhner found an ally in the chief district administrator of Upper
Bavaria, Gustav von Kahr, who made no secret of his fundamental aversion to the presence of East European Jews. Thus, Kahr rejected a Galician Jew's request for permission to settle in Munich, for two reasons:
the petition was turned down on general economic grounds and also
"out of consideration for how the entry of East European Jews is quite
especially disagreeable to us. It should not be underestimated how the
ill humor directed against Jews, deriving from experiences only too
well-known from the period of war and revolution, is capturing ever
wider circles of the population and also proliferating more and more in
worker's circles, which were originally indifferent about this question.
But since it is the East European Jews who activate in the most evident
way the racial characteristics that are so unbearable to so many Germans, and since it was frequently East European Jews who were most
prominent during the period of the Council Republic about inciting the
masses, it is only natural that the population's indignation, frequently

worked up to the point of hatred, is chiefly directed against this portion of the Jewish race." Hence it was also in their own interest to have them "kept away from here."[66]

Shortly afterwards, Kahr had become Bavarian prime minister, and in this capacity, he pushed through the expulsion of East European Jews. Beginning with his first government statement, Kahr had emphasized that he regarded "taking strict action against foreign infiltration by tribal strangers, maintaining the purity of our own people from contamination by foreign elements," as the order of the day.[67] On March 20, 1920, four days after he took office, Kahr made one of his first measures the expulsion of unwelcome foreigners from Bavaria within five days. Officially, the ones most affected by this measure were all those foreigners who had arrived since August 1, 1914, and who were not in possession of an explicit residency permit. So that it would be clear just who was intended as the target of these measures, Pöhner appended an announcement to the expulsion order stating that it was aimed at "those of foreign origin who were driven into the country only by greed for profit and who are the carriers of Bolshevik ideas."[68] As *Das Jüdische Echo* wrote, it was an open secret "that by the superfluous foreigners, by the Polish and Galician 'Bolsheviks and traffickers,' only 'the members of a foreign race,' only the Jews were meant." For the broad masses, these measures represented nothing more than "a hounding of Jews, quite simply."[69] Preceding the expulsion measures was a targeted public campaign conducted by völkisch circles, especially in the *Völkischer Beobachter*, but also from among the ranks of the right-wing German National People's Party (DNVP).

Once again, Jewish organizations pulled out all the stops in order to block the expulsions. The Welfare Office of Jewish Organizations petitioned against those measures that were promoting expulsion and "unjustifiable hardship."[70] Once again, Pöhner brought out the heavy artillery. He designated the welfare organization a kind of consular office for Munich's Jews and thus branded the entire community collectively as foreigners. Pöhner rejected any kind of cooperation with this and other Jewish organizations, since in the past they had refused to provide him with lists of the names of East European Jews residing in

FIGURE 24. Kahr, Ludendorff, and Pöhner at the Bavarian Flyer Memorial Days, 1921.
BArch Bild 183-R41120, photographer: not indicated, Bundesarchiv.

Munich. "What Bavaria needs to avoid by all means are the same conditions prevailing in Prussia, where the Ostjuden cannot be mastered at all any longer," asserted the March 20 administrative decree, which had to be implemented, it declared, "ruthlessly and quickly."[71] The Welfare Office thereupon complained to the Interior Ministry "that our well-intentioned efforts have been honored so little, and as a result any successful implementation of our work program has been rendered impossible."[72] Yet the office did succeed, initially, in blocking the measures planned by Pöhner. Frustrated, Assessor Lang from the Munich Police Headquarters wrote in June 1920 that the Jewish Welfare Office had "understood how to use constant complaints lodged with all the authorities and repeated applications to drag out and prevent the execution [of the expulsion orders] for three months now. . . . It is not apparent to what end the Jewish Welfare Office might still make further use of the already high level of activity in favor of the East European Jews."[73]

In the end, police chief Pöhner had to concede that he was not always successful in his attempt to deport most of the East European Jews targeted for removal from Bavaria. "To deal with them, there is only one more method that can prove effective: ruthless removal by force."[74] Yet the Interior Ministry did not give in to Pöhner's pressure, and only a few persons were deported.[75] *Das Jüdische Echo* described these deportees— some of whom got only a few days' notice before the date of their expulsion—in detail. They included persons who had lived in Munich for seventeen years, some of them since they were two years old. Among them was a girl apprentice, a tailor, an engineer, and a medical student. The group contained a decorated war veteran from the Austrian army, the father of a family of nine, and a man whose pregnant wife was close to confinement. Some of them no longer had any ties to Poland or Russia or family members there.[76]

In the rest of Bavaria, too, there was an increase in measures taken against East European Jewish immigrants during the spring of 1920. In March, the police station for Northern Bavaria reported to the office for foreigners at the Munich Police Authority about measures taken by the surveillance office for the Hof-to-Lichtenfels railway line against East European Jews whom they had selected and who were described as people "who are virtually becoming a dangerous plague on the country."[77] The documents are also full of petitions from Bavarian citizens in the style of this anonymous letter: "If Munich and Bavaria are someday purged of this riff-raff, hopefully better times are coming, God willing."[78] Outside of Bavaria, there were also isolated instances of anti-Jewish measures being taken by authorities; thus, in March 1920, General Hans von Seeckt, head of the Reichswehr, ordered a raid in the East European Jewish neighborhood of Berlin known as the Scheunenviertel.[79] In the Reichstag, the center-right German People's Party (the Deutsche Volkspartei, DVP) issued a proposal to prevent the mass immigration of "foreign-born elements," especially along Germany's eastern border. And Prussia's Social Democratic interior minister, Carl Severing, acting against his own convictions, felt compelled to order that foreigners who could not be deported be housed in refugee camps. In a dispatch to London, the British consul general in Frankfurt am Main described the impact on public perceptions above all by the events in Bavaria: "Private reports, which I am unable to control, state that the Jews are leaving Bavaria in considerable numbers in order to take up their residence here. It is possible, however, that even in Frankfort their position may not prove as safe as they would consider desirable."[80]

The calls to deport East European Jews did not cease. In February 1921, the NSDAP presented a catalog of demands to the Bavarian government, at the top of which was the demand to deport all East European Jews who had immigrated after 1914. That there was no huge expulsion of Ostjuden is partly attributable to the reaction of those states that feared them now pouring over their borders. This list of states included, in addition to Poland and Austria, Bavaria's German neighbors, Prussia and Württemberg. The Prussian envoy in Munich sent dispatches to Berlin expressing his concern about the expulsions, and for this reason he also met with Kahr. He let Kahr know that "serious countermeasures are threatened from abroad." By this he meant the danger of Bavarian citizens also being deported. Kahr assured him that the only foreigners affected were those for whom there were "serious grounds" for expulsion. Moreover, just announcing expulsion had had a salutary effect; he pointed out that some of these undesirable foreigners had already left Munich without a whimper. Kahr left no doubt whom he had in mind, namely, "first and foremost Galician Ostjuden."[81] He hereby adopted as his own a widely accepted position in Germany that sought to lay the blame for every visible malady since 1918 on East European Jews as a collective scapegoat. Many prominent Germans had taken note of this at an early stage. In 1921, Albert Einstein wrote: "Eastern European Jews are made the scapegoats for certain defects in present-day German economic life, things that in reality are painful after-effects of the war. The confrontational attitude toward these unfortunate refugees, who have escaped the hell that Eastern Europe is today, has become an efficient and politically successful weapon used by demagogues."[82]

"Travelers, Avoid Bavaria!"—Manifestations
of Violence

In Munich, discussions about Jewish traffickers and Bolsheviks, about war profiteers and draft dodgers or shirkers on the front, and about the possible expulsion of Ostjuden were now affecting the public climate—and this kind of talk was hardly confined to a preoccupation with the East European Jews.[83] Those Jews who had been residents of Munich for a long time felt equally threatened. As early as the autumn of 1919, the pogrom atmosphere had disseminated more widely, as the intelligence department of the Munich police reported to police headquarters: "As we have learned from reliable sources, pogroms against Jews are supposed to take place in Munich at the end of October. Like those in Vienna and Russia. Jewish families who are informed about the matter have already left Munich."[84] In February 1920, the Social Democratic *Münchener Post*—in an article headlined "Antisemitism, a Protective Measure?"—complained that "junior police stations" saw in the antisemitic movement a suitable protective measure against the socialist activism of workers.[85] Conservative circles around the BVP were also attempting in this way to undermine the Social Democrats.

A month later, the lead article of *Das Jüdische Echo* was simply headlined "Pogrom." That word, the article stated, "had taken on a reality for Jews never thought imaginable." This new reality had already become clear since the revolutionary days of November 1919: "But in these times the catastrophe stands before us threateningly like never before. More and more are the storm signals manifesting themselves and the conditions evolving that previously seemed conceivable only in darkest semi-Asia." Nowhere was this more clearly discernible than in Munich. "Since the new prime minister in his very first speech . . . placed himself on the ground of antisemitic demands . . . one must now be prepared for the worst. We Jews have to count on not being able to expect with certainty any kind of effective, energetic protection from law and order: as soon as it occurs to the rabble of all sorts to make good on the threats buzzing through the city." The author Jakob Koppel lamented the persistently tepid attitude of the Jewish community, whose members often preferred hiding behind a distinction between Bavaria's native Jews and the Ostjuden, imagining that would save them.[86]

In a letter to the editor of *Das Jüdische Echo*, Helene Cohn, who had recently arrived in Munich, agreed with Koppel: "Never before in my life have I sensed around me such a degree of hate-filled passion as in the streets of this city. When I buy newspapers on the street corner, look at bookstore displays, hear a conversation in a tram or restaurant—everyone is filled with hate and inflammatory defamations of Jews." No distinction was really made anymore between German and East European Jews. It bordered on madness that the people, afflicted with hardship, could not think about anything else besides "hating and annihilating the 2,500 Jewish families within the walls of the city of Munich."[87] These words written by an observer who had only recently moved to Munich very clearly expressed what was happening at that time and place. For the first time in a German city, the "Jewish question" had moved to the center of daily life. In his study of postwar Munich, Martin Geyer comes to the conclusion: "What was only marginally successful (including in Munich) before the war, in spite of the campaigns waged incessantly by the largely nationalistic and antisemitic wing of the Conservative party—namely turning antisemitism into a central component of debate and speech—was now being accomplished with astonishing speed. The 'Jewish question' was on everyone's lips."[88]

The young Gerhard Scholem, who had just begun his scholarly career as an expert researcher into Jewish mysticism at the Ludwig-Maximilians-Universität in Munich, experienced the start of Munich's rise to becoming the "capital of the movement" this way: "In Munich I had a chance to get acquainted with incipient Nazism at the university from close up. The atmosphere in the city was unbearable and the antisemitism—usually still assuming the conservative forms of crude Bavarian-ness—obvious; this is something that is often disregarded today and presented in more mutable colors than it actually was. There was no disregarding the huge, blood-red posters with their no less bloodthirsty text, inviting people to attend Hitler's speeches. . . . But it was frightening to encounter the blindness of the Jews who refused to see and acknowledge all that. They all regarded this as a temporary phenomenon. This greatly encumbered my relations with Munich Jews, for they became extremely jumpy and angry when someone broached the subject."[89]

As early as the first large mass meeting held by antisemites in Munich's Kindl-Keller in January 1920, there was talk about a pogrom atmosphere against Jews and "Marxism." A background report from the Bavarian State Recruitment Agency of the Reichswehr Group Commando 4 noted: "There is hatred in the broadest circles directed increasingly against the Jews, who are snatching up most of the trade for themselves and, in the view of everyone, are enriching themselves mostly at the expense of their fellow human beings in the must unscrupulous manner. In railways and streetcars and on every possible occasion, one hears people grumbling about the Jews."[90]

The organ of the German Nationalists in Munich was the *München-Augsburger Abendzeitung*, an evening paper published on behalf of the media mogul Alfred Hugenberg by the Protestant pastor and German Nationalist politician Gottfried Traub. It rebuffed the advances made by the National Socialist movement. But the publication's owner did believe they could harness Hitler to their own wagon, and they tried attracting the antisemitic public to the German Nationalists themselves.[91] While the newspaper did not advocate a violent kind of antisemitism, it did not want to grant Jews complete equality. An article written by Traub after the assassination of foreign minister Walther Rathenau typifies the paper's attitude: "We are not antisemites of the rowdy street. Many of these antisemitic goings-on cripple any kind of political judgment, because people think that as soon as the Jew has simply been beaten to death, everything will be just fine, and then they forget how many Christians are acting 'Jewish.' But as Germans we are resolute advocates of our people's right to be governed by Germans."[92]

In April 1920, there was a nine-day ban on the publication of the *Völkischer Beobachter* after its reporting exceeded even the usual level of antisemitic agitation. The paper had asserted that "Levien, Levine, and Toller" had allowed the kind of savagery to prevail "that is prescribed for them by their religious law books against every non-Jew. And they have also gotten assistance from the local Israelite religious community." That same religious community issued a libel action against the antisemitic paper. In the ensuing trial, accompanied by a lengthy discussion about whether the Munich Jewish Community could be permitted to give out the names and addresses of other Jews, the authors of the article were sentenced to a fine for defamation.[93] This shows that there were also judges in Bavaria who either did not let themselves be intimidated by right-wing radicals or did not sympathize with these extremists.

Alongside the vocal antisemites, of course, there were also influential moderate voices. One may cite the BVP's parliamentary leader in the Bavarian Landtag, Heinrich Held, Minister of Culture Franz Matt, and Interior Minister Franz Xaver Schweyer, whose aversion to the growth of National Socialism and of the antisemitism that followed in its wake could not be doubted. Most Social Democrats took a clear position against antisemitism. The same was true of many Liberals. There were even broad segments of the population who rejected antisemitic excesses. Yet the antisemitic atmosphere extended well beyond the usual völkisch circles, especially when war profiteers and the economic problems of the young republic were being discussed. Even in the Communist circles of the KPD, an "antisemitic tendency was clearly discernible," as it was said in reports from police informers.[94] Under these circumstances, Jewish politicians who otherwise had decent prospects for a parliamentary career preferred not to run for office. At the primary election for the Independent Social Democrats' nominees to the Bavarian Landtag in 1920, the attorney Max Hirschberg was fourth on the party list, but he turned down a candidacy because "the current agitation against Jews was not in accordance with his feelings."[95]

There was no sign that things were going to calm down in the new year, even after the collapse of the Kahr government. In April 1921, the most visible monuments to Jewish life, the synagogues, became targets of antisemitic graffiti. In his memoirs, Emanuel Kirschner, the cantor of Munich's main synagogue (and also one of the most important contemporary composers of Jewish liturgical music), related one of these incidents: "It was the second night of Passover that the representatives of the Aryan race had selected in order to besmirch the façade of our synagogue and that of Ohel Ya'akov [the Orthodox synagogue] with meter-high, pitch-black swastikas visible from afar. It was (and still is now) the time in which small paper slips have been pasted onto the doors and windows of Jewish homes with provocative and obscene insults against Jewish taxpayers . . . bearing witness to the rampant coarsening and inhumanity spreading throughout the country of poets and thinkers." Kirschner was also in immediate proximity to the speaker when, a few days later, Rabbi Baerwald gave a lecture before the Gnosis Society that was interrupted by troublemakers. The *Bayerischer Kurier* reported about the incident this way: "About 30 accomplices who were spread across the hall surged toward the speaker's stage while shouting wildly, the speaker along with his table was torn from the podium, the chairman and honorary chairman . . . maltreated. Hurriedly, the audience, including a number of women, left the hall. The police arrived too late for the actual racket and only cleared the street." Kirschner gives a detailed account of how the mob "attacked the public with clubs and chair legs." "The rowdy Aryan heroes were practicing a special kind of roughness by their dreadful maltreatment of the nearly blind Ludwig Aub, a grandson of the former Munich rabbi."[96]

On June 2, 1921, Alwin Saenger, a Social Democratic member of the Bavarian Landtag mistakenly identified as a Jew, was assaulted and knocked down on the street. As in the case of Max Levien, it did not matter if the victims really were Jewish. As long as they were regarded as Jews by those around them—or, as in Saenger's case, had defended Jews in court—they were targeted by antisemites. This message soon got out beyond Munich. The *Berliner Tageblatt* was now also taking note of "the denominational agitation in Munich."[97] The American ambassador in Berlin, Alanson B. Houghton, made this entry in his diary: "Something is brewing in Bavaria and no one seems to know exactly what it is."[98] The lack of solidarity with the victims of violence was reflected in Lion Feuchtwanger's novel *Success*: in one scene, there is this terse reaction to a brutal assault on the attorney Geyer (a character only partly corresponding to that of Saenger): "These Jews have only themselves to blame. Who asks them to interfere with our affairs? None of their business!"[99]

The diaries of the Orientalist Karl Süßheim testify to the room made in 1920s Munich for everyday antisemitism. This conservative university lecturer, who had once voted for the nationalist DNVP, now became witness to numerous antisemitic rallies by students. And owing to the "Aryan clause" in the organization's statutes, he was initially prevented from joining the Bavarian Association of Philatelists. On January 22, 1922, he was present when antisemitic students disrupted a speech by Rabbi Benno Jacob from Dortmund at a meeting of the Central Association of German Citizens of the Jewish Faith. According to Süßheim, these disrupters were representative of the student fraternities that sympathized with the antisemites.[100] A former police official recalled "that in the winter of 1921/1922 antisemitic hate rallies were held every evening in the Neuhauser Straße in Munich by lots of students, which ultimately ended up in rowdiness, rioting, and fighting and that soon caused a sensation well beyond the borders of Bavaria."[101] Indeed, these events reverberated well beyond the borders of Germany and Europe.

The antisemitic wave in Munich rolled as far as Buenos Aires. From there the *Argentinisches Tag- und Wochenblatt* reported in 1921:

It seems to have become almost something of a criminological principle that, for every misdemeanor and crime that can be connected in any way to right-wing parties, the first traces need to be sought in Munich. Munich may be regarded as the bastion of the reactionary movement that aspires to bring back the rule of the Kaiser and the princes and thus also restore class privileges. That here is where not only Ludendorff lives, but also a number of well-known reactionary politicians, that in Munich the nationalist parties of every shade control an especially large number of newspapers and journals whose tone has from time to time become quite severe; that certain lines of political thought were second nature to the Civil Defense Guard, in spite of its statutory non-partisanship; that the animosity toward Jews is especially strong even for the average citizen of Munich; and finally that the German National People's Party specifically moved its convention to Munich as a kind of demonstrative gesture; all this has amplified even further the assessment of Munich as the center of reaction."[102]

The language of another article in this German-language Argentine newspaper was even catchier: "The original poison of our domestic politics in Germany today is agitation against Jews; its derivative, no less befuddling to our minds, is the fear of Bolshevism. . . . Whatever one finds unsuitable is called Jewish or Bolshevist, and that settles things in a cozy and effective manner."[103]

French diplomats in Munich reported repeatedly about the antisemitic climate in Munich. Above all, they complained that the police and leading politicians were not energetic enough about intervening against the anti-semitic aggression emanating from the National Socialists.[104] To reassure concerned American Jews who were complaining about antisemitism in Bavaria, the American embassy in Berlin also had to step in. While the April 1920 report of a commission headed by A. W. Dulles, who would later become director of the CIA, did admit that antisemitism had begun to assume menacing proportions, some share of the blame was laid on the Jews themselves. Dulles wrote: "As a result of the participation in and the leadership of Communism in Bavaria by Jews, the pre-war tolerance has now changed and a strong anti-Semitic movement has developed." Dulles added that the intended expulsion of East European Jews "was directed chiefly against Jewish war profiteers. . . . This anti-Semitic movement is especially pronounced among the students, the military and the peasants of south Bavaria."[105] This appraisal was certainly in line with other reports about antisemitism from the US State Department around that time.[106] It is no surprise that Ellis Loring Dresel, the US commissioner in Berlin, sent a very similar report a year later to the State Department listing the follow-ing four points as causes of the new kind of antisemitism: war-profiteering behavior, fear of Bolshevism, the presence of Jews in politics, and the flood of East European Jews.[107] All these purported reasons for rising antisemi-tism ultimately assign blame for it to the Jews themselves, either because of how some of them behaved or by virtue of their mere presence.

The violence directed against Jews in Bavaria was hardly confined to the capital. On August 6, 1922, there was a pogrom-like incident in

Memmingen, the Swabian gateway town to the Alpine Allgäu region, seventy miles west of Munich. Initially about thirty people had gathered in front of the villa of the Jewish cheese wholesaler Wilhelm Rosenbaum to protest against what they alleged were his extortionate prices and profiteering. Very soon the protests assumed an antisemitic guise, and the crowd grew to over one hundred. At first they were shouting, "Out with the Jews." Within a short period of time, the mob in front of the house grew to three hundred people, and calls to violence were escalating. Now the crowd was chanting: "All Jews to the gallows!" Activists from the German Nationalist Protection and Defiance Federation (Deutschvölkischer Schutz- und Trutzbund) had now taken control, but there was also a Communist city councilor who stood out among the demonstrators. The police were either unable or unwilling to dissolve the crowd. Instead, they took Rosenbaum into protective custody. As he was led across the Kaiserpromenade, the crowd had swelled to two thousand. The police had to exert every effort to prevent the prisoner from being torn away from their "protection." Under deafening noise and the ringing of cowbells, Rosenbaum was beaten multiple times on the way to the courthouse in spite of the efforts of the police. Along the way, the mob threatened other Jewish citizens as it passed by their homes. The affair ended with Rosenbaum being taken into pretrial detention for a week and finally sentenced to five weeks in jail and a fine of 3,000 marks for price advantages he allegedly pocketed, while the riot instigators and ringleaders got away with small fines or minor prison sentences.[108]

As an inmate in the Niederschönenfeld prison, revolutionary poet Erich Mühsam was an attentive observer of the events in Memmingen: "They're having a jolly time in Bavaria. Pogroms against Jews are not too far off. The riot in Memmingen was a promising prelude. The profiteer who has to serve the cause of amusing the people is not somebody I begrudge any lesson of the heart; it's just pathetic that he was castigated not for profiteering, but instead for his Jewish name, and because one is now afraid that, the next time this happens, the agitated Bavarians won't be humiliating a cheese speculator, but will instead lunge at some poor Jewish junk dealer who might not, needless to say, be able to count on protection from the Kahr-Roth government. What is being done to

Jews or revolutionaries is sacrosanct in this 'Free State': just look at [Eisner's assassin] Count Arco!"[109]

In the summer resorts of Upper Bavaria too, travelers could not fail to notice antisemitism. Bavarian resort towns had been among the most popular vacation destinations of Jewish travelers. In contrast to many northern German seaside bathing resorts and Austrian summer resorts, Jews had been left at peace in the Bavarian Alps. This changed at the beginning of the 1920s. Even Bavarian Jews were now advising against vacationing in Bavaria. In 1922, Hans Guggenheimer from Munich published "A Word of Warning to Jewish Travelers," an article in the newspaper of the Centralverein in which he conceded "that our once so gemütlich [cozy] Bavaria is today home to the most persistent and ardent hostility toward Jews, and that in no other German state is the Jew at the mercy of so much bitter insipidness as in Bavaria."[110] A year later, the same newspaper repeated its concerns: "In general anyone who can do without Bavarian summer resorts should definitely avoid them. It is especially advisable to keep a stay in Munich as short as possible. Most of the smaller towns are infested with Jew-hatred. Frequently the movement recedes, only in order to arise with greater intensity in the winter. Therefore we advise Jewish non-Bavarians: Keep away from all Bavarian spas and places to summer if you do not strictly know that their management, especially their mayors and their municipal and spa administrations, wish to have Jewish visitors."[111]

As early as 1921, the journalist Kurt Tucholsky had written a plea in the Berlin journal *Die Weltbühne* headlined "Travelers, Avoid Bavaria!": "The constitution certainly sees the German Republic as a unified entity—but the Bavarian police doesn't quibble over such trifles. It imposes orders and penalties on visitors, prescribes a registration period for travelers, demands entry permits that are harder to obtain than a passport for Nicaragua, and harasses Germans in the most outrageous manner. Whoever doesn't have a national beer belly of Bavarian provenance is a 'foreigner.' Munich's chief of police Poehner abuses the existing, wrongful ordinances for political chicaneries—in brief: the non-Bavarian traveler is subjected to the torments of a megalomaniacal states rights blister. There is only one weapon against this. Don't travel to Bavaria!"[112]

In a reply to Tucholsky that appeared in the *Miesbacher Anzeiger*, the popular Bavarian writer Ludwig Thoma denigrated his Berlin colleague as "Chaim Wrobel, alias Teiteles Tucholsky, alias Isak Achselduft [meaning "Armpit Scent"] . . . from Krotoschin in Galicia. . . . We want to tell the smut writer that we regard every Prussian dog as a thousand times more valuable than every Galician statesman."[113]

Thoma was incessantly agitating against Prussians, Social Democrats, and Jews in this Upper Bavarian provincial paper. He glorified "the execution of Eisner," boasted that "we finished off Landauer," and defended the "corporal punishment against Magnus Spinatfeld [meaning "Spinach Field"]," by which he meant Magnus Hirschfeld, the sex researcher brutally beaten up in Munich.[114] Yet what agitated him most of all was anything having to do with East European Jews, whom he now suspected of wanting to usurp power in Germany. In case of doubt, as already seen in the case of Eisner, all Jews supposedly came from Galicia.

For Thoma, "Galicia" represented the spawn of backwardness, but at the same time it was the provenance of all Jews.

As our upright soldiers marched through Poland and Galicia, they saw for the first time the horrible conditions of a country and a people under Jewish rule. No fruit tree bloomed in valleys that could have been paradises; if one looked at a village from afar and immediately thought of a certain homeliness, one was horrified as soon as one entered these breeding grounds for plague and cholera. One house to another inhabited by scabrous Jews; if a door was open, then a stench of decomposition was given off that infected everything living. Stout, lazy Jewesses who were breeding their behinds into cushions of fat crept out of the doors . . . in Germany there wasn't even a mangy dog so full of vermin as was the case here with the richest Jew or the rabbi. . . . Why was one making war on the good-natured, decent Russians instead of joining them to eradicate this plague? . . . The sons and grandsons of these lepers— that is Berlin W. They slipped through the sewer tubes into the city, nestling down; today they own the sea of houses behind the [wealthy quarter of] Tiergarten, the press, the theater, commerce, art, trade, and—since 1918—the regiment. From here they want to enslave Germany.[115]

Here there is already a preliminary sketch of all those images that would be presented two decades later to the German viewing public in one of the vilest of antisemitic films, *Der ewige Jude* (The Eternal Jew): the Jew as a parasite invading from Eastern Europe in order to achieve cultural and political domination over the German people. Thoma, the follower of Kahr, viewed Bavaria as a bulwark against the Jewish "plague" and Prussian expansionism. In summarizing the sources for his story at the end of his novel *Success*, Lion Feuchtwanger wrote sarcastically about the forum for Thoma's tirade of hate, the *Miesbacher Anzeiger*: "Two copies of this newspaper have been preserved: one is in the British Museum, the other in the Institute for Research on Primitive Cultural Forms in Brussels."[116]

Erich Mühsam may not have been reading the *Miesbacher Anzeiger* in his jail cell, but he certainly was on the receiving end of the charged antisemitic atmosphere outside the prison's walls. Thus, he noted that, "until the rage boils up again, we can only fix our gaze on the decay of the economy, and I do not share the view of all my friends that the general collapse will have to be borne longer in Bavaria than elsewhere because of the diversionary actions of the National Socialists. That the attempt will be made to shift everything onto the Jews is certain, and it is also quite possible that the rage of the starving population will be discharged in pogrom activities in the bigger cities (in Silesia, persecuting the Jews has already assumed the form of pogroms)."[117]

At a time when antisemitic agitation was assuming ever more drastic forms, and when the government was undertaking few measures to reassure Bavaria's Jewish communities and their members, these communities felt the need to band together into an umbrella organization to protect themselves against external dangers. To this end, in 1920, they founded the Association of Bavarian Israelite Communities (the Verband Bayerischer Israelitischer Gemeinden or VBIG). The chairman of the association, Bavarian Higher Court judge Alfred Neumeyer, who also chaired the Munich Jewish Community, made the aims of the federation clear in the foundation's inaugural speech: "We want to unite for the sake of internal consolidation and external defense." He left no doubt that the Jewish communities also wanted to "highlight the conservative forces concerned with maintaining public order" that "are based in Judaism and that place themselves at the service of the Fatherland."[118]

Jewish organizations in Munich reacted to the agitation against Jews by sponsoring public events. In particular, the local affiliate of the Central Association of German Citizens of the Jewish Faith (the Centralverein) tried to counter antisemitism with efforts at persuasion, and to this end it also issued invitations to conservative circles. For the first time, in April 1920, the Centralverein organized a discussion about the numerous accusations directed against the Jewish community. The chairman of the local Munich affiliate emphasized that Jews, just like Christians, had only one urgent task: quickly rebuilding the fatherland. Ludwig Holländer, the managing director who had traveled to Munich from Berlin to attend the discussion, refuted the three most frequent prejudices against Jews: their belief in chosenness, their internationality, and their foreignness. That the association of Jews with the revolutionaries of 1918 was still strongly reverberating two years later may be discerned from the clarification that Holländer felt he had to offer about allegedly Jewish revolutionaries who in reality were not Jewish at all, such as Karl Liebknecht and Karl Kautsky in Berlin or Max Levien in Munich. Holländer pointed out that the revolutionaries who actually were of Jewish descent, such as Landauer, Toller, and Mühsam, "came out of a milieu that had nothing to do with Judaism." In general, Holländer firmly repudiated the notion that an especially large number of Jews was linked to the socialist parties.[119]

One year later, the general counsel of the Centralverein, Alfred Wiener, was invited to a similar discussion. In the meantime the situation had become even worse. Wiener also pointed out that, even in Russia, Jews were especially to be found among the opponents of Bolshevism and revolution. And, once again with reference to Munich, Wiener emphasized that, in spite of well-known revolutionaries of Jewish descent, the majority of Munich's Jews had been opponents of the revolution and the council republics, "and that two Jews sacrificed their lives in the fight to liberate Munich [from rule by the council regime]." If there really was a disproportionate number of Jews on the political left, the right-wing parties and their antisemitism were to blame, since they left Jews no other option in the way of political action. But at this event one member of the Munich Chamber of Commerce also complained about the behavior of some Jews, which he claimed was hampering the fight against antisemitism. This behavior included the "leadership of Jews among the parties, which toppled the old, lovely Germany, the strong leftward swing taken by the *Frankfurter Zeitung* and that well-known Berlin paper, and the flashy appearance the Jews are making, especially in the countryside, and the protrusion of the war profiteers." Also present was the president of the Bavarian parliament, the BVP representative Heinrich Königbauer, who urged the Jews "to move far away from those elements who view it as their essential business to plunge the German people into misfortune and also now to sow discord among the people."[120]

The Centralverein published notices in the press with arguments against these antisemitic prejudices. In contrast to a widely held assumption, one of these ads said that Germany also had craftsmen who were Jewish. "If their number is small, this is attributable to centuries-old restrictions based on outdated legislation." Here, too, the discussion immediately turned again to the Jewish revolutionaries of 1918–1919: "In order to whip up the passions of [the revolution's] opponents, Jewish-sounding names among the leaders of the Independent [Social Democrats] and Communists are repeatedly named. But most of them dissolved their affiliation with Jewry a long time ago, are outside any Jewish community, and are pursuing their party's goals but not Jewish aims."[121] In one brochure from June 1920, the Centralverein pointed out "that neither in the Reich nor in Prussia is a Jew a [cabinet] minister or any kind of leading statesman." And looking back at the revolutionary events in Munich, the brochure stressed that Jews were to be found on both sides of the barricades. Thus, among those accused of murdering the hostages in the Luitpold Gymnasium during the Red Terror, there had not been a single Jew, while one of the murdered hostages was a Jewish professor at the Arts Academy, Ernst Berger.[122]

The lawyer Max Hirschberg was critical in his assessment of the efforts made by these official representatives of the Jewish community to combat antisemitism: "All attempts to curry favor with the reactionaries have done the Jews in Germany no good. Everywhere, the Central Association of German Citizens of the Jewish Faith is seeking to avoid giving offense. It hasn't helped them. My battle against the Nazi and fascist counterrevolution met with disapproval from the majority of Jews. I have almost no Jewish clients."[123]

Outside Bavaria, individual Jews from Munich were also drawing attention to what was happening there. The leader of Munich's Orthodox Jewish community, Siegmund Fraenkel, whom we have already encountered several times, turned to the readers of the *Berliner Tageblatt* in order to make it clear that Munich's Jews could expect nothing good from the leadership of the Munich police: Fraenkel began his remarks by saying that "German-völkisch acts of violence are the order of the day right now in Bavaria and especially in Munich." He then pointed out that the police let this public agitation against Jews in Munich— especially the posters from the antisemitic German Nationalist Protection and Defiance Federation "that positively incite pogroms"—go unpunished.

In reminding readers of his own public letter against the Jewish members of the council republic, Fraenkel could then point out that he had never shied away from "forewarning the leading men of the Bavarian government today with equal candor that the German-völkisch wrong track now being taken by another extreme, with the silent approval of the Munich police headquarters, must unfailingly lead us into a new chaos of destruction and devastation." Munich's reputation as a city for tourists was unfortunately suffering, Fraenkel wrote, in what had become an insufferably antisemitic atmosphere. Previously, the governing parties under Herr von Kahr had not been able to prevent the chief of police from tolerating all theses antisemitic actions. Now they really had to decide "if the insane exploits of the swastika politicians are finally going to be stopped by a top-to-bottom reform in Munich's police headquarters."[124] It did not take long until the antisemites reacted to Fraenkel's cry for help. Ludwig Thoma cited the very words of this self-same Siegmund Fraenkel, who had so clearly disassociated himself from the Jewish revolutionaries during the Bavarian Council Republic, as proof that Munich's Jews had "placed themselves on the side of the demagogic Ostjuden who abused Munich for five months with the assistance of the worst rabble." The Jews should not get so upset if there were now attacks on them, since the people believed, understandably enough, that the Jews "want to take over the reins of government with the assistance of the proletariat." The Jews, according to Thoma, were not victims of agitation, but rather the real agitators.[125]

The Social Democrats proved largely resistant to the spreading anti-semitic wave. In their official statements, they defended the rights of Jews against a variety of attacks, and during the 1920s several Jewish Social Democrats sat on the Munich city council. Yet even the Social Democrats were not entirely immune to antisemitism. Looking back, one Social Democratic opponent of Bavaria's council republic, Carl Landauer (no relative of Gustav Landauer), conceded that "during those years of rapidly surging Hitler agitation, waves of antisemitism also spilled into Bavarian Social Democracy, and antisemitic feelings combined with the resentment that party functionaries of a proletarian background held against the intellectuals in the party." Even the party chairman, Erhard Auer, was not free of antisemitic sentiments, yet Landauer felt that Auer deserved respect for having taken up the fight, more than any other Bavarian politician, against the right, especially after the Hitler putsch. Looking back to this period, Landauer related the astonishing fact that, when it came to financing measures against the right, it did not require much thinking "for us to become aware that only Jewish circles were willing to help us financially without regard for differences in economic aims." Through the intervention of the main organization among German Jews, the Centralverein in Berlin, Landauer succeeded in arranging for a source of funding. "The political risk of this connection was evident to us, of course. As morally unobjectionable as the whole matter was, we certainly knew what the Nazis would make out of this link between 'Jewish capitalists and Social Democratic bosses' if they ever got their hands on any evidence about this." And, in fact, the correspondence between the Social Democrats and the Centralverein was leaked—with all the consequences anticipated by Landauer.[126]

Thus, what Erich Mühsam had described in *Ein Mann des Volkes* (A Man of the People), the fragment of a novel he wrote while a prisoner in Niederschönenfeld, became reality. Here Mühsam drew a picture of the Jewish physician Dr. Blumenthal, who is active as a socialist agitator "and wants to implant class consciousness into the dull-staid journeyman" he coaches. Blumenthal tells his most "proficient pupil," the simple-minded worker Heini Kunde: "When the people find out that I am the mixer of poisons who administers drops of proletarian class to the journeymen, then it is over for the medical practice of the Jew Blumenthal in Kersching."[127]

In the meantime, the situation in Munich had become so acute that, on April 8, 1922, a delegation from the Association of Bavarian Israelite Communities called on Prime Minister Lerchenfeld and Interior Minister Schweyer and, using drastic language, got right to the point about their situation: "Our very existence in Germany, as dreadful as this sounds, is called into question."[128] This entreaty did not, however, seem to have made an impression on Lerchenfeld. He brought up his encounter with the Jewish delegation briefly in a cabinet meeting and, partly out of fear of his coalition partners on the right, continued to abstain from introducing concrete measures against antisemitism.[129]

In June 1922, Germany's foreign minister, Walther Rathenau, was shot to death near his home in Berlin by members of the right-wing Organization Consul, an antisemitic group that had long been allowed to operate out of Munich, since it was tolerated by Ernst Pöhner, the chief of police.[130] Lion Feuchtwanger had just finished his novel *Jud Süß*. There is considerable irony in Feuchtwanger's writing plans at this juncture in his career. Originally, in lieu of the early eighteenth-century court Jew who was the subject of his novel, the life he wanted to portray was that of Rathenau, which had now ended just as tragically as Joseph Süß Oppenheimer's.[131] In his less well-known story "Conversations with the Eternal Jew," from 1920, Feuchtwanger has his protagonist complain that antisemitism is waning; nevertheless, his interlocutor replies hopefully, there are signs that it is reviving. "'And, even in Munich, you believe?' 'I believe? I know.'"[132]

"Now Germany Has Its Dreyfus Trial"—A Legal Scandal and a Scandalous Legal System

The Bavarian legal system was notorious for the important role it played in Hitler's rise. That the judiciary during the Weimar Republic was blind on its right eye has been demonstrated often enough by both contemporaries and scholars. Here, too, Bavaria—and above all its capital city—took a leading and ignominious role. As the former chairman of the Bavarian Bar Association, Max Friedländer, observed in retrospect: "These were dark times. There were courts for summary court martials and, in addition, the so-called People's Courts. What these remnants of the revolutionary period, transformed by the new government into a rather reactionary institution, mostly had in common with their namesake was the badness of their procedural rules and the lack of any legal guarantees for the accused. A number of trials took place that did not do any credit to the German legal system."[133]

Soon it became very clear that the political offenses of the left were judged by a different standard than those on the right. In a study from 1924, the pacifist Emil Julius Gumbel, who taught statistics at the University of Heidelberg, summed things up this way: "The juxtaposition of severe punishment for the supporters of the Bavarian Council Republic and complete impunity for these political murders [on the right] provides perhaps the clearest evidence about the nature of the Bavarian People's Courts." Barely 21 people were sentenced for the 164 political murders committed following the collapse of the council republic, in contrast to 2,209 sentences against people connected with the council republic, even though significantly more human lives were lost to the White Terror than had been victims of the Red Terror.[134]

In his foreword to Gumbel's book, Arnold Freymuth, chief justice of the Prussian Court of Appeals, remarked: "For all of this supposedly 'patriotic'—but in reality criminal—activity, which is severely endangering Germany's lot both abroad and at home, Bavaria is the predominant

FIGURE 25. Book cover for Erich Mühsam, *Das Standrecht in Bayern* (Martial Law in Bavaria) (1923).

local hub. Even if a major share of the especially serious incidents did not take place in Bavaria, or did not emanate directly from Bavaria . . . there is a ubiquitous connection to Bavaria, whether the perpetrators came from Bavaria or fled to Bavaria after the crime, or were aided or abetted from there, or whether there are other threads running to and from Bavaria."[135]

That perpetrators on the right were celebrated as patriots at the same time that perpetrators on the left were regarded as traitors was a double standard already clearly manifested in the trial conducted against Count Arco, Eisner's murderer, during the tenure of the Social Democratic Hoffmann government. The numerous witnesses for the defense were given the opportunity to abuse the courtroom for political propaganda. Arco's former teacher and his fellow students, as well as comrades and commanders from his time as a soldier in the First World War, outdid each other in depicting his strength of character and patriotism. The chief witness to the crime, Eisner's secretary Felix Fechenbach, was not even summoned to testify, since it was feared that he might make a political statement before the court in favor of Eisner and his socialist ideals. By contrast, the well-known surgeon Ferdinand Sauerbruch, who operated on the severely wounded Arco following the assassination and saved his life, had only words of praise for his patient: "The manly conduct of Count Arco is in accord with his general character traits." The doctor went on to say: "For me there is no doubt that this man committed this deed out of a conviction that he was thereby doing his Fatherland a service. If only one single person in the Revolution had done his work with such clean hands."[136]

Rarely had a prosecuting attorney praised a defendant accused of murder as highly as in the trial against Arco, when the prosecutor explained in his closing argument: "It's not for me to say: It was true, profound, deeply ingrained love of Fatherland that moved the defendant to his deed, nor is it for me to add: If our youth as a whole were to be animated by such ardent love of Fatherland, then we could hope to look forward with joyful confidence to the future of our Fatherland."[137] The presiding judge saw things much the same way. Although, owing to the clear circumstances of the case, he had to pronounce a death sentence, he refused to strip Arco of his civil rights, "since the conduct of the young, politically immature man did not arise from a lowly disposition, but from the most ardent love of his people and his Fatherland."[138] After he was sentenced, Arco emphasized his patriotism. As the *Münchner Neueste Nachrichten* reported: "In response to these words of Arco's, there was an eruption of rapturous applause from all the seats in the overcrowded auditorium, continuing for minutes with repeated calls of bravo and clapping of hands."[139] It was no surprise that, on the following day, the Bavarian government passed a unanimous resolution reducing the sentence to life imprisonment.

Arco became a hero to large sections of the population, and the reporting of the mainstream press, in newspapers like the *München-Augsburger Abendzeitung*, expressed similar adulation: "It was a positively elevating mood that suffused the widest circles of the population in unison during those days. For a while the misery of the present was mitigated, and one sensed again that spirit that permeated the entire people during the great days of August 1914. Should the profound impression made by Count Arco's fiery commitment to the Fatherland persist, then the highest and sacred aim of his fearless sacrifice is fulfilled." The sympathies of Munich's students, who were solid backers of a pardon for Arco, were expressed in an unprecedented rally at the university. "Not since the new building [an addition to the university's nineteenth-century main building] was constructed has the auditorium seen such a mass of people; students from the Technical University also put in an appearance." When the rector arrived to announce the pardon, "an unparalleled storm of applause and jubilation" erupted.[140]

In contrast to their glorification of Arco as a hero, the Bavarian People's Courts were severe in the way they proceeded against purportedly leftist offenders. Two such cases from 1922 stand out. Both revolved around the man who was deliberately not summoned to testify at the Arco trial: Eisner's secretary, Felix Fechenbach. Two years after that trial, Fechenbach had to appear on his own account before a Bavarian People's Court. This case—described by Emil Julius Gumbel in 1924 as "the most interesting case of the Bavarian People's Courts"—is extremely relevant to the theme of this book.[141] Not unlike the unequal pairing of Eisner and Arco, this case involved a confrontation between two people whose destinies illuminate twentieth-century German-Jewish history in its entire complexity. Although both came from a Jewish family and both met a violent end as Jews under Nazi terror, at the beginning of the 1920s they could not have been further apart.

In charging Felix Fechenbach, the authorities were prosecuting Kurt Eisner's former secretary and closest aide. The accuser suing him for libel, Paul Nikolaus Cossmann, was one of the most powerful men in

Fechenbach, der Sekretär Eisners
und Aktenmitfälscher

FIGURE 26A AND 26B. Felix Fechenbach (left) and Paul Nikolaus Cossmann (right).
Bayerische Staatsbibliothek München / Bildarchiv.

Kahr's Bavaria. Fechenbach was a pacifist and Social Democrat. Cossmann, one of the initiators of the "stab in the back" legend, saw in Social Democracy and Jewry potential dangers to conservative Bavaria. Fechenbach, who had briefly been in the innermost circles of power, was washed ashore and left stranded in political isolation after Eisner was murdered and the Bavarian Council Republic toppled. As the publisher of the *Süddeutsche Monatshefte* and the most powerful man at Munich's most influential daily newspaper, the *Münchner Neueste Nachrichten*, Cossmann had direct access to the new inner circles of power in counterrevolutionary Munich. Raised in a strictly religious family, Fechenbach sympathized for a brief time with Zionist socialism and traveled to Palestine in the mid-1920s. While in his thirties, Cossmann converted from Judaism to Catholicism and, for the rest of his life, disassociated himself from the community into which he had been born.

Who was Paul Niklaus Cossmann, this man who is nearly forgotten today but was such a central player in the Munich of the 1920s? He was born in 1869 to German-Jewish parents living in Moscow, where his father, the cellist Bernhard Cossmann, held a professorship of music from 1866 to 1870. After university studies in Frankfurt and Munich, he settled in the Bavarian capital, where in 1903 he was one of the founders of the *Süddeutsche Monatshefte*, whose editor he remained from 1904 to 1933. Initially a liberal, cosmopolitan paper mainly covering cultural affairs, this periodical became increasingly mired in nationalism during the war. In the postwar years, it provided an open forum for all those eager to talk about Germany's betrayal by the Treaty of Versailles, and its pages made the case for the "stab in the back" legend, according to which Germany was not defeated on the battleground but at home by its internal enemies. After 1918, the *Süddeutsche Monatshefte* focused on Germany's innocence in the outbreak of the war, the country's defeat at the hands of domestic enemies, and the injustice perpetrated by the Allies.

Cossmann shifted increasingly to the right during the war and supported the conservative German Fatherland Party, which rejected any attempt at reaching a compromise peace. The historian Karl Alexander von Müller (who would later play a crucial role in Nazi Germany by leading a pseudo-scientific institute on the "Jewish Question") depicts his friend Cossmann's baptism as an essential precondition for becoming an "ardent German": "He had come out of Judaism and its highly cultivated abstract way of thinking and had become a deeply convinced Catholic Christian and ardent German; the antagonism between these two worlds, it often seemed to me, ignited that paradoxical quality that was characteristic of him in thought and speech."[142]

During the early 1920s, Cossmann finally rose to become one of Munich's most influential people. He had access to the innermost circles of Bavarian politics and close ties to Ruhr industrialists at the same time that he was esteemed among the city's conservative academics and intellectuals. In 1920, he became the political adviser to, and thus the decisive voice behind, the *Münchner Neueste Nachrichten*, the most important daily newspaper in the city. He was at the center of the secret Gäa Circle (named after Gaia, the ancient Greek word for "land" and the name of the primordial earth goddess). The circle was a group bringing together the leading minds of German heavy industry, the Farmers' Association, and Munich politics—as well as independent personalities like the surgeon Ferdinand Sauerbruch, the philosopher of history Oswald Spengler, and the historian Karl Alexander von Müller—for annual retreats, including a meeting in 1923 to hatch plans for a dictatorship in Bavaria.[143] Via Cossmann and his close contacts in influential business and political circles, Spengler was then nurturing ambitious plans to influence the Munich press, with the ultimate aim of attaining "liberation from the forms of Anglo-French democracy" and establishing a German-style national socialism.[144]

Politically, Cossmann was close to Kahr and the Bavarian Order Bloc, a loose association of over forty nationalist and völkisch movements. Spengler, himself entrenched in the right-wing camp, wrote a letter in December 1923 accusing Cossmann of not doing enough to disassociate his *Münchner Neueste Nachrichten* from the NSDAP and of taking an uncritical stance toward Hitler's activities.[145] The Social Democratic lawyer Philipp Löwenfeld went so far as to characterize Cossmann, in spite of his Jewish origins, as an antisemite, and he added: "One of world history's bad jokes was that the two most important catchwords of the Nazis and the other nationalists fighting against the German republic came from an honest-to-goodness Jew."[146] His law partner Max Hirschberg arrived at a similar assessment: "Coßmann was a highly educated man, but of substandard character, for whom no means, neither breach of promise nor breach of trust nor denunciation, was low enough in the fight against progress. He was a baptized Jew with a strongly Jewish intellectual face."[147] Hirschberg thought that Cossman belonged to that category of Jews with a keen self-hatred, a group the lawyer despised: "The patriotic Jews who allied themselves with völkisch chauvinism in order to destroy a Jew, who were then deservedly spat upon under Hitler and nevertheless treated like Jews, are a sad spectacle that always filled me with disgust and contempt."[148] For the left-wing *Weltbühne*, Cossman was "one of those antisemites who is himself of Jewish descent."[149] On another occasion, the journal quoted approvingly from Munich's *Allgemeine Zeitung*, which had chastised Cossmann because he did not offer even "the most timid public comment against antisemitism. . . . He disowns his blood and the blood of his fathers and is ashamed of taking a stand. . . . Coßmann, the Jew who cloaks himself in Aryan garb, who knows that his former coreligionists are good Germans for the most part, and nonetheless he fosters a pogrom atmosphere by his positively glaring passivity in a position of responsibility—this Coßmann falls short on manliness."[150]

Looking back, Karl Alexander von Müller confirmed that his friend Cossmann had an inner aversion to the community from which he came. On several occasions, Cossmann spoke to him with no holds barred "about his rejection of Judaism, indeed of his often 'physical aversion to everything Jewish.'" The spiritual warfare conducted "against what Spengler called metropolitan civilization" was one of Cossmann's crusades against "that part of the metropolitan Jewish intelligentsia who struck him as doubly dangerous, because they combined brilliant wit with great artistic talent." There is no lack of irony in Karl Alexander von Müller, of all people, then adding this remark: "I defended the Jewish sort more than once against him." Müller, who never had any scruples after 1933 about holding all kinds of offices under the Nazi regime, actually wrote after 1945 that the National Socialist doctrine to which he was least receptive was its ideology of "racial theories bloated with pseudo-scientific pretensions." Yet there was certainly nobody, at least not in Munich, more responsible for making race theories socially acceptable in academic circles than the selfsame Müller, who in 1936 made himself available to run the newly founded Research Department for the Jewish Question at the Reich Institute for the History of the New Germany. In retrospect, however, he claimed to have found "the dull hatred of anti-semitism repugnant all along."[151] It is hard to imagine a historian tinkering more shamelessly with his own past than this.

Cossmann's activity during the early 1920s, as well as his role in the Fechenbach trial, can only be understood by taking a closer look at his position in the Munich press. As general manager of the publishing house that put out Munich's most important daily newspaper, Cossmann had close relationships with industry and politics throughout Germany. The files from his estate provide insight into his ties to the conservative representatives of heavy industry from the Ruhr and to the highest circles of Bavarian politics. In July 1920, a conglomerate of several Ruhr industrialists took over majority stakes in the publishing house that published the *Münchner Neueste Nachrichten*. Forty-five percent of the publishing house was acquired by Karl Haniel, chairman of the board of the Gutehoffnungshütte in Oberhausen (partly on behalf of the coal and shipping magnate Hugo Stinnes), while another share of almost 23 percent was acquired by the conglomerate of the right-wing nationalist press czar Alfred Hugenberg. The general public did not know about these acquisitions, since the new owners were hiding behind a special-purpose trust company, the Süddeutsche Treuhandgesellschaft, created for the takeover.[152]

Behind the scenes, however, people were thinking out loud about the paper's transformation. Thus, the Prussian legation in Munich sent this complaint to Berlin in a report from December 1920: "In all of Bavaria there is not one newspaper that rises above the level of a provincial rag. . . . The unifying band that entwines Bavaria's bourgeois papers is . . . carping about the Reich and Berlin." The once-liberal *Münchner Neueste Nachrichten*, the report went on to say, had taken a sharp turn to the right, especially on the subject of Bavaria's autonomy. "In its relationship to the Reich, even today the 'Münchner Neueste Nachrichten' follows its old tradition of writing what the majority of its leaders are glad to hear. And since the Bavarian public in general loves grumbling about Berlin, the [paper] valiantly grumbles along, though not with the severity that the [even more right-wing] 'Bayerischer Kurier' or the 'Vaterland' prefer."[153]

Cossmann's correspondence with the paper's new owners makes it clear that they wanted to keep their new role as secret as possible. It would not look good to the Bavarian public if "foreign elements" were seen controlling the Munich press. Thus, Karl Haniel wrote to Cossmann: "Any prominence of Rhenish firms must naturally be avoided for obvious reasons." The immediate task at hand would be to make sure "the [future of the newspaper] 'Das Bayerische Vaterland' is discreetly secured."[154] Acting on behalf of the industrialists Hugenberg, Haniel, and Stinnes, Martin Spahn, the German nationalist history professor and founder of the conservative Political College for National-Political Training and Pedagogy, sounded a very similar note in a letter to Cossmann in which he sketched out some preliminary ideas about founding "our own society for the south," only to abandon the idea a few days later. It would be better, Spahn now argued, just to deploy confidants in order to make the takeover look as anonymous as possible.[155] Aside from Cossmann, of course, Bavaria's leading politicians had been let in on these takeover plans. It warrants our attention that the same political circles that had condemned Kurt Eisner from Berlin, the Karlsruhe native Gustav Landauer, and Erich Mühsam, who had grown up in Lübeck, as "foreign elements" had few qualms about industrialists from Duisburg and Mülheim, Essen and Dortmund, Oberhausen and Rinteln taking over Munich's most important paper, whose fate was now decided by a general manager who had been born in Baden and brought up in Russia.

These conservative industrialists saw in the monarchically inclined Bavarian government a political partner in their fight against the hated Weimar Republic. Munich was a location they envisioned as a fitting playground for their economic interests. And in the publisher Paul Nikolaus Cossmann they saw their most suitable representative in Germany's south. They supported measures taken by the Bavarian government that frequently clashed with the policy of the Reich government in Berlin, such as raising battalions of Civil Defense Guards.[156] Spahn assured Cossmann that Kahr had a "political instinct that was absolutely reliable. Hopefully, in all his beautifully masculine modesty, he will not let himself be deterred in this either by Berlin or any other place."[157] Cossmann also cultivated a direct contact with Alfred Hugenberg, the press czar and cofounder of the German National People's Party, and he attempted via Hugenberg to wield influence over the Reich economics minister Johann Becker, another industrialist from the Ruhr region.[158]

Stinnes, Hugenberg, and the other owners of the publishing group— who mistrusted each other[159]—intervened in the newspaper's daily business, either directly or by way of their representatives. They made it clear that their priority was adhering to the paper's conservative course, as agreed on between Cossmann and his financiers. It was suggested to Cossmann that he pay close attention to keeping Fritz Gerlich, the editor-in-chief who was also a conservative nationalist but not always politically reliable, in line: "Herr Dr. Gerlich had . . . in general lent the paper a direction of the kind that we agreed upon in Munich back in the day." But as Hugenberg's close confidant, retired naval captain Johann Bernhard Mann, complained to Cossmann, for the last two to three months there had been unfriendly attacks on the DNVP (the far-right-wing German National People's Party) as well as a stance toward moderate Center Party Reich chancellor Joseph Wirth that was much too friendly. Mann asked Cossmann to keep him apprised about "how the stance of the M.N.N. can be put back on the right track."[160] After Kahr's resignation, Mann made it clear that the priority now was, at the very least, making sure not to lose the ultraconservative police chief: "I believe I share your view that every effort must be made to keep Pöhner in his job."[161]

Bavarian politicians also gave clear directives to Cossmann. Justice Minister Christian Roth, for example, urged him to work toward getting the newspaper to adopt an even stronger nationalistic point of view.[162] A few months later, in June 1921, when an attack on the Social Democratic parliamentary deputy Alwin Saenger and the assassination of the USPD parliamentary chairman Karl Gareis triggered a political crisis in Bavaria, the German nationalist Roth finally expressed his enormous satisfaction with the direction Cossmann was taking. The subject came up in a discussion he had with Kahr. "We also got to talking about the attitude of the Munich press over the last several critical weeks. His Excellency von Kahr agrees with me that the M.N.N. has performed a most inestimable service through its determined, and not particularly partisan, attitude; [the paper has] made a major contribution toward facilitating the treatment of the Civil Defense Guard question and the Sänger case, warding off political and parliamentary action on account of the murder of Deputy Gareis, and thus securing the continuation of the coalition."[163]

Cossmann also kept supporting Kahr when the latter, in his new function as state commissioner general, adopted a more autonomous Bavarian posture and set out on a course of confrontation with the

Reich government in Berlin. Cossman did explain to Max Graf von Montgelas "that in everything we do, the pan-German idea is decisive. We support Herr von Kahr because we know that he also wishes nothing more than to cooperate with a Reich government in the making. But what is to be done when one realizes that the breakdown of the Reich, if only for economic reasons, is advancing from day to day? Is loyalty to the Reich then preserved by dispensing with criticism while watching, or by attempting to create something new in one sub-territory and thereby providing an example for the rest of the Reich?"[164]

The reputation of the once-cosmopolitan *Münchner Neueste Nachrichten* in liberal and leftist circles sank continuously in the 1920s. Just how much Cossmann and his paper represented Bavaria's political decline from a center-left perspective was made clear by this commentary in the *Weltbühne*: "It is a defamatory rag, to be sure, thoroughly worthy of the man who inspired it, Paul Nikolaus Coßmann, and it is chiefly responsible for the putrefaction of Bavaria and solely responsible for the Fechenbach affair."[165] From his jail cell, Erich Mühsam wrote: "Here it is said that the Jews of Munich had, out of solidarity, canceled their subscription to the Münchner Neueste Nachrichten and withdrawn their advertisements so that this filthy rag, sailing under a democratic false flag, closed its annual balance sheet with a deficit of 70 million. The Jews would have done well there—if they keep the bargain."[166] It is highly unlikely that there was really any kind of arrangement like this among Munich's Jews. It is more likely that a number of individual initiatives added up to produce this outcome.

The publishing forum closest to Cossmann, the print venue in which he could act without outside influence, was not the *Münchner Neueste Nachrichten* but the *Süddeutsche Monatshefte*, which he had founded.[167] After the war, it became one of the most important platforms for the intellectual crusade against the "war guilt lie," and it was among the loudest champions of the "stab in the back" legend. It was in this journal that the campaign against Fechenbach got under way. Immediately after the end of the war, Cossmann was incapable of admitting that Germany had been defeated. He had seen it coming, yet (as he wrote in the *Monatshefte* toward the end of 1918) "now that it seems to have come to

FIGURE 27. Title page of the *Süddeutsche Monatshefte* with the motif of the "stab in the back" legend (April 1924).

this, we still cannot believe it. . . . We are convinced that our enemies have nothing else to do than carry out the permanent annihilation of the German people and jointly enrich themselves at the expense of the former Central Powers."[168] The prospects were catastrophic: "We regard what's going on not as an act of construction, but as decay."[169]

The pages of the *Süddeutsche Monatshefte* were now conjuring up sponsorship of Bolshevism by radical Jews as the worst danger facing

Germany. In the same issue, in December 1918, Cossmann's co-editor Josef Hofmiller picked up on this theme. He lamented "that the chief backers of nihilism both in Russia and Germany are deracinated Jews. There is nothing more cowardly than the way in which our newspapers are deliberately closing their eyes to this fact, for fear of being regarded as antisemitic. As if the solid, respectable Jewry and the Germany that, without wanting to be conservative, at least wants to conserve itself against everything that threatens to destroy both, were not natural allies! One really needs, finally, to name Messieurs Radek, Trotsky etc. by their real names!"[170]

This debate continued in the next several issues. Jewish authors such as Elias Hurwicz, by trade a legal scholar and translator of the historian Simon Dubnow's works, and David Eliasberg, whose brother Alexander was active in Munich as a writer in Thomas Mann's circle of acquaintances, quietly gave voice to an opposing position. Eliasberg, for example, wanted "to point out the little-noticed fact that Russian Jews also play a major role in the anti-Bolshevik movement: indeed, they show up there as active fighters, while the Jewish Bolshevik leaders in most cases are not championing their idea with their blood. One need only think about the assassination attempts on Lenin and Uritsky that were committed by Jews. In this case the Jewish people is actually producing, alongside cowardly careerists, heroes willing to make sacrifices."[171]

Cossmann insisted on intervening forcefully in the debate. With the zeal of a Jewish renegade, he examined the ideas of Judaism and Christianity from the vantage point of classical Christian theology: one was the religion of hate, the other that of love; and in contrast to the religion of materialism was that of idealism. This is one of the few articles from that time that attempted—with a deliberately hostile attitude—to explain "Jewish socialism" in theological terms: "Jewish socialism, the system of the Pharisees and the scribes, was an attempt at setting the world to rights by changing the distribution of goods or changing convictions. It was capitalist, i.e., materialistic, searching for the origins of human suffering and the means to remedy this in the material realm, while Christianity searches for both in conviction. Only once has there been true communism, in the first few centuries of Christianity. Jewish socialism, whose strategic goal was achieved with the socialist republic, used hatred as a tactical instrument. Its adherents, who had been drilled in hatred on a daily basis, could not adapt themselves to loving once the next goal, the socialist republic, had been achieved. According to Jewish socialism's materialistic view of history, human beings could not be anything other than the necessary product of their economic conditions." This theologically based contrast between the vilified religious community into which he was born and the idealized religion he had joined is certainly the key to Cossmann's anti-Jewish attitude.

Given the revolutionary tensions of the time, words like the following simply further inflamed the highly charged atmosphere and spread the thesis of Bolshevism as the "mature form of Jewish socialism." More specifically, Cossmann was shifting the focus from general categories to Bavarian particulars: "Compare a man like Tolstoy with one like Eisner. There introspection and non-resistance to evil, here shifting all blame onto others, self-aggrandizement, striving for power." Cossmann was toying with two common anti-Jewish stereotypes when he characterized Bolshevism as "a joint-stock company" that had no cares about individual human beings or even about the dead. Here Judaism represented not only communism but capitalism as well. On the other side of this contrast was his picture of an idealized Christianity: "Christianity regards possessions as nothing, the soul as everything."[172] In an atmosphere increasingly charged with racism, Cossmann tried to clarify which camp he belonged to—and above all, which side he was no longer to be be associated with. Here theological, political, and economic arguments were thrown together in a colorful mix.

The anti-Jewish invectives appearing in the *Süddeutsche Monatshefte* raised objections from the journal's remaining Jewish readers. The pediatrician Karl Oppenheimer and his wife Klara were especially outraged at what Cossmann had written: "All the Jews are supposed to be made liable and responsible for everything bad and reprehensible that one Jew in the entire world does. Can one imagine anything more unjust and heartless, but also more nonsensical?" The Jewish couple concluded, certainly based on their own political posture, that "[t]he Jew is hardly a revolutionary by nature. . . . We do not believe we are wrong when we maintain that nobody hates the Jewish revolutionary more fiercely than that Jew who is politically on the right. What he hates about the Jewish subversive is not only the enemy of order, but also the source of his personal misfortune, since he surely knows that he is going to be held co-responsible for the contemptible behavior of the other one."[173] This statement reveals the dilemma of politically conservative German Jews who were no less unhappy about the loss of the monarchy than their Christian neighbors but now had to experience political homelessness.

Cossmann was certainly aware of this and insisted on responding directly. He assured his Jewish readers: "Many Germans, indeed a rapidly growing number of them, are of the view that every misfortune for Germany comes from the Jews. We cannot share this view." Nevertheless, as he went on to say, entirely in the spirit of the "stab in the back" legend, "it cannot be denied that, among the many causes of the collapse, the attitude of one segment of German Jews—an attitude partly hostile to Germany, partly just opposed to a clear-cut German victory, from which it feared a strengthening of antisemitism and of antisemitic circles—was the most effective." And then he takes another swing against the Jews: "The difference of which we are speaking here, compared to the period of a hundred years ago, is only that, at that time, the enemies of the German idea in Germany were just as clumsy, disjoined, and leaderless as its defenders, whereas now they possess agile leaders in Jewish lawyers, willing financiers in Jewish capitalists, and above all a superior propaganda instrument in the Jewish Press."[174] With this reply to the Oppenheimers, Cossmann rendered the dilemma of Jews like them, worried about their conservative homeland, even more visible. Once again he availed himself of the standard anti-Jewish terminology, and in so doing he was going back on his own assurance at the beginning of his article that he was disassociating himself from antisemitism. One could sum up his conclusion this way: not all of Germany's misfortunes emanated from the Jews, but a huge share of them certainly did.

Nearly the entire annual volume of the *Süddeutsche Monatshefte* in 1920 was preoccupied with refuting the Versailles Treaty and propagating the "stab in the back" legend. Against this backdrop, the articles appearing in the journal brewed up a poisonous mixture that fully took effect during the Fechenbach-Cossmann dispute. Ironically, the tirade of publications claiming to be patriotic and calling for a revision of the "war guilt clause" in the Versailles Treaty began with an article by Georg Karo, another author with a Jewish family background. Karo was the director of the German Archaeological Institute in Athens. In spite of his German nationalist views, he was later forced into early retirement by the Nazis "on racial grounds" and driven into exile. The archaeologist first issued his demand for a revision of Versailles in the September 1919 issue of the *Monatshefte*. But then, in May 1921, he struck a real blow for this cause, while also helping to spread the "stab in the back" legend, by drawing the conclusion that "our most dangerous enemies" were "not outside, but inside this country."[175] These words were still being used in a very general way. Yet, in the context of the reporting that appeared in the pages of the *Süddeutsche Monatshefte*, the intended target of this language soon became very clear.

The campaign against Kurt Eisner's former secretary Felix Fechenbach began to take shape when the *Süddeutsche Monatshefte* published its July 1921 issue. Professor Karl Alexander von Müller started it off by taking up the question of war guilt. His argument involved a letter from the councilor for the Bavarian legation in Berlin, Hans von Schön (a communication that had originally been attributed to the Bavarian emissary Count Lerchenfeld), that had served as proof of German war guilt. Müller reiterated what Schön had already asserted in 1919, namely, that the letter as published by Eisner had been forged using "refined deletions and truncations."[176] Fechenbach indignantly countered the accusation by saying that, in light of this "essay that was truly shameful for a serious scholar, political fanaticism was stronger than the search for scholarly objectivity."[177] For the antisemites following this story, it was only a short step from there to seeing the culprits not simply as two characters named Eisner and Fechenbach but as two Jews accused of forgery. The conservative Catholic newspaper *Das Bayerische Vaterland*, for example, published an article with the title "How the Jews Eisner and Fechenbach are perpetrating a heinous crime on the German people."[178]

Cossmann himself spoke up on the matter in a footnote where he added that Eisner's wife had claimed "that it was not her husband who made the forgery, but his secretary Fechenbach."[179] The *Süddeutsche Monatshefte* kept on taking shots at Eisner and his secretary Fechenbach. In February 1922, it was the turn of Pius Dirr, Munich's city archivist and Bavarian Landtag deputy for the liberal DDP, who also touched on the "stab in the back" legend in his allegation of forgery.[180] The *Süddeutsche Monatshefte* accused Eisner and his secretary Fechenbach of having deliberately forged documents in order to prove Germany's war guilt.

In the words of his attorney Philipp Löwenfeld, Fechenbach was being called to account as a stand-in for Eisner: "This was intended to have Eisner's living student be accused of an alleged moral and national crime so that the German people could finally know that it was not just 1 Jew but 2 Jews who could be held responsible for the Versailles Treaty. The accusation of an anti-national forgery was leveled by one Jew against another at a time when countless political assassinations had already taken place because of the murder victims' alleged national unreliability. It triggered a rush of murders in Bavaria."[181]

This trial was not Fechenbach's first encounter with the judicial authorities of the Free State of Bavaria. In 1919, after the fall of the council republics, Fechenbach was briefly arrested but then released after it became clear that he had not been a participant in either of the two council republics.[182] In July 1920, when he was supposed to answer to the district court in Munich about files that had disappeared from the Bavarian Foreign Ministry, he did not show up. Instead, he first decamped to Czechoslovakia and was released again after posting bail.[183] Thereafter, a period of calm surrounded Fechenbach. With the publication of the false assertions against him, however, his name made a public comeback in Munich. At first it was Fechenbach who accused Cossmann of slander, yet the court turned this into a show trial against the forgery allegedly concocted by Eisner and Fechenbach. The libel trial that began on April 27, 1922—a trial Fechenbach had sought—was unable to confirm Cossmann's assertion that Fechenbach was the actual author of the forgery. Yet it also exonerated Cossmann on the charge against him of defamation.[184]

Fechenbach conceded that the letter had been abridged, but he vehemently denied any kind of forgery distorting its meaning. He also ruled out any possibility that Eisner's widow "had begotten any such frivolous slander of my person." Rather, he accused the *Süddeutsche Monatshefte*, "which had taken a lease on the 'historical truth' about the war for the next several years," of having turned Schön's genuine letter into a forgery by Eisner.[185] In court, Cossmann was allowed to continue his unhindered attacks against the dead Eisner: "Unfortunately I have to say I have the impression that Eisner was the most untruthful personality who has ever played a part in Germany history." Eisner and Fechenbach had "helped maintain the devils's empire on earth" and should be held responsible for one of "the greatest crimes of German history."[186] Thus, in the end, Fechenbach had to accept a defeat at court in Munich. But this would prove to be just the first act in an unfolding, painful drama for him.

Georg Neithardt, the same judge who had presided over the trial against Count Arco and would later be responsible for the mild sentence given Hitler after the Beer Hall Putsch, had Fechenbach arrested on the basis of a denunciation from his ex-wife. On August 10, 1922, a few weeks after the murder of Walter Rathenau, Fechenbach was arrested, and now he was suddenly before the court no longer as a plaintiff but as a defendant. The charge was treason—and it came from Cossmann. Fechenbach was indicted for passing on documents that incriminated Germany about the outbreak of the war to a Swiss journalist. And he was also indicted, because of his cooperation with the information office run by Sigismund Gargas out of Berlin, on matters pertaining to monarchist and right-wing extremist activities in Bavaria; allegedly, the documents were forwarded to British government circles via a news agency in Rotterdam with which Gargas was cooperating.[187]

At court, there were additional Jewish actors participating in this trial on both sides. Philipp Löwenfeld (in the first trial) and Max Hirschberg, along with Max Bernstein (in the second trial), acted as Fechenbach's attorneys, while Cossmann, in addition to using the services of the Catholic Count Josef von Pestalozza (the same lawyer who had defended the revolutionaries Eugen Leviné and Erich Mühsam!), was also represented by Otto Pflaum, the publishing director of the *Münchner Neueste Nachrichten*. Fechenbach's ex-wife Martha Czernichowski played an important role as a witness for the prosecution against her ex-husband. She had written a nine-page denunciation that played a major role in Fechenbach's arrest. Under the pretext that it was Jewish revolutionaries who were encouraging antisemitism, her attorney, David Weiler, who was Jewish like her (and would also later emigrate to Palestine), advanced the argument that his client's and his own cause was the protection of Bavarian Jews.[188] He wrote a letter to the public prosecutor saying that he felt "honor-bound as a patriot . . . to expose [the man] who was to blame for so much misfortune for us Germans and especially for Bavarian Jewry." He also conceded publicly that his client, at his instigation, had offered incriminating material for Cossmann to evaluate in order "to lend support to this champion opposing the guilt lie out of patriotic motives."[189] So once again, as in the past, the old argument that Jews had to make a special effort to prove their patriotism served as a motif for the incrimination of Jewish revolutionaries.

The Fechenbach trial, which was also intended to be a Bavarian counterpart to the trial under way in Berlin against the murderers of Walther Rathenau, was conducted before a People's Court, with Karl Hass as the presiding judge. It ended with a judgment that was devastating for Fechenbach. The accused was sentenced to eleven years in prison and being deprived of his civil rights for ten years. The pacifist and former Reichstag deputy Hellmuth von Gerlach stated in the Social Democratic paper *Vorwärts*: "The living Fechenbach has to atone for the dead Eisner."[190]

Antisemitism did not play a role in the trial, at least not on the surface. But it clearly overshadowed the trial, as was evident from a question that Judge Hass addressed to Hirschberg: the judge wanted the defense attorney's assurance that Hass had conducted himself properly with respect to the "Jewish question." In the same vein, Hass condemned every pogrom not only as an affront to Jews, but also as an injustice against the German fatherland.[191] Yet even if Hirschberg absolved Hass of the charge of antisemitism, he complained about the "total lack of rights for the defendant" in this trial, which was held before a People's Court that initially denied the defense an opportunity even to inspect the indictment: "All guarantees of an impartial verdict that go without saying in a modern state founded on the rule of law were suspended in this unconstitutional and unlawful proceeding."[192] The judge, according to Hirschberg, had himself assumed the role of prosecuting attorney.

There was an interesting kind of punch line concluding the entire affair, if one bears in mind which judges were assigned, at the insistence of the Reichstag, the task of writing up a report on this trial to the Bavarian Court of Appeals. The report was meant to settle the matter of whether there had been procedural errors in the trial and whether Judge Hass had been guided by political motives. The fate of a Social Democratic Jewish defendant accused of treason now lay in the hands of three judges, two of whom would just a few months later themselves participate in Hitler's attempt to topple the republic in Bavaria in preparation for a nationwide National Socialist upheaval. One of these judges was Erich Pöhner, the right-wing former police chief, and another was Theodor von der Pfordten, a close confidant of Justice Minister Franz Gürtner.[193] Four months later, when Fechenbach's attorney Max Hirschberg finally received a copy of the report (issued on October 30, 1923) confirming the legality of the trial, Pöhner was in jail and the report's author, von der Pfordten, was no longer alive. On November 9, 1923, he had been marching with Hitler and Pöhner to the Feldherrnhalle, where he was shot dead. The "Emergency Constitution" found in his coat pocket—clearly intended as a provisional constitution for the Reich in case the putsch succeeded—included a clause stating that the property of all "members of the Jewish people" could be confiscated.[194] Von der Pfordten was treated as one of the National Socialist movement's first martyrs and was among the persons to whom Hitler dedicated his book *Mein Kampf*.

Max Friedländer, who had once had a friendly relationship with the Bavarian Court of Appeals justice, recalled a conversation from 1922 in which von der Pfordten, one of the highest-ranking judges in the Free State of Bavaria, had justified the murder of Walther Rathenau to him: "As I expressed my horror at this, he replied to my surprise that political murder is sometimes necessary in turbulent times if it involves political parasites. I took the liberty of asking who should get to decide whether the victim was a political parasite; he preferred to leave that up to the Messrs. Murderers." Friedländer finished this observation by mentioning von der Pfordten's role in the Hitler putsch: "The same man who had presented the Jew Friedländer as a model and teacher to the younger generation 1½ years ago fell in front of the Feldherrnhalle as an enthusiastic adherent of Adolf Hitler."[195]

Talk of a German Dreyfus trial quickly made the rounds.[196] *Die Weltbühne* lamented just one difference between Fechenbach's trial and the sensational trial of the innocent French-Jewish officer Alfred Dreyfus thirty years earlier: there was no German Émile Zola defending Fechenbach (a reference to the French writer who was the best-known public champion of the wrongly accused Jewish officer). While there was a great deal of protest, where, the journal wondered, was the outcry from a leading German intellectual? Where was Heinrich Mann in all this?[197] In a number of German cities, at least, there were some protest demonstrations and expressions of solidarity, even from prominent intellectuals, and a petition calling for Fechenbach's release was signed by thirty thousand citizens.[198]

The political dimension of the sentence against Fechenbach could be seen not only in the extensive press coverage but also in its prominence as a subject of parliamentary debates: one in the Bavarian Landtag lasted for two days in November 1922, and a second debate took place in the Reichstag in July 1928. In the Landtag, Justice Minister Gürtner defended the sentence, as did deputies from the BVP and German Nationalists.[199] Outside Bavaria, the Bavarian government's treatment of the Fechenbach sentence and the conclusions drawn from the trial about Germany's innocence in the outbreak of the war drew disconcerted reactions and a certain sarcasm. The representative of the Reich government in Munich reported back to Berlin: "Justice Minister Dr. Gürtner from the Middle Party [the Bavarian wing of the German Nationalists] responded to the inquiry in a speech whose scope and wordiness was not entirely in conformity with the substantive content." The government in Berlin saw "the best guarantee for the impartiality

in the administration of justice . . . in an objectively dispassionate juris-
prudence as ensured by the training and character of Bavarian judges."
Gürtner himself had to admit that Judge Hass "had often deviated from
the strict line of wise restraint; yet this was humanly excusable, given
the temperament of the judge in question and the long duration of the
trial."[200]

In a more critical judgment, the historian Friedrich Thimme, summoned as an expert witness, faulted Judge Hass in a memorandum for
hardly even trying "to liberate himself from that Bavarian mentality that
intrinsically sees a traitor in every one of Eisner's followers."[201] The Austrian consul general registered his consternation in a report to the Foreign Ministry in Vienna: "In the case of Fechenbach (Eisner), today's
Bavarian politicians are convinced that there is no way things could have
been done any better, and in response to the objection that foreign
countries are hardly even taking notice of the trial taking place, Bavarian
cabinet ministers and parliamentary deputies declare, with a naiveté
that is positively delightful, that Germany's innocence has been proven
for good, since it has been established, after all, by a court of law.'"[202] For
a leftist journal like *Die Weltbühne*, it was clear after the Fechenbach
sentencing "how in Bavaria, ever since Müller-Meiningen has been Justice Minister, there arose a variety of judges less concerned with substantive legal findings in the practice of their profession than with manifesting an ambition to solve political problems. The courtroom became
a political stage."[203]

The antisemites, however, were feasting their eyes on the spectacle
of a Jewish socialist condemned for treason. Max Maurenbrecher,
editor-in-chief of the *Deutsche Zeitung*, a newspaper inclined toward
pan-German nationalism, had reported on the Fechenbach trial under
the headline "The Jewish Forgery" and discussed Jewish collective guilt
for harm inflicted on the German people. As punishment, he demanded
that Jews' civil rights be rescinded. When a lawsuit ensued, the Berlin
District Court acquitted him, "since, according to the court, no incitement to violence can be found in the incriminating article."[204]

The expert legal opinions that were able to demonstrate a wrongful
conviction also allowed a new Bavarian government, which embarked

on a more moderate course under Prime Minister Heinrich Held following Kahr's resignation, to stop insisting that Fechenbach serve out
the rest of his sentence.[205] He was set free on December 20, 1924, the
same day Erich Mühsam and others sentenced for offenses during the
council republic left the prison in Niederschönenfeld. Even more in-
triguingly, Adolf Hitler and Ernst Pöhner were set free the same day,
barely a year after they had attempted to bring about a violent overthrow
of the government in Bavaria.

A personal epilogue to the trial explicitly touched on the Jewishness
of the parties to this case. The attorney Philipp Löwenfeld felt personally assaulted by Cossmann. After he had been repeatedly characterized
as "unpatriotic" (*vaterlandslos*) in the *Münchner Neueste Nachrichten*,
Löwenfeld addressed an open letter to its editor. In this letter, he told
Cossmann that the paper's characterization amounted to "an accusation
of which you know only too well the kind of consequences it can have
in a time as agitated as the current one." Löwenfeld suspected that Cossmann was directly behind this denunciation, as a way of rendering the
attorney harmless. Löwenfeld thought it was especially pathetic that it
was a person with a Jewish background (Löwenfeld continued to call
Cossman a Jew) who was supplying the antisemites with ammunition.
If Cossmann was not prepared within three days to disassociate himself
from this accusation, Löwenfeld would take the liberty of "characterizing him as a man who, under cover of anonymity, is plying malicious
and murderous propaganda against an objective opponent, [a man]
who, as a Jew, also ignites murderous antisemitic instincts."[206]

The words coming at the end of the Fechenbach trial demonstrate
once again the full extent of what Martin Buber, writing three years
earlier, had called a "nameless Jewish tragedy." This was not just about
revolutionaries like Eisner and Fechenbach, or Landauer and Toller. It
was also about those who, by word or deed, were trying as hard as they
could to disassociate themselves from their Jewish family backgrounds,
as Arco and Cossmann were doing.

In 1930, the philosopher and journalist Theodor Lessing wrote a book
entitled *Jewish Self-Hatred*. With this publication, Lessing took up a
question that had been a prominent topic of conversation in Jewish

circles. There had always been Jews who turned their back on their own community and, as renegades, became the Jewish community's worst enemies.[207] Heretofore their number had been small, and it remained so even in the twentieth century. Nevertheless, it seemed hard to believe that there were now Jewish people who were allying themselves, however sporadically, with their mortal enemies on the far right. Paul Nikolaus Cossmann was not among the cases treated by Lessing. But his book does discuss more radical Jewish exponents of antisemitism like Arthur Trebitsch, who was born in 1880 to a Viennese silk manufacturer. Trebitsch would come under the influence of his contemporary Otto Weininger, who was regarded as the prototype of the modern Jewish antisemite. At a young age, Weininger took his own life, not least out of despair over his Jewish ancestry. Trebitsch did not follow his mentor on the path to suicide, but he was antagonistic toward his Jewish surroundings and his own family, even taking them to court, and in the 1920s he promoted the emerging Nazi Party in Austria.[208]

He was not related to Ignaz Trebitsch-Lincoln, who also turned up briefly in Munich and was one of the most impenetrable figures in an era that certainly did not lack inscrutable characters.[209] His appearance on the scene gives a clear sense of the wide range of actors perceived as Jewish in the Munich of the early 1920s, reaching all the way into the far right political scene. Trebitsch-Lincoln was born in 1879 in Hungary but converted to Protestantism in England before working as a missionary to Jews in Canada. In the next stage of his checkered career—while a newly naturalized British subject—he ran for office as a virtually unknown Liberal Party candidate in 1910, contesting a House of Commons seat that represented the Darlington constituency in Durham County in northeast England. Surprisingly, Trebitsch-Lincoln won this election and became an English member of Parliament for a few months. After some of his commercial ventures failed, he offered his services to the Germans as a spy in the First World War. Picked up by the British authorities, he then spent three years in an English prison for different fraud crimes. In 1919, he was deported and surfaced in Germany. This was where the former Canadian missionary and ex-MP, born a Hungarian Jew, got involved in the German nationalist and Munich scene.

In 1920, Trebitsch-Lincoln seems to have backed the Kapp Putsch in Berlin, according to the extant sources. After the coup's failure, he fled to Munich, where Ernst Pöhner, the police chief, protected him from the detective sent by the Reich government in Berlin. Although there was a reward for Trebitsch-Lincoln's capture, Pöhner equipped him with new papers and a new name, Heinrich Lamprecht.[210] Two days later, he showed up at the Hungarian consulate in Munich and received an additional passport, this time under the name of Vilmos Ludwig, a journalist by profession residing in Munich. Equipped with these new papers, he made his way to the town of Rosenheim, near the Austrian border, with the aim of joining Ludendorff and his followers, who were hatching their conspiratorial plans there in the general's house. The conspirators included the Freikorps leader Lieutenant-Commander Hermann Ehrhardt and Major Franz von Stephani, who was under indictment for murder. The plans, to which the Organization Escherich (or Orgesch, named after its leader Georg Escherich) was also privy, were meant to bring about a staunchly right-wing nationalist, Bavarian-Austro-Hungarian state, an annulment of all the peace treaties, and a "White International" of counterrevolutionaries.[211]

Those on the right and on the left were now accusing each other of supporting this dubious character going by the name of Trebitsch-Lincoln. When the liberal *Frankfurter Zeitung* and the Social Democratic *Münchener Post* pointed out the close ties between Trebitsch-Lincoln and the conservative *Münchner Neueste Nachrichten*, the latter paper countered: "In their partisan zeal, the socialist papers that are using the 'Frankfurter Zeitung' as a prop, overlook how it is this paper, with its unnational and racially alien views, that nationalist working-class circles clearly see through and reject." The *Bayerischer Kurier* outdid these anti-semitic allusions of the *Münchner Neueste Nachrichten* regarding the center-left newspapers' references to a link between Trebitsch-Lincoln and the Organization Escherich: "These papers have only overlooked the fact that Herr Trebitsch-Lincoln—a Hungarian Jew by birth and, as such, closely linked to the circles who, for their part, are linked to the people from the 'Frankfurter Zeitung' and the [Social Democratic newspaper]

'Münchener Post'—was and still is actually collaborating with Social Democracy."[212] As if this were not enough, in 1921 the Communist paper *Rote Fahne* claimed a direct link between Trebitsch-Lincoln and "Herr Mussolini, editor-in-chief of 'Popolo d'Italia,'" (even though the future Duce was not that well known at the time).[213]

Munich police files testify to the utter confusion that the confidence man Trebitsch-Lincoln was also causing for the authorities in this case: "By birth he is a Hungarian Jew. . . . He played a quite terrible part during the Kapp Putsch, where he was the right hand for the [provisional Kapp government's] chief press officer at the time," the Munich police report says. In that position, according to a report from the Civil Defense Guard "Orka" (short for Organization Kanzler, named after another Freikorps member who collaborated with Escherich's Orgesch militia) located in the Chiemgau region of Upper Bavaria, Trebitsch-Lincoln had been conducting propaganda on behalf of England. "As time went on he brought all the participants in the Kapp Putsch . . . to Budapest. Here he attempted, via Colonel Bauer, to gain influence over Hungarian politics."[214]

In fact, Trebitsch-Lincoln used the identity papers forged for him by the Munich police chief to flee the city. Initially, he went to Vienna, where he received a new ID from the Hungarian ambassador—this time he would be known as Dr. Tibor Lehotzky, an attorney—before heading to Budapest, where a short time earlier Admiral Miklós Horthy had been elected regent for life. There Trebitsch-Lincoln met with his German allies and a Hungarian delegation that included the former cavalry officer Pál Prónay, who had been accused of involvement in pogroms against Jews, although he continued to enjoy Horthy's trust. The description of Trebitsch-Lincoln from Prónay's perspective does not sound very flattering. Max Bauer, the Ludendorff adviser and participant in the Kapp Putsch, "introduced me to a fat, small, dark, very Jewish-looking man whom he called Herr Lincoln. As soon as the man started to speak German, it was clear to me that he was a Jew." Thereupon Prónay took Bauer aside and told him the German's friend was a Jew, and that the Hungarian officer did not talk to Jews. Bauer assured him he could absolutely trust Herr Lincoln, but Prónay refused: "One cannot trust any Jew so long as there is even the slightest breath in his body."[215] For his part, Trebitsch-Lincoln saw his grandiose plans failing. These plans had envisioned uniting "all the right-wing elements of Germany who are ready for this counterrevolutionary action and who were already behind the Kapp putschists, then the Hungarians, and furthermore all the Russian monarchists, the Ukrainian and Belorussian emigrés, the Sudeten Germans, and the right-wing-oriented elements of Austria." But when, in the end, it was decided to carry out just one coup restricted to Bavaria rather than this broader joint action encompassing all of central Europe, Trebitsch-Lincoln withdrew—out of disappointment (according to his own statements).[216] According to another account, however, he feared for his life because of the personal attacks on him owing to his Jewish ancestry. So he absconded—not for the first time during his checkered career—into the enemy camp, taking important files along with him.[217]

What were Trebitsch-Lincoln's motives for his involvement in right-wing extremist causes? In considering the answer he himself gave to this question, one is reminded of Eisner's murderer Count Arco, who wanted to become socially accepted in right-wing radical circles by committing an antisemitic act. Trebitsch-Lincoln formulated his position this way: "I wanted to show people that a man 'of Jewish ancestry' had more honor and decency in his body than this whole society taken together. And I already had my plan prepared."[218] From Arco through Cossmann to Trebitsch-Lincoln, the picture that emerges is one of extremely different figures who nonetheless had one thing in common: the rejection of their family background that was at least partly Jewish.

The Munich police reported on Trebitsch-Lincoln one more time when he resurfaced in the Bavarian capital—as it happened, just a few days before the Hitler-Ludendorff putsch. He was spotted at the Hotel Regina accompanying a deputation that included supposedly Chinese diplomats, General Ludendorff, and Erwin von Scheubner-Richter, a former diplomat and friend of Hitler who would be killed only days later at the Feldherrnhalle. The police report once again mentioned

Trebitsch-Lincoln's ties to Cossmann: "Upon departing General Ludendorff's villa, Trebitsch mentioned the 'Münchner Neueste Nachrichten' as the next destination. Trebitsch actually had himself driven in front of the Neueste Nachrichten."[219] Finally he disappeared from Munich, as clandestinely as he had suddenly resurfaced there. But like so much else about Trebitsch-Lincoln, his connection to Cossmann and the *Münchner Neueste Nachrichten* remained murky.

5

The City of Hitler

Munich is the city of Hitler, the leader of the German *fascisti*; the city of the *Hakenkreuz* [swastika], this symbol of popular defiance.[1]

—THOMAS MANN, JUNE 1923

Sukkoth 5684 (September 1923)

Sukkoth, the Feast of Tabernacles for the Jewish year 5684, began on the evening of September 23, 1923, on the Gregorian calendar. Especially in the neighborhoods of Lehel and Isarvorstadt, where many families from Eastern Europe had settled and lived a very traditional Jewish life, a self-built hut called a sukkah would typically be set up in a back courtyard or on a balcony. The sukkahs, often comfortably furnished, provided a visible sign of the Jewish presence in these neighborhoods. For a whole week Orthodox Jews would eat their meals in these temporary accommodations that recalled the story of the exodus from Egypt, when the Israelites had no time to build solid houses. This year Sukkoth was an ill-starred celebration.

As reported in the local press, a sukkah in a courtyard on Wagmüllerstraße burned down during the night of September 28. "The hut was about 4 meters long, 3 meters wide, and 3 meters high, with homely furnishings: a table, chairs, rugs etc. Also catching fire were the residential building's window frames; the windows shattered up to the second floor, and thick clouds of smoke penetrated into the lodgings." An anti-semitic motive was immediately suspected and later corroborated because, on the same night, several windows in the nearby Ohel Jakob synagogue had been shattered by stones. "The perpetrators could not be identified," said a laconic press statement. That same night, "the old men who had gathered in an Israelite prayer room on Reichenbach-straße [were] insulted in a crude manner by several young people."[2]

"All the Lazy and the Vicious . . . Rushed, as if Magically Drawn, to Munich"—The Capital of Antisemitism

The events on Sukkoth in 1923 were directly related to the transfer of government, only days before, to Gustav von Kahr as Bavaria's state commissioner general, a powerful office invested with extensive political authority. Jews already knew from his first tenure in office in 1920 that he was not kindly disposed toward them. Now he attempted to implement what he had been unable to do in 1920: the expulsion of East European Jews from Bavaria. The event-filled autumn of 1923 culminated in the National Socialists' failed attempt to place an openly antisemitic movement in charge of the Free State of Bavaria and the German Reich.

Numerous writers recognized the signs of the times and abandoned Munich and Bavaria in the 1920s. In 1924, Bertolt Brecht moved to Berlin, Lion Feuchtwanger followed in 1925, Ricarda Huch in 1927, and Heinrich Mann in 1928. From a safe distance, Feuchtwanger wrote his novel *Success*, in which, as early as the end of the 1920s, he was already mercilessly describing Hitler's rise in Munich when he wrote: "In former times the beautiful, comfortable, well-beloved city had attracted the best brains in the Empire. How was it that all these had left now, and that all the lazy and the vicious, who could not find a home in the Empire or anywhere else, rushed, as if magically drawn, to Munich?"[3] Not surprisingly, National Socialists had the exact opposite perspective on this same transformation of the city: "Bavaria became the hope for all nationalist circles, Munich the asylum for all persecuted freedom fighters."[4]

Thomas Mann was already making Munich's transformation a matter for public discussion in June 1923 when he characterized his adopted hometown as "the city of Hitler." He deliberately placed this change in the context of antisemitism's rise. For him, Judaism represented above all the spirit of literary criticism in which the values of a democratic Europe were expressed. But in Munich—according to what Mann wrote half a year before the Hitler putsch (and published in the literary magazine *The Dial* in October)—this spirit hardly existed anymore by 1923. What dominated instead was völkisch thinking, symbolized by the swastika. In the city of Hitler, Judaism had "become exposed to a popular disfavour which on occasion takes on the most drastic forms."[5] This son of a Hanseatic patrician from Lübeck who remained in Munich until 1933 increasingly disassociated himself from the city's political developments and cultural decline. He wrote later in his novel *Doctor Faustus* that Munich "would change its cozy sociability into chronic depression."[6]

Influenced by Germany's hyperinflation, economic distress, and political crisis, as well as by Mussolini's successful March on Rome in Italy, right-wing radical forces in Munich felt as if they were on the rise. The year 1923 began with several clearly visible anti-Jewish acts in the cultural sphere. On January 5, 1923, Nazi riots disrupted the premiere of Lion Feuchtwanger's play *The Dutch Merchant* at the Residenztheater. He had spoken prophetically in 1920 in the story "Conversations with the Eternal Jew" (see chapter 4) about a group of right-wing radicals interrupting a staging of the dramatic poem *Nathan the Wise* by the Protestant German Enlightenment writer Gotthold Ephraim Lessing with the argument that "Lessing's real name was Levi."[7] Three years later, this vision became reality—not on the stage, but in a movie house.

Nothing did more to highlight the cultural difference between Munich and Berlin than the (non-)screening of the film *Nathan der Weise* at the beginning of 1923. Basing his movie on Lessing's classic tale of tolerance, the German-Jewish director Manfred Noa filmed this material with a very elaborate staging that involved huge battle scenes and a

monumental set of an "Oriental" character. The title role was played by
Werner Krauß, who would later compromise himself by helping to
make the Nazi film version of *Jud Süß*, in which he portrayed a number
of Jewish characters. In *Nathan*, however, his acting was still free of antisemitic stereotypes. The producer was Erich Wagowski, using his
Bavaria-Filmkunst firm. Although the film was shot in Munich's Emelka-
Studios, the premiere took place in Berlin, on December 29, 1922. The
response to the movie in Berlin was extremely positive. One review
said: "With these recordings, which demanded very serious and detailed preparations lasting weeks, director Manfred Noa has earned a
glorious chapter in the history of filmmaking. Everything was set up so
splendidly and appropriately that this can only be appreciated and admired!" The magazine *Film-Echo* interpreted the "spontaneous applause
at the end" as an indication "that the [movie's] general tone is clearly
fleshed out and undoubtedly deserving of recognition." The tabloid *B.Z.
am Mittag* praised "the humanity that penetrated the hearts of the audience."[8] The attendance figures in Germany as well as abroad were so
overwhelming that stock prices for Emelka, which owned Bavaria-
Filmkunst, rose to the top of all German film industry shares.[9]

In Munich the situation was completely different. There a hostile attitude began to take shape against a film that was preaching tolerance
toward Jews at a time when a pogrom atmosphere was prevailing in the
city. The film also had a Jewish director and producer. The movie's rejection in Bavaria had already started to take shape in September 1922,
when the two censors evaluating it for the Film Review Board, Councilor Wilhelm Werberger and Father Schiele, gave the film a negative
rating. The officer in charge of public order and security in the Munich
police department criticized the positive depiction of the Jewish protagonist, which hearkened back to Lessing's own Enlightenment-era
classic: "The naked truth about this film's content is that it says: The Jew
is everything, the others, whether Christian or Turk, are nothing. . . .
Not only in Munich, where this can almost be said with certainty, but
elsewhere as well, the film is bound to elicit opinion and counter-
opinion straightaway in the cinema. In all probability this will result in
agitated debate and, if experience is any guide, also to acts of violence,

so that the film seems to be unusually suited to endangering public order and security." Father Schiele made it clear that the film was bound to be provocative in antisemitic Munich: "The overwhelming accentuation of the Jew as the best human being by far, behind which all the others have to take a distant second place, is bound—especially at this time, where opinions about this are quite the opposite, especially among the broad masses—to hurt the religious feelings of both the Catholic and the Protestant part of the population."[10] The *Völkischer Beobachter* expressed its revulsion even more clearly. Especially "in Munich, the stronghold of the antisemitic movement," the Nazi paper said, it was "a crime—at this time when an enemy lashed on by the furies of revenge is brutally suppressing the most elementary human rights—to drive out with all their might the last remnant of the German people's will to shake off its servitude via this kind of mendacious Jewish concoction dripping with hypocritical humanity."[11]

In spite of the two censors' dismissive view, the Film Review Board let the film be released for public presentation in Munich, on the grounds that antisemitic incidents were not attributable to the film's contents but rather to "the people's mistaken conception" about the movie. Yet since the owner of the Regina-Lichtspiele, the movie house where the premiere took place on February 9, received threats to destroy the cinema if there were additional showings, the film was immediately taken off the program. Previously, National Socialists had already tried without success to destroy the film's negative. The Bavaria-Filmkunst director had even arranged to give the editor of the *Völkischer Beobachter*, Hermann Esser, a private showing in order to convince him—in vain, as it turned out—that the film's political material was harmless. It was telling, for this period, that the owner of the cinema did not even bother to turn to the Munich police for help. It was known that this police force was riddled with National Socialists. Following the Regina-Lichtspiele's cancellation, no other movie house in Munich was prepared to show the film.

Screening the film version of a German literary classic that preached the idea of religious tolerance had become impossible in "the city of Hitler." This tells us something about the power structure in Munich, where the NSDAP had now risen to become the dominant group among the city's numerous right-wing extremist organizations and where the Nazis, supported by a police leadership favorably disposed to them, could successfully intimidate movie house proprietors.[12]

Yet it was not only on the stage and screen but also on the city's streets that Jews in Munich no longer felt secure. In March, therefore, the Association of Bavarian Israelite Communities sent a letter to the Bavarian state government in which it stated that for months Munich's Jewish population had been "injured in its honor, livelihood, and peaceful engagement on the job and in society by public assaults and in the press, by public assemblies and individual terrorist acts, by threats and preparations to carry them out."[13] Once again, a delegation of Jewish communities met with the government, this time with the new prime minister, Eugen Ritter von Knilling, in order to demand that the authorities offer protection against the threat of antisemitic violence. And once again the outcome was as sobering as it had been the year before. The prime minister "received" the delegation's concerns "with interest and goodwill." But no effective measures were taken by the government.[14]

In spite of supplications like this, tensions kept escalating. At the very beginning of 1923, there was a press report about an attack on an American citizen in Schwabing, an incident that prompted Erich Mühsam to comment (from the Munich quarter of his jail cell):

[A] really grave incident just took place on Georgenstraße in Munich. There, around 11 o'clock in the evening, a man was stopped by National Socialists who demanded that he prove he wasn't a Jew. His passport, which identified him as an American, was not enough for the Teutons, and the man had to unbutton the fly of his pants and prove that he was not circumcised. It is inconceivable what would have happened to him if, say, a small foreskin operation had been performed for hygienic reasons, as is the case for countless non-Jews. Only it is clear what would have then been done to the pigs who were manifesting their Germanness with this compulsory exhibition; the same thing that is now being done to them: nothing at all. It will be explained that they could not have been investigated, which is also true, since nobody will try to make sure they are sought. In America they will be pleased about the opportunities to which peaceable travelers are subjected in the once so hospitable Munich. We may also tell ourselves: things like this are already the immediate precursors of pogroms, which poor devils of Jewish hawkers and junk dealers will have to find convincing. For the rich Jews will be protected by the stock exchange and industry, which they use because of their common interest in helping to finance the exploitation of the poor, and it is also from these very circles that the propaganda about killing Jews is financed. There is this difference between Jew and Jew, the same as between rich and poor, between bourgeois and proletarian, between the accused on the right and the accused on the left. But one hand does not cut off the other hand's fingers, even if the hands' bearers are Swastika-Hitler and the Nationalist Jew Siegmund Fränkel.[15]

Here, once again, Erich Mühsam was lunging out with another sideswipe at the same Siegmund Fraenkel who, as spokesman for Orthodox Jewry in Munich, had previously engaged in a war of words with him and who, in that earlier exchange, had refused to acknowledge Mühsam as a Jew. A few months later, however, Fraenkel himself became the victim of a brutal antisemitic attack. As vice president of the Chamber of Commerce and a member of the Bavarian and Reich Railway Council, Fraenkel, as mentioned earlier, did not shy away from publicly denouncing the methods of police chief Pöhner, and right-wing extremists never forgave him for this.

When Fraenkel and his family returned from a trip on June 23, 1923, he was mobbed as he exited a streetcar and accused of having only "stolen goods" in his luggage. He was then hit on the head with a blunt object. His son was also injured at the time. "When Fraenkel jr. confronted the speaker [accusing him] while alighting with the others, he received a blow in the face.... The perpetrators fled without being identified." The Fraenkel family went immediately to the police to report the incident. Once they finally arrived home, the assaults continued. Frau Fraenkel was now beaten in front of her own front door "by a local merchant known to the police" in an act accompanied by an antisemitic tirade: "If one more Yid were to be turned out, I would also have enjoyed it."[16] The *Münchner Neueste Nachrichten* condemned this "cowardly and unfounded attack on a deserving, strictly nationalist man." He "was one of the very few men, both during the time of the councils and afterward, who stood up courageously and resolutely against the rule of Levien, Leviné, and comrades, against Bolshevism. This opposition arose out of the strictly patriotic, state-upholding attitude held by Fränkel, who had been economic adviser to Reich Chancellor Hertling during his chancellorship." But above all, there was one thing the *Münchner Neueste Nachrichten* feared: the perpetrators of this crime were damaging the city's reputation.[17] Thus, a few days later the paper noted: "Such acts of brutality are unfortunately already the order of the day in Munich: they endanger public security in an intolerable manner and damage our tourist town at its most sensitive."[18]

The Social Democratic *Münchener Post*, by contrast, openly admitted: "The perpetrators escaped: does anybody wonder why?"[19] A few days later, the newspaper answered its own question: "The person responsible for order here is the senior bailiff Frick, who makes no secret of his antisemitic convictions. . . . The assault was on Thursday night. But an official report has not reached us until today, early on Saturday!"[20] The *Völkischer Beobachter* was openly rejoicing. It said that Fraenkel's son had behaved impudently, his father had stood by him, and they were only receiving their just punishment: "If the 'Münchner Neueste Nachrichten' regrets that these kinds of things diminish Munich's standing and cause it to suffer damage, we must admit that we are happy if Munich gradually gets the reputation of being a place where it is better for Jews and other strangers not even to enter the city."[21]

Shortly afterward, the kind of strangers who were more than welcome in these circles were coming to Munich en masse, and they were hardly upset by this attack on a Jew. In July 1923, the city was host to three hundred thousand participants in the German Gymnastics Festival, which was almost like a preview of future Nazi Party rallies. It turned into a demonstration of the völkisch German spirit—and into an event seized by the National Socialist movement for its own aims.[22]

In the late summer and autumn of that year, the number of antisemitic incidents increased throughout Bavaria.[23] Not even prison inmates were exempt, as noted by Erich Mühsam in his diary on August 14, 1923: "The day before yesterday in the evening, in front of the fortress [Nieder-schönenfeld prison], there was yet another antisemitic demonstration that, it goes without saying, did not encounter any interference from the armed forces of the administration. . . . It blared with this resounding final serenade: 'Throw out the Jewish gang, out of the German Father-land, we do not want and we do not need any Jew republic.'"[24]

As was also the case with the Munich police, nobody expected that the Bavarian government would take any action against this. One incident from the resort town of Bad Kissingen documents the state government's rejection of taking any action against antisemitic acts, out of political considerations. In September 1923, the district rabbi from Bad Kissingen had complained about acts of violence in a beer garden and about antisemitic remarks made by the administration of the spa there with regard to the "rich Israelites." The rabbi told the Ministry for External Affairs: "On the basis of these facts, many spa guests have already departed, and others are thinking of doing so if the authorities are not energetic about taking measures against this."[25] He expressed his worries about the reputation of the spa resort and asked the ministry to clarify publicly that the government disassociated itself from antisemitism, so that the international reputation of Bad Kissingen would not suffer. He himself would be glad, he said, to publicize a statement to this effect in the Jewish press in Germany and abroad.

There was an immediate reaction from inside the government, though it turned out to be different from what the rabbi was hoping for. Any such public statement "against this antisemitic behavior . . . would certainly be extremely dangerous, since it could be interpreted as the Bav. Government taking a position in the racial dispute, which would have to cause the biggest and most unpleasant stir in those circles that cultivate völkisch German thinking." Apparently, there was a greater fear inside government circles of losing völkisch-German travelers than of losing Jewish tourists. Besides, having the latter come to Bavarian spas did not seem opportune as far as this government was concerned. For, as it went on to say in an internal communication from the ministry, taking a public position against antisemitism "could be interpreted as an invitation to Jews from outside to come to Bavaria." But this was precisely what they wanted to avoid. Instead of issuing a declaration against antisemitism, the ministry and police headquarters sought "to produce a register of East European Jews who, since early 1923, have received entry visas from the German mission in Moscow to take a cure in Bad Kissingern or Reichenhall. Their number is not insubstantial." In fact, the police headquarters immediately complied with this demand and sent both a list with the names of Jewish spa visitors in general who were staying in Bad Kissingen on August 9, 1923, and a list "of Ostjuden for whom an entry visum has been granted by the German mission in Moscow since early 1923."[26] Thus, the Jewish petitioners' request backfired on them. Instead of disassociating itself from antisemitism, the Bavarian government used this opportunity to get rid of unwanted Jewish spa guests from abroad.[27]

"Tomorrow You'll All Be Hanging"—
The Hot Autumn of 1923

By the end of September, the situation had become even more aggravated for Bavaria's Jews. Gustav von Kahr, whose term as prime minister in 1920 had already been characterized by anti-Jewish actions, was brought back into office as a strong man after the abandonment of passive resistance in the Ruhr by the national government under Chancellor Gustav Stresemann. As state commissioner general, he was practically furnished with dictatorial powers. Kahr had also been appointed to this post in order to curb the influence of Hitler and the National Socialists. Yet even his first speech, in which he remarked that he wanted to rely "only on men of the German tribe," was an affront to the Jewish community. They understood all too well that this poorly coded sideswipe was aimed at them—so well that the paper *Das Jüdische Echo* published an open letter to Kahr saying: "At a terribly difficult moment, in which you assume the authority of the state and political responsibility in

Bavaria, the statement announcing your assumption of these public duties places us Jews outside the circles on which you—meaning the authority of the state—want to rely." The paper affirmed that Germany's Jewish citizens "have for ages played a part in the life of the German state and people," and that they had also proved this on the battlefield. In the future, too, they would only have Germany's well-being in mind. "If we have repeatedly neglected responding to all antisemitic attacks, we cannot silently endure having the most responsible office of state intending for us to be placed outside the state."[28]

When this letter went unheeded, *Das Jüdische Echo* published another article, full of bitterness, a week later: "It is the first time in the history of the German Reich that a responsible statesman in an official announcement makes a distinction between citizens of different kinds, and we repeatedly and emphatically raise the strongest objection against this attempt, a violation of the German constitution's basic rights, to place us Jews outside the state, to make us citizens with lesser rights." If the state commissioner general was going to oppose the "poisoning of public opinion," the paper asserted, then he should condemn the antisemitism that found expression in papers like the *Völkischer Beobachter* and the *Miesbacher Anzeiger*.[29]

Kahr did not respond to this plea from the Jewish community. Instead, he tried even harder to win allies in völkisch German circles. In so doing, he once again found easy scapegoats to target among the Ostjuden. Having failed at his first attempt to deport East European Jews during his earlier term as prime minister, he made a renewed attempt in this direction immediately after being appointed state commissioner general. On October 13, he issued a decree to deport foreigners for behavior damaging to the economy and for other offenses so vaguely defined that he could deport entire families who had already lived in Bavaria for decades. Their houses and apartments accrued to the state, a convenient side benefit during a housing shortage. As in 1920 during Kahr's first attempt at mass expulsion, this action was not applied to foreigners in general but was directed almost exclusively at Jews with an East European background, many of whom were longtime residents of Munich. In the early morning of October 17, 1923, police constables showed up to search a number of homes from among the roughly fifteen hundred East European Jews living in Munich. According to their own records, they issued orders for forty expulsions; other sources put the number at around seventy. Those affected by the orders had to leave Bavaria within fourteen days. The right to decide about complaints against the expulsions was reserved by Kahr for himself—and these personal decisions were unequivocal. From among the fifty-seven complaints lodged, he granted relief from the order in only two cases.[30]

On October 25, the Reich Chancellery in Berlin received a letter from the Reich Commissioner for the Supervision of Public Order with this announcement: "Yesterday, 60 prominent Jewish families were expelled from Munich with a deadline of 5 days. A number of Jews were imprisoned. Additional expulsion orders are pending. Without question it is intended to proceed more energetically against the Jews in Munich."[31]

The antisemitic press was completely on track with the new government's course, and in October 1923 it had stepped up its campaign against the East European Jews. On October 14, these jubilant headlines were splashed across the front page of the *Miesbacher Anzeiger*: "Out with the Jews!" and "The Ostjuden Danger."[32] But the most prominent daily newspapers in Munich were also backing Kahr. Only the Social Democratic *Münchener Post* protested against the unjustified expulsions.[33] The *München-Augsburger Abendzeitung*, which was close to the Bavarian branch of the German National People's Party, welcomed the expulsions, since "they include the most damaging elements, which as a rule have come to Munich completely indigent, or were even completely indigent before the war, and lived in dirty holes but now own stately homes, villas, autos etc.," which they had procured, the paper claimed, through usury and profiteering. It was predicted that the expulsion action would have a "welcome impact."[34] A similar tone was struck by the *Münchner Neueste Nachrichten*, which confidently reported that "among the deportees there are a number of Ostjuden who arrived in Munich penniless and figured out how to acquire huge fortunes through dubious business transactions." The newspaper did complain, however, that "this opportunity is also being used again for foolish agitation" and that no distinction was being made between the Ostjuden and the "old-established Israelites." Thus, the famous Bernheimer furniture and art store had to issue a public declaration defending itself against unfounded accusations.[35] The *Münchner Zeitung* cited Max Naumann, chairman of the Federation of Nationalist German Jews, whose main program was disassociating his group from the East European Jews. He, too, fundamentally supported the expulsions, "which are targeting real pests on German nationhood, especially those with a foreign background, even if those affected are Jews, so long as only senseless hardships [are] avoided."[36] The Jewish press closed ranks in rejecting the expulsions, with the exception of the Orthodox *Deutsche Israelitische Zeitung*, published in Regensburg, whose conservative positions were mentioned earlier. In contrast to the rest of the Jewish press, it basically approved of Kahr's policy and opposed only expulsions against those Jews who had been living in Bavaria since before the war.[37]

In contrast to the planned measures of 1920, the expulsions antici-pated in 1923 no longer counted personal fault as a decisive criterion. The distinction between Ostjuden and German Jews (or German citi-zens) also became increasingly unimportant. Thus, Jakob Reich, the chairman of the General Committee of East European Jews, depicted his encounter with an adviser to the Police for Foreign Nationals this way: "We asked: 'So do you want to deport all the East European Jews?' He replied: 'It is certainly going to be pretty much all of them, but we are not restricted to East European Jews.' Counter-question: 'So can you deport German citizens?'—to which he replied: 'It doesn't exactly have to be expulsion; we are going to order compulsory stays in the country-side in which one will have to report to the police twice daily.'"[38] Reich also evoked the forced internment of "troublesome foreigners," mostly indigent East European Jewish families, at Fort Prinz Carl outside of Ingolstadt.[39] "While housing accommodations were bearable, nutrition was quite unsatisfactory."[40] An October 1923 report said that the provi-sions had become so bad that potatoes were about the only food left over.[41] In addition, housing conditions in the old, damp, chilly camp were often described as extremely unpleasant.[42] Kahr had a telling reply to a query from the Jewish community as to why so many inmates were of the Jewish faith: offenses of this kind, Kahr said, just seemed to occur more frequently "in these circles."[43]

Many of the expulsions could only have happened because, in contrast to Prussia and other German states, Jews who were foreign nationals in Bavaria were not naturalized as a rule.[44] Philipp Löwenfeld's comment on Kahr's measures was unequivocal: "The text [of Kahr's expulsion decrees] was the most horrid and despicable ever produced in the way of antisemitic smut in Bavaria." Together with Orthodox rabbi Heinrich Ehrentreu, he made his way to Kahr to see if they could bring about a delay in the expulsions, or at least get an opportunity to seek legal remedies against them. Kahr maintained that the action was directed only against "pests," though it could certainly happen that he caught the wrong one. He insisted that he was no antisemite, but "rather was only obeying 'necessities of state.' . . . At this reception, Kahr behaved toward me with an unpleasantly tacky friendliness." It was "less important that these arbitrary acts were carried out than that he could prove himself to his antisemitic competitors by ordering them." Löwenfeld then relayed the wording of one such decree against a sixty-year-old cigarette manufacturer: "You immigrated to Munich in 1887 as a poor tobacco worker. You now own, according to what's stated here, a thriving factory and three houses in Munich. In a search of your house, two golden watches were also found. You are, accordingly, a pest to the Bavarian people and were to be deported. You have to hand over your firm within one week to a sequester to be appointed by the state commissioner general; failing that, it will be confiscated without compensation for the benefit of the Bavarian people." No provisions were made for legal remedies against these kinds of decrees. The Jewish community hesitated to go out on a limb, as Löwenfeld observed, since there was a prevailing fear "that this arbitrary antisemitic abuse of power might expand if one advocated too vigorously on behalf of the 'Ostjuden.'"[45]

In her memoirs, Lion Feuchtwanger's wife Marta recalled the case of a highly respected Austrian who owned a large lingerie and lace store in Munich. The businessman, moreover, stood out as a benefactor because he had his wares made in a monastery that also took in ailing prostitutes who had no other place to stay or who had no income. "But since he was

Das Jüdische Echo

| Erscheinungszeit: Jeden Freitag. Bezug: Durch die Postanstalten oder den Verlag. — Bezugspreis: Jährlich Grundpreis Mk. 1.—, Teuerungszahl 1 650 000 000, Einzelnummer Mk. 35 000 000. / Verlag, Auslieferung des „Jüdischen Echo": München, Herzog Maxstr. 4. | **Die Austreibung der Juden aus München** | Anzeigen: Die viergesp. Millimeter Zeile: Grundpreis 15 ₰, Teuerungszahl 1 650 000 000 / Familien-Anzeigen Ermäßigung/Anzeigen-Annahme: Verlag des „Jüdisch. Echo", München, Herzog Maxstr. 4 Fernsprecher 580⁹ Postscheck-Konto: München 398 |

Mit der Beilage: Mitteilungen des Israelit. Lehrervereins für Bayern

| Ausgabe A | Nr. 48 / 30. November 1923 | 10. Jahrgang |

FIGURE 28. *Das Jüdische Echo*, November 30, 1923: "The Expulsion of the Jews from Munich."

an Austrian Jew, he was deported along with his beautiful, elegant daughters."[46] This case, according to Marta Feuchtwanger, was one of the critical factors informing the decision that she and her husband Lion made to leave Munich and move to Berlin.

Another deportee was the dry goods and toy exporter Isaak Gelberger from Fürth, who had lived in Bavaria for more than twenty years. In January 1924, he received a summons from police headquarters in Nuremberg-Fürth ordering him to leave the Free State of Bavaria within fourteen days. As an Austrian citizen, he would not be allowed to wind up his business; instead, it would have to be continued by a manager to be appointed by the police. One of Gelberger's "crimes" went back to 1903 when, as a seventeen-year-old on the tramp, he had been twice sentenced to a few days in jail after begging for bread; a second offense had come in 1912 following a legal dispute with his former employer, for which he was fined 50 marks.[47]

Who could come to the aid of the Jews in this situation? As in 1920, those affected by the Bavarian order initially hoped that there would be protests from the governments of the states to which the Jews were to be deported. These included neighboring German states like Prussia and Württemberg.[48] In France, too, there were reports coming from the consulate general that, although nobody was surprised about Kahr's antisemitism, his attempts to deport East European Jews were being viewed as only the beginning of a wave of expulsions against foreigners as a whole.[49] The states primarily affected, Poland and Austria, were apprehensive about having to take in the deportees. The Polish consul general in Munich had clearly conveyed to the Bavarian government his state's resistance to the planned expulsions, to the point of threatening that Poland would deport German families in numbers equal to the number of Polish families the Bavarian government was expelling.[50]

The report of the Austrian consul general to the Foreign Ministry in Vienna about the "systemic expulsion of Israelite families from Bavaria" made it clear what Austria's concerns were; this report was also clearer about the anti-Jewish dimension of the operation. "To be sure, police headquarters here denies that the expulsions are directed against Jews alone, yet all the cases of which I'm aware affect Jews exclusively." The consul then described the case of Jakob Kalter, who had lived in Munich since he was twelve, was married, and had five children. For twenty years he had been the owner of a thriving clothing business. His expulsion was justified on the grounds of multiple previous convictions and because he was regarded as an economic pest. Kalter added that he had been punished with minor fines before the First World War because of offenses involving newspaper advertisements; in the old clothes trade this kind of thing was unavoidable, "which I readily believe." Regarding the accusation that he should be regarded as an economic pest, he presented several letters from which it emerged that in 1917 he had donated his entire stock of old clothes to the Clothing Office and that the prices he was asking for were regarded as exemplary.

The consul continued: "Among the Jewish members of our colony, this expulsion, taken together with the previous and ongoing expulsions of Jews, has elicited a strong element of unrest and insecurity. For if an Austrian Jew who has resided here for 20 years, who owns a business, whose children were born here and have attended schools here can be deported under such transparent pretexts, then every Austrian Jew must feel as if he is outlawed and his livelihood threatened. Hence I, too, attach great importance to this expulsion." The consul wanted to complain personally to Kahr but was received only by his deputy, Undersecretary Ernst Freiherr zu Aufsess, who pointed out—again, with an antisemitic undertone—that all the commotion was attributable to reporting in the Viennese press, "which with very few exceptions is in Jewish hands."

The representative of Austria in Munich concluded, unequivocally, "that Herr von Kahr's decree about the expulsion represents a concession to the radical antisemitic tendency of the Hitler group. . . . It is well known that Hitler's enthusiastic supporters are openly preaching the extermination of Jewry in Germany, and their talk and propaganda material are an open invitation to pogroms. Since the radical tendency . . . threatens to overwhelm Herr von Kahr, he may have decided to make this concession." The consul general concluded with a barely disguised threat to Munich: he let Herr von Kahr know than Austria was considering countermeasures.[51]

In addition to banking on pressure from Austria and other neighboring states, those affected by the expulsions hoped for pressure from the new great power emerging on the global political horizon, the United States of America. When Kurt Eisner was trying to prevent harsh peace conditions from being imposed on Germany, he had already placed high hopes in President Woodrow Wilson's liberal-minded approach. Even after the Wilson era had passed, America remained the repository of hope for all the opponents of reaction and antisemitism. There was also the fact that the significant Jewish community in the United States had direct channels to Washington. In 1923, some of its representatives who were concerned about developments in Bavaria turned directly to the State Department, which in turn asked the US embassy in Berlin and the consulate general in Munich to issue a report. The American Jewish press had reported on the incidents in Munich. An article put out by the *Daily News Bulletin* of the Jewish Telegraphic Agency on October 26, 1923, under the (exaggerated) headline "Jews Deported from Bavaria by Hundreds" claimed: "Bavarian Jewry is in the throes of an unspeakable panic. . . . The Hitler spirit controls not only the Government but also all public opinion."[52]

The acting consul in Munich was the diplomat Robert Murphy, who had arrived at the age of twenty-seven when the consulate general that had been closed in November 1917 was reopened after the war. Murphy was at the start of a long diplomatic career that would later take him to many other posts, including one as ambassador to Japan; he would continue to act as a foreign policy adviser well into the Carter administration. Looking back on 1923 in his memoirs, he complained about Washington's lack of interest in the reports he sent the State Department, forecasting the storm looming over the blue-and-white skies of Munich: "But while we were sending in our reports so earnestly, we never knew whether or not anybody in Washington read them. They were accepted in total silence. . . . No comment came from Washington when I sent an eyewitness report of the Hitler group's attempt to overthrow the government of Bavaria in 1923."[53]

When one reads Murphy's report on the antisemitic incidents from that time, however, it is hard to avoid the impression that he was trying to ease his own conscience. Rabbi Stephen Wise, president of the American Jewish Congress, sent an inquiry on October 31, 1923, to Secretary of State Charles Evans Hughes about the "most alarming situation which has developed within the German Republic. We have advices that several hundred Jewish families have been expelled from Bavaria and that many more are awaiting expulsion by order of the Dictator on the ground of their putative inability to establish the right of domicile." Murphy confirmed the danger to Bavaria's Jews, but on December 13, 1923, a month after the Hitler putsch with all its anti-Jewish excesses, he held the Jews themselves partly responsible for the anti-Jewish mood: "The existing anti-semitic feeling in Bavaria is principally the result of excesses indulged in by certain of the revolutionaries under Kurt Eisner during and after the coup d'etat of November 8, 1918. A number of Eisner's supporters were non-German Jews, including Galician, Russian, and Hungarian nationals." Commenting on the reaction of Munich's Jews to the expulsion of the East European Jews, he wrote: "It is a curious [sic] fact that among certain of the older Jewish families at Munich no objection or protest against the action was made. Several have confidentially informed me that they did not object since, in their opinion, the Jews expelled were undesirable because of dishonest business methods." And as late as January 18, 1924, Murphy's report to the State Department repeated the notion that the measures were not extreme. Murphy did not convey to Washington, however, the quite unequivocal stance against the expulsions taken by the Jewish community in Bavaria. Rabbi Wise was not satisfied with Murphy's reply and wrote to Secretary of State Hughes on January 24, 1924: "Such information as came to me does not tally with that which has been brought to you and I am trying to secure documentary information."[54]

As in earlier emergencies, another potential recipient of calls for help was the Catholic Church. Relations between representatives of the Jewish and Catholic religious communities in Bavaria were frequently less burdened than were relations between Jews and the Protestant population, since Bavarian Lutherans and their spiritual representatives had been drawn earlier toward National Socialist thinking.[55] As we have already seen, the stance taken by the Catholic Church's most important representative, Archbishop Michael Faulhaber (who had been elevated to a cardinalship in 1921), was extremely ambivalent. On the one hand, he disassociated himself from the brutal antisemitism of the street. On the other hand, he made a point of emphasizing his distance from Judaism, which he often associated with seditious tendencies. In 1922, at the sixty-second German Catholic Convention in Munich, he made the statement that would be much quoted later (and that at the time elicited opposition from Konrad Adenauer, then mayor of Cologne and later to become the first chancellor of the Federal Republic of Germany in 1949): "The revolution was perjury and high treason, suffering from a hereditary condition and branded with the mark of Cain."[56] Liberal observers detected, both at the Catholic conference in general and in Faulhaber's peace speech in particular, "antisemitic reverberations."[57] The association of revolution with Jews continued to shape Faulhaber's understanding of contemporary Judaism, as his address at the dedication of a denominational school that same year underscored: "In Bavaria there is still an army that won't let the Christian denominational school be robbed by the revolutionary Jews. The people has spoken now, and now we will see if we live in a people's state or in a Jews' state."[58]

Openly anti-Jewish violence, by contrast, was not something he would tolerate. When the situation worsened dramatically in the autumn of 1923, Faulhaber followed up on a request made to him by Gustav Stresemann, who regarded the pogrom atmosphere as extraordinarily dangerous. Stresemann had become Reich chancellor of a center-left coalition in Berlin for four months in August 1923 and was himself a target of antisemitic attacks because of his wife's Jewish ancestry. Faulhaber addressed the chancellor in a letter published simultaneously in national and local newspapers. What mattered, he wrote, was breaking down the hate that came "over our Israelite fellow citizens . . . without proof of guilt from one head to another."[59] This was similar to a formulation he had made in his All Saints' Day sermon on November 4, 1923: "With blind hatred against Jews and Catholics, against peasants and Bavaria, no wounds will be healed. . . . Every human life is something precious."[60]

Faulhaber was confronted with antisemitic reactions to his sermon and even insulted by völkisch nationalists as a "Jew cardinal" (*Juden-Kardinal*). These attacks from the right might have had something to do with the following statement by the Central Committee of Munich Catholics that appeared—certainly not without the cardinal's approval—in the *Bayerischer Kurier* on December 12, 1923: "The Herr Cardinal said nothing in his sermon other than what the commandment to love your neighbor announces and demands, [the commandment] that excludes no human being from love. Of course, he never wanted to excuse the sins committed by Jewish revolutionaries and profiteers against the German people and their well-being over the last few years."[61]

This was the same spirit in which Faulhaber spoke to Rabbi Leo Baerwald, who sought out the cardinal to thank him "for the announcement in favor of the Israelites" and to request his assistance because of his community's acute anxiety about the expulsions. Faulhaber's diary entry makes clear how great the distance was between him and his Jewish colleague: "[He] should not make so much fuss, since that impedes my broader mission. From a general Christian point of view. No contradiction to my statement about the Jewish press at the Catholic Conference. Expulsions are a political matter."[62] Munich's Jews waited in vain for any public word from Faulhaber against the expulsion of the East European Jews.

As the historian Olaf Blaschke has persuasively explained, many Catholics at that time drew a distinction between a "Christian antisemitism" that was permissible and an "un-Christian antisemitism" that should be rejected. This distinction was articulated, for example, in the entry on "Antisemitism" in the *Kirchliches Handlexikon* (a household ecclesiastical reference work) from 1907: "One can distinguish between two kinds of A[ntisemitism]. The one kind fights against Jewry as a race that includes everything this involves (meaning the O[ld] C[ovenant] as well); this Racial A. is anti-Christian." But what about the other kind of antisemitism? "The other tendency only demands special laws for the protection of the Christian population against the harmful advances of Judaism; among those holding this view are Cathol. social policy makers. Judaism has indeed . . . shown how far it has become alienated . . . from its original purpose; the greedy chase for material goods is precisely what lends it its characteristic imprint."[63]

This "permissible antisemitism" also resonated in Bavarian clerical circles during the 1920s. Take, for example, the essays written by Father Edmund Schlund, lecturer in religion at the theological-philosophical university of the Franciscan order in Munich. Schlund was clear about rejecting National Socialist antisemitism: "Catholic Christianity has never been and cannot ever be 'extremely' anti-Jewish. On the contrary, whoever attacks a people in such a programmatic fashion cannot—in spite of all reservations against the Jews—be a good Christian, since he is not acquainted with the all-embracing Christian kind of love and is preaching hatred." Nevertheless, in his book *Katholizismus und Vaterland*, Schlund had no problem characterizing Judaism in very general terms (and as a single entity: *"das" Judentum*): "Even in the antisemitic movement, the Catholic who loves his Fatherland will again have to make a clear choice. He will be at one with the antisemites in his pain about the ever-growing influence of Judaism, specifically in Germany, and in the wish to see this influence more and more curtailed. He will, above all, regret and combat the greedy hunt for money and material goods, domination in the financial realm, the destructive influence of the Jews on religion, manners, literature, and political and social life. He will certainly also have to be ever-conscious of how the Jews are racially alien. But he will not go so far as wanting to combat and drive out the Jews only because of their race, and even less so will he reject the Old Testament."[64]

This kind of attitude culminated in a 1923 statement put out by the press commission of the Catholic Associations of Rosenheim that lumped together followers of the swastika, freethinkers, Freemasons, and Jews in a single stew of "Jewish, anti-Christian spirit." The logic was simple: all those who denied the divinity of Christ were "on the side of the Jews."[65] Here National Socialism was clearly rejected, yet mentioned in the same breath as Judaism. Two years later, Siegmund Fraenkel, the spokesman for Orthodox Jews who had been so vehement about disassociating himself from the Jewish revolutionaries, was also complaining about religious agitation in Bavaria. And as early as 1919, even Rabbi Seligmann Meyer's *Deutsche Israelitische Zeitung*, which always defended political Catholicism, had to note the "attempts at agitation against Jews in Lower Bavaria" coming from nationalistic clerical circles.[66]

There were also individual voices of radical racial antisemitism inside the Catholic Church. Among the loudest of these was Joseph Roth, ordained as a priest in 1922 by Faulhaber. As early as 1919, while still a student, he had published wildly anti-Jewish articles in the *Münchener Beobachter*. In one article he wrote: "But the individual German Catholic, as a German, must also see in Jewry the alien race, the enemy of German culture and the German nation, and must fight it."[67] He subsequently joined the antisemitic German Nationalist Protection and Defiance Federation. Even as an ordained priest, Roth was publishing inflammatory antisemitic articles and calling for Catholics to emerge from their "catacomb antisemitism" and openly embrace hostility toward Jews in an act of what he saw as "self-defense." It was a matter of "deactivating the Jews," for otherwise "downfall" threatened the German people and the world. He quite openly signed his articles in the renamed Nazi paper *Völkischer Beobachter* as a curate from Indersdorf outside of Munich.[68]

Unlike public opinion at the time of Kahr's first attempt at deporting Jews in 1920, the prevailing antisemitic mood had by now put down deep roots. This time, neither the Catholic Church's official calls for moderation nor the threats of countermeasures from abroad had any effect on Kahr. In contrast to the situation he had faced three years earlier, Kahr now had almost dictatorial powers. By setting up the office of the state commissioner general, Bavaria had broken with fundamental principles of the new democracy. On top of that, the state government in Munich had fallen out with the national government in Berlin. As far as the lawyer Max Hirschberg was concerned, Kahr had established a "miniature dictatorship" that was preparing fertile ground on which the völkisch-nationalist movement could flourish.[69] According to Hirschberg, the "total dissolution of law in Bavaria under the fascist dictatorship [was] . . . already complete before the Hitler putsch of November 8–9, 1923."[70] The Munich attorney left no doubt as to what he really thought about Kahr: "This obstinate bureaucrat [Kahr] with the low, flat forehead sympathized openly with the rebels and their plans for a fascist coup in Bavaria. But, in addition, this statesman was pursuing monarchist plans that he sought to combine somehow with this völkisch coup. He was seriously turning over in his stupid brain the March on Berlin by way of the Bavarian rebels."[71]

Hirschberg may have been formulating his view especially brusquely, yet by no means was he alone in his fears. As early as the beginning of 1923, the Reich government's representative in Munich was warning about the growth of the National Socialist movement and expressing his view that the Bavarian government "is too indulgent, has proven itself too weak, at the critical moment, to keep the movement within lawful boundaries."[72] In another report, also from January 1923, the same representative informed the Foreign Office back in Berlin: "The enthusiasm of the people for the National Socialist idea surpasses by far that of the Eisner era. In general, there is a firm conviction that there will soon be a total victory for National Socialism throughout Germany. People whose sobriety and healthy political sense is tried and tested are letting themselves be swept along by the general storm. . . . Reichswehr and police of all kinds are rendering homage [to Hitler]. More and more, workers are turning to him. . . . Somebody who three years ago was infatuated with Eisner is today going through fire for Hitler."[73] As early as 1922, there was already talk in Bavaria of a possible putsch by Hitler and his allies. At the beginning of 1923, the region was thick with rumors along these lines. On March 7, 1923, the representative of the Reich government in Munich shared with the Foreign Ministry in Berlin concrete evidence of a possible National Socialist putsch.[74]

With the appointment of Kahr as state commissioner general, and against the background of a situation that was already fraught with tension throughout the country, the conflict between the Bavarian government and the Reich government escalated. Elements of this highly stressful situation included the climax of the postwar hyperinflation, the dismantling of resistance in the Ruhr region, the removal of the governments in Saxony and Thuringia made up of Communists and Social Democrats, and the Communist putsch attempt in Hamburg. Reich president Ebert had transferred executive power to the liberal democratic army minister Otto Gessler. Kahr, however, suspended the Law for the Defense of the Republic and did what he could to protect the powerful Patriotic Leagues (most of which had emerged from the Civil Defense Guards), which the Reichswehr minister wanted to disband. In addition, the Bavarian regional commander of the Reichswehr, Otto von Lossow, resisted implementing the ban on the *Völkischer Beobachter* ordered by Gessler. In the conflict between Lossow and the Reich government, Kahr backed the Bavarian commander. In a speech he delivered on October 19 at the Army District Command (Wehrkreiskommando) before the most senior on-site officers, Kahr made it clear that the "Jewish question" played a role even against the background of this conflict between Bavaria and the national government in Berlin. At stake was a "great struggle between the two world views that are decisive for the fate of the entire German people, the international-Marxist-Jewish and the national German view." Bavaria was "fated to assume leadership in the struggle for this great German goal."[75] Rumors about an imminent coup by Kahr and the formation of a Reich-wide "national dictatorship" were making the rounds.

What happened in the Bürgerbräukeller on the night of the eighth and morning of the ninth of November 1923 is well known.[76] While Gustav von Kahr was delivering a speech, Hitler stormed into the hall, silenced the crowd with a pistol shot to the ceiling, and seized control. During a roughly fifteen-minute discussion held in an adjoining room under circumstances never fully clarified, he secured assurances from Kahr and his closest comrades, Otto Lossow and Hans von Seißer, that they would support a new Reich government led by Hitler. Kahr was slated to be a stand-in for the monarchy in Bavaria, while Lossow and Seißer were to hold cabinet posts. Hitler promised his closest confidant, former police chief Pöhner, the office of Bavarian prime minister, while General Ludendorff was to have control over the "National Army." A few hours later, Kahr, Lossow, and Seißer retracted their assurances and got to work suppressing the putsch. The march undertaken by about two thousand putschists the following morning was forcibly stopped in front of the Feldherrnhalle. Fifteen of Hitler's supporters, one civilian bystander, and four policemen lost their lives. Hitler himself fled to the villa of the businessman Ernst Hanfstängl at nearby lake Staffelsee, where he was arrested two days later.

While these events can be thus summarized, some questions pertaining to the putsch will surely remain forever unresolved. Kahr's stance in particular remains obscure. His version of events—whereby he only supported Hitler outwardly, against his own convictions, and at gunpoint in the first few hours of the putsch—was treated skeptically by some contemporaries.

On the morning of November 9, numerous conservative newspapers were at first reporting approvingly about a seemingly successful putsch and about the cooperation between Kahr and Hitler. Paul Nikolaus Cossmann and the editor-in-chief of the *Münchner Neueste Nachrichten*, Fritz Gerlich, were themselves present as the events unfolded in the Bürgerbräukeller. Gerlich assured Pöhner of his solidarity, had Hitler's and Ludendorff's speeches typeset for his papers, and apparently wrote an editorial enthusiastically welcoming the new government. These were withdrawn at the last moment, however, when news of Kahr's rejection of Hitler came through. The German Nationalist *München-Augsburger Abendzeitung* also sided with the putschists, and its editor, Pastor Gottfried Traub, was still assuring Pöhner of his support the next morning.[77] That morning even the readers of the *Bayerischer Kurier*, the mouthpiece of the Catholic BVP party, learned about the "proclamation of the national revolution" and about how Kahr was now to become Bavaria's regent and Pöhner prime minister, while Hitler would be political leader of a provisional national government. In addition, they could read the following sentences from Hermann Göring's speech: "Today begins the national revolution. In no way is this aimed against Herr von Kahr, revered by all. It is not aimed against the troops, not against the police who even now are marching out of the barracks in front of our flags. This revolution is aimed exclusively against the Berlin Jew government (rapturous, unending applause and clapping of hands) . . . The government of Hitler, Ludendorff, Pöhner, Kahr, hooray!"[78]

A few days later, the Austrian consul general reported to Vienna that, according to "very reliable information," the version about Kahr and Lossow being forced by revolver to join Hitler did not correspond to the facts.[79] The attorney Philipp Löwenfeld subsequently noted: "When I set eyes on the proclamation by means of which Kahr turned his back on Hitler, I had a disagreeable feeling, which was shared by many people, namely that one criminal was seeking to gain the upper hand in a race with the other."[80] Two months after the events, a publication by the respected Munich law professor Karl Rothenbücher with the title *Der Fall Kahr* (The Case of Kahr) caused a stir because the author accused the former state commissioner general of high treason. Rothenbücher tried to prove that it was by no means under pressure from Hitler's pistol that Kahr was forced into acknowledging the putschist's leadership.[81]

How did Munich's Jews experience the events that night of November 8 and morning of November 9, 1923? Here, too, as in any situation, the experiences of Jewish contemporaries varied widely. Without a doubt, among the thousands listening to Kahr's speech in the city's Bürgerbräukeller that evening, there were some conservative Munich Jews who were surprised by the turn of events. We know about the presence of at least one such person in the audience: Dr. Ludwig Wassermann, chairman of the local branch of the Central Association of German Citizens of the Jewish Faith. Wassermann was an alcohol manufacturer who was politically close to the BVP. Max Hirschberg had this to say about him: "On the evening of November 8, 1923, a mass meeting was convened in the Bürgerbräukeller in which Kahr was supposed to proclaim a national revolution. Sitting devoutly at his feet was the Jewish Commercial Councilor W., who was then led out under arrest. To me he always will seem a symbol for the political insensitivity of many wealthy Jews who had placed their hopes in the reactionaries and then got kicked as their just deserts."[82]

In the hours that followed, the National Socialists and their supporters went on a rampage and set upon their enemies. Numerous Social Democrats were roughhoused and taken as hostages, while the offices of the Social Democratic *Münchener Post* were almost completely destroyed; in that newspaper's building alone, some 380 windowpanes were broken.[83] For most of Munich's Jews, this night represented their first real confrontation with the life-threatening horror of National Socialist terror. They came to realize that, should there be a real seizure of power by Hitler, the National Socialists seriously intended to turn their antisemitic rhetoric from words into deeds. From the vantage point of later observers, some of the details about these incidents already sound like a test run for what would happen on the same date fifteen years later, when a Nazi regime in power burned hundreds of synagogues, destroyed thousands of Jewish businesses, and deported tens of thousands of Jewish men to concentration camps.

Undoubtedly spurred on by pogrom-like scenes in Berlin's Scheunenviertel, with its large East European Jewish population, Hitler's followers started arresting a number of Jews and Social Democrats "indiscriminately as hostages."[84] Members of the right-wing Oberland League in particular scoured Munich's directory of addresses for Jewish-sounding names or looked for them next to doorbells. Occasionally, their name hunt led them to inadvertently arrest some prominent non-Jewish citizens.[85] Kahr himself wrote about this in his memoirs: "[W]hen Hitler had power in his hands for a few hours in November, his subordinates called on the suspect families at 4 o'clock in the morning in their homes, and the Social Democrats and Jews arrested during an attack on the Rathaus [town hall] under the leadership of Hitler officers in uniform were insulted and so spit upon that the swinish mess ran across their faces and down their clothes, and they were thrown like calves onto the flatbed trailer that apparently was supposed to transport them to their place of execution."[86]

In some cases the intruders smashed windowpanes, fired shots at the ceilings, and stole weapons and valuables from the homes they plundered. The police summoned for assistance reacted passively. While it was still night, numerous Jews hastily took flight from the city. Prominent Jews and Social Democrats like Carl Landauer and Erhard Auer went into hiding at nighttime. The arrests continued the following morning, although some of the "hostages" had already been released. Then things moved on to the Bogenhausen district, where the seventy-four-year-old department store owner Isidor Bach, a longtime target of antisemitic attacks, was arrested along with the attorney Julius Heilbronner. East European Jews were also a convenient target group for the Nazis to apprehend. The Jewish hostages, most of whom were brought to the Bürgerbräukeller, were threatened with being shot until the Bavarian state police finally came by to free them. The Nazi putschists broke into the city hall, where they targeted Social Democratic and Communist city councilors for arrest and gave the floor leader of the Social Democrats, Albert Nußbaum, a bloody beating.[87]

Especially hard-hit was the rabbi of the Jewish community. According to Schalom Ben-Chorin, Leo Baerwald was hauled out of his home at night, taken to a field outside the city, tied to a tree, and threatened with being shot. "But no murder was attempted at the time. Things went no further than this grey comedy, and the victim was left with a nervous shock that left its mark by causing his right eyelid to blink."[88]

The physician Rahel Straus and her husband Eli also experienced November 9, 1923, with horror. That day she received an anonymous call warning her that her husband should go into hiding; otherwise he would be picked up. Then a note was slipped under her door: "Don't send your children to school, it's too dangerous." Her account brings to mind the descriptions of the events that would take place exactly fifteen years later during the so-called *Kristallnacht*: "All along the Ring, they were picking up all Jewish men—we had been spared. And all were told: 'Tomorrow you'll all be hanging, the entire Jewish community.' . . . The street was in a complete uproar. Streicher, the wild antisemitic elementary school teacher from Nuremberg, was standing on Sendlingertor-platz and holding a vile inflammatory speech against the Jews. One was just walking by: 'Strike him down,' Streicher screamed." In retrospect Straus felt that this day was a major turning point in the life of Munich's

FIGURE 29. Julius Streicher speaking on November 9, 1923, on Marienplatz.
Bayerische Staatsbibliothek München / Bildarchiv.

Jews: "This time things turned out well, but this event did leave its mark.
It taught us what the world around us looked like. My Isa, fourteen years
old at the time, never forgot that schoolgirls in her class with whom she
had lived and learned together all these years were flinging their arms
around each others' necks [and saying]: 'Thank God, tomorrow all the
Jews are leaving the class.'"[89]

A good stroke of fortune allowed the attorney Philipp Löwenfeld to
escape that night's terror by the skin of his teeth. On the evening of
November 8, an acquaintance rang him up at his office half an hour
before midnight to tell him that he was in personal danger and should
go into hiding. There were "already Jewish hostages [who had been]
arrested in large numbers." At the last minute, Löwenfeld fell back on
an offer made by a Nazi supporter who wanted to save him and who
drove him through the city in an automobile flying a swastika flag.[90]

On the night before November 9, the Orientalist Karl Süßheim encountered the angry crowds on Marienplatz. The following morning he was at the university before seven o'clock, but a student assembly had already convened to voice their support for Hitler and Ludendorff and then join the remaining putschists marauding through the city. "They stopped in front of the Hotel Regina and vented their antisemitic feelings by shouting 'out with the Jews.'"[91]

Schalom Ben-Chorin, ten years old at the time, later wrote something that undoubtedly summarized what many of Munich's Jews felt: "This scary night is something I have committed to memory. I was overcome by horror and surprise in equal measure. The incomprehensible confronted me at close quarters. What was going on in this city in which I was born, in which my parents and grandparents lived? A section of our fellow citizens has sallied forth—to strike us dead. It was utterly incomprehensible." In Poland and Russia one was used to this, Ben-Chorin reflected; there Jews lived as strangers among the native population and spoke a different language. "But we? At home and on the street we spoke the same Bavarian-tinged German as those around us. We went to the same school as our fellow Christians of the same age and played with them . . . in the English Garden and did gymnastics together in the Turnverein Jahn."[92]

The National Socialist attempt to stage a putsch had failed. The Jewish hostages had escaped the horror one more time and gotten another reprieve. For the state commissioner general, however, the government's suppression of Hitler would prove to be a Pyrrhic victory. Only recently, Kahr's popularity had started to wane, but now his reputation, as the Reich government's representative in Munich put it, had "taken an incurable blow."[93] The Austrian consul general wrote back to Vienna in a similar vein: "The popular mood is definitely opposed to Kahr. The military and police are greeted everywhere by the crowd with howls, are booed and mocked. All around, one hears only voices against Kahr. If he were to show his face in public, he would be lynched. There is no doubt that Kahr had resolved to march toward Berlin and that Hitler merely pre-empted him."[94]

Kahr tried to slip his neck out of the noose by banning the NSDAP and its mouthpiece, the *Völkischer Beobachter*, and by simultaneously taking the Communist and Social Democratic press and Munich's only Jewish newspaper, *Das Jüdische Echo*, out of circulation. While the Social Democratic *Münchener Post* was already back on the newsstands by the end of November, the next edition of *Das Jüdische Echo* had to wait until April 1924, following Kahr's resignation. There was a clear verdict on Kahr in the paper's first new edition that spring: "Winning Jewish sympathies was something Kahr never tried." Although he had attempted to establish law and order up until the Hitler putsch, the state commissioner general could "hardly be exonerated from being guilty of having let the combat associations reach such heights that he could only keep them down by armed force."[95]

The press was reporting about solidarity rallies for Hitler, especially among Munich's students. The university had to stay closed for several days. The *Bayerischer Kurier* described a student assembly held in the atrium of the university's main building a few days after the suppression of the putsch as a "desecration of the rooms in which it convened. One inflammatory speech followed another. The Rector His Eminence Dr. Kraus, as well as Prof. Dr. Sauerbruch and Dr. Kisch, who admonished in favor of calm and prudence, were shouted down with catcalls, while every inflammatory word was celebrated with Hail and Hooray." The students reviled both the Catholic Church and Cardinal Faulhaber, whom they called a "Jew friend" and "Jew cardinal."[96]

In November, Julius Walter Levi, who worked as a spa physician in the nearby resort town of Bad Tölz, was in Munich to help his parents with their business, which had already suffered losses in the months before the putsch as a result of antisemitic calls for a boycott. He noticed that anti-Jewish agitation following the failed putsch was also being aimed against Kahr himself. Kahr, of all people, was now even said to have Jewish ancestry: "The 'street' is agitating against Kahr, and naturally the most badly behaved are again the 'Flower of the Nation,' the scamps of the University and the Technical College. The Catholics are insulted as 'Faulhaber Vassals'; it is said that the Cardinal has been bought by the Jews, who offered to pay him to renovate the Cathedral; Kahr is of Jewish ancestry (!) and has received a gift of seven Persian carpets from Gernheimer [*sic*] [the Jewish-owned Bernheimer store]."[97]

Cardinal Faulhaber, above all, was repeatedly accused of having persuaded Kahr to change his mind on the night in question and of having encouraged him to break with Hitler. The cardinal vehemently refused these accusations.[98] Undoubtedly, in order to escape any suspicion of being regarded as a "Jew lover" (*Judenfreund*), the Catholic circles engaging in anti-Jewish polemics kept upping the ante after November 9, 1923. Thus, the *Bayerischer Kurier* printed a series of articles whose antisemitic gist is hard to overlook. These articles expressed themselves in the language of "good" antisemitism, the kind that felt superior to "evil" racial antisemitism. Thus, under the headline "Lessons of November 8," we find Hans Rauch, a BVP member of the Bavarian Landtag, writing:

What would be the reason for Catholics like us to set ourselves up as special protectors of Jewry? Have we ever received any kind of promotion from them, or is what we have gotten from them rather more like hostility, partly open, partly hidden? No, we Catholics, too, take the view that the numerous East European Jews who pounced on the mortally wounded German people during and after the war should, as irksome parasites, be forced to return to their Eastern homeland as soon as possible. And we are also of the opinion that all Jews and non-Jews who can be shown to have participated in the November revolution of 1918, whether through active participation or through donations of money, should be subjected to the full severity of the law as elements endangering the state. The German people is a Christian people, is tolerant toward people of different faiths, but it demands that its Christian character be respected, and must treat everyone who openly or secretly fights against this character as harmful foreign bodies. We Catholics therefore combat in the strongest possible way the moral filth and spiritual confusion that is poured as a daily poison by a Jewish-dominated press and literature into the soul of our people. We combat this poison when it is turned against our people's German spirit, but also against its Christian spirit, combat it when it is proffered by Jewish forces, but also when put forward by other forces hostile to faith, even if dressed up in nationalist garb. We Catholics want this, but there is one thing we do not want, in contrast to the others; we do not want to join in the chorus of the general, indiscriminate hatred against that person who cannot be accused of anything more than that he was born on German soil as the child of Jewish parents. That would go against the commandment of our Savior, who certainly preached justice against all wrongdoers, but not hatred against followers of a different faith.[99]

The anti-Jewish mood that had been building since the revolution came to a head in 1923. It began to take shape slowly when the screening of *Nathan the Wise* was blocked by the increasingly influential National Socialists, emitted clearly disquieting signals when the Fraenkel family was attacked, assumed a menacing semblance with the expulsion action directed against East European Jews, and became part of a constitutional crisis with Hitler's putsch attempt. Only seemingly did the arrest of Hitler and his comrades in arm put an end to the threats against Munich's Jews. For them, 1924 began the same way 1923 had ended.

"A Mockery of the German People"—
Reverberations of 1923

The year 1924, which saw the Weimar Republic appear to stabilize after years of hyperinflation and political turmoil, did little to help Munich's Jews feel that they could now resume living in peace and security. Even if Hitler's putsch had come to naught, the house painter from Braunau was now regarded as a hero in the city, while the state commissioner general was seen as a spoilsport. "Hanging in the stationery stores are images of our 'heroes' Hitler and Ludendorff in any desired size and layout between the portrait format and postcard size, from 10 pennies up." Lodged bashfully between the two was a small portrait of Kahr, his "black hair anointed with a lot of oil," as the *Argentinisches Tag- und Wochenblatt* reported from Munich.[100] In February 1924, Kahr resigned from his office as state commissioner general and ended his career with the same position his father had once held, president of the Bavarian Administrative Court, until he was pensioned off at the beginning of 1931. He was not granted a lengthy retirement. Once in power, Hitler would avenge himself for Kahr's behavior in Munich's Bürgerbräukeller. In the course of the "Night of the Long Knives," Kahr was carried off to the Dachau concentration camp, where he was shot on June 30, 1934.

Hitler's rise was made possible by the Bavarian justice system of the 1920s, which was favorably disposed toward him. It sounded like an April Fool's joke when a Bavarian People's Court chaired by Georg Neithardt—the judge whose mild sentence for Eisner's murderer Arco had already created a sensation—scheduled April 1, 1924, as the day to pass judgment on the leaders of the failed November putsch from the year before. Hitler received the minimum sentence of five years in prison, of which he—like Pöhner—only had to serve six months; Hitler used the short term practically as a writing sabbatical to compose *Mein Kampf* in a comfortable setting. Although, as an Austrian, he should have been extradited, Judge Neithardt declared that he had proved himself by his deeds to be a German. Neithardt attributed a "pure patriotic spirit and the most noble will" to Hitler. The judge also made allowances for the thirty-seven insurrectionists among Hitler's shock troops who were accused of "abetting high treason" because they had "acted out of honorable conviction and trusting in the participation of Bavaria's leading men and patriotic circles." Their sentences to a year and three months in prison were turned into suspended sentences on probation by taking into account the time spent in detention while awaiting trial. Ludendorff was acquitted.[101] In a news flash, the *Frankfurter Zeitung* spoke of high treason being transformed into an "excusable, light felony." The sentence, said the paper, revealed Bavarian judges' lack of identification with the constitution of the German Reich under the Weimar Republic.[102] In its regular issue the following day, the publication issued its own verdict on the trial: the People's Court in Munich had issued a "mockery of the German people."[103]

For the most part, too, the members of the Oberland League who forced their way into Jewish houses on November 9, 1923, destroyed valuables, plundered, and took hostages got away with impunity. The proceedings against them did not advance beyond the pretrial stage. On September 27, 1924, the Munich Regional Court declined to issue a penal order against the persons involved, since they had not acted on their own initiative but on the orders of their commander and could not have known that those orders were not being carried out on Kahr's instructions. The prosecuting attorney's objection—that there was no written order, that the accused had looked up the names of the hostages themselves from a Munich directory, and that they should have been skeptical as far as any "order" was concerned, "if only because of its vagueness"—went unheeded. That the court was not in the least concerned about any sentencing is also evident from the fact that no procedure of any kind was even introduced against Ludwig Oestreicher, the group's commander.[104]

A few days after the mild sentence issued against Hitler, he was also rewarded politically. While the NSDAP was initially banned, its cover organization, the Völkisch Bloc, received a share of votes in Munich for the Bavarian Landtag elections on April 6, 1924, that, at 35 percent, was twice as high as in Bavaria overall. By the time of the national election in December 1924, the share of votes for this Bavarian Nazi Party affiliate receded to only 9 percent (of the Bavarian electorate voting for the Reichstag this time, as opposed to 3 percent for all Nazi Party groupings throughout the Reich). Yet even this decline hardly sent a clear signal that the failure of the putsch spelled an end to the National Socialist movement and its wave of antisemitism. Among the insurrectionists, Ernst Röhm and Erich Ludendorff obtained Reichstag seats, and Ernst Pöhner a seat in the Landtag.

That is how Kurt Tucholsky, the Jewish journalist in Berlin, was already seeing things at the beginning of 1924. He now repeated his previous advisory warning travelers to avoid Bavaria:

In the summer of Bavaria's deepest shame, fifty-one Socialist and Communist Reichstag deputies were sitting in the Bavarian mountains during their summer vacation because, after all, you can't let politics get in the way of your private life. Eisner had been murdered, Landauer crushed and plundered. Toller locked up, Mühsam tormented, Fechenbach ruined—but these fifty-one and thousands of German Jews, republicans, and dissidents of all shades gave the Bavarians the chance to make some money. Until these [Bavarians] were so dumb as to prevent every kind of tourism by increasingly crude shenanigans. . . . . Berliners who are Israelite to boot, strangers who are interested in recreational travel and not some guerilla war, foreigners who want their peace and quiet—all of them will beware of letting their travels be spoiled by Bavarians, who, moreover, are also government bureaucrats.[105]

Yet even the Jews who did not want to heed Tucholsky's warning felt increasingly ostracized whenever they wanted to travel to the mountains. For the numerous Jewish mountain climbers who lived in Munich and Bavaria, the expulsion of the Donauland Section from the German and Austrian Alpine Club in 1924 was a harsh slap in the face. The Academic Section of the Munich alpine club had already introduced an Aryan clause in 1910, and other sections followed suit. In 1921, after an avowed National Socialist was elected chairman of the alpine club, Jewish mountain climbers had found a home in the Donauland Section, which was open to climbers of every religious denomination. But now banishing this section from the larger alpine club was more than a symbolic setback for people living in a city where mountain climbing fervor ran as high as it did in Munich.

Munich's university was another area in which the city's antisemitism received nationwide attention in 1924. One of its most important researchers, the Nobel Prize–winning chemist Richard Willstätter, resigned from his chair at the University of Munich that year. The move made headlines both nationally and internationally because Willstätter insinuated that the reason for his resignation, in addition to symptoms of fatigue, lay in the appointment practices of his colleagues. On multiple occasions, he claimed, they had refused to appoint the best experts in the field because they believed that with Willstätter, the mathematician Alfred Pringsheim (Thomas Mann's father-in-law), and the physicist Leo Graetz already on the faculty of twenty-three tenured professors, there was no room for any additional Jewish professors, especially given the city's charged atmosphere after the Hitler putsch. Addressing his

Die Angeklagten des Hitler-Prozesses

Pernet   Weber   Frick   Kriebel   Ludendorff   Hitler   Brückner   Wagner
Röhm   phot. Hoffmann Mchn.

FIGURE 30. The defendants in the Hitler trial. Bayerische Staatsbibliothek München / Bildarchiv.

successor Heinrich Wieland in 1925, Willstätter made the reasons for his resignation clear: "Whenever I am in the company of friends and colleagues and a Jew knocks on the door and there are shouts from here and there saying: not at any price should a Jew be let in, then I either throw out the shouters or leave myself."[106] One part of the faculty subsequently made an effort to persuade Willstätter to change his decision, and they drew up a statement about the need to guarantee absolute objectivity in the appointment of new professors. But in the end the lack of support for this statement from all the professors led to more negative press coverage.[107] In his 1941 memoirs, Willstätter reflected once more about the occasion for his resignation, and he stuck to his earlier assessment. The atmosphere in the academic milieu also played an important role: "The universities had lapsed into a kind of right-wing radicalism." Willstätter had in mind, above all, the students who were now shouting: "No young German man should sit at the feet of a Jewish teacher in the future." Yet he was equally concerned about the attitude of his colleagues on appointment questions when the faculty refused to put the best-qualified colleagues on an appointment list "because they did not want a colleague of presumably Jewish (or partly Jewish, I know nothing about this) descent in their midst."[108]

In the following years, Bavarian politics did stabilize under the conservative government of Heinrich Held, yet even bourgeois intellectuals saw no reason to breathe a sigh of relief. In 1926, Thomas Mann warned that if Munich did not get back to its prewar liberal tradition, it would "be a provincial patriotic city with lots of war clubs moving in and nailing of flags and here and there a stab-in-the-back trial, but utterly without significance for the life, the times, and the future, for the German spirit and for the wide world outside."[109]

Munich's Jews also detected growing Nazi Party influence on local and state politics regarding religious matters. In 1925, the NSDAP in the Munich city council started its attack on kosher slaughter. Although the proposal was rejected there, the subject came up repeatedly during the following year in Landtag debates. In January 1930, the state legislature passed a ban on kosher slaughter in Bavaria with the combined votes of Nazis and Social Democrats (!) against the votes of the conservative BVP. For Orthodox Jews, the voting record of the Social Democrats was a special slap in the face and gave additional impetus to thoughts of emigration among the very observant.[110]

Yet many of Munich's Jews saw a shimmer of hope once again after the Landtag elections of 1928, when the Nazi Party's share of votes fell to only 6 percent. Even the Zionists shared this hope, as Rahel Straus recalled in retrospect:

It is odd how little we Jews, of all people, noticed the looming danger. After the period of inflation, a quiet, orderly period of construction had arrived, yet thousands had lost their last reserves, entire classes had become impoverished. . . . One was ready to recognize anybody as a leader [Führer] who promised an improvement in the situation, who named the "guilty ones": the Versailles Treaty, the Social Democrats, and above all and in the first place the Jews. We knew all of this, every week we saw the red posters that announced Hitler's speeches.

We walked past the boxes with the "Völkischer Beobachter," read the inflammatory articles, and kept moving, full of indignation. We did not realize that this "Völkischer Beobachter" was one of the most widely read newspapers in Germany at the time.[111]

It was increasingly difficult for Munich's Jews to escape proximity to the *Völkischer Beobachter* and its pernicious spirit. They kept on celebrating Sukkoth in the years to come. Yet now they had to get used to the increasing difficulty of achieving the kind of peaceful coexistence they had known before the war. Antisemitic incidents had become routine. As Schalom Ben-Chorin, the philosopher of religion who grew up in the Lehel district of Munich as Fritz Rosenthal, put it:

> Never did I feel more strongly as a Jew living in exile than on the first evening of Sukkoth, when a real Munich-style persistent rain made it impossible to take the first festive meal inside the Sukkah. ... The Rotter family and I therefore waited for the rain to end. Over and over again, one stuck one's nose out and finally, around ten o'clock in the evening, we could visit the wet and fragrant Sukkah, covered with pine twigs, on the balcony. But no sooner was the festival soup on the table than there poured down from above ... not the rain, but a garbage can intended for us by our dear neighbors. That was not at all surprising, for immediately across from the home of my pious landlord and landlady were the editorial offices of the "Völkischer Beobachter."[112]

That the Jewish Feast of Tabernacles should be celebrated within range of the editorial office of the *Völkischer Beobachter* may symbolize the new everyday life of Munich's Jews in the late 1920s. Even more of a cloud would be cast over the lives of Munich Jews by the triumph of the National Socialists in the Landtag and Reichstag elections of 1932, and their lives would experience a major rupture the following year with Hitler's appointment as Reich chancellor. But in contrast to their co-religionists in most other German cities, Munich's Jews already had a concrete notion of what was now in store for them.

6

A Variety of Perspectives

Wherever he looked things were the same as ever; they were all there again. There had been a war and a revolution, and then the last five years with their bloodshed and their stupidities; with the Liberation of Munich at the beginning and the inflation in the middle and Kutzner *coup* at the end. But the same people were sitting in office, in the Nurnberger Bratwurstglöckel, in the Club, and in the Tyrolean Café. . . . The green Isar was still rolling rapidly, and the song of Munich still went on blithering about old Peter and the never-ending good fellowship [*Gemütlichkeit*] of its citizens. It was a tough, peasant persistence; the eternal recurrence of sameness. The city simply would not admit that the last ten years had happened; it had forgotten them; it put on a candid air and shut its eyes and would not admit that anything had happened. It believed that everybody else would also forget. But in that it was wrong.[1]

—LION FEUCHTWANGER, *SUCCESS*

Gravestones

The New Israelite Cemetery in the north of Munich, dedicated in 1908, is not one of the city's sightseeing highlights. Situated between housing blocks, entry roads, and the autobahn, the graveyard has an address in the Freimann district that the visitor needs to look up very deliberately in order to locate it. The new burial ground was abused during the Second World War when parts of it were worked as a vegetable garden. For some Jews at this time, it also served as a hiding place. With the assistance of a couple who administered a Lutheran cemetery, seven of Munich's Jews were able to survive the war unnoticed by the National Socialists.

Visitors to the cemetery today can walk through rows of splendidly ornamented mausoleums replete with German sayings from a more hopeful time before the First World War; glance at the Hebrew characters on plain graves for Polish immigrants from the period of hyperinflation in the early 1920s; pass by the memorials for the Jewish soldiers killed in action during the First World War and for the victims of the Holocaust; and see a row of graves honoring the names of those who refounded the Jewish community after the Second World War, as well as the numerous new memorial slabs with Russian inscriptions for those who immigrated from the former Soviet Union after 1991.

The New Israelite Cemetery reflects the highly diverse chapters making up more than a century of Jewish life in Munich. A tour focused on one chapter in particular, the revolution and the Bavarian council republics, would take the visitor past three gravestones that serve as exemplars of this episode in Munich's Jewish history.

Only a few visitors today would notice the small stone gravestone with a completely weather-beaten inscription that lay fallen over for years. For a long time nobody bothered taking care of this gravestone or commemorating the people buried there. In 2015, a few history-conscious Munich citizens cleaned the memorial slab for the first time, and two years later they saw to it that the gravestone was erected again.[2] Exercising some powers of deduction, the visitor could make out a legible fragment of words on the stone from Nietzsche's poem "Ecce Homo" and the beginning of the inscription: "Here rests my wife Sara [sic] Sonja Lerch née Rabinowitz Dr. Phil."

Here, then, lies buried that comrade in arms of Kurt Eisner, the woman who stood by his side during the munitions workers' strike of January 1918 and who took her own life two months later in her jail cell at Munich's Stadelheim prison. The news that her husband Eugen Lerch was going through with divorcing her had just been disseminated by the Munich press. Here, in April 1918, Eugen Lerch mourned at the open grave, accusing himself of causing his still not divorced wife's death, of sacrificing her for the sake of his own career.[3] Standing alongside the Protestant widower Lerch at the grave, the elderly Rabbi Cossmann Werner, who would be buried there himself a few months later, recited the mourner's prayer. He spoke about the mental derangement of the dead, not only to comfort the widower but also, undoubtedly, to justify carrying out a Jewish ritual at the grave of a suicide. A representative of the Independent Social Democrats laid down a wreath, whereupon the anarchist Josef Sontheimer pushed his way forward and tried to give a political speech of his own. The police were on hand, however, and immediately led him away.[4]

Not far away is a significantly more imposing gravestone made of black marble. In contrast to the grave of Sonja Lerch, this one has no stones placed on it, as is the custom for Jewish mourners who are relatives and friends of the deceased. Instead, a brief and simple inscription is clearly legible: "Eugen Levine" (without the accent mark), and underneath: "5 June 1919." Here one of the most radical figures of the Second Council Republic found his final rest. Cossmann Werner's successor, Rabbi Leo Baerwald, held a brief service at this site a year after Sonja Lerch's burial. Once again, there was a commotion at the open grave, as would happen annually. Since Leviné's grave had become a pilgrimage site for local Communists, the Jewish community found itself caught on the front line of a war between the Communist Party and the Munich police. In 1924, the *Münchner Neueste Nachrichten* reported on a Communist rally planned for Leviné's gravesite, which the police prevented.[5] And two years later the Communist paper *Neue Zeitung* carried this story: "A number of Communists made their way to the grave of Leviné at the Jewish Cemetery in Schwabing on the anniversary of his death; after 20 comrades had entered the cemetery, the gate was closed by the police." The newspaper left unanswered the outstanding question: Did this happen by arrangement with the official Jewish community?[6]

The visitor needs to move on to the very edge of the cemetery, near the wall, to chance upon the third grave. On a block of natural stone

FIGURE 31. The gravestone of Sarah Sonja Lerch-Rabinowitz.
Thomas Hauzenberger, Munich.

erected there in 1946, two names have been engraved: "Kurt Eisner" and, just underneath, "Gustav Landauer." On small black jambs surrounding the grave, numerous stones have been laid down as memorial symbols. Neither of the two revolutionaries had been originally buried at the Jewish cemetery. In February 1919, when one hundred thousand people followed Eisner's body, they were heading to the city's Ostfriedhof (Eastern Cemetery). The urn containing Landauer's ashes was

FIGURE 32. The gravestone of Eugen Leviné. Thomas Hauzenberger, Munich.

initially interred at the cemetery in Schwabing (Schwabinger Friedhof); in 1923 his remains were transferred to the Waldfriedhof (the Woodland Cemetery), on the edge of the Hadern district. There, in 1925, a stele built with donations from the Free Workers' Union (the anarcho-syndicalist Freie Arbeiter Union Deutschlands) was erected to commemorate Landauer.

Immediately after Hitler was appointed Reich chancellor, the mayor and city council received letters from outraged citizens complaining that Munich's cemeteries had a tomb of honor and a memorial stele, dedicated to those "impudent Jews" Eisner and Landauer, and plans commenced for the forcible reburial of their remains to another site. On June 22, 1933, the city council then declared that the graves purchased for Eisner and Landauer for the period through 1935 and 1938, respectively, had now passed their expiration dates. The demolition of the memorials and removal of the mortal remains was to take place "forthwith." But where should the mortal remains contained in those urns go? Eisner's son Hans was trying to look after the delivery of his father's remains at the same time that the Nazi government was holding him in "protective custody" in Berlin. The young Eisner was told by

FIGURE 33. The gravestone of Kurt Eisner and Gustav Landauer.
Thomas Hauzenberger, Munich.

the Munich city magistrate that urns could not be handed over to private persons. The vessels containing the remains were sent instead to Munich's Jewish community. The community expressed its reservations about this move. For one thing, cremation is regarded as incompatible with traditional Jewish religious practice. But in addition, as in 1918–1919, the Jewish community in 1933 did not want to be associated with revolutionaries. The Jewish community's chairman, Dr. Alfred Neumeyer, wrote to the city council that he did not know if the two deceased men were affiliated with "the Israelite denomination" at the time of their death. But it was obvious that the community had no choice in the matter. Thus, Neumeyer's letter ends with words reflecting the realities of the new era: "But we do not want to create any difficulties and therefore declare that we are prepared to receive the urns and consign them to the earth for now." There was even some discernible and sporadic protest against removing the grave of Bavaria's first prime minister. An anonymous handwritten report received by the NSDAP city council caucus on June 28, 1933, stands out among the municipal documents. It says "Monsters of culture!!! You're idiots, it must be said / no rest left even to the dead / the spirits of the dead survive / though brown plague and Nazi murder thrive!!! / The spirits of the dead from Munich's East and Woodland Cemetery" ("Scheusale der Kultur!!! Ihr seid doch echte Idioten / lasst nicht einmal in Ruh die Toten / der Geist der Toten lebt fort / trotz brauner Pest u. Nazimord!!! / Der Geist der Toten vom Münchener Ost und Waldfriedhof").[7]

Life Journeys

The three gravestones at the New Israelite Cemetery reveal the fate of the Jewish protagonists in our story who met their deaths in Munich in 1918 and 1919. The life journeys of our other protagonists of Jewish descent mostly ended far away from Bavaria: in New York and London, in Jerusalem, Shanghai, and Ortaköy (in Turkey), in the Oranienburg and Theresienstadt concentration camps, and on the way to the Dachau camp.

Ernst Toller was released from the Niederschönenfeld prison on July 15, 1924. All his petitions for an earlier release were unsuccessful, even when he was slated to take over the seat of the USPD deputy Karl Gareis in the Bavarian Landtag after that Independent Social Democrat had been murdered. During his internment, Toller wrote four dramatic plays in addition to his poetry. The dramas were successfully staged at several German theaters, although their author was only able to see them for himself years later. They included the revolutionary drama *Man and the Masses*, in which he immortalized Sarah Sonja Lerch-Rabinowitz ("Sonja L.") and Eugen Leviné ("The Nameless One"). In 1925, just a few months after his release from prison, he undertook a journey to Palestine. He did not become a Zionist, yet he later once proposed founding a fund to support Jewish workers in Palestine.[8] By 1932, he had already left Germany, initially going to Switzerland, then moving via Paris to London and California. At the beginning of May 1939, he gave his last public speech at the International PEN Congress in New York, and a few days later he was introduced to President Roosevelt. Deeply depressed about the political triumphs of Hitler and Franco in Europe, he hanged himself on May 22, 1939, in his New York hotel room. For years nobody picked up his ashes; they were finally interred in a mass grave of funeral urns.

Erich Mühsam was released from prison at the Niederschönenfeld fortress a few months after Toller. In Berlin he published the anarchist newspaper *Fanal* and became involved with the prisoner aid organization Rote Hilfe (Red Aid), which was close to the KPD (the German Communist Party). In spite of his earlier assurance that he could never really leave Judaism, in 1926 he took the formal step of leaving the Jewish community as an institution. Until 1933, he went his own way, which was anarcho-communist and not supported by any organization. He was among the first to be arrested by the Nazi regime. After six months of "protective custody" in the Oranienburg concentration camp, he was brutally maltreated and murdered on July 10, 1934. Officially, it was announced that he had hung himself. His disfigured corpse was handed over to his widow and interred in the Waldfriedhof Berlin-Dahlem (Dahlem forest cemetery).

Felix Fechenbach was released from jail on the same day as Erich Mühsam—as well as Adolf Hitler—and before his full term had been served. During his imprisonment, which he first spent in solitary confinement at the Ebrach penitentiary, he wrote a novel about Würzburg, the city that was his childhood home.[9] After an initial refusal, he attended lectures on religious philosophy that the Bamberg rabbi, Adolf Eckstein, gave to the small number of Jewish prisoners every five weeks. At the same time, Fechenbach also began studying the Hebrew language.[10] After his release, he chiefly turned his attention to his interest in Jewish political matters. In 1926, he and his wife, Irma Epstein, spent their honeymoon in Palestine.[11] Just before that trip, he had joined the Zionist socialist movement Poalei Zion.[12] The 1928 edition of the *Jüdisches Lexikon* wrote about Fechenbach: "He left Judaism, yet he is now Jewishly interested again."[13] After his release from jail, Fechenbach worked for a while in Berlin, then as editor for a Social Democratic newspaper in Detmold. His attorney Philipp Löwenfeld managed to obtain from the Reichsgericht, Germany's highest criminal and civil court, a partial annulment of the judgment against Fechenbach. In March 1933, Fechenbach was arrested by the Nazis. On August 7, apparently as he was being transported to the Dachau concentration camp, he was shot to death in a forest near Detmold. His family was told that he had been shot while trying to escape. Fechenbach was interred at the Jewish cemetery in the small town of Rimbeck.[14] Two of his brothers were murdered during the Holocaust, while his widow was able to escape to Switzerland.

After 1933, neither his exaggerated nationalism nor his disassociation from the religious community into which he had been born helped Paul Nikolaus Cossmann protect himself from the attacks of the National Socialists. In April 1933, during a stay at a health spa in Bad Wörishofen (a resort town in the Allgäu hills west of Munich), he was arrested upon leaving church. It was quite an irony of history that Cossmann, who had often enough accused others of treason, should now have the same charge hurled at him. His crime was to have advocated a restoration of the monarchy under the auspices of the Bavarian crown prince as a way of blocking Hitler's rule. He was released a year later, and for several years he lived a reclusive life in Ebenhausen, south of Munich. While his sister was still able to escape to England in 1939, Cossmann was taken to the collection camp in Berg am Laim in southeastern Munich shortly after the start of Munich's deportation of Jews in 1941.[15] In the summer of 1942, he was transferred from there to Theresienstadt, where he died shortly after his arrival. The pious Catholic was interred according to Jewish ritual.[16] As far as his erstwhile opponents were concerned, Cossmann's tragic death changed nothing about his ominous life work. Thus, Max Hirschberg wrote: "The tragic end of this peculiar writer and politician should not prevent us from observing that he was one of the most disastrous figures in the counterrevolution and in the German Republic."[17]

The path taken by Count Anton von Arco auf Valley after his release on April 24 from the Landsberg prison, where he had enjoyed the same generous conditions of detention as his short-time fellow inmate Adolf Hitler, hardly displayed much evidence of the heroic career his backers had once prophesied for him. While still in prison, he wrote a polemical treatise on behalf of a South German–inflected federalism meant to break the dominance of Prussia.[18] Immediately following his release, he was celebrated enthusiastically in his Upper Austrian hometown of St. Martin im Innkreis. For a brief period in 1926, he was the publisher of the conservative-antisemitic newspaper *Bayerisches Vaterland*, but in this position he was attacked by völkisch nationalists—among other reasons, because of his partly Jewish background. The same thing happened after he had been accepted into the Catholic student fraternity Rhaetia as an "honorary philistine" (one of the membership categories for pledges).[19] A few years later, he held an attractive position as director of Lufthansa's southern German operations, until he was suddenly fired from that job as well. Arco's police files during the 1920s and 1930s do not reveal any conspicuous political activities, though there were plenty of traffic violations for reckless behavior at the wheel and repeated incidents of drunken driving, and he was also accused of being responsible for the venereal disease contracted by a woman with whom he had an affair.[20] Little was left of what his right-wing followers had once claimed as their role model for his supposedly impeccable conduct. If anything, that reputation had been superseded by that of a playboy and bon vivant whose behavior in his various professional functions was rarely responsible. Because of his political activity on behalf of conservative-monarchist circles and some remarks he supposedly made right after Hitler came to power, Arco was briefly taken into protective custody in 1933. Reportedly, he claimed that he could imagine killing others besides Eisner, which some interpreted as being directed against the new Führer. Yet, owing to his "heroic deed" of 1919, he was able to survive the era of National Socialism unscathed, in spite of an ancestry that was not exactly "purely Aryan." In 1941, at the personal instigation of Hitler, his sentence from 1920 was removed from court records. Arco died shortly after the end of the war as the result of an automobile accident.[21] He was interred in St. Martin in the crypt of the von Arco auf Valley family.

The life of Ignaz Trebitsch-Lincoln—who mutated from Hungarian Jew to Canadian missionary, from British MP to German radical, and who in 1920 was first supplied with fake identity papers by Munich police chief Pöhner before helping General Ludendorff forge plans for a united anti-Bolshevik front—took yet another unexpected turn in the early 1920s. In November 1921, he made his way to China, where he became adviser to a private army. Occasionally, and accompanied by Chinese diplomats, he would also show up in Munich, where he would visit General Ludendorff and probably Paul Nikolaus Cossmann as well. The Munich press had not forgotten him and reported about one of "the greatest international adventurers and political confidence men of our time . . . who has had his hand in play in almost all the cases of political scandals and coups of the last several years. His versatility in the field of political crime and the concomitant chameleon-like capacity for metamorphosis he has developed border on the miraculous."[22] After his son was condemned to death and executed in England, Trebitsch-Lincoln studied Buddhist culture in Sri Lanka and, until his death in Shanghai in 1943, spent the rest of his life as a Buddhist monk.[23] But at the same time he appeared to have been working for Japanese intelligence, to the extent that this secret service employment—or anything else in his life for that matter—can be confirmed with any degree of certainty. And nothing can be proven for sure from his memoirs, which were published under the not-so-modest title *The Greatest Adventurer of the Twentieth Century?!* (The English translation published in London in 1931 was less grandiloquently called *The Autobiography of an Adventurer*.) All we can definitively say is that Trebitsch-Lincoln's gravestone is located in the municipal cemetery in Shanghai.

Commercial councilor Siegmund Fraenkel—the representative of Munich's Orthodox Jews who conducted a public campaign on two fronts, opposing both the Jews in the council republic and the antisemites in Munich's police and Bavarian government—never recovered fully from the attack on him in June 1923. His son claimed that "the political events of 1921–1923, especially the assault in 1923, shattered his health."[24] Fraenkel died in September 1925. In its obituary, the *Bayerische Staatszeitung* wrote: "He was a specialist for major international transit traffic, well-known and respected as such."[25] Yet in spite of the high regard in which Fraenkel was held, the Bavarian prime minister had rejected the recommendation made in 1924 by the trade minister to make him president of the Chamber of Commerce. Appointing a Jew struck him as an unnecessary provocation to antisemitic forces in the state.[26] Fraenkel is interred in Munich's Old Israelite Cemetery. His son, Adolf

Abraham Fraenkel, became a professor of mathematics in Jerusalem, and it was there that he composed his memoirs about his Bavarian hometown.

Karl Süßheim, the lecturer in what was then called "Oriental" studies, became a senior adjunct professor (*Außerordentlicher Professor*) at the University of Munich. In 1933, he lost his job and had to earn a living giving private lessons. In his diaries, which he continued to compose in Turkish and Arabic, he chiefly wrote about the acts of discrimination against him and other Jews. Hedwig Süßheim, the widow of his brother, the longtime Social Democratic Landtag deputy Max Süßheim, took her own life after the pogrom night of November 9, 1938. Karl Süßheim, who had once voted for the conservative-liberal DVP, was taken along with other Jews from Munich to the Dachau concentration camp. He managed, as one of the last Jews from his city able to emigrate, to find refuge in Turkey by 1941. There he lived frugally, continuing his research and offering private tutorials. He died from cancer in January 1947 and is buried in the Jewish cemetery in Ortaköy, in northeastern Istanbul.[27]

In 1933, after mourning for her husband Eli, who had died at a young age of cancer, Rahel Straus left with her two children for Palestine, where she wrote her memoirs about her life before emigrating. After a difficult first few years, she established herself as a physician and social worker there. She died in 1963 in Jerusalem. Her grave is located in the city's Sanhedrin Cemetery.

Philipp Löwenfeld and Max Hirschberg continued working as attorneys in Munich until the start of the Nazi era. In 1933, Hirschberg was taken into "protective custody" for five months before emigrating to Italy. Löwenfeld left Germany right away in 1933, going initially to Switzerland. Both lawyers emigrated in 1938 to the United States, where they died in 1963 and 1964, respectively. They both wrote extensive memoirs about their lives in Munich and are buried in New York. Another important memoir was written by the attorney Max Friedländer from his exile in London, to which he had fled in 1939 via Switzerland. His seminal commentary on the lawyer's code was disseminated in Nazi Germany as a plagiarized work under another name. He died in London in 1956. He never returned to Germany.

Interpretations

Historical events do not change retrospectively. The overthrow of the monarchy on November 7, 1918; the murder of Kurt Eisner on February 21, 1919; the proclamation of the First Council Republic on April 7, 1919, and of the Second Council Republic a week later; the victory of the White Troops on May 1–2, 1919; the breakdown of the Hoffmann government on March 14, 1920; and the thwarted putsch of Hitler and Ludendorff on November 8–9, 1923—there can be no doubt that all these things happened. Yet in the twenty-first century historians can no longer associate themselves with Ranke's stipulation that they must try to describe "how it actually happened." As Johann Martin Chladenius was already noting in the middle of the eighteenth century, how a historical event is described always depends on the viewpoint of the observer.[28] We know that different contemporaries perceive the same events differently and that historical perception is also repeatedly changed by the experiences of subsequent generations.[29]

Did Kurt Eisner create the People's State or the Free State of Bavaria? Was he the first prime minister of this state or the chairman of its "Gesamt-ministerium," as the Council of Ministers was labeled in 1918? Was he willing to accept a parliamentary system, or did he want to establish a parallel system based on the councils? Was the council republic headed by Ernst Toller, Gustav Landauer, and Erich Mühsam a dreamland for unworldly idealists, or might it have provided some impetus for a democracy-in-the-making had it lasted longer? Did Gustav von Kahr accede to Hitler's demands in Munich's Bürgerbräukeller only because he was being held at gunpoint, or was he deliberately getting involved in a possible collaboration for at least a brief moment? Did Cardinal Michael Faulhaber and Nuncio Eugenio Pacelli contribute to the anti-semitic climate of that time, or were they trying to counteract it? Did Hitler become a National Socialist because of the Jewish revolutionaries, or did this play only a minor role in the formation of his worldview? Was November 1923 a necessary precondition for January 1933, or might it have delayed Hitler's path to power for several years?

These are just a few of the questions to which both contemporaries and historians have found—and continue to find—different answers. The vantage point for the perception of historical events shifts over the course of time and is also closely tied to the circumstances of every observer's own era. One way to chart this change in perspective is to look at the revolution's anniversaries as commemorated at ten-year intervals.

When Erich Mühsam's "Personal Report" about the emergence of the Bavarian council republic appeared under the title *From Eisner to Leviné* in time for the council republic's tenth anniversary, the Weimar Republic had just stabilized itself. At the Reichstag elections in May 1928, the NSDAP received only 2.6 percent of the vote, and even in Bavaria it had slipped to 6.1 percent in the Landtag election that took place simultaneously. Here the conservative Held government was now firmly in the saddle. The political turmoil of the initial postwar years looked like a thing of the past, and the danger emanating from Hitler, as well as the economic distress and inflation of the postwar period, seemed to have been remedied. On July 14, 1928, the Reich Amnesty Law went into effect, a measure that also granted Mühsam immunity from punishment and thus facilitated the publication of his "Personal Report." Mühsam was certainly aware of how time had also changed the perspective of the chronicler. Thus, in the new foreword he composed in 1929 for a report originally written in 1920 he emphasized: "Today there are some things I would certainly express differently, and also some things I would assess differently. . . . Ten years after the event I do not want to tell the world mostly about what I think today, but rather about what I, as a participating contemporary, had to say in the immediate aftermath."[30]

There were no official state holidays in Munich to celebrate the tenth anniversary of the revolution or the council republic. The governing Bavarian People's Party disassociated itself from the politicians who had toppled the monarchy, and conservative papers like *Das Bayerische Vaterland* also talked about Eisner as a "man guilty of high treason" on the occasion of the tenth anniversary of his murder. Meanwhile, the Social Democratic *Münchener Post* mourned Eisner as an "idealist and revolutionary."[31]

On the twentieth anniversary of the Bavarian revolution, by contrast, major festivities were held in Munich's Old City Hall. Germany's new Nazi rulers did not celebrate the downfall of the monarchy on November 8, 1918, but rather the glorified, though failed, putsch attempt of November 8, 1923. In the official reading, the Beer Hall Putsch had now overshadowed the events of 1918. On that eighth of November in 1938, the new regime came up with something very special: on the pretext of supposedly spontaneous popular outrage over the murder of a German embassy official in Paris, all synagogues throughout the Reich were to go up in flames within a few hours as part of an action that had been carefully planned in advance, while thousands of Jews would be shipped off to concentration camps and their businesses and homes demolished. In the "Capital City of the Movement" (as the Nazis officially labeled Munich), only the smaller synagogues were destroyed that night, as the grand synagogue that had been dedicated with such ceremony fifty years earlier had already been demolished in the summer of 1938 at Hitler's personal orders. The assassin in Paris, Herschel Grynszpan, was reacting to his parents' deportation from Germany to the no-man's-land between Germany and Poland, where only days before they had been forced to join without any notice seventeen thousand other Jews with Polish citizenship. With this action, the National Socialists had succeeded in implementing those expulsions of East European Jews that Gustav von Kahr had twice failed to accomplish. In the interim, Kahr himself had also fallen victim to Hitler's thirst for revenge: in the course of the "Night of the Long Knives" in 1934, he had been murdered at the Dachau concentration camp.

By no means was commemoration of the revolution and council republic obliterated in the Nazi state. Instead, observing the anniversary of these short-lived regimes was quite deliberately abused for political purposes. The Jewish revolutionaries provided Germany's new masters with a useful image of the enemy, a convenient bogeyman. In the Nazi-tinged history writing of those years, the narrative was about "those wretched, unscrupulous fellows who in November 1918 knew how to use criminal treason and subversion to seize the rudder of the state."[32] Such language was accompanied by constant warnings about a supposedly imminent danger posed by the "Jewish Bolsheviks" and by caricatures of the "November criminals" that routinely appeared in the press. In 1936, a dedicated research division dealing with the Jewish question was founded at the National Socialist Reich Institute for the History of the New Germany, a department now devoted specifically to taking up these themes of Jewish menace. At its head stood Karl Alexander von Müller, from whom Adolf Hitler had once taken his first training course in history; in the meantime, Müller had become not only a professor of history at the University of Munich but also president of the Bavarian Academy of Sciences. When his former close associate Paul Nikolaus Cossmann was being deported to Theresienstadt, Müller received the Goethe Medal and was waxing lyrically about Germany's military triumphs.

In the period following the Second World War, historians in the western part of Germany shied away from approaching this topic, not least because of the lingering effects of antisemitic images of the revolution and the council republic.[33] In Germany's eastern half, interest in Bavaria's council republic focused mostly on this short-lived regime as an early, if incomplete, forerunner of the Communist state later established east of the Elbe.[34] So it is telling that the first comprehensive—and in many respects still definitive—history of the revolution was written in English as a dissertation at Harvard. In the introduction to *Revolution in Bavaria*, its author, Allan Mitchell, wrote this about how the events in Bavaria were assessed in the mid-1960s when the book based on his thesis was published: "The handbooks and textbooks of Bavarian history invariably lament the passing of the monarchy rather than celebrate the founding of the republic."[35] Mitchell was interested above all in the origins of a democratic system in Germany. This same interest guided the historians who contributed to *Bayern im Umbruch* (Upheaval in Bavaria), the collection of essays edited by Karl Bosl in 1969.[36] This study not only celebrated the fiftieth anniversary of the council republic but also reflected a new interest in the history of that year's revolution at a time that many of the contributors also felt was revolutionary. The "68-er" movement, with its longing for social renewal, was rediscovering figures like Kurt Eisner, Gustav Landauer, and Erich Mühsam. A spate of new studies and collections of writings were published in connection with the New Left's revival of an older revolutionary Marxism, but for understandable reasons this postwar generation of scholar-activists tended to evade questions about the earlier revolutionaries' Jewish identity.[37]

The fiftieth anniversary of Eisner's murder and the council republic also set off new debates among the general public in Munich. Against the background of new student unrest, the old fault lines of ideological trench warfare from the past were still there to see. On the centenary of Eisner's birth a year earlier, in 1967, the *Süddeutsche Zeitung* (postwar Munich's center-left newspaper of record, and Germany's highest-circulation non-tabloid daily today) commented that "assessments of him still frequently fluctuate between transfiguration as an idealist and the verdict that he was a traitor."[38] The storm of letters to the editor that followed, either accusing or defending Eisner, underpinned the writer's point. On the fiftieth anniversary of his death, the SPD parliamentary caucus in Munich's city council proposed naming a street after Kurt Eisner. Hardly any other question ever led to city council discussions as heated as this one. Fifty years after his death, Eisner was identified with the Bavarian Council Republic that had not been established until after his death and whose deeds were confounded with the White Terror that followed its defeat. The CSU (Christian Social Union, the Bavarian sister party of Germany's Christian Democratic Union, CDU) fought back against the proposal to name a street after a "Communist," an advocate of the radical left-wing council ideology "based on the Russian model," and a man allegedly responsible for "hundreds of deaths." One city council member said that it would be better to commemorate Eisner's victims, citing the widow of Count Arco in this context.[39] In the course of the debate, which also raged among the general public in Munich, the CSU city councilor (and later chief municipal adviser on social welfare policy), Hans Stützle, disassociated himself from his own caucus, saying: "On the whole, it might be very good if people in Munich would now, 50 years after these turbulent times born of war and hunger, take another look at the events of those times. For it is astonishing how imprecise are the recollections of many people."[40] What Stützle "encountered in the way of accusations and defamations all but overwhelmed him," according to Christian Ude, later Munich's (Social Democratic) mayor.[41]

The street finally named after the founder of the Free State of Bavaria (this was the formulation decided upon for the street signs after another drawn-out discussion) was placed in an inconspicuous corner of Neuperlach, a new satellite town of high-rise apartments on the southeastern edge of metropolitan Munich. Incidentally, it was right next to Karl-Marx-Ring. At the spot where Eisner was killed, in front of the Hotel Bayerischer Hof, an outline of the murder victim was later engraved on the sidewalk after the owner of the building refused to let a plaque be placed on the wall. But just above the sidewalk memorial, on the sign showing the building's address, a passerby would see a mention of the man for whom the street is named, the same cardinal for whom Eisner's revolution meant falsehood and high treason. Just a few blocks away from Kardinal-Faulhaber-Straße, near the Ordinariate for the Archdiocese of Munich and Freising, and also much more centrally located than Kurt-Eisner-Straße on the edge of town, one finds the street named after the nuncio and later Pope Pius XII, Pacelli-Straße. As accident would have it, what is for now the last Eisner memorial, a glass sculpture dedicated in 2011 on a small pedestrian space along the Oberanger promenade in downtown Munich, lies exactly halfway between the headquarters for the SPD, the political party Eisner once exited, and the new Ohel Jakob synagogue, dedicated in 2006 to replace the former house of worship in which he certainly never set foot.[42]

One hundred years after the original events, the view has shifted once again. Now numerous books, largely narrative nonfiction, recall the founder of the Free State as well as the "Republic of Poets" that followed.[43] In Munich, a huge Eisner exhibition was held in the Municipal Museum, and then there was another exhibition (also under municipal auspices) in the Monacensia Library about the Jewish revolutionaries Eisner, Landauer, Mühsam, and Toller, with the title "Poetry Is Revolution." In addition, there were countless anniversary events. Even Bavaria's governing party, which had long resisted identifying Kurt Eisner as a "founder of the state," reversed course: the CSU has now incorporated him, however cautiously, into the positive legacy of Bavaria.[44]

Each one of these anniversaries—whether it was 1928, 1938, 1968, or 2018—represented a different time in which to illuminate the events of 1918–1919 by placing different aspects of those years center stage. Historians, like the general public, envisaged these events from their respective vantage points, each closely tied to the developments of its own time. In this book, too, a very special perspective has come into play. Its paramount concerns have been the Jewish actors and the antisemitism of those years. Needless to say, this focus is not intended to imply that everyone in Munich at that time was either a Jew or an antisemite. The aim is rather to show that the significance of the events described in this book—the acts pertaining to the revolution, the council republic, and the reaction in Bavaria between 1918 and 1923—belong to a larger picture of Jewish history in the twentieth century that extends well beyond the temporal and geographic framework depicted here.

In the first place, this chapter of Germany history makes it clear that many German Jews were mistaken in their conviction that the equality they had enjoyed on paper since 1871 would turn into de facto equality with the fall of the monarchy and that their religion or ancestry would no longer stand in the way of their political activity. Thus, immediately after the revolution, some Jewish commentators regarded the fact that a Jewish prime minister was heading a German state for the first time as the successful culmination of emancipation. But hopes that the invisible barriers still present in Imperial Germany would disappear—if not owing to the shared experience of war, then at least because Jews were now living in a new democratic state—would very quickly prove illusory. Jews' participation in Bavarian life at the government level, after what turned out to have been no more than a brief interlude, picked up at exactly the same spot where it had stopped in November 1918. After May 1919, no Jewish politician would again hold government office in Bavaria, neither before 1933 nor after 1945. At the level of Reich politics, the basic picture did not look very different. After Walther Rathenau, at the end of barely five months in office as Reich foreign minister, was murdered in June 1922 by members of the Organization Consul (a terrorist group residing in Munich, where it was protected by police chief Pöhner), only one Jew, Finance Minister Rudolf Hilferding, held office in any national government.[45] In everyday life, too, Jews and non-Jews remained confined to their old prewar trenches. In spite of integration inside the city council and the political parties, the boundaries between Jewish and Christian society hardly disappeared in sports clubs and other social gatherings. "In domestic company, most Jews remained among themselves," Werner Cahnmann recollected. "In the houses of the Christian upper bourgeoisie, religiously observant Jews were not to be found. . . . One met in associations, but not in the family."[46]

In the second place, this historical episode is a textbook lesson in the complexity of the question, "Who is a Jew?" For antisemites, the question was easy to answer: they simply decided the question at their own discretion. If one had a Jewish-sounding name (like Max Levien), if one was married to a Jew (as Else Eisner was), or if one was an attorney defending a Jew (like the Landtag and later Reichstag deputy Alwin Saenger), then that was enough for them. Just as easily as non-Jews could be branded as Jews, German Jews were turned into foreigners, foreigners into East European Jews (Ostjuden), Ostjuden into Galicians, and Galicians into East Galicians. The antisemites printed cartoons showing caricatures of Jews with hooked noses, thick lips, and names that sounded as foreign as possible, while the German they spoke was distorted with a Yiddish accent. The fact that in reality most of the revolutionaries like Eisner, Landauer, Mühsam, and Toller had grown up in Germany, with German as their mother tongue, hardly bothered their accusers. At the same time, most of the National Socialist activists in Munich at the time did not exactly have roots in Bavaria. Hitler was from Austria, Rosenberg came from Estonia at a time when it belonged to the Czarist Empire, and Heß grew up in Egypt and later went to school in Bad Godesberg, a suburb of Bonn in the Prussian-governed Rhine Province.

Yet inside the Jewish community, too, there was a variety of views about who should count as a member. Membership in the city's official Jewish Community, the Israelitische Kultusgemeinde München, gave only a formal answer to the question of who was a Jew. For an Orthodox Jew like Siegmund Fraenkel, revolutionaries like Toller and Mühsam had sinned against their Jewishness. They themselves, by contrast, saw this quite differently. Kurt Eisner affirmed that he was not disassociating himself from a persecuted community whose prophetic ideals as conveyed by Hermann Cohen were dear to him. Erich Mühsam and Gustav Landauer also invoked the biblical prophets and the Hebrew Bible's teachings of social justice as the core of their Jewish identity. Ernst Toller professed his support for the "community of fate" from which he sprang. Things were even more complicated among those people who, as the children of Jewish mothers, were actually Jews according to the traditional definition, even if they had themselves baptized as Christians and spoke out or acted against the Jewish community, like Paul Nikolaus Cossmann and Ignaz Trebitsch-Lincoln. And what about Eisner's murderer Arco, whose grandparents had already converted but who would always remain a Jew in the eyes of the antisemites in spite of the count's "liberating act"? The answer to the question of who should be viewed as a Jew lies—like so much else—in the eye the beholder.

In the third place, the story recounted here is a textbook example of the fragility of historical interpretations. A frequent reading of our story could be summed up this way: The revolution and council republics caused an antisemitic reaction of a kind previously unknown in Bavaria and Germany. The presence of numerous Jewish politicians on the left led to the formation of notions about "Judeo-Bolshevism," which in turn became one of the formative myths for the subsequent emergence of the National Socialist ideology.

Another reading, however, calls into question any such direct causality behind these events. Alan Mitchell, in the first systematic account of this history, had already warned against a simple causality linking the chain of events in the sequence: "because of Eisner, the Soviet Republic; because of the Soviet Republic, a conservative reaction; because of reaction, the appearance of Nazism." For "in each instance," Mitchell cautioned, "the contingencies outweigh the certainties."[47] But the question we should be posing is not whether there was a council republic *because* of Eisner, or whether National Socialism arose *because* of the council republic and the conservative reaction to it. Instead, we should be asking whether there could have been a council republic *without* Eisner and a rise of National Socialism *without* the reaction. And in any event, perhaps we should locate the starting point for this causal chain earlier and ask instead: Had there been no political antisemitism in Imperial Germany, would there have been such a sudden emergence of Jewish revolutionaries? And without the long prehistory of hatred against Jews, would it have been possible to point the finger at a tiny minority for everything that went wrong after the First World War?

In generations to come, historians will certainly find still more and different answers to these questions. It is certain that we will not be able to understand the events that followed the interwar revolution and reaction without comprehending those that preceded them. The emergence of the "Jewish question" as a routine topic for public discussion in Germany after the First World War can be observed for the first time in Munich. To be sure, there was no direct path leading from here to 1933. But whichever way we look at it, the city of Munich—with its increasingly anti-socialist and anti-Jewish atmosphere following the suppression of the council republic—served Hitler as a stage for the political development he sought and proved to be an ideal laboratory for his subsequent plans.

Purim 5693 (March 1933)

Let us end this book the way we have begun every chapter: with a Jewish holiday. On March 12, 1933, the 14th of Adar in the year 5693 on the Jewish calendar, the Jews of Munich, as has been the custom on the festival of Purim in all Jewish communities for centuries, read the biblical Book of Esther. It tells about the conspiratorial plans of Haman, by profession an adviser at the court of the Persian king Xerxes (Ahasuerus), to kill all the Jews in the empire. Since Purim is close to the time when Christians celebrate Fasching (as "Carnival" is called in Bavaria), it is customary on this holiday—when the biblical narrative ends with a miraculous rescue from the imminent danger of Haman's nefarious plot—for Jews to wear costumes. In Munich, too, on that March night in 1933, Jewish girls ran around in the synagogues dressed as Queen Esther, and Jewish boys as Esther's Uncle Mordecai or as the villain Haman. Whenever the name Haman came up during the reading from the Book of Esther, they loudly whirled their rattles and stomped on the floor with their feet. One week after the Reichstag election that consolidated Hitler's position as chancellor, it does not require much imagination to guess who it was that German Jews were thinking of when the name Haman was mentioned.

But in Munich there was yet another peculiarity in 1933: an additional Purim festival was going to be celebrated for the last time, exactly ten years after it had been introduced. In the Jewish tradition, fast days are often called for to commemorate and give thanks for redemption from some great danger on the anniversary of that day, and these days are then designated as a local Purim celebration. The best known of these local Purim festivals was celebrated in Frankfurt am Main, recalling those rescued from the so-called Fettmilch Uprising of 1614 in that city's Judengasse, its Jewish ghetto. The threat to Munich's Jews of Hitler's attempted putsch of November 8–9, 1923, had such an impact that the city's Orthodox rabbi, Heinrich Ehrentreu, decreed that the first day in the month of Kislev would be a day of fasting and prayer "to commemorate the prevention of a pogrom against Bavaria's Jews." For the next ten years, this day was highlighted in religious services by the recitation of psalms of thanks. The Jewish Telegraphic Agency commented: "Devout Jews are inclined to regard the failure of the putsch as nothing short of a divine miracle."[48] What irony that 1933 would be the very year in which this local holiday commemorating the catastrophe averted ten years earlier would be celebrated for the last time!

We do not know if Munich's Orthodox Jews really did celebrate their local Purim festival up until the last one scheduled for 1933, nor do we know if they extended the observation beyond that date, in light of the most recent developments. Yet it seems certain that they took little joy in celebrating the main Purim festival in 1933. A few days later, on March 22, and right outside the city gates—quite officially and certainly not concealed by the press—the first German concentration camp was opened in Dachau, a small town famous for its artist colony. Two days earlier, Heinrich Himmler had announced the opening of the camp at a press conference, and now the first 150 prisoners were transported to Dachau. The first four murders of Jewish inmates in a concentration camp followed a few weeks later. The prisoners Rudolf Benario and Ernst Goldmann, along with the brothers Arthur and Erwin Kahn, after having been bloodily beaten, were shot to death in a forest outside the camp. In contrast to what happened in the biblical narrative from the Book of Esther, the Jews in the years after 1933 were unable to avert the murderous fate planned for them. The brief but menacing storm cloud that had sailed over Munich ten years before would now develop into a powerful tempest that, after first engulfing Germany, would darken all of Europe for many years to come.

TIMELINE

1918

November 2	Constitutional reform published calling for a constitutional monarchy with proportional representation and restrictions on the powers of the Chamber of Imperial Councilors
November 7	Peace demonstration on the Theresienwiese, followed by Kurt Eisner's proclamation of the People's State of Bavaria
November 8	Pending elections to the Bavarian parliament (Landtag), the Provisional National Council represents the interests of the people; Independent Social Democrat Kurt Eisner, as chair of the Joint Ministry (*Vorsitzender des Gesamtministeriums*), becomes the first prime minister of the Free State of Bavaria
November 12	Promulgation of women's suffrage and the eight-hour workday
November 15	Ernst Toller and Gustav Landauer arrive in Munich
December 6	Interior Minister Erhard Auer (from the Majority Social Democrats) is briefly forced to resign

1919

January 5	The German Workers' Party (Deutsche Arbeiterpartei, later National Socialist German Workers' Party [Nationalsozialistische Deutsche Arbeiterpartei, or NSDAP]), is founded
January 12	Elections to the Bavarian parliament (February 2 in the Bavarian Palatinate) result in the conservative Bavarian People's Party (BVP) becoming the strongest party, winning 66 of 180 seats, followed by the Majority Social Democrats (SPD), who win 61 seats; the Independent Social Democrats (USPD) receive only three seats
January 19	Elections to the Constituent National Assembly that will write the constitution for the Weimar Republic
February 19	Putsch by the sailor Konrad Lotter against the Eisner government fails
February 21	Eisner is shot dead by Count Anton von Arco auf Valley on the way to opening the new Bavarian parliament; in the parliament building, SPD chairman Erhard Auer suffers severe gunshot wounds

February 25	The Congress of Workers', Soldiers', and Farmers' Councils convenes through March 8 and proposes a government under Martin Segitz (SPD); the Segitz government never materializes
February 26	Kurt Eisner's funeral
March 17	The Bavarian parliament elects the Majority Social Democrat Johannes Hoffmann as prime minister
April 7	The Bavarian Council Republic is declared under the leadership of Ernst Niekisch, Ernst Toller, and Erich Mühsam; Gustav Landauer becomes people's commissioner for public education, science, and arts
April 13	A putsch attempt by the Republican Guard (Republikanische Schutzwehr), known as the Palm Sunday Putsch, tries but fails to reinstall the Hoffmann government, which has fled to Bamberg; the Communist Council Republic begins under Eugen Leviné and Max Levien
April 28	Dictatorship of the Red Army under City Commandant Rudolf Egelhofer
April 30	"Hostage murder" in the Luitpold Gymnasium
May 2	Capture of Munich by Reichswehr and Freikorps units ends the council republics; Gustav Landauer is murdered in the Stadelheim prison
June 5	Eugen Leviné is executed
July 12	Erich Mühsam is sentenced to a prison term of fifteen years
July 16	Ernst Toller is sentenced to a prison term of five years
August 1	Summary executions are revoked; People's Courts are set up
August 4	Adoption of Bavarian constitution

1920

January 16	Eisner's murderer Count Arco is sentenced to death; the Council of Ministers commutes the sentence to life in prison, from which he will be released after serving five years
March 14	The Hoffmann government resigns
March 16	Gustav von Kahr is elected Bavarian prime minister
March 20	Kahr orders the expulsion of "undesirable aliens"
June 2	The SPD Bavarian parliament deputy Alwin Saenger is attacked on the street
June 6	In elections to the Bavarian parliament, the Bavarian People's Party remains the strongest party, with sixty-five seats, while the Majority Social Democrats, winning only twenty-six seats, and the German Democratic Party, picking up just thirteen seats, suffer major losses; the Independent Social Democrats and parties on the far right register major gains
June 9	Karl Gareis, head of the Independent Social Democratic caucus in the Bavarian parliament, is shot to death in front of his house
October 4	During a visit to Munich, sex researcher Magnus Hirschfeld is beaten up on the street and severely wounded

1921

April 23	Antisemitic graffiti appears at Munich synagogues
August 6	Anti-Jewish riots in Memmingen
September 15	Gustav von Kahr resigns as prime minister
September 21	The Bavarian parliament elects Hugo Graf von und zu Lerchenfeld as prime minister
November 5	Funeral for King Ludwig III

1922

April 27	Start of the trial in the libel suit brought against Paul Nikolaus Cossmann by Felix Fechenbach
July 24	With the departure of the German Democratic Party and subsequent entry of the Bavarian Middle Party (Bayerische Mittelpartei, the Bavarian affiliate of the right-wing German National People's Party), the Bavarian government shifts to the right; German Nationalist Franz Gürtner becomes justice minister in Bavaria
August 10	Arrest of Fechenbach, who will be sentenced after the trial to eleven years in prison for high treason
November 8	Eugen von Knilling becomes the new prime minister

1923

January 5	The opening performance of Lion Feuchtwanger's *The Dutch Merchant* at the Residenztheater is disrupted
February 9	The Munich opening of the film *Nathan the Wise* is immediately canceled, owing to threats of violence
June 22	Attack on the merchant Siegmund Fraenkel and his family
September 26	Gustav von Kahr is appointed state commissioner general with dictatorial powers
September 27	Antisemitic incidents, including the smashing of windows in the Orthodox synagogue
October 13	Expulsion of foreigners for "behavior damaging to the economy"
November 9	Putsch attempt by Hitler and Ludendorff leads to acts of violence against Jews and political opponents

1924

February 16	Gustav von Kahr resigns as state commissioner general
April 1	Adolf Hitler is sentenced to five years' imprisonment, of which he is required to serve only six months

April 6	In elections to the Bavarian parliament, the Völkisch Bloc (Bavarian electoral alliance standing in for the temporarily banned Nazi Party) receives 35 percent of the vote in Munich, and 17 percent in Bavaria overall
June 24	As a reaction to the antisemitic hiring policy at the University of Munich, Richard Willstätter, winner of the Nobel Prize for Chemistry, asks to be released from his position as a professor
July 15	Ernst Toller released from prison
December 20	Hitler released from prison, as are Mühsam and Fechenbach

ACKNOWLEDGMENTS

THIS BOOK HAS a long prehistory. In 1987, as a student at the College for Jewish Studies in Heidelberg, I started research for what was supposed to be a master's thesis on the Jewish revolutionaries in Munich in 1918–1919. After finding archival material that ultimately led me in a different direction, I decided to let the topic I had originally chosen rest for a while. Although this subject matter kept cropping up on the margins of my other research, for one reason or another I was ultimately and repeatedly pulled each time along a different trajectory. Shortly before the centenary of the revolution, two things became clear to me. For one, a rich literature had since emerged on the revolution and the council republics in Bavaria, on antisemitism in the early 1920s, on the rise of Hitler, and on the early history of the Bavarian Free State. Yet it was also evident that, in spite of this abundant new scholarship, the special complex of themes I had originally envisioned tackling had still been explored in only a fragmentary way. The hundredth anniversary struck me as a welcome opportunity to take up again the research I had started some thirty years earlier.

My thanks go first of all to the late Michael Graetz, who was my first academic teacher and the scholar with whom I wanted to approach this topic three decades ago. His commitment to linking Jewish history with issues of social justice led me to this question many years ago in Jerusalem and Heidelberg and has led me back there again after numerous detours. The fact that I have been working as a historian in Munich for over two decades fortified this decision to revisit the matter. At the Ludwig-Maximilians-Universität, I have always been able to profit from the inspiration of my students, colleagues, research associates, and staff. In two seminars on the subject, students raised many of the questions and stimulated much of the research reflected in this book. Special thanks are owed to those colleagues who took the time to share their expertise and critical scrutiny of portions of the manuscript, thereby saving me from committing several errors. For this collegial assistance I am especially grateful to Matthias Bischel, Martin Geyer, Ferdinand Kramer, and Philipp Lenhard.

From Bernhard Grau, director of the Bayerisches Hauptstaatsarchiv (Bavarian Main State Archive) and Eisner's biographer, I received not only valuable advice about archival holdings but also important suggestions for my manuscript. I am grateful to Andreas Heusler from the Stadtarchiv München (Munich City Archive) for profound insights into Jewish life in Munich during this period and for permission to view the holdings of the Stadtarchiv. Laura Mokrohs granted me access to the holdings of the Monacensia (Munich's literary archive) as well as to her own research on the subject. Antonia Leugers generously made her unpublished manuscripts and notes on the subject available to me. I thank Christian Dietrich for unpublished material by Eugen Leviné, and Douglas Morris for American newspaper articles by Max Hirschberg. They also took time for a critical examination of lengthy portions of the manuscript. I found Mirjam Zadoff's advice on the Jewish revolutionaries most helpful, as were Dirk Heißerer's expertise on Thomas Mann, Cornelia Naumann's and Michael Schmidt's advice about the Rabinowitz family, and Carmen Sippl's assessment of the Eliasberg brothers.

A "book incubator" forum at American University in Washington provided me with the opportunity to discuss the manuscript with several colleagues. Their constructive criticism found its way into this book. Richard Breitman, Peter Jelavich, Susanna Schrafstaetter, Andrea Sinn, Alan Steinweis, Eric Weitz, and Richard Wetzell sacrificed many hours of their own research time to participate in these helpful sessions.

During the critical phase of preparing this manuscript for its initial publication in Germany, Julia Schneidawind and Lukas Ruser assisted me with research and editing work. Thomas Hauzenberger, with his customary keen eye, took the pictures of the Jewish Cemetery. I thank Thomas Sparr and Sabine Landes for accepting this as a publication with the Jüdischer Verlag imprint at Suhrkamp and for editorial supervision.

I am grateful to Brigitta van Rheinberg for her continued trust in my research. As with my previous books, I have had once again an excellent experience with the editorial staff of Princeton University Press and would like to express my thanks to Priya Nelson and Mark Bellis. Cynthia Buck has been an amazing copyeditor. As always, Jeremiah Riemer was so much more than a translator for this book as well. His close reading helped to improve the original German text.

Without Michelle Engert's patience, this book would probably have gotten stuck somewhere in the initial years of the revolution. Her constant encouragement, her original ideas, and her analytical eye sharpened my own questions. I dedicate this book to the memory of my mother, who was born one year after the events described here. The seeds sown during those years in Munich were reaped during her childhood and youth in Dresden. When, during the bombing attack on Dresden, she was able to rip off her yellow Star of David and look around at the inferno surrounding her, the "Capital City of the Movement" (as the Nazis styled Munich) had already been largely destroyed and the end of the horror that got its start there was in sight. With her unconditional will to life and optimism, in spite of all the horrors she experienced, she has remained an ever-present inspiration to me and my family.

ABBREVIATIONS

Archives

BA	Bundesarchiv, Berlin-Lichterfelde
BayHStA	Bayerisches Hauptstaatsarchiv, Munich
EAM	Erzbischöfliches Archiv, Munich
LBINY	Archives of the Leo Baeck Institute, New York
LoC	Library of Congress, Washington
MLA	Monacensia Literaturarchiv, Munich
ÖStA	Österreichisches Staatsarchiv, Vienna
StA München	Staatsarchiv, Munich
StdA	Stadtarchiv, Munich
UAM	University Archives, Ludwig-Maximilians-Universität, Munich
USHMM	United States Holocaust Memorial Museum, Washington
USNA	United States National Archives, Washington
SAPMO	Stiftung Archiv der Parteien und Massenorganisationen der DDR, Bundesarchiv, Berlin-Lichterfelde

Newspapers, Journals, and Periodicals

AZJ	*Allgemeine Zeitung des Judentums*
BIGZ	*Bayerische Israelitische Gemeindezeitung*
BK	*Bayerischer Kurier*
BSZ	*Bayerische Staatszeitung*
BT	*Berliner Tageblatt*
BV	*Bayerisches Vaterland*
CVZ	*C.V.—Zeitung*
DIZ	*Deutsche Israelitische Zeitung*
HZ	*Historische Zeitschrift*
IdR	*Im deutschen Reich*
JE	*Das Jüdische Echo*
JM	*Jüdische Monatshefte*
JR	*Jüdische Rundschau*
LBIYB	*Year Book of the Leo Baeck Institute*
MA	*Miesbacher Anzeiger*

MAAZ	München-Augsburger Abendzeitung
MB	Münchener Beobachter
MMP	Münchner Morgenpost
MNN	Münchner Neueste Nachrichten
MP	Münchener Post
MS	Münchner Stadtanzeiger
MZ	Münchner Zeitung
NFP	Neue Freie Presse
NJM	Neue Jüdische Monatshefte
NZ	Neue Zeitung
SM	Süddeutsche Monatshefte
SZ	Süddeutsche Zeitung
VB	Völkischer Beobachter
VfZ	Vierteljahrshefte für Zeitgeschichte
VZ	Vossische Zeitung
ZBLG	Zeitschrift für Bayerische Landesgeschichte

NOTES

Preface

1. Brenner, "Pre–Nazi Germany Tells Us the Fight to Save American Democracy Is Just Beginning."

2. Mann wrote his article in June 1923; it was published in October; Mann, *Essays II, 1914–1926*, vol. 15.1 of *GKFA*, 694. The writer's "German Letter" first appeared in English in *Dial Magazine* 75, no. 4 (October 1923): 374. This is the first public mention of Hitler in the published work of Thomas Mann. See Heißerer, "Bruder Hitler?," 66. Mann's 1923 "German Letter" is discussed in chapter 5.

1. A Change of Perspective

1. Landauer to Buber, December 2, 1918, in Buber, *Briefwechsel* 2:15; Buber, *Letters*, 234. We depart slightly here from the English translation by Richard and Clara Winston and Harry Zohn.

2. Gustav Landauer, eulogy for Kurt Eisner, reprinted in *MNN*, February 27, 1919.

3. Buber to Ludwig Strauss, February 22, 1919, in Buber, *Letters*, 242.

4. Landauer to Buber, February 2, 1918, in Buber, *Briefwechsel*, 2:15; Buber, *Letters*, 234. The Winston-Zohn translation is slightly altered here.

5. See, for example, the classic 1965 account by Allan Mitchell, *Revolution in Bavaria*, along with works published in 2017 and 2018: Appel, *Die letzte Nacht der Monarchie*; Höller, *Das Wintermärchen*; Schaupp, *Der kurze Frühling der Räterepublik*; Weidermann, *Träumer*. The designation "council republic" (capitalized when referring to a specific regime, such as the "First Council Republic" in April 1919) will be used throughout this book, except in cases where an English-language writer using the term "soviet republic" is being quoted. "Soviet"—the Russian word for "council"—has long been used by historians and journalists writing in English as the adjective to designate the revolutionary governments that sprung up in Germany after the First World War. The term is rarely used outside the Russian context in Germany itself, where *Räterepublik* (literally, "council republic") is standard. The radical council movement did draw some inspiration from the Bolshevik Revolution in 1917. But this does not necessarily imply that every council (or "soviet") republic outside of Russia was backed by the Communist rulers in Moscow.

6. Grau, *Kurt Eisner*; Gurganus, *Kurt Eisner*; Haug, *Erich Mühsam*; Hirte, *Erich Mühsam*; Hug, *Erich Mühsam*; Kauffeldt, *Erich Mühsam*; Distl, *Ernst Toller: Ein Leben in Deutschland*; Dove, *He Was a German: A Biography of Ernst Toller*; Lixl, *Ernst Toller*.

7. Among the numerous contemporary writings, see, for example: Rosenberg, "Die russisch-jüdische Revolution"; Eckart, *Totengräber Rußlands*; Eckart, *Der Bolschewismus von Moses bis Lenin*; Kriegsgeschichtliche Forschungsanstalt des Heeres, *Die Niederwerfung der Räteherrschaft in Bayern 1919*; Tharaud and Tharaud, *Die Herrschaft Israels*.

8. Hitler, *Mein Kampf*, 1:561. One of many English translations, Ralph Manheim's translation of *Mein Kampf* renders *Judenherrschaft* as "reign of the Jews" (207).

9. Mann, "Über Antisemitismus," in Mann, *Geschichte und Geschichten*, 187–88. An especially troubling interpretation is that offered by Johannes Rogalla von Bieberstein in his book *Jüdischer Bolschewismus*. The book is also unreliable. Within a few pages, Gustav Landauer is described as having grown up in a religious household (169), Erhard Auer becomes Frank Auer (170), and Max Levien's father is turned into a Jew (171). On the formation of the motif of Jewish Bolshevism, see Herbeck, *Das Feindbild vom "jüdischen Bolschewiken."*

10. Meinecke, *Die deutsche Katastrophe*, 53. The translation used here from Meinecke's *The German Catastrophe* was found in Winkler, *1933–1990*, 104.

11. Toller, *I Was a German*, vii.

12. A clear statement of this position can be found in Bernstein, *Foregone Conclusions*.

13. See the following studies, which adduce extremely different motives and evaluations: Joachimsthaler, *Hitlers Weg begann in München*; Plöckinger, *Unter Soldaten und Agitatoren*; Reuth, *Hitlers Judenhass*, 147; Weber, *Wie Adolf Hitler zum Nazi wurde*, 164–66. For more on this subject, see chapter 4.

14. Joachimsthaler, *Hitlers Weg begann in München*, 177–78.

15. Wirsching, "Hitlers Authentizität," 406. On the same point, see also Walser Smith, "When Was Adolf Hitler?"

16. Brenner, "What if the Weimar Republic Had Survived?"

17. Geyer, *Verkehrte Welt*, 59–123; Large, *Where Ghosts Walked*, 123–230; Gordon, *Hitlerputsch 1923*; Hürten, "Revolution und Zeit der Weimarer Republik"; Walter, *Antisemitische Kriminalität*, 41. See also the essay by Benz, "Ressentiment und Trauma."

18. Paula Winkler converted to Judaism in 1907. She also published under the nom de plume Georg Munk. See the catalog for the exhibition *"... zäh, genial, unbedenklich ...,"* 7.

19. Eisner, "Zum 70. Geburtstag des Philosophen (4 Juli 1912)," 125; excerpt published in *MP*, July 5–6, 1912.

20. On the reluctance of historians to investigate this question, see Haberer, *Jews and Revolution in Nineteenth-Century Russia*, xi–xiv; Zadoff, "Shades of Red."

21. Deutscher, *The Non-Jewish Jew*, 26–27.

22. Freud, "Ansprache an die Mitglieder des Vereins B'nai Brith (1926)," 51–53; see also Yerushalmi, *Freuds Moses*.

23. Bauman, "Pawns in Other People's Games," 35.

24. There is an extensive literature on the subject of Jewish involvement in leftist and revolutionary movements. To mention just a few: Diner and Frankel, *Dark Times, Dire Decisions*; Mendes, *Jews and the Left*; Mendelsohn, *Essential Papers on Jews and the Left*; Wistrich, *Revolutionary Jews from Marx to Trotsky*; Haberer, *Jews and Revolution in Nineteenth-Century Russia*; Gerrits, "Jüdischer Kommunismus."

25. For Germany, see Pulzer, *Jews and the German State*, 122; Toury, *Die politischen Orientierungen der Juden*.

26. Löwy, *Redemption and Utopia*; Wolin, "Reflections on Jewish Secular Messianism."

27. Friedländer, "Die politischen Veränderungen," 52. Friedländer, "Political Transformations," 160.

28. Scholem, *The Messianic Idea in Judaism*, 19.

29. Mosse, *German Jews beyond Judaism*, 70–71.

30. Deutscher, *Der nichtjüdische Jude*, 66.

31. Kreiler, *Die Schriftstellerrepublik*, 7.

32. The exception that would seem to prove the rule in this case was the finance minister in Baden, Moritz Ellstätter. See Pulzer, *Jews and the German State*, 91.

33. Angress, "Juden im politischen Leben der Revolutionszeit," 307.

34. Kayser, "Der jüdische Revolutionär," 96–98; see also Zadoff, "Shades of Red," 285–86.

35. In the most comprehensive account of German Jews' involvement in politics, Peter Pulzer writes: "No doubt the most spectacular and controversial example of Jewish revolutionary participation took place in Munich." Pulzer, *Jews and the German State*, 209.

36. Déak, "Jews and Communism," 97.

37. Ibid., 113.

38. "The Communist Terror in Munich" was the title given to Max Hirschberg's article in the July 19, 1919, issue of the American periodical *The Nation*. At the same time, he wrote a more than 100-page renunciation of Russian Bolshevism under the title *Bolschewismus: Eine kritische Untersuchung über die amtlichen Veröffentlichungen der russischen Sowjet-Republik* (1919). See also Morris, *Justice Imperiled*, 29–35.

39. Among Klemperer's many diaries, the best known is *I Will Bear Witness*, about surviving the Nazi era in Dresden.

40. Lessing, *Der jüdische Selbsthaß*.

41. StA München, Akten der Polizeidirektion München (Munich police files) 10110: "Eugen Leviné-Niessen, Mitteilungen des Vollzugsrats der Betriebs- und Soldatenräte" (Announcements of the Executive Council of the Workers' and Soldiers' Councils), April 15, 1919, p. 3.

42. Toller, *Eine Jugend in Deutschland*, 168; Hoser, *Die Revolution 1918/19 in der Provinz*, 178–79; on Paul Mühsam, see Mühsam, *Mein Weg zu mir*, 45–47; Flemming and Schmidt, *The Diary of Karl Süßheim*, 186–88. The diary is written in Turkish and Arabic.

43. Mann, untitled piece in *Kampf um München als Kulturzentrum*, 9. The translation of the quote, from "hotbed of reaction" to "stupidest city of all," is found in Winkler, *Age of Catastrophe*, whose translator is Stewart Spencer. All other quotes from Mann here are translated by Jeremiah Riemer.

44. Feuchtwanger, *Success*, 28.

45. *VZ*, October 21, 1923.

46. Specht, *Die Feuchtwangers*, 131–34.

47. For a contextualization, see Bauer and Brenner, *Jüdisches München*. To situate this in religious terms, see Stadtarchiv München, *Beth ha-Knesset*.

48. Franzos, *Halb-Asien*.

49. Brenner, "Warum München nicht zur Hauptstadt des Zionismus wurde."

50. Tiedemann, "Erscheinungsformen des Antisemitismus."

51. Heusler, *Das braune Haus*, 66. On the anti-Jewish sculpture at the city hall, see ibid., 69.

52. Deuerlein, *Aufstieg der NSDAP*, 49–50; Zuber, "Im Netz bayerischer Eliten," 245; Jelavich, *Munich and Theatrical Modernism*, 280.

53. Bauer and Piper, *München: Die Geschichte einer Stadt*, 216–52; Niehuss, "Parteien, Wahlen, Arbeiterbewegung."

54. Angress, "The German Army's 'Judenzählung' of 1916," remains a standard work on the subject. See also more recent literature: Fine, *Jewish Integration in the German Army*; Grady, *The German-Jewish Soldiers of the First World War*; Penslar, *Jews and the Military*; Rosenthal, *Die Ehre des jüdischen Soldaten*; Sieg, *Jüdische Intellektuelle im Ersten Weltkrieg*

55. Angermair, "Eine selbstbewusste Minderheit."

56. Zuber, "Im Netz bayerischer Eliten," 145–46.

57. See Rohrbacher, *Gewalt im Biedermeier*; Harris, *The People Speak!*

58. Schröder, "Der Erste Weltkrieg und der 'jüdische Bolschewismus," 86–88; Kellogg, *The Russian Roots of Nazism*; Baur, *Die russische Kolonie in München 1900–1945*; on Rosenberg, see Piper, *Alfred Rosenberg*, esp. 45–93.

59. Mann, "German Letter," 374. This is the first public mention of Hitler in the writings of Thomas Mann. See Heißerer, "Bruder Hitler?," 66; see also chapter 4. Mann wrote his article in June 1923, and it was published in the October issue of *Dial*.

2. Jewish Revolutionaries in a Catholic Land

1. Wassermann, *My Life as German and Jew*, 218.

2. So far there has been no systematic account looking more closely at the Jewishness of those involved in the events in Munich. A brief and useful overview of their activities, as well as those of Rosa Luxemburg, Leo Jogiches, and Paul Levi in Berlin, is provided by Bronner, "Persistent Memories of the German Revolution," 83–94.

3. Erich Mühsam, *Gedichte, Prosa, Stücke*, 41. The English translation is by Jeremiah Riemer, who thanks Barbara Kreuzer for helpful improvements. The German original is:

> Geboren ward zu Bethlehem
> ein Kindlein aus dem Stamme Sem.
> Und ist es auch schon lange her,
> seit's in der Krippe lag,
> so freun sich doch die Menschen sehr
> bis auf den heutigen Tag.
> Minister und Agrarier,
> Bourgeois und Proletarier—
> es feiert jeder Arier
> zu gleicher Zeit und überall
> die Christgeburt im Rindviehstall.
> (Das Volk allein, dem es geschah,
>   das feiert lieber Chanukah.)

4. Bernhard Grau reminds us that the revolt in the north began as a military strike and only later acquired a political thrust, while in Bavaria, where it started with a huge political peace

rally on October 23 at Munich's Theresienwiese, it took the opposite course. See Grau, "Revolution in Bayern," 208–9.

5. *BK*, November 9, 1918. See, too, the memoirs of the parliamentary deputy Ernst Müller-Meiningen, who left the Theresienwiese and arrived at the Bavarian parliament just as they were "debating a 'parliamentary inquiry about potatoes' as sociably as if nothing was happening." Müller-Meiningen, *Aus Bayerns schwersten Tagen*, 31.

6. Kritzer, "Die SPD in der bayerischen Revolution von 1918," 435–36; see also Schmalzl, *Erhard Auer*, 265–69.

7. Graf, *Prisoners All*, 327.

8. Schaupp, *Der kurze Frühling der Räterepublik*, 63.

9. The office of prime minister or minister-president was officially established only later. But, in addition to his function as the first chair of the Workers' and Soldiers' Councils, which would soon be expanded to include Farmers' Councils, Eisner also came to be called the "chair of the Joint Ministry" (*Vorsitzender des Gesamtministeriums*) and is usually referred to, by both friend and foe, as "minister-president" (prime minister). In the documents providing for his surviving dependents, he is designated as the "provisional Minister-President." See also the chapter "Eisner als Ministerpräsident" in Grau, *Kurt Eisner* (346–448), and Kramer, "Bayerischer Ministerpräsident."

10. Hofmiller, *Revolutionstagebuch 1918/1919*, 33.

11. Hirschberg, "The Communist Terror in Munich," 29.

12. *BK*, November 9, 1918.

13. Hofmiller, *Revolutionstagebuch 1918/1919*, 58.

14. Müller-Meiningen, *Aus Bayerns schwersten Tagen*, 41.

15. Fishman, "The Assassination of Kurt Eisner," 143.

16. Kahr, "Lebenserinnerungen," 213.

17. Klemperer, *Munich 1919: Diary of a Revolution*, 18–30.

18. Brentano, *Mein Leben im Kampf*, 350.

19. BA SAPMO NY/4060/129, p. 34. Hedwig Eisner died on November 21, 1918.

20. BA SAPMO NY/4060/1, pp. 3–38, 66.

21. BA SAPMO NY/4060/113, Beglaubigte Abschrift der Aufnahms-Urkunde in den bayerischen Staatsverband (28.10.1908) (notarized copy of certificate of admission to the Bavarian Federation [October 28, 1908]).

22. BA SAPMO NY/4060/121, Beglaubigte Abschrift aus dem Heiratsregister des Standesamtes III München, Nr. 2 der Heiratsurkunde vom 31.5.1917 (notarized copy from the marriage registry of Registry Office III Munich, no. 2 of the marriage certificate from May 31, 1917). His wife Else Belli is designated there as unaffilliated with any denomination (*konfessionslos*); the copy of the death certificate is located in BA SAPMO NY/4060/121. Because there is no archive for the Jewish religious community in Munich, it cannot be determined whether he left the Jewish community during his final year of life or the designation on his death certificate was in error. In a letter from June 27, 1933, regarding the reinterment of Eisner's urn, the Munich Jewish Community (Israelitische Kultusgemeinde München) informed the Munich city council that it could not determine at the time whether Eisner belonged to the religious community at the time of his death. StdA München, Bürgermeister und Rat 1659/3.

23. Gurganus, *Kurt Eisner*, 12.

24. On Eisner's political activities in Marburg, see Gurganus, *Kurt Eisner*, 33–35.

25. Sperans [Kurt Eisner], "Sporen," 26.

26. Sperans [Kurt Eisner], "Ein Fäulnisprozeß," 47.

27. Schade, *Kurt Eisner*, 104, note 209, quoting "Frau Pfarrer Börner." Grau, *Kurt Eisner*, 494, mentions a similar quote from Eisner's daughter Ruth. It is also mentioned as early as 1930 in volume 6 of the German-language *Encyclopedia Judaica*, where it is asserted that Eisner had never left the Jewish community; see Weyl, "Eisner."

28. Eisner, "Zum 70. Geburtstag des Philosophen," 125. Excerpts appeared in *MP*, July 5–6, 1912.

29. BA SAPMO NY/4060/67, p. 8.

30. Treitschke, "Unsere Aussichten." See also Meyer, "Great Debate on Antisemitism," and Sieg, "Bekenntnis zu nationalen und universalen Werten," 612–18.

31. Eisner, "Zum 70. Geburtstag des Philosophen," 127.

32. Sieg, "'Der Wissenschaft und dem Leben tut dasselbe not.'"

33. Hackeschmidt, "Die hebräischen Propheten und die Ethik Kants."

34. Schmolze, *Revolution und Räterepublik in München 1918/19*, 21.

35. Eisner, "Religion des Sozialismus," 201–2.

36. Eisner, "Zum 70. Geburtstag des Philosophen," 127.

37. Ibid., 134. On the secularization of Messianic thought among the Jewish revolutionaries, see Löwy, *Redemption and Utopia*, as well as the problematic work of Knütter, *Die Juden und die deutsche Linke*, 57–67.

38. BA SAPMO NY/4060/65, Cohen to Eisner, August 14, 1902.

39. Grau, *Kurt Eisner*, 49, 52.

40. Schade, *Kurt Eisner und die bayerische Sozialdemokratie*, 105, note 209.

41. On the full range of German-Jewish affiliations and senses of belonging, see Brenner, "Religion, Nation oder Stamm."

42. Freud, "Ansprache an die Mitglieder des Vereins B'nai B'rith (1926)," 52. The translation used here is from the Standard Edition of Freud's works translated and edited by James Strachey (*SE* 20: 273–74).

43. The letter from the War Ministry on May 26, 1917, explicitly mentions the Jewish religious affiliation of Emilie Landauer and Richard Kämpfer (but not the religious affiliation of Christian party members). A letter from June 9, 1917, is similar, and a letter from August 28, 1917, refers explicitly to the frequent participation of Jewish women in the meetings of the USPD. BayHStA Abtl. IV, Kriegsarchiv, 11528, 3261.

44. BA SAPMO NY/4060/79, pp. 12–13, 336.

45. BA SAPMO NY/4060/77, p. 162, Eisner to Else Belli, April 27, 1909.

46. BA SAPMO NY/4060/79, p. 316, Eisner to Else Eisner, January 16, 1918.

47. Grau, *Kurt Eisner*, 373; Löffelmeier, "Besaß Kurt Eisner die bayerische Staatsangehörigkeit?," 405.

48. Sebottendorff, *Bevor Hitler kam*, 66–67.

49. Faulhaber, "Kritische Online-Edition der Tagebücher Michael Kardinal von Faulhaber (1911–1952)," EAM, NL Faulhaber 10003, 11, diary entry for November 11, 1918, https://www

.faulhaber-edition.de/dokument.html?idno=10003_1918-11-11_T02&collid=1918 (accessed June 10, 2021).

50. Hauck to Faulhaber, November 17, 1918, quoted in Leugers, "'weil doch einmal Blut fliessen muss, bevor wieder Ordnung kommt,'" 90.

51. Hirschberg, *Jude und Demokrat*, 118.

52. Loewenfeld, *Recht und Politik in Bayern*, 205.

53. ÖStA/AdR/NPA/Liasse Bayern 2/1, Österreichisch-Ungarische Gesandtschaft, Anonymes Schreiben an das Deutschösterreichische Staatsamt für Äußeres, 21.12.1918 (anonymous letter to the German-Austrian State Office for External Affairs, December 21, 1918).

54. Grau, *Kurt Eisner*, 345; Schmalzl, *Erhard Auer*, 453.

55. Haffner, *Die verratene Revolution*, 177; Haffner, *Failure of a Revolution*, 165.

56. Haffner, *Die verratene Revolution*, 180; Haffner, *Failure of a Revolution*, 167.

57. Geyer, *Verkehrte Welt*, 58.

58. Brentano, *Mein Leben im Kampf*, 355.

59. Eisner, "Revolutionsfeier," 278.

60. Isolde Kurz, "Aus den Tagen der Münchener Räterepublik," *NFP*, July 12, 1919, *Morgenblatt*, no. 19713.

61. Sternsdorf-Hauck, *Brotmarken und rote Fahnen*, 24. For more on this subject in general, see Grebing, *Frauen in der deutschen Revolution 1918/19*.

62. Kampf, "Frauenpolitik und politisches Handeln," 304.

63. Ibid., 307.

64. Graf, *Prisoners All*, 341.

65. *MB*, May 31, 1919.

66. Kampf, "Frauenpolitik und politisches Handeln," 73–77.

67. Ibid., 198–214.

68. Straus, *Wir lebten in Deutschland*, 220–21.

69. Benz, *Süddeutschland in der Weimarer Republik*.

70. See, for example, Fechenbach, *Der Revolutionär Kurt Eisner*, 61. The translation of the line from Schiller's *Wilhelm Tell* is taken from the account of this incident in Grunberger, *Red Rising in Bavaria*, 74.

71. Fechenbach, *Der Revolutionär Kurt Eisner*, 62.

72. Pranckh, *Der Prozeß gegen den Grafen Anton Arco-Valley*, 13, 28.

73. Sebottendorff, *Bevor Hitler kam*, 82.

74. Ibid., 84.

75. Huch, "Kurt Eisners Todestag," 436–37.

76. *MB*, March 15, 1919.

77. Stürmer, Teichmann, and Treue, *Wägen und Wagen: Sal. Oppenheim jr. & Cie*, 333.

78. Ibid., 382.

79. Gossman, *The Passion of Max von Oppenheim*, 184–85.

80. Haffner, *Die verratene Revolution*, 184; Haffner, *Failure of a Revolution*, 170.

81. Mühsam, *Tagebücher 1910–1924*, diary entry for July 22, 1919, 206.

82. Graf, *Prisoners All*, 369.

83. *JE*, February 28, 1919.

84. Haffner, *Failure of a Revolution*, 171.

85. Graf, *Prisoners All*, 379.

86. Eulogy by Gustav Landauer, reprinted in *MNN*, February 27, 1919. Landauer had also explicitly characterized Eisner on previous occasions as a Jew, as when he referred to him as "Eisner, this courageous Jew," in a letter to Fritz Mauthner of November 28, 1918. Landauer, *Sein Lebensgang in Briefen*, 1:322.

87. Pringsheim, *Meine Manns*, 238.

88. Huch, "Kurt Eisners Todestag," 438. Huch was one of the most prominent non-Jewish proponents of Zionism. See *JE*, March 1914, 26.

89. *MP*, March 13, 1919, 7.

90. Mann, "Kurt Eisner," 174 and 170; reprinted in Schmolze, *Revolution und Räterepublik in München 1918/19*, 246.

91. Although Fechenbach had grown up in Würzburg, he was born in Mergentheim and was thus a citizen of Württemberg; he did not become a Bavarian citizen until 1921. See his certificate of admission from March 10, 1921, in LoC, Rehse Collection, "German Captured Documents," box 185, p. 132.

92. Quoted in Schueler, *Auf der Flucht erschossen*, 53.

93. Ruppert, "Felix Fechenbach als Soldat," 11–13, 21–22.

94. See Schopf, "Blende auf! Josef Breitenbach."

95. Ruppert, "Felix Fechenbach als Soldat," 8.

96. Roth, "Edgar Jaffé and Else von Richthofen," 152. The children of the Protestant Jaffé–von Richthofen marriage, regarded as "half-Jews" in National Socialist terminology, fled Germany after 1933 to escape possible persecution.

97. Loewenfeld, *Recht und Politik in Bayern*, 186. The Zionist Rahel Rabinowitz also described Jaffé as a Jew. *BK*, December 11, 1918; see also chapter 3.

98. USNA, Records of the Department of State Relating to Internal Affairs of Germany, 1910–1929, microcopy 336, roll 33 862.00 (Political Affairs), 862.01 (Government). See also Briggs, *George D. Herron*, 67.

99. ÖStA/AdR/NPA/Liasse Bayern 2/1, Österreichisch-Ungarische Gesandtschaft, Schreiben an das Deutschösterreichische Staatsamt für Äußeres, 21.12.1918 (letter to the German-Austrian State Office for External Affairs, December 21, 1918).

100. BA SAPMO NY/4060/66, p. 4, Landauer to Eisner, November 22, 1918.

101. Brenner, "A Tale of Two Families."

102. Landauer, *Rechenschaft*, quoted in Löwy, *Redemption and Utopia*, 128.

103. Landauer to Ida Wolf, June 16, 1891, quoted in Wolf, "'. . . der Geist ist die Gemeinschaft, die Idee ist der Bund,'" 87.

104. Landauer to Rafael Seligmann, September 17, 1910, in Landauer, *Sein Lebensgang in Briefen*, 1:324. See also Löwy, *Redemption and Utopia*, 132; and Breines, "The Jew as Revolutionary."

105. Landauer, "Die Legende des Baal Schem," cited in Löwy, "Romantic Prophets of Utopia," 71.

106. Scholem, *Von Berlin nach Jerusalem*, 65.

107. Seemann, *Lachmann-Landauer*, 76.

108. Hausberger, "My Father, Gustav Landauer."

109. *BK*, May 30, 1919.

110. Angress, "Juden im politischen Leben der Revolutionszeit," 267; Landauer, *Aufruf zum Sozialismus*, 57–58.

111. Quoted in Heydorn, "Vorwort," 23.

112. See Landauer to Margarete Faas-Hardegger, October 20, 1908, in Buber, *Gustav Landauer: Sein Lebensgang in Briefen*, 1:218.

113. Quoted in Heydorn, "Vorwort," 23.

114. Landauer to Mauthner, November 20, 1913, in Delf, *Gustav Landauer—Fritz Mauthner: Briefwechsel*, 282–83.

115. Landauer, "Sind das Ketzergedanken?" 172–73; originally in Verein jüdischer Hochschüler Bar Kochba in Prag, *Vom Judentum: Ein Sammelbuch*, 250–57.

116. Landauer, "Ostjuden und Deutsches Reich."

117. Landauer to Mauthner, May 18, 1906, in Delf, *Gustav Landauer—Fritz Mauthner: Briefwechsel*, 129.

118. Landauer, "Sind das Ketzergedanken?" 173.

119. Bernstein, *Die Aufgaben der Juden im Weltkriege*; "Vom Mittlerberuf der Juden," *NJM* 14 (April 25, 1917).

120. Landauer, "Sind das Ketzergedanken?" 170–74.

121. Landauer to Buber, May 12, 1916, in Buber, *Briefwechsel*, 1:433; Buber, *Letters*, 189.

122. Buber, *Briefwechsel*, 1:437; Buber, *Letters*, 192.

123. Landauer to Buber, February 5, 1918, in Buber, *Letters*, 230–31. Landauer is referring to the short-lived rule of Prince Wilhelm of Wied from the Prussian Rhineland; after being appointed ruler of Albania in 1914, he lasted only six months on the throne until civil war broke out in that part of the Balkans.

124. Landauer to Buber, November 22, 1918, in Buber, *Letters*, 234.

125. Buber, "Die Revolution und wir," 345–47.

126. Landauer to Buber, December 2, 1918, in Buber, *Letters*, 234.

127. Verhandlungen des provisorischen Nationalrats, Nr. 5 (minutes of Provisional National Council, No. 5), 109, quoted in Linse, *Gustav Landauer und die Revolutionszeit 1918/19*, 90; Angress, "Juden im politischen Leben der Revolutionszeit," 266.

128. Landauer to Hauschner, December 25, 1918, in Buber, *Gustav Landauer: Sein Lebensgang in Briefen*, 2:341.

129. Zweig to Buber, March 6, 1919, in Buber, *Briefwechsel*, 2:30 (translation by Jeremiah Riemer).

130. Landauer to Buber, March 20, 1919, ibid., 2:33–34.

131. An overview covering some of these passages about Landauer is provided by Lunn, *Prophet of Community*, 352, note 7.

132. So wrote Landauer in the foreword to the second edition of his book *Aufruf zum Sozialismus* (1919); see Löwy, *Redemption and Utopia*, 138.

133. Quoted in Geyer, *Verkehrte Welt*, 60.

134. BA SAPMO NY 4060/101, Linse, "'Poetic Anarchism' versus 'Party Anarchism,'" 59.

135. Landauer to Buber, March 20, 1919, in Buber, *Gustav Landauer: Sein Lebensgang in Briefen*, 2:402.

136. Kurz, "Aus den Tagen der Münchener Räterepublik," *NFP*, July 12, 1919, *Morgenblatt*, no. 19713, 1.

137. Kurz, "Aus den Tagen der Münchener Räterepublik," *NFP*, July 11, 1919, *Morgenblatt*, no. 19712, 1.

138. For details on the persons involved, see Köglmeier, *Die zentralen Rätegremien in Bayern 1918/19*.

139. Mauthner to Buber, Easter Sunday 1919, in Buber, *Briefwechsel*, 2:36 (translation by Jeremiah Riemer)

140. "Aus den letzten Tagen Landauers." *BT*, June 2, 1919.

141. Landauer to Mauthner, April 7, 1919, in Delf, *Gustav Landauer—Fritz Mauthner: Briefwechsel*, 364.

142. *JE*, May 9, 1919, 212–13.

143. *MNN*, September 24, 1920. See also Mühsam, "Zur Judenfrage"; and chapter 3.

144. On Mühsam and Judaism, see Baron, "Erich Mühsam's Jewish Identity"; Kauffeldt, "Zur jüdischen Tradition im romantisch-anarchistischen Denken Erich Mühsams und Gustav Landauers"; Goette, *Erich Mühsam und das Judentum*.

145. Quoted in Hug, *Erich Mühsam*, 2.

146. Klatt, "Siegfried Mühsam und seine Erzählungen," 39.

147. Hirte, "Erich Mühsam und das Judentum," 58.

148. Guttkuhn, "Jüdische Neo-Orthodoxie 1870 bis 1919 in Lübeck." Mühsam was not elected either time.

149. Mühsam, *Die Killeberger*.

150. Mühsam, *Neu-Killeberg*; see Klatt, "Siegfried Mühsam und seine Erzählungen," 42–51.

151. Hug, *Erich Mühsam*, 2.

152. Ibid., 3.

153. Mühsam, *Tagebücher 1910–1924*, diary entry for March 23, 1915, 150.

154. Ibid., 152.

155. Ibid., 98, diary entry for October 29, 1912.

156. For his thoughts on leaving the Jewish community and the consequences of such a decision for his inheritance, see ibid., diary entry for July 27, 1915, 153–54.

157. The standard translation (in a dual-language edition) is Kafka, *Letter to His Father* (*Brief an den Vater*).

158. See the biography of Werner Scholem by Mirjam Zadoff, *Der rote Hiob*, along with these works on Gershom Scholem: Biale, *Gershom Scholem*; Noam Zadoff, *Gershom Scholem*; Engel, *Gershom Scholem*.

159. Reinhold Scholem to Gerhard Scholem, November 25, 1919, in Scholem and Scholem, *Mutter und Sohn im Briefwechsel, 1917–1946*, 58.

160. Mühsam, *Mein Weg zu mir: Aus Tagebüchern*, 45–47.

161. Landau-Mühsam, "Meine Erinnerungen," 22, memoirs in manuscript collection, LBINY.

162. Ibid., 33. In her memoirs, Charlotte Landau-Mühsam depicts her commitment to women's rights and Zionism.

163. "Ritualmord," *Kain* (November 1913): 125–26, reprinted in Goette, *Erich Mühsam und das Judentum*, 25.

164. Luxemburg, *Das Menschliche entscheidet*, 13.

165. Mühsam, *Die Jagd auf Harden*, 226–27, reprinted in Goette, *Erich Mühsam und das Judentum*, 23. On the concept of race within the Jewish community, see Efron, *Defenders of the Race*.

166. Mühsam, *Tagebücher 1910–1924*, 28–29.

167. Mühsam to Kreszentia Mühsam, May 7, 1919, quoted in Baron, "Erich Mühsams jüdische Identität," 163. See also *Von Eisner bis Leviné*, the book Mühsam wrote in 1920 while he was in jail; it is dedicated to the memory of Landauer (10).

168. Hug, *Erich Mühsam*, 8. "Through Separation to Community" is the translation given to Mühsam's essay "Durch Absonderung zur Gemeinschaft" by Gabriel Kuhn in Landauer, *Revolution and Other Writings*.

169. Landauer to Hedwig Mauthner, November 15, 1913, in Buber, *Gustav Landauer: Sein Lebensgang in Briefen*, 1:449; Landauer to Fritz Mauthner, November 20, 1913, in ibid., 1:451.

170. Jelavich, *Munich and Theatrical Modernism*, 270–84.

171. Mühsam to Johannes Knief, December 1, 1918, in Jungblut, *Erich Mühsam: Briefe an Zeitgenossen*, 102. Mühsam's version cannot be corroborated with other sources.

172. On Toller's Judaism, see Bodenheimer, "Ernst Toller und sein Judentum."

173. Toller, *I Was a German*, 2–3.

174. Toller, *Eine Jugend in Deutschland*, 20–21 (only the last sentence of the English version is from Toller, *I Was a German*, 13). On Konitz, see Walser Smith, *Die Geschichte des Schlachters*. Edward Crankshaw's otherwise excellent translation is faulty on page 12 when it comes to describing the blood libel and the Gentile children's taunt. He gives "matzos" the erroneously Christological term "passion cakes" and has the Christian children saying "Yah to you, dirty Jew!" instead of the traditional antisemitic slogan "hep, hep!" that Toller describes.

175. Toller, *I Was a German*, 92ff.

176. Dbid, *Ernst Toller, Ein Leben in Deutschland*, 19, 33

177. Hug, *Erich Mühsam*, 22.

178. Graf, *Prisoners All*, 282.

179. Toller, *Seven Plays*, 63.

180. ibid., 100.

181. Kraepelin, "Psychiatrische Randbemerkungen zur Zeitgeschichte," 178.

182. Kraepelin, "Persönliches," in *Selbstzeugnisse*, 41–43; quoted in Becker, *Bürgerliche Lebenswelt und Politik in München*, 341–42. See also Geyer, *Verkehrte Welt*, 97–99.

183. A "Memorandum on the Soviet Governments in Munich and the Suppression" from the British government's Political Intelligence Department said, on June 3, 1919: "A student, appropriately named Toller (madman), emerged as leader of the Independent Socialists and commander of the Red Guard . . . ," in USNA, Records of the Department of State Relating to Internal Affairs of Germany, 1910–1929, microcopy 336, roll 33 862.00 (Political Affairs), 862.01 (Government).

184. Wadler, *Der Turm von Babel*, 3.

185. Pacelli's report to Gasparri, April 18, 1919, quoted in Fattorini, *Germania e Santa Sede*, 323, and in Pacelli, "Kritische Online-Edition der Nuntiaturberichte (1917–1929)," document 157, April 18, 1919, http://www.pacelli-edition.de/Dokument/257.

186. Sternsdorf-Hauck, *Brotmarken und rote Fahnen*, 26.

187. Kampf, "Frauenpolitik und politisches Handeln," 261; Fähnders, "Rubiner," 147.

188. Kampf, "Frauenpolitik und politisches Handeln, 105.

189. Höller, *Das Wintermärchen*, 219–21.

190. MLA, F.Mon. 2629, "An die Bürger der Republik!" Toller's leaflet reads:

> To the citizens of the Council Republic!
>   Leaflets are being distributed in Bavaria that are attempting in the most disgraceful and criminal manner to incite the passions of the masses against the Jews. At the same time, bourgeois provocateurs are agitating against Jews on the streets. Behind this organization there lurks an organization of reactionary conspirators all across Germany that wants to entice the masses into pogroms against Jews in order to open the way for Prussia's Freikorps to enter Bavaria and put down the proletarian revolution. The population is urged to exercise strictest discipline and, acting on its own, immediately arrest every member of this vile group so that they can be brought before the Revolutionary Court. Every citizen can see how despicable the entire agitation is because of how this whole vile provocation of the masses is being undertaken by people lying in wait under the cover of cowardly anonymity.
>   The Provisional Revolutionary Council
>   [signed] Ernst Toller

191. Ben-Chorin, *Jugend an der Isar*, 61–62.

192. Birnbaum, "Juden in der Münchner Räterepublik," 371; Birnbaum, "Thomas Mann und die Münchner Revolution." I thank Dr. Dirk Heißerer for referring me to this document. See also Mann, *Essays II, 1914–1926*, vol. 15.2 of *GKFA*, 156–57.

193. Toller, *Eine Jugend in Deutschland*, 227–28. I mostly follow the translation by Crankshaw in Toller, *I Was a German*, 280–82, but depart from Crankshaw in the opening sentence; he changes Toller's original present tense to the past and renders "that people" (*jenem Volk* in the original) to whom Toller feels he belongs as "that great race."

194. StA München, Akten der Polizeidirektion München (Munich police files) 10110, "Eugen Leviné-Niessen, Stadtkommandantur Fahndungsabteilung" (City Headquarters Investigations Department), May 19, 1919, p. 76.

195. Leviné, "Rede vor Gericht," 162.

196. StA München, Akten der Polizeidirektion München (Munich police files) 10110, "Eugen Leviné-Niessen Stadtkommandantur Fahndungsstelle" (City Headquarters Investigations Office), May 7, 1919, p. 45.

197. StA München, Akten der Polizeidirektion München (Munich police files) 10110, "Eugen Leviné-Niessen Stadtkommandantur Fahndungsstelle, Personalbeschreibung" (City Headquarters Investigations Office, Personal Description), May 11, 1919.

198. StA München, Akten der Polizeidirektion München (Munich police files) 10110, "Eugen Leviné-Niessen, Betriebsräteversammlung am 1 und 2. Ostertag, 20 und 21.4.1919" (Works Council Assembly, Easter Sunday and Monday, April 20–21, 1919), p. 3.

199. BA SAPMO NY 4094/6, p. 42. I thank Christian Dietrich for making this document available to me. The poem comes from the period between 1903 and 1905.

200. This fragment, "Der Spion: Eine Skizze aus dem russischen Studentenleben," may be found in Dietrich, *Eugen Leviné*, 12–17.

201. Meyer-Leviné, *Leviné: The Life of a Revolutionary*, 83–84.

202. Meyer-Leviné, *Leviné: The Life of a Revolutionary*, 85, 90. See also Kistenmacher, *Arbeit und "jüdisches Kapital."*

203. StA München, Akten der Polizeidirektion München (Munich police files) 10110: "Eugen Leviné-Niessen, Mitteilungen des Vollzugsrats der Betriebs- und Soldatenräte" (Announcements of the Executive Council of the Workers' and Soldiers' Councils), April 15, 1919, p. 3.

204. StA München, Akten der Polizeidirektion München (Munich police files) 10110, "Eugen Leviné-Niessen, Vollzugsrat d.B.S.R., Sitzung 17.4.1919" (Records of Council Meeting, April 17, 1919), p. 6.

205. Angress, "Juden," 293.

206. Distl, *Ernst Toller: Ein Leben in Deutschland*, 73–74.

207. Mühsam, *Tagebücher 1910–1924*, 197.

208. Morris, *Justice Imperiled*, 40–41.

209. Meyer-Leviné, *Leviné: Leben und Tod eines Revolutionärs*, 126–27; Lerner, *Ernst Kantorowicz*, 46; Schönhärl, *Wissen und Visionen*, 63–65.

210. Vatlin, "Weltrevolutionär im Abseits." On Pollock's support both for Leviné and Axelrod, see Philipp Lenhard, *Friedrich Pollock: Die graue Eminenz der Frankfurter Schule*, 58.

211. Krull, *La Vie mène la danse*, 107–9.

212. Loewenfeld, *Recht und Politik in Bayern*, 349–50.

213. StA München, Akten der Polizeidirektion München (Munich police files) 10110: "Eugen Leviné-Niessen, Protokoll der öffentlichen Sitzung des standrechtlichen Gerichts München, 2.6.1919" (Minutes of Summary Court-martial, June 2, 1919), p. 119.

214. Flemming and Schmidt, *The Diary of Karl Süßheim*, 198. Flemming and Schmidt erroneously state that Leviné was Roman Catholic.

215. BayHStA Abtl. IV, Kriegsarchiv, Freikorps—Höhere Stäbe 6, "An den Herrn Staatskommissar für Südbayern," July 1, 1919, p. 103.

216. Löwenthal, "Ein unveröffentlichter Brief aus dem Jahr 1920." I am grateful to Philipp Lenhard for referring me to this letter by Löwenthal from 1920.

217. Heusler, *Lion Feuchtwanger*, 149.

218. Feuchtwanger, *Success*, 723–24.

219. Friedländer, "Memoiren," 70.

220. Ibid., 76.

221. Cahnmann, "Die Juden in München 1918–1943," 413–14.

222. Birnbaum, "Juden in der Münchner Räterepublik," 369.

223. Landauer, "Erinnerungen an die Münchner Sozialdemokratie 1921–1923," 380–81.

224. BayHStA Abtl. IV, Kriegsarchiv, Freikorps—Höhere Stäbe 6, "Staatskommissariat für Südbayern" (letter with no date or name of sender). The letter says: "If Herr Walter Löwenfeld was so convinced about the success of his venture, one has to ask why, already on 11 o'clock that Sunday morning, he preferred escaping to safety by escorting the prisoners' train after he had previously tried without success to obtain a machine for his departure."

225. BayHStA Abtl. IV, Kriegsarchiv, Freikorps—Höhere Stäbe 41, "Schreiben der Politischen Abteilung an das Oberkommando Ulm" (letter from the Political Department of the Ulm Supreme Command), April 25, 1919: "Bericht über Versammlungen in Kempten und Memmingen" (report on meetings in Kampten and Memmingen).

226. Loewenfeld, *Recht und Politik*, 276.

227. Ibid., 295–96.

228. Birnbaum, "Juden in der Münchner Räterepublik," 370.

229. Weber, *Becoming Hitler*, 61–63, and esp. 354–55, notes 45–46. He refers to an unpublished work by his student Reinout Stegenga, according to which at least 158 Freikorps combatants were Jews. It is not clear, though, what being Jewish means in his account.

230. Sinn, *"Und ich lebe wieder an der Isar,"* 17.

231. See chapter 5.

232. Wassermann, *My Life as a German and Jew*, 217–19.

3. A Pogrom Atmosphere in Munich

1. Kafka, *Briefe 1902–1924*, 274–75; Kafka, *Letters to Friends, Family, and Editors*, 237.

2. Straus, *Wir lebten in Deutschland*, 229. On Agnon's time in Munich, see Laor, "Agnon in Germany, 1912–1924."

3. Fraenkel, *Recollections of a Jewish Mathematician in Germany*, 115. As a student and teacher in Germany, the young mathematician published under his boyhood name Adolf Abraham Fraenkel. After leaving for the Hebrew University of Jerusalem, he wrote as Abraham A. Fraenkel.

4. Reprinted in Lamm, *Vergangene Tage*, 373–75.

5. Fraenkel, *Recollections of a Jewish Mathematician in Germany*, 32.

6. *MNN*, September 14, 1920.

7. *MNN*, September 24, 1920; Mühsam, "Zur Judenfrage."

8. Cahnmann, "Die Juden in München," 38.

9. Graf, *Prisoners All*, 385.

10. Max Weber to Else Jaffé, in Krumeich and Lepsius, *Max Weber Gesamtausgabe*, 303–4.

11. On Mann's Munich period, see Brenner, "'Wir haben einander böses Blut gemacht'"; Darmaun, *Thomas Mann, Deutschland und die Juden*, esp. 108–14.

12. Mann, *Tagebücher 1918–1921*, entries for November 8, 16, 18, and 19, 1918, 63, 81–85; translation of "big-city piss elegance of the Jew-boy" and "Jewish scribblers" from Mann, *Diaries 1918–1939* (translated by Richard and Clara Winston), 19–20; "neither a Jew, nor a war profiteer, nor anything else that is bad," from Mann, *Diaries 1918–1939*, 84; Eisner as "little long-bearded Jewish man" mentioned as something "reported" by "Mann's friends" in Prater, *Thomas Mann: A Life*, 119. Other translations of excerpts from Mann's diary entries cited here by Jeremiah Riemer.

13. Hedwig Pringsheim's mention of "privy councilor" is a reference to her husband's honorific title. As to her application of the term "race" to her husband, although Alfred Pringsheim no longer regarded himself as practicing "the Mosaic persuasion," he was never baptized. Hedwig's own father, by contrast, had converted his family to Protestantism a generation earlier.

14. Hedwig Pringsheim letter from December 12, 1918, in Pringsheim, *Meine Manns*, 237.

15. Deuerlein, *Der Hitler-Putsch*, 25.

16. Müller-Meiningen, *Aus Bayerns schwersten Tagen*, 49. See also *AZJ*, "Der Gemeindebote" (supplement), November 29, 1918, 3.

17. Müller-Meiningen, *Aus Bayerns schwersten Tagen*, 48, 108.

18. Ibid., 72.

19. Ibid., 80, 106, 109.

20. Kahr, "Lebenserinnerungen," 572. I thank my colleague Ferdinand Kramer for allowing me to use Kahr's memoirs in the partly edited and digital form being prepared for publication: Ferdinand Kramer, with the assistance of Matthias Bischel, "Lebenserinnerungen von Gustav von Kahr: Bezirksamtmann—Ministerialbeamter—Regierungspräsident—Bayerischer Ministerpräsident—Generalstaatskommissar." The page numbers refer to the manuscript in the Kahr Papers (Nachlass Kahr) held at the BayHstA.

21. Kahr, "Lebenserinnerungen," 587.

22. Report by Moser von Filseck, December 6, 1918, quoted in Hermann, "Im Visier der Diplomaten," 42.

23. ÖStA/AdR/NPA/Liasse Bayern 2/1, Österreichisch-Ungarische Gesandtschaft, Anonymes Schreiben an das Deutschösterreichische Staatsamt für Äußeres, 21.12.1918 (anonymous letter to the German-Austrian State Office for External Affairs, December 21, 1918). On December 16, 1918, Karl Bernauer had become provisional office head for what was still the Austro-Hungarian Consulate General in Munich, which as of June 1919 became the German-Austrian Consulate General and then, as of May 1920, the Austrian Consulate General. Bernauer, who was reporting panic attacks during the revolutionary turmoil, was already removed from office by 1921. See Weigl, *Bayernbild*, 181–82.

24. *Neue Preußische Zeitung (Kreuzzeitung)*, February 21, 1919. See also Sebottendorf, *Bevor Hitler kam*, 49: "As we were told, the Independent Social Democratic Party of Munich is nominating the writer Kurt Eisner for by-election in the Reichstag electoral district Munich II. Eisner will surely not be elected, but that a party would even dare to nominate a Russian Jew condemned for treason is certain to make the worker blush with shame!"

25. *AZJ*, "Der Gemeindebote" (supplement), November 29, 1918, 3.

26. Weidermann, *Träumer*, 79.

27. BA SAPMO NY/4060/129, p. 29, Kurt Eisner, Rede vor Bayerischen Soldatenräten, 30.11.1918 morgens 10 Uhr (speech before the Bavarian Soldiers' Councils, November 30, 1918, 10 a.m.), in *Die neue Zeit*, 97.

28. A.B. (Antibavaricus = Victor Klemperer), in Klemperer, *Man möchte immer weinen*, 11; translation here by Jeremiah Riemer. The same passage may be found, in a different translation by Jessica Spengler, in Klemperer, *Munich 1919: Diary of a Revolution*, 1.

29. BA SAPMO NY 4060/1/116–118, 121.

30. Löffelmeier, "Besaß Kurt Eisner die bayerische Staatsangehörigkeit?," 401–6.

31. See, for example, Kriegsgeschichtliche Forschungsanstalt des Heeres, *Die Niederwerfung der Räteherrschaft in Bayern 1919* (Berlin: E. S. Mittler, 1939), 1. Here Eisner is characterized as a "Jew from Galicia who was formerly called Kosmanowsky."

32. Schwend, *Bayern zwischen Monarchie und Diktatur*, 574; in this book's index, there is an entry for "Eisner = Kosmanowski." Likewise in Ritter, *Staatskunst und Kriegshandwerk*, 4:572; here, as late as 1968, the index entry for Eisner is followed by: "correct name: Kosmanowski." See Angress, "Juden," 236.

33. *MB*, March 22, 1919.

34. Faulhaber, "Kritische Online-Edition der Tagebücher Michael Kardinal von Faulhabers (1911–1952)," diary entry for November 8, 1918, EAM, NL Faulhaber 10003, 5–6, https://www.faulhaber-edition.de/dokument.html?idno=10003_1918-11-08_T01 (accessed February 10, 2021).

35. Grau, *Kurt Eisner*, 345. Cossmann, "Vom Munitionsarbeiterstreik zur Revolution," 92.

36. *AZJ*, "Der Gemeindebote" (supplement), November 29, 1918, 3; see also *DIZ*, "Die Laubhütte" (supplement), November 21, 1918, 10.

37. Hofmiller, *Revolutionstagebuch 1918/1919*, 136–37.

38. BA SAPMO NY/4060/64, pp. 38, 53, 88, 95, 165, 214; see also Altieri, *Der Pazifist Kurt Eisner*, 126–37; and Jacob, "Kurt Eisner, der unvollendete Revolutionär," 839–40.

39. BA SAPMO NY/4060/64, pp. 83–85.

40. BA SAPMO NY/4060/64, pp. 115, 124.

41. BA SAPMO NY/4060/64, pp. 213.

42. BA SAPMO NY/4060/64, pp. 280, 331.

43. Hofmiller, *Revolutionstagebuch 1918/1919*, 153, 156.

44. *Kreuzzeitung*, February 21, 1919.

45. Busching, *Die Revolution in Bayern*, 217.

46. Ibid., 229–31.

47. Doeberl, *Sozialismus, Soziale Revolution, Sozialer Volksstaat*, 31, 34, 43; Weisz, "Die Revolution von 1918," 565. On Doeberl, see Weigand, *Münchner Historiker zwischen Politik und Wissenschaft*, 179–84.

48. Doeberl, *Sozialismus, Soziale Revolution, Sozialer Volksstaat*, 12.

49. *BK*, July 28, 1920.

50. *BV*, July 28, 1921.

51. Preußische Gesandtschaft München an das Auswärtige Amt, München, 17.12.1920 (Prussian envoy in Munich to the Foreign Office, Munich, December 17, 1920), Bundesarchiv, R 43 I/2213, pp. 135–38, reprint, https://www.bundesarchiv.de/aktenreichskanzlei/1919-1933/0000/feh/feh1p/kap1_2/para2_139.html (accessed December 27, 2020). This is document 139 at "Das Kabinett Fehrenbach—Band 1—Dokumente," 354, https://www.bundesarchiv.de/aktenreichskanzlei/1919-1933/0000/feh/feh1p/kap1_2/index.html.

52. *VB*, November 8, 1919.

53. *VB*, October 1, 1919.

54. Toller, *I Was a German*, 212.

55. Mühsam, *Tagebücher 1910–1924*, diary entry for July 27, 1915, 153.

56. Mühsam, diary entry for July 6, 1919, at Erich Mühsam, "Diaries," http://www.muehsam-tagebuch.de/tb/diaries.php#d_1919_07_06.

57. Mühsam, *Der Krater*, 148.

58. Scholem, *Von Berlin nach Jerusalem*, 180; Scholem, *From Berlin to Jerusalem*, 144. On Werner Scholem, see the biography by Mirjam Zadoff, *Der rote Hiob*.

59. *AZJ*, November 29, 1918, 566.

60. Mühsam, *Mein Weg zu mir: Aus Tagebüchern*, diary entry for December 31, 1918, 49.

61. Mann, *Tagebücher 1918–1921*, entry for November 16, 1918, 80–81.

62. Hitler, *Mein Kampf*, 2:1423. The English version here is adapted from the original James Murphy translation.

63. Graf, *Prisoners All*, 360 (with minor punctuation and spelling changes to the translation).

64. Ibid., 339.

65. Wolf, *Pope and Devil*, 80. Two strongly condemnatory accounts of the nuncio who would later become pope and his role during the Holocaust are offered by Cornwell, *Hitler's Pope* and Goldhagen, *A Moral Reckoning*.

66. Pacelli, "Kritische Online-Edition der Nuntiaturberichte Eugenio Pacellis (1917–1929)," Eugenio Pacelli to Pietro Gasparri, November 15, 1918, document 302, http://www.pacelli-edition.de/Dokument/302.

67. Pacelli, "Kritische Online-Edition der Nuntiaturberichte Eugenio Pacellis (1917–1929)," Pacelli to Gasparri, November 20, 1918, document 234, http://www.pacelli-edition.de/Dokument/234. This is similar to an earlier letter from Pacelli to Gasparri dated November 15, 1918, in Gasparri, Apostolische Nuntiatur, Bayern no. 10856.

68. Pacelli, "Kritische Online-Edition der Nuntiaturberichte Eugenio Pacellis (1917–1929)," Schioppa to Gasparri, April 6, 1918, document 2152, http://www.pacelli-edition.de/Dokument/2152. See Hermann, "Im Visier der Diplomaten," 56–57.

69. Pacelli, "Kritische Online-Edition der Nuntiaturberichte Eugenio Pacellis (1917–1929)," Schioppa to Gasparri, November 28, 1918, document 3042, http://www.pacelli-edition.de/Dokument/3042.

70. Pacelli, "Kritische Online-Edition der Nuntiaturberichte Eugenio Pacellis (1917–1929)," Schioppa to Gasparri, December 7, 1918, document 905, http://www.pacelli-edition.de/Dokument/905.

71. Faulhaber, "Autobiographie" (copy made by W. A. Ziegler).

72. So far the text of the speech has not come to light. Yet Faulhaber himself repeatedly referred to it. For instance, he mentioned it in 1925 in a speech given in the Löwenbräukeller before the Katholischer Akademikerausschuss der Münchner Hochschulen (Catholic Committee of Scholars in Munich's Universities), published under the title "Deutsches Ehrgefühl und katholisches Gewissen" (German Sense of Honor and Catholic Conscience) (Munich 1925, 22), and again in 1939 in an (unpublished) apologia vis-à-vis the National Socialists. See "Die Myrrhen meiner Bischofsjahre," 1ˢᵗ copy, January 15, 1939, in EAM, NL Faulhaber 9269/1, 2. See also Leugers, "'weil doch einmal Blut fliessen muss, bevor wieder Ordnung kommt,'" 93. For an apologetic treatment of this topic, see Generaldirektion der Staatlichen Archive Bayerns, *Kardinal Michael von Faulhaber 1869–1952*, 181; and Kornacker, "Regierung von Jehovas Zorn."

73. Faulhaber, "Kritische Online-Edition der Tagebücher Michael Kardinal von Faulhaber (1911–1952)," EAM, NL Faulhaber 10003, 25, http://www.faulhaber-edition.de/dokument.html?docidno=10003_1918-12-07_T01 (accessed September 10, 2018).

74. "Arbeitsausschuß für Volksaufklärung," October 5, 1919, EAM, NL Faulhaber 7090.

75. Archbishop Michael von Faulhaber, pastoral letter, January 29, 1919, read out on February 2, 1919, quoted in Leugers, "'weil doch einmal Blut fliessen muss, bevor wieder Ordnung kommt,'" 74–75. The verse from the Gospel According to Matthew is taken from the Douay-Rheims (Catholic Bible) translation.

76. Faulhaber, "Kritische Online-Edition der Tagebücher Michael Kardinal von Faulhaber (1911–1952)," EAM, NL Faulhaber 10003, 51–52, http://www.faulhaber-edition.de/dokument.html?docidno=10003_1919-02-21_T01 (accessed September 10, 2018).

77. Faulhaber, "Kritische Online-Edition der Tagebücher Michael Kardinal von Faulhabers (1911–1952)." EAM, NL Faulhaber 10003, 57, http://www.faulhaber-edition.de/dokument.html ?docidno=10003_1919-03-03-T01 (accessed September 10, 2018).

78. Leugers, "'weil doch einmal Blut fliessen muss, bevor wieder Ordnung kommt,'" 87.

79. Faulhaber, "Kritische Online-Edition der Tagebücher Michael Kardinal von Faulhaber (1911–1952)," EAM, NL Faulhaber 10003, 55–56, http://www.faulhaber-edition.de/dokument .html?docidno=10003_1919-02-07_T01 (accessed September 10, 2018). See also Faulhaber, "Autobiographie Faulhaber," EAM, PD 4401/4, 484. "Landauer gave the funeral speech for Kurt Eisner with the blasphemous remark that Eisner had died like Jesus, crucified and banished by stupidity" (484).

80. Faulhaber, "Kritische Online-Edition der Tagebücher Michael Kardinal von Faulhaber (1911–1952)," EAM, NL Faulhaber 10003, 77, http://www.faulhaber-edition.de/dokument.html ?docidno=10003_1919-04-18_T01 (accessed September 10, 2018); Leugers, "'weil doch einmal Blut fliessen muss, bevor wieder Ordnung kommt,'" 96.

81. Leugers, "'weil doch einmal Blut fliessen muss, bevor wieder Ordnung kommt,'" 97, note 173.

82. Faulhaber, "Autobiographie Faulhaber," EAM, PD 4401/4, 142.

83. Faulhaber, "Kritische Online-Edition der Tagebücher Michael Kardinal von Faulhaber (1911–1952)," EAM, NL Faulhaber 10003, 10, 13, http://www.faulhaber-edition.de/dokument .html?docidno=10003_1918-11-13_T01 (accessed September 10, 2018).

84. Quoted in Greive, *Theologie und Ideologie*, 41–42.

85. Ibid., 236, note 105.

86. *JE*, January 3, 1919.

87. *JE*, February 28, 1919.

88. "Bayerische Volkspartei! Wähler und Wählerinnen! Passt auf!," undated, MLA, FMon, no call number.

89. Moser von Filseck, report, January 8, 1919, quoted in Hermann, "Im Visier der Diplomaten," 45.

90. *BK*, April 9, 1919.

91. Pacelli, "Kritische Online-Edition der Nuntiaturberichte Eugenio Pacellis (1917–1929)," Pacelli, report to Gasparri, April 18, 1919, document 257, http://www.pacelli-edition.de /Dokument/257; also quoted in Fattorini, *Germania*, 323.

92. Mann, *Tagebücher 1918–1921*, entry for May 2, 1919, 223. The translation here is from Friedländer, "'Europe's Inner Demons,'" in Wistrich, *Demonizing the Other*, 215.

93. Hofmiller, *Revolutionstagebuch 1918/1919*, 164 (February 25), 177–78 (April 18), 188 (April 16), and 206 (April 30).

94. Klemperer, *Munich 1919*, 63.

95. Klemperer, *Munich 1919*, 75–76.

96. Klemperer, *Munich 1919*, 100.

97. Hitzer, *Der Mord im Hofbräuhaus*, 394, 397. On Niekisch, see Elsbach, "Irrwege eines Antisemiten."

98. Niekisch, *Gewagtes Leben*, 68–69.

99. Quoted in Pulzer, "Die jüdische Beteiligung an der Politik," 208–9; Noske, *Erlebtes aus Aufstieg und Niedergang einer Demokratie*, 27.

100. Karl, *Die Schreckensherrschaft in München*, diary entries for April 7 and 12, 1919, 13 and 24.

101. Ibid., 244, 247, 249, 256.

102. Knütter, *Die Juden und die deutsche Linke*, 77–79; see also Grimpen, *Judentum und Sozialdemokratie*, 16–17.

103. Loewenfeld, *Recht und Politik in Bayern*, 366; *Der Freistaat* (Bamberg), June 18, 1919.

104. Walter, *Antisemitische Kriminalität*, 54.

105. Quoted in Schueler, *Fechenbach 1894–1933*, 93.

106. Doeberl, *Sozialismus, Soziale Revolution, Sozialer Volksstaat*, 34; see also Geyer, *Verkehrte Welt*, 59.

107. BayHStA Abtl. IV, Kriegsarchiv, Freikorps—Höhere Stäbe 6, Staatskommissar für Südbayern an das Gesamtministerium in Bamberg (State Commissioner for Southern Bavaria to the Joint Ministry), June 26, 1919, p. 101. See also the letter from the same day to the Bayerisches Gruppenkommando 4 (Bavarian Group Commando 4) detachment, ibid., p. 102.

108. Jelavich, *Munich and Theatrical Modernism*, 301–4.

109. *MS*, November 26, 1918.

110. *MS*, December 14, 1918.

111. *MS*, January 4, 1919.

112. *MS*, March 1, 1919.

113. Blessing, "Kirchenglocken für Eisner?" 407.

114. *MS*, May 10, 1919.

115. *MS*, May 24, 1919.

116. *MS*, August 23, 1919.

117. *MS*, May 29, 1920.

118. *AZJ*, "Der Gemeindebote" (supplement), November 29, 1918.

119. Müller-Meiningen, *Aus Bayerns schwersten Tagen*, 206.

120. Meyer-Frank, "Erinnerungen an meine Studienzeit," 212; Specht, *Die Feuchtwangers*, 128.

121. Feuchtwanger, *Zukunft ist ein blindes Spiel*, 12; Specht, *Die Feuchtwangers*, 131.

122. *Israelitisches Familienblatt*, December 13, 1918.

123. *AZJ*, November 22, 1918.

124. Ibid.

125. *NJM*, November 10 and 25 and December 10, 1918.

126. *JR*, November 15, 1918.

127. *AZJ*, November 22, 1918.

128. *AZJ*, November 29, 1918.

129. Ibid.

130. *AZJ*, January 17, 1919.

131. *IdR*, January 1919.

132. *AZJ*, December 6, 1918.

133. *AZJ*, December 27, 1918.

134. *JE*, November 22, 1918, 567, reprinted in *AZJ*, December 6, 1918.

135. Ben-Chorin, *Jugend an der Isar*, 61.

136. Flemming and Schmidt, *The Diary of Karl Süßheim*, 186, 192.

137. *Die neue Zeit*, March 5, 1919.

138. BA SAPMO NY/4060/64, p. 94. Max Dreyfus Schwarz to Kurt Eisner, November 28, 1918.

139. BA SAPMO NY/4060/64, p. 260, Jakob Kramer to Kurt Eisner, undated.

140. Blumenfeld, *Erlebte Judenfrage*, 142–46.

141. Eisner, correspondence card to Herr Kommerzienrat J. Mayer, November 12, 1918, copy belonging to Else Eisner, in Kurt Eisner folder, Schwadron Collection, Hebrew National Library, Jerusalem; reprinted in Toury, *Die politischen Orientierungen der Juden*, 344. See also Kirschner, "Erinnerungen aus meinem Leben," 128.

142. Falk, *Juden, Regierung und Spartakus*, 23.

143. Ibid., 10.

144. *IdR*, December 1918; *JE*, November 29, 1918.

145. *IdR*, March 1919.

146. Ortsgruppe München, "An alle ehrlichen Volksgenossen!," pamphlet from the Munich local group of the "Zentralverein deutscher Staatsbürger jüdischen Glaubens," April 10, 1919, MLA, FMon 2649. A similar proclamation was also published by the Centralverein in the local press. See, for example, *MNN*, April 11, 1919.

147. Quoted in Schmolze, *Revolution und Räterepublik in München 1918/19*, 293.

148. *MS*, July 19, 1919.

149. *MS*, November 22, 1919.

150. Kirschner, "Erinnerungen aus meinem Leben," 128.

151. Straus, *Wir lebten in Deutschland*, 225.

152. Ibid., 229; see also Neumeyer, *Lichter und Schatten*, 61–67.

153. Neumeyer, *Lichter und Schatten*, 164.

154. Ibid., 167.

155. Wachsmann, "Hitler wurde in Bayern nicht allzu ernst genommen," 387.

156. Bilski, "Ein Facit meiner 61 Jahre," 52, memoirs in manuscript collection, LBINY.

157. Loewenfeld, *Recht und Politik in Bayern*, 206.

158. *JM*, no. 5 (1918).

159. *JM*, nos. 1 and 2 (1919).

160. *DIZ*, October 31, 1918.

161. *DIZ*, November 28, 1918.

162. *DIZ*, December 5, 1918.

163. *DIZ*, January 9, 1919.

164. *DIZ*, December 12, 1918.

165. *DIZ* (supplement), February 6, 1919.

166. *DIZ*, April 24, 1919.

167. *MP*, January 18–19, 1919.

168. *AZJ*, March 14, 1919.

169. *BK*, April 20, 1922.

170. For her biography, see Gurganus, "Sarah Sonja Lerch, née Rabinowitz." On her time at Gießen, see Naumann, "Exkurs über die Gießener Jahre." Cornelia Naumann's novel about the life of Lerch-Rabinowitz, *Der Abend kommt so schnell*, explores her family background.

171. Eisner, "Aus Tagheften 1914–18," 201–92, quoted in Gurganus, "Sarah Sonja Lerch, née Rabinowitz," 613, and in Gerstenberg, *Der kurze Traum vom Frieden*, 294.

172. Toller, *I Was a German*, 84.

173. *MNN*, April 2, 1918.

174. Gurganus, "Sarah Sonja Lerch," 614.

175. Klemperer, *Munich 1919*, 101–3.

176. *BK*, November 25, 1918.

177. *Die Laubhütte* (supplement to *DIZ*), November 29, 1918.

178. *JE*, November 29, 1918. The same comment is made in Walter, *Antisemitische Kriminalität*, 26.

179. *JE*, November 29, 1918.

180. *BK*, December 11, 1918.

181. *JE*, December 13, 1918.

182. Jochmann, *Adolf Hitler*, 245.

4. The Hotbed of Reaction

1. *JE*, September 10, 1920.

2. *JE*, October 8, 1920; Walter, *Antisemitische Kriminalität*, 97. See also the report from one of the Jewish witnesses present in Klugmann, "Mein Leben in Deutschland."

3. *Jahrbuch für sexuelle Zwischenstufen mit besonderer Berücksichtigung der Homosexualität*, nos. 3 and 4 (double issue) (July and October 1920): 124, 127.

4. Rilke, *Briefe zur Politik*, 268; also found in the translation of Rilke's letters by Jane Bannard Greene and M. D. Herter, *Letters of Rainer Maria Rilke 1910–1926*, 194.

5. Rilke, *Briefe zur Politik*, 268, translated by Jeremiah Riemer.

6. Rilke, *Briefe zur Politik*, 268, as found in the Greene and Herter translation, *Letters of Rainer Maria Rilke 1910–1926*, 194.

7. Kurz, "Aus den Tagen der Münchener Räterepublik," *NFP* July 11, 1919, *Morgenblatt*, no. 19712, 1–2.

8. Straus, *Wir lebten in Deutschland*, 233.

9. Friedländer, "Memoiren," 76–77.

10. Heusler, *Das Braune Haus*, 92.

11. Thomas Mann, *Kampf um München als Kulturzentrum*, 9. As in chapter 1, we are again using the translation of Munich as a *Hort der Reaktion* found in Winkler, *Age of Catastrophe*, 243.

12. See Hillmayr, *Roter und Weißer Terror in Bayern nach 1918*; and Thoß, "Weißer Terror, 1919." Details on the White Terror are provided by Jones, *Founding Weimar*, ch. 8: "Death in Munich."

13. On Kahr's biography up to 1921, see Bischel, "Auf der Suche nach Stabilität" and Deutinger, "Gustav von Kahr: Regierungspräsident von Oberbayern."

14. As early as his government declaration of 1920, Kahr was talking about how outsiders could look at Bavaria and "see the cell from which calm and order [will] break through." In his memoirs, he writes that he will be held responsible for having created the "Cell of Order" in Bavaria. See Kahr, "Lebenserinnerungen," 488, 569.

15. Hinterberger, "Unpolitische Politiker?", 486.

16. Loewenfeld, *Recht und Politik*, 379.

17. Schwend, *Bayern zwischen Monarchie und Diktatur*, 151, quoted in Geyer, *Verkehrte Welt*, 114.

18. Bischel, "Klischeehafte Überzeichnung als Erkennungsmerkmal?".

19. Sammartino, *The Impossible Border*, 127–29.

20. Loewenfeld, *Recht und Politik*, 502.

21. See Kramer, "Kirchen und Religion in den 'Lebenserinnerungen' von Gustav von Kahr," 226–28.

22. Kahr, "Lebenserinnerungen," 59–60.

23. Ibid., 313.

24. Ibid., 569.

25. Ibid., 353–54.

26. Ibid., 631.

27. Ibid., 1061.

28. Kahr, 1921 diary entry (vol. 1), 206 and 196, quoted in Hinterberger, "Unpolitische Politiker?," 77–78. The image of the Jewish profiteer was hardly restricted to Munich. Shortly afterwards, the Jewish entrepreneurs Julius Barnat and Jakob Michael in Berlin were associated with this figure. See Geyer, *Kapitalismus und politische Moral in der Zwischenkriegszeit*, 114–21.

29. Robert Murphy, Consul General in Munich, report to the Secretary of State, December 13, 1923, in USNA, Records of the Department of State Relating to Internal Affairs of Germany, 1910–1929, microcopy 336, roll 79 862.00, 862.4016.

30. Walter, *Antisemitische Kriminalität*, 130.

31. Gruchmann, *Justiz im Dritten Reich, 1933–1940*, 16–48.

32. Feuchtwanger, *Success*, 61.

33. Walter, *Antisemitische Kriminalität*, 113–14.

34. Nickmann and Schröder, "Revolution und 'Ordnungszelle Bayern,'" 19–24.

35. Neliba, *Wilhelm Frick*, 29.

36. Plöckinger, *Unter Soldaten und Agitatoren*, 11–14; Joachimsthaler, *Hitlers Weg begann in München*, 177; Weber, *Wie Adolf Hitler zum Nazi wurde*, 160–90; Wirsching, "Hitlers Authentizität." For a sharply formulated discussion, see Reuth, *Hitlers Judenhass*, 72–152. See also the new biographies by Kershaw, *Hitler, 1889–1936*; Longerich, *Hitler: A Biography*; Pyta, *Hitler*; Ullrich, *Ascent: 1889–1939*. For an overview, see Large, *Where Ghosts Walked*.

37. Joachimsthaler, *Hitlers Weg begann in München*, 188–89. Plöckinger is cautious in his assessment in *Unter Soldaten*, 42–44. By contrast, a more unambiguous answer to the question suggesting Hitler's sympathies for the new regime is given by Reuth, *Hitlers Judenhass*, 88–91; Reuth even views Hitler as a "functionary in the machinery of the Communist world revolution" (94).

38. Hitler, *Mein Kampf*, 561, 531. The translation used here is by Ralph Manheim from the Houghton Mifflin edition of *Mein Kampf*, 194.

39. Plöckinger, *Unter Soldaten und Agitatoren*, 42–65.

40. Weber and Plöckinger arrive at different conclusions on the development of Hitler's antisemitism. See Weber, *Wie Adolf Hitler zum Nazi wurde*, 137–59; and Plöckinger, *Unter Soldaten und Agitatoren*, 113–68. It is in Lechfeld—the town south of Augsburg where Hitler received Reichswehr education training, was appointed an instructor himself, and had an opportunity to try out his speaking skills in the summer of 1919—that Wirsching, in "Hitlers Authentizität," 401–2, locates the origins of Hitler's ideological formation.

41. See Plöckinger, *Unter Soldaten und Agitatoren*, 209–17.

42. On the complex circumstances of Hitler's approach to the DAP, the party he took over and transformed, see ibid., 145–53.

43. *MAAZ*, August 10, 1919.

44. The letter is reproduced in Joachimsthaler, *Hitlers Weg*, 231.

45. See Plöckinger, *Unter Soldaten*, 331–35; see also Walter, *Antisemitische Kriminalität*, 36–37.

46. Piper, *Alfred Rosenberg*, 48–52.

47. Large, *Where Ghosts Walked*, 195. On the Bruckmanns, see also Martynkewicz, *Salon Deutschland*.

48. See Heusler, *Das Braune Haus*, 110–26.

49. "General-Mitgliederversammlung und Partei-Tagung der Nationalsozialistischen Deutschen Arbeiterpartei am 29. und 31. Januar in München" (General Assembly of Members and Party Conference of the National Socialist German Workers' Party on January 29–31 in Munich), in LoC, Rehse Collection, "German Captured Documents," box 271.

50. Hitler, "Rede auf NSDAP-Führertagung in Plauen i.V. am 12.6.1925" (speech at the NSDAP Leader Conference in Plauen im Vogtland, June 12, 1925), in Hitler, *Reden Schriften Anordnungen*, 99. See Andreas Heusler, "Hauptstadt der Bewegung," Historisches Lexikon Bayern, January 23, 2018, https://www.historisches-lexikon-bayerns.de/Lexikon/Hauptstadt_der_Bewegung,_München (accessed January 1, 2021).

51. On East European Jews in Germany, see Maurer, *Ostjuden in Deutschland, 1918–1933*; Wertheimer, *Unwelcome Strangers*; Aschheim, *Brothers and Strangers*. On the history of the Ostjuden in Munich, see Stadtarchiv München, *"Ich lebe! Das ist ein Wunder."* On the number of pogrom victims, see the new book by Jeffrey Veidlinger, *In the Midst of Civilized Europe: The Pogroms of 1918–1921 and the Onset of the Holocaust*. I am grateful to Professor Veidlinger for allowing me to see the manuscript (titled "Pogrom: The Origins of the European Genocide of the Jews") before its publication by Metropolitan Books in 2021.

52. Brenner, "The Jüdische Volkspartei"; *JE*, November 22, 1918.

53. In electoral districts with a high concentration of East European Jews, by contrast, the JVP obtained two-thirds of the votes. *JE*, March 18, 1921.

54. *JE*, March 18 and 21, 1921. See Brenner, "The Jüdische Volkspartei," 219–41; and Specht, "Zerbrechlicher Erfolg," 154–56.

55. *JE*, November 22, 1918.

56. *JE*, December 20, 1918.

57. Meining, "Ein erster Ansturm der Antisemiten: 1919–1923," 58. See also Maurer, *Ostjuden in Deutschland, 1918–1933*, 403–59; and Knütter, *Die Juden und die deutsche Linke*, 85–86.

58. StA München, Pol. dir. München, verz. 241/II, Fasz. 43, no. 122b, Fremdenpolizei: Ostjüdische Zuwanderer (Aliens Police: Eastern Jewish Immigrants), "Denkschrift zur Verordnung des Stadtkommandanten vom 3.6.1919 betr.: 'Aufenthaltsverbot für Ausländer' vom 21. Mai 1919 von Rechtanwalt Dr. L. Ambrunn namens des Gesamtausschusses der Ostjuden in München" (memorandum on decree from City Commanding Officer dated June 3, 1919 re: "Residence Ban for Foreigners" dated May 21, 1919 by attorney Dr. L. Ambrunn on behalf of the General Committee of Eastern Jews in Munich).

59. BayHstA Abt. II 99902, Akten des Staatsministeriums des Äußern (files of the State Ministry for External Affairs), Maßnahmen zur Wiederherstellung geordneter Verhältnisse in Bayern, Besprechung im Ministerium des Innern am 26.6.1919 (measures to restore orderly conditions in Bavaria, meeting in the Ministry of the Interior, June 26, 1919); Ehberger and Bischel, *Das Kabinett Hoffmann II: Teil 1: 31. Mai-1. September 1919*, 290–92.

60. BayHstA Abt. II, 99902, Akten des Staatsministeriums des Äußern (files of the State Ministry for External Affairs), Maßnahmen zur Wiederherstellung geordneter Verhältnisse in Bayern. Kommandantur der Landeshauptstadt München Abteilung IIIa Nr. 2921: Schreiben der Kommandantur an den Ministerpräsident Hoffmann und verschiedene Ministerien, betr. Schutzhaft, Ausweisungen (measures to restore orderly conditions in Bavaria, Headquarters of the City of Munich, Department IIIa, no. 2921: letter from the headquarters to Prime Minister Hoffmann and various ministries, re: protective custody, expulsions). See also Knütter, *Die Juden und die deutsche Linke*, 85–86.

61. StA München, Polizeidirektion München (Munich Police Headquarters), 4118, Pol. dir. München, verz. 241/II, fasz. 43, no. 122b, Fremdenpolizei: Ostjüdische Zuwanderer (Aliens Police: Eastern Jewish Immigrants), Schreiben: Pol. dir. München an das Staatsministerium des Inneren 8.12.1919 (Ne. 3785/II) (Letter: Munich police headquarters fo State Ministry of the Interior, December 8, 1919), B. 301–31.

62. Even after 1945, the writer Hans Carossa was describing Kahr's expulsion of Ostjuden as "fair and justified," since, he claimed, they had come to Germany after the First World War "in order to enrich themselves at the expense of the impoverished people." Quoted in Becker, *Bürgerliche Lebenswelt und Politik in München*, 345.

63. StA München, Polizeidirektion München 4118, p. 10, Vorschläge zur Handhabung des Aufenthaltsverbots für Ausländer (proposals for handling the residence ban for foreigners).

64. StA München, Polizeidirektion München 4118. On the subject of expulsions of East European Jews out of Munich more generally, see Walter, *Antisemitische Kriminalität*, 59–70.

65. Meining, "Ein erster Ansturm der Antisemiten: 1919–1923," 58–60. See also the depiction from the perspective of Reich, "Eine Episode aus der Geschichte der Ostjuden Münchens," 402.–3.

66. StA München, Polizeidirektion München 4118 (Pol. dir. München verz. 241/II, fasz. 43, no. 122b), Fremdenpolizei: Ostjüdische Zuwanderer (Aliens Police: East Jewish Immigrants), Reg. von Oberbayern an das Staatsministerium des Innern, 25.1.1920: "Zuzug von Ausländern, hier des Moses Laus aus Przemysl in Galizien" (Govt., admin. of Upper Bavaria to the State Ministry of the Interior, January 25, 1920, "Immigration of Foreigners, here from Moses Laus from Przemysl in Galicia").

67. Walter, *Antisemitische Kriminalität*, 64.

68. *JE*, April 9, 2020.

69. *JE*, April 23, 1920.

70. StA München, Polizeidirektion München 4118, Fürsorgestelle der jüdischen Organisationen an das Ministerium des Innern, 12.4.1920 (Welfare Office of Jewish Organizations to the Ministry of Internal Affairs, April 12, 1920).

71. StA München, Polizeidirektion München 4118, Polizeidirektion München (Pöhner) an das Ministerium des Innern, 19.4.1920 (Munich Police Department [Pöhner] to the Minister of Internal Affairs, April 19, 1920).

72. StA München, Polizeidirektion München 4118, Fürsorgestelle der jüdischen Organisationen Münchens an das Staatsministerium des Innern, 21.6.1920 (Welfare Office of Jewish Organizations to the Ministry of Internal Affairs, June 21, 1920).

73. StA München, Polizeidirektion München 4118, letter from Assessor Lang, June 30, 1920.

74. StA München, Polizeidirektion München 4118, Polizeidirektion München (Pöhner) an das Ministerium des Innern, 23.6.1920 (Munich Police Department [Pöhner] to the Ministry of Internal Affairs, June 23, 1920).

75. Meining, "Ein erster Ansturm der Antisemiten: 1919–1923," 66.

76. JE, April 23, 1920.

77. StA München, Polizeidirektion München 4118.

78. StA München, Polizeidirektion München 4118, anonymous letter, November 11, 1920.

79. Large, "'Out with the Ostjuden.'"

80. Pommerin, "Die Ausweisung von 'Ostjuden' aus Bayern 1923," 321.

81. USHMM Washington, R 98632, Bericht vom 3.6.1920. Politisches Archiv des Auswärtigen Amts (report from June 3, 1920, Political Archive of the Foreign Office) (microfilm).

82. JR, June 21, 1921, 352; translation available in the Einstein Papers held at Princeton University at "How I Became a Zionist," document 57, pp. 234–37, 236, in vol. 7 of "The Berlin Years: Writings, 1918–1921" (English translation supplement), https://einsteinpapers.press.princeton .edu/vol7-trans/252.

83. See Walter, Antisemitische Kriminalität, 64–70; Plöckinger, Unter Soldaten, 194–209.

84. The letter from October 13, 1919, is quoted in Meining, "Ein erster Ansturm der Antisemiten: 1919–1923," 61.

85. MP, February 9, 1920.

86. JE, March 26, 1920. The term "semi-Asia" (Halb-Asien) should not be confused with "Asia Minor." The designation was popularized by the Austrian-Jewish writer Karl-Emil Franzos in his book Halb-Asien: Land und Leute des östlichen Europa. The anthropologist Ivan Kalmar, Early Orientalism, 23, describes it as the "the contemptuous term used in twentieth-century German . . . to imagine Eastern Europe as a marginal region between Occident and Orient."

87. JE, April 9, 1920.

88. Geyer, Verkehrte Welt, 280.

89. Scholem, Von Berlin nach Jerusalem, 153; Scholem, From Berlin to Jerusalem, 135–36. Zohn's translation omits Scholem's description of the "crude Bavarian-ness" of antisemitism in Munich and his comment that Munich's Jews "all regarded this as a temporary phenomenon," so we include these references from the German edition to the Bavarian setting in our own translation. On Scholem's time in Munich, see Rees, "Ein Dichter, ein Mädchen und die jüdischen Speisegesetze."

90. Geyer, Verkehrte Welt, 280–86.

91. Hoser, Die politischen, wirtschaftlichen und sozialen Hintergründe, 472. For background on the Bayerische Mittelpartei (Bavarian Middle Party, BMP), the Bavarian affiliate of the Nationalist party, the DNVP, see Kiiskinen, Die Deutschnationale Volkspartei (Bayerische Mittelpartei).

92. MAAZ, October 22, 1922, 365; quoted in Hoser, Die politischen, wirtschaftlichen und sozialen Hintergründe, 1036.

93. MNN, September 25, 1920; see also StA München, Polizeidirektion München 4118, Amtsgericht München an die Polizeidirektion München, 21.9.1920 (Munich District Court to Munich Police Department, September 21, 1920).

94. Geyer, *Verkehrte Welt*, 280–86.

95. Reinhard Weber, "Einleitung," in Hirschberg, *Jude und Demokrat*, 15. An additional reason may also have been resistance from his newly wedded wife, who feared for his safety. See Morris, *Justice Imperiled*, 58.

96. Kirschner, "Erinnerungen aus meinem Leben," 136–37; see also *BK*, April 28, 1921.

97. *BT*, June 11, 1921. Of the reports that he was Jewish, Saenger, who was the defense lawyer for numerous East European Jews, wrote: "It is not true that I am a Jew. What is true, by contrast, is that neither I nor any of my ancestors ever belonged to an Israelite religious community" *VB*, January 17, 1920. The register of births, deaths, and marriages from the Staatsarchiv Hamburg and the Niedersächsisches Landesarchiv in Stade confirm Saenger's Christian family background. On the assault itself, see Walter, *Antisemitische Kriminalität*, 283.

98. Nagorski, *Hitlerland*, 22.

99. Feuchtwanger, *Success*, 122.

100. Flemming and Schmidt, *The Diary of Karl Süßheim*, 201–2.

101. Hinterberger, "Unpolitische Politiker?," 254.

102. Bry, *Der Hitlerputsch*, 28.

103. Ibid., 107–8.

104. Müller, *Die französische Gesandtschaft in München*, 169, 232–38.

105. USNA, Records of the Department of State Relating to Internal Affairs of Germany, 1910–1929, microcopy 336, roll 15 862.00 (Political Affairs), vol. 9, American Commission Berlin to State Department, "Report on the Present Situation in Bavaria Prepared by A. W. Dulles, April 10, 1920," April 12, 1920.

106. Weil, *A Pretty Good Club*.

107. USNA, Records of the Department of State Relating to Internal Affairs of Germany, 1910–1929, microcopy 336, roll 79 862.00, 862.4016.

108. Hoser, "Die Rosenbaumkrawalle von 1921 in Memmingen."

109. Mühsam, "Niederschönenfeld, Saturday, d. August 13, 1921," diary entry for August 13, 1921, at the website Erich Mühsam: Diaries, issue 28, May 26–September 14, 1921, http://www .muehsam-tagebuch.de/tb/diaries.php (accessed January 4, 2021).

110. *CVZ*, May 26, 1922.

111. *CVZ*, May 11, 1923. This and the previous *CVZ* quote may be found in Bajohr, "Tatort Bayern—die 'Arisierung' der Alpen" (Crime Scene Bavaria—the "Aryanization" of the Alps), in Bajohr, *"Unser Hotel ist judenfrei,"* 62–69.

112. Ignaz Wrobel (aka Kurt Tucholsky), *Die Weltbühne*, no. 4 (January 27, 1921): 114.

113. *MA*, February 2, 1921, reprinted in Volkert, *Ludwig Thoma*, 131–32.

114. *MA*, April 8, 1921, reprinted in Volkert, *Ludwig Thoma*, 222–23.

115. *MA*, April 7, 1921, reprinted in Volkert, *Ludwig Thoma*, 216–18. "Berlin W." is a reference to the affluent western parts of Berlin. Whereas Ostjuden often lived in older neighborhoods, like the Scheunenviertel in the eastern part of the city, newer districts in western Berlin were becoming home to more affluent German Jews.

116. Feuchtwanger, *Erfolg*, 773, translated here by Jeremiah Riemer. This sarcastic remark about the *Miesbacher Anzeiger* does not appear to be in the English translation of *Success* by Willa and Edwin Muir.

117. Mühsam, "Niederschönenfeld, Sonntag, d. 27. August 1922," diary entry for August 27, 1922, at the website Erich Mühsam: Diaries, issue 34, August 21–October 2, 1922, http://www.muehsam-tagebuch.de/tb/index.php (accessed January 4, 2021).

118. Alfred Neumeyer, VBIG inaugural speech, reprinted in Lamm, *Vergangene Tage*, 379.

119. *MNN*, April 29, 1920.

120. *MNN*, May 3, 1921.

121. "An alle ehrlichen Volksgenossen!" *MNN*, April 11, 1919; MLA, F.Mon. 2649, Die Ortsgruppe München des Zentralvereins Deutscher Staatsbürger jüdischen Glaubens (Munich branch of the Central Association of German Citizens of the Jewish Faith), "An alle ehrlichen Volksgenossen! Eine offene Erwiderung" (To all honest fellow citizens! An open reply), April 10, 1919.

122. Falk, *Juden, Regierung und Spartakus*, 8–11.

123. Hirschberg, *Jude und Demokrat*, 247.

124. *BT*, June 11, 1921, reprinted in Lamm, *Vergangene Tage*, 375–79.

125. *MA*, July 14, 1921, reprinted in Volkert, *Ludwig Thoma*, 393–95.

126. Landauer, "Erinnerungen an die Münchner Sozialdemokratie 1921–1923," 380–83. See also Landauer's more detailed account, Landauer, Carl. "The Bavarian Problem in the Weimar Republic."

127. Quoted in Hirte, "Erich Mühsam und das Judentum," 68.

128. BayHStA, MA 102386, Verband Bayerischer Israelitischer Gemeinden to Lerchenfeld, April 30, 1922.

129. BayHStA, MA 99517, Council of Ministers meetings, May 5, 1922, and October 18, 1921. See also Hinterberger, "Unpolitische Politiker?," 253.

130. Sabrow, *Die verdrängte Verschwörung*.

131. Heusler, *Lion Feuchtwanger*, 159; Feuchtwanger, "Vom Sinn und Unsinn des historischen Romans," 19–23; Small, "In Buddha's Footsteps."

132. Feuchtwanger, "Gespräche mit dem Ewigen Juden," 58.

133. Friedländer, "Memoiren," 128.

134. Gumbel, *Verschwörer*, 159.

135. "Vorwort," in Gumbel, *Verschwörer*, 33–35.

136. Pranckh, *Der Prozeß gegen den Grafen Anton Arco-Valley*, 30–31. This brochure put out by the right-wing extremist publisher J. F. Lehmann Verlag and written by a loyal Arco supporter marks the beginning of an entire literature glorifying Eisner's murderer. In 1919, Ludwig Holländer wrote: "The worst poison is being disseminated in Munich by the publisher Lehmann." Holländer, *Der Antisemitismus in der Gegenwart*, 5.

137. *MNN*, January 16, 1920; see also the collection of newspaper clippings on Arco in StdA ZA-P-12-4.

138. *MNN*, January 16, 1920.

139. *MNN*, January 17, 1920.

140. *MAAZ*, January 19, 1920.

141. Gumbel, *Verschwörer*, 165.

142. Müller, *Mars und Venus: Erinnerungen*, 56.

143. Selig, *Paul Nikolaus Cossmann und die Süddeutschen Monatshefte*, 46–47; Geyer, *Verkehrte Welt*, 117.

144. Spengler, *Preußentum und Sozialismus*, 98. On Spengler's economic plans, see Hoser, *Die politischen, wirtschaftlichen und sozialen Hintergründe*, 172–94.

145. See Spengler to Cossmann, December 2, 1923, in Koktanek, *Oswald Spengler*, 289–93. See also Selig, *Paul Nikolaus Cossmann*, 69; and Hoser, *Die politischen, wirtschaftlichen und sozialen Hintergründe*, 468.

146. Loewenfeld, *Recht und Politik*, 434.

147. Hirschberg, *Jude und Demokrat*, 160.

148. Ibid., 167.

149. Monacensis, "Und immer wieder Fechenbach," 241.

150. *Die Weltbühne*, June 26, 1924, 907–8.

151. Müller, *1919–1932*, 226. On Müller, see Berg, *Karl Alexander von Müller*.

152. Hoser, *Die politischen, wirtschaftlichen und sozialen Hintergründe*, 87; Hoser, "Münchner Neueste Nachrichten."

153. Preußische Gesandtschaft München an das Auswärtige Amt. München, 17.12.1920 (the Prussian envoy in Munich to the Foreign Office, December 17, 1920), Das Bundesarchiv, R 43 I/2213, pp. 135–38, reprint, https://www.bundesarchiv.de/aktenreichskanzlei/1919-1933/0000 /feh/feh1p/kap1_2/para2_139.html (accessed December 27, 2020), document 139 at "Das Kabinett Fehrenbach—Band 1—Dokumente," 354, https://www.bundesarchiv.de/aktenreichskanzlei /1919-1933/0000/feh/feh1p/kap1_2/index.html. The circulation figures for Munich newspapers in 1920 were *MNN*, 120,000; *MZ*, 120,000; *MP*, 60,000; *MAAZ*, 48,000; *BSZ*, 30,000; *BK*, 25,000; and *VB*, 10,000. Hoser, *Die politischen, wirtschaftlichen und sozialen Hintergründe*, 981–83.

154. BayHStA NL Cossmann, folder 7, Karl Haniel to Cossmann, September 13, 1920.

155. BayHStA NL Cossmann, folders 12 and 14, Prof. Dr. Martin Spahn to Cossmann, November 15 and 22, 1920.

156. The Civil Defense Guards had already been established under the revolutionary government. Their earliest members included Jewish defenders of democracy like the attorney Max Friedländer. See Friedländer, "Memoiren," 77. On the Civil Defense Guards, see Large, *The Politics of Law and Order*.

157. BayHStA NL Cossmann, folder 12, Prof. Dr. Martin Spahn to Cossmann, November 15, 1920. On the Cossmann-Spahn relationship, see also Hübner, *Die Rechtskatholiken*, 325–31.

158. BayHStA NL Cossmann, folder 10; see, for example, Cossmann to Hugenberg, April 18, 1923 (about his visits to Munich and their future collaboration) and Hugenberg to Cossmann, April 24, 1923 (about the possibility, however difficult, of influence over "the man from Ludwigshöhe" that Cossmann had asked for). This was a reference to Becker's hometown; at that time, the economics minister was also on the executive board of the Rheinische Stahlwerke Duisburg-Meiderich. Hugenberg was often characterized by Cossmann only according to his residence, either as "Rohbraken" (the site of Hugenberg's estate near Kükenbruch north of Detmold) or as the man from the Weser (the nearby river).

159. Hoser, *Die politischen, wirtschaftlichen und sozialen Hintergründe*, 83.

160. BayHStA NL Cossmann, folder 7, Mann to Cossmann, June 28, 1921.

161. BayHStA NL Cossmann, folder 7, Mann to Cossmann, September 24, 1921.

162. BayHStA NL Cossmann, folder 7, Roth to Cossmann, September 29, 1920.

163. BayHStA NL Cossmann, folder 7, Roth to Cossmann, July 19, 1921.

164. BayHStA NL Cossmann, folder 14, Cossmann to Max Graf von Montgelas, October 22, 1923.

165. *Die Weltbühne*, October 2, 1924, 523.

166. Mühsam, "Niederschönenfeld, Sonntag, d. 20. August 1922," diary entry for August 20, 1922, at the website Erich Mühsam: Diaries, issue 33, June 7–August 20, 1922, http://www.muehsam-tagebuch.de/tb/index.php.

167. In 1921, Cossman personally controlled 75 percent of the company capital for the *Süddeutsche Monatshefte*. Hoser, *Die politischen, wirtschaftlichen und sozialen Hintergründe*, 181.

168. Cossmann, "Der Zusammenbruch," 146–47.

169. Ibid., 156.

170. Hofmiller, "Nietzsche und der Bolschewismus," 292.

171. Eliasberg, "Russischer und Münchner Bolschewismus," 72; see also Hurwicz, "Die Weltexpansion des Bolschewismus." Little is know about David Eliasberg. He died in February 1920 on a "quarantine ship" outside Königsberg at the age of twenty-three. I thank Dr. Carmen Sippl for this information. On Alexander Eliasberg, see Sippl, "Der 'Bote von außen.'" On Hurwicz, see Terpitz, "Simon Dubnow und seine Übersetzer."

172. Cossmann, "Bolschewismus und Christentum," 75–77.

173. Oppenheimer and Oppenheimer, "Der Antisemitismus," 129.

174. Cossmann, "Der Friede," 257.

175. Karo, "Deutsche Schuld und deutsches Gewissen," 99–100.

176. Müller, "Neue Urkunden," 52. This assertion was first published in the August 2, 1919 issue of the *Deutsche Allgemeine Zeitung* by Hans von Schön. See Dreyer and Lembcke, *Die deutsche Diskussion um die Kriegsschuldfrage*, 74.

177. *MMP*, 29 July 1921.

178. *BV*, 28 July 1921. This was similarly reported in the *MA*, August 4, 1921. The conservative Catholic newspaper *Das Bayerische Vaterland*, for example, published an article with the title "How the Jews Eisner and Fechenbach are perpetrating a heinous crime on the German people."

179. Müller, "Neue Urkunden," 52, editor's footnote.

180. Dirr, "Auswärtige Politik Kurt Eisners."

181. Loewenfeld, *Recht und Politik*, 446–47. On the political assassinations, see the two books by Gumbel, *Zwei Jahre Mord* (1921) and *Vier Jahre politischer Mord* (1922).

182. *MAAZ*, June 17, 1919.

183. *MNN*, October 7, 1920.

184. The most extensive account of the trials between Fechenbach and Cossmann is found in Morris, *Justice Imperiled*, 67–155.

185. *MMP*, July 28, 1922. Immediately after Schön's initial accusation, Eisner had contradicted the charge of forgery. See *Der Kampf*, September 16, 1919.

186. *MNN*, 5 May 1922, 5

187. A contemporary account of the trial from the perspective of Fechenbach's defense attorney may be found in Hirschberg, *Der Fall Fechenbach vor dem Münchner Volksgericht*. Another contemporary account is Dreyfus and Mayer, *Recht und Politik im Fall Fechenbach*.

188. Czernichowski emigrated in 1933, Weiler in 1936.

189. StA München stanw. 1682, quoted in Schueler, *Fechenbach 1894–1933*, 172–74. Dr. E. Darmstädter made a similar remark on 14 July 1919 to the prosecuting attorney Mathäus Hahn;

see Staatsarchiv für Oberbayern, Staatsanwaltschaft München I, no. 2242/II, im Strafverfahren gegen Ernst Toller (in the criminal proceedings against Ernst Toller), quoted in Knütter, *Die Juden und die deutsche Linke*, 92.

190. *Vorwärts*, October 5, 1922.

191. See Morris, *Justice Imperiled*, 95–96.

192. Hirschberg, *Jude und Demokrat*, 174. Hirschberg published his own account of the trial in the book *Der Fall Fechenbach vor dem Münchner Volksgericht*.

193. The third judge was the former Bavarian justice minister Ernst Müller-Meiningen, who had also played an unfortunate part in the restoration phase and had threatened Fechenbach's attorney Max Hirschberg in 1920 with withdrawal of his license to practice law. See Morris, *Justice Imperiled*, 128.

194. Walter, *Antisemitische Kriminalität*, 114.

195. Friedländer, "Memoiren," 72; see also Morris, *Justice Imperiled*, 128.

196. Loewenfeld, *Recht und Politik*, 466.

197. *Die Weltbühne*, July 5, 1923, 30. See Morris, *Justice Imperiled*, 134. One of the few significant statements made by a jurist was that of Professor Heinrich Kitzinger, "Der Fall Fechenbach."

198. Flade, "Leben und Tod Felix Fechenbachs," 22.

199. *MNN*, November 18, 1922.

200. USHMM Washington, R 98549, Po. 15 Fechenbach, Schreiben des Gesandten Frerichs vom 18.11.1922. Politisches Archiv des Auswärtigen Amts (letter from envoy Frerich, November 18, 1922, Political Archive of the Foreign Office) (film version).

201. USHMM Washington, R 98549, Po. 15 Fechenbach, Denkschrift Dr. Thimme, Politisches Archiv des Auswärtigen Amts (memorandum Dr. Thimme, Political Archive of the Foreign Office) (film version), 14.

202. ÖStA/AdR/Konsulat München, Pol.Korr. 1919–1930, Bericht des Generalkonsuls an das Bundesministerium für Äußeres in Wien, 14.7.1922 (report of the Consul General to the Federal Ministry for External Affairs in Vienna, July 14, 1922).

203. Monacensis, "Und immer wieder Fechenbach," 242.

204. *MZ*, December 2–3, 1922.

205. Hirschberg, *Der Fall Fechenbach vor dem Münchner Volksgericht*.

206. *MP*, January 31, 1923. The letter may be found in LoC, Rehse Collection, "German Captured Documents," box 183.

207. Lessing, *Der jüdische Selbsthaß*; see also Gilman, *Jewish Self-Hatred*.

208. Hamann, *Hitlers Wien*, 329–33.

209. See the biography by Wasserstein, *The Secret Lives of Trebitsch Lincoln*.

210. StA München, Polizeidirektion München 10166, p. 1. A letter from Berlin to the Munich police department, dated July 4, 1920, contains a wanted-persons photo as well as a note remarking that a reward of 100 marks was offered for Trebitsch-Lincoln's capture.

211. Kerekes, "Die 'Weiße Allianz.'" I am grateful to Matthias Bischel for drawing my attention to these plans and for other valuable suggestions.

212. StA München, Polizeidirektion München 10166, pp. 7–11. See also *MP*, November 29, 1920; and *BK*, December 12, 1920.

213. *Rote Fahne*, January 14, 1921. StA, Polizeidirektion München 10166, p. 13.

214. StA München, Polizeidirektion München 10166, p. 2.

215. Wasserstein, *The Secret Lives of Trebitsch Lincoln*, 162–68; Trebitsch-Lincoln, *Der größte Abenteurer des XX. Jahrhunderts!?*, 193–205.

216. Trebitsch-Lincoln, *Der größte Abenteurer des XX. Jahrhunderts!?*, 196–97.

217. Thoß, *Der Ludendorff-Kreis 1919–1923*, 429.

218. Trebitsch-Lincoln, *Der größte Abenteurer des XX. Jahrhunderts!?*, 213.

219. StA, Polizeidirektion München 10166, p. 23, Polizeidriektion Abteilung (Police Department) VI a. F., November 5, 1923.

5. The City of Hitler

1. Mann, *Essays II, 1914–1926*, vol. 15.1 of *GKFA*, 694, first published in English in the American literary periodical *Dial Magazine* 75 (October 1923): 374. This is the first public mention of Hitler in the published work of Thomas Mann. See Heißerer, "Bruder Hitler?," 66.

2. *JE*, October 5, 1923.

3. Feuchtwanger, *Erfolg*, 31–32; Feuchtwanger, *Success*, 27.

4. Schricker, *Rotmord über München*, 192, quoted in Piper, *Alfred Rosenberg*, 37.

5. Mann wrote these lines in June 1923 for the third of his letters later to appear in *Dial Magazine* 75 (October 1923): 374; see Mann *Essays II, 1914–1926*, vol. 15.1 of *GKFA*, 694. I am grateful to Dr. Dirk Heißerer for showing me this and other texts by Thomas Mann.

6. Mann, *GKFA*, vol. 10.1, 295; see also Heißerer, "Bruder Hitler?," 68. The quote may be found in *Doctor Faustus*, translated by John E. Woods, 217.

7. Feuchtwanger, "Gespräche mit dem Ewigen Juden," 85.

8. All quotes in Drößler, "'Nathan der Weise'—ein klassisches Drama und die öffentliche Gewalt," 215–17. See also Loiperdinger, "Nathan der Weise."

9. Motz and Seeßlen, "Erich Wagowski und seine 'Tilmlnus Bavaria CmbH,'" 16.

10. Loiperdinger, "Nathan der Weise," 63.

11. *VB*, February 16, 1923.

12. In May 1923, the staging of Bertolt Brecht's drama *Dickicht* (In the Jungle of the Cities) at Munich's Residenztheater was sabotaged by gas bombs. See Heißerer, "Bruder Hitler?," 68. In February 1921, the tenth performance of Arthur Schnitzler's *Reigen* (La Ronde) had already been disrupted by a planned action coming from the audience. In contrast to the authorities in Berlin and Hamburg, who saw to it that additional performances took place, the Munich police immediately banned the piece. See Pfoser, Pfoser-Schewig, and Renner, *Der Skandal*, 176–77.

13. BayHStA, no. 2745/X, March 16, 1923, MA 100116, Verband Bayerischer Israelitischer Gemeinden an die bayerische Staatsregierung (Association of Bavarian Israelite Communities to the Bavarian state government), quoted in Pommerin, "Die Ausweisung von 'Ostjuden' aus Bayern 1923," 322.

14. *BSZ*, March 20, 1923.

15. Mühsam, diary entry for January 2, 1923, at the website Erich Mühsam: Diaries, issue 35, October 3, 1922–January 10, 1923, http://www.muehsam-tagebuch.de/tb/index.php.

16. *BSZ*, June 23, 1923. This article and the following ones may be found in the newspaper clipping collection, StdA ZA-P-134-36.

17. *MNN*, June 23, 1923.

18. *MNN*, June 27, 1923.

19. *MP*, June 22, 1923.

20. *MP*, June 23–24, 1923.

21. Quoted in *MNN*, June 29, 1923.

22. Geyer, *Verkehrte Welt*, 126.

23. These incidents culminated in violent riots in the Franconian towns Untermerzbach and Autenhausen, in which Jewish citizens were physically assaulted by members of paramilitary organizations. See BayHStA, Minn 73725, "Antisemitische Bewegung"; Walter, *Antisemitische Kriminalität*, 115–18.

24. Mühsam, *Tagebücher 1910–1924*, 333.

25. BayHStA, Minist. Akten 1919–1932, MA 100403, letter from August 6, 1923.

26. BayHStA, Minist. Akten 1919–1932, MA 100403, Ministry of External Affairs to the Justice and Interior Ministry, September 12, 1923.

27. On the long history of antisemitism at swimming and bathing resorts, see Bajohr, *"Unser Hotel ist judenfrei."*

28. *JE*, September 28, 1923, 459.

29. *JE*, October 5, 1923, 469.

30. BayHStA, Generalstaatskommissariat, "1. Rundschreiben Kahrs" (Kahr's first circular), October 19, 1923; Pommerin, "Die Ausweisung von 'Ostjuden' aus Bayern 1923," 323; Geyer, *Verkehrte Welt*, 342; Hinterberger, "Unpolitische Politiker?," 415; Maurer, *Ostjuden in Deutschland, 1918–1933*, 405–16.

31. Pommerin, "Die Ausweisung von 'Ostjuden' aus Bayern 1923," 315.

32. *MA*, October 14, 1923.

33. *MP*, October 27–28, 1923.

34. *MAAZ*, October 27, 1923.

35. *MNN*, October 27, 1923.

36. *MZ*, November 15, 1923.

37. *DIZ*, November 6, 1923.

38. Reich, "Eine Episode aus der Geschichte der Ostjuden Münchens," 403.

39. This was the place were, as early as 1920, East European Jews and other foreigners who could not be deported were housed. See Walter, *Antisemitische Kriminalität*, 70–75.

40. Reich, "Eine Episode aus der Geschichte der Ostjuden Münchens," 403.

41. BayHStA, MInn 71741, Commander Sommermann to the Munich Police Department, October 21, 1923. See also Kraftzick, "Das Sammellager Fort Prinz Karl bei Ingolstadt 1920–1924."

42. BayHStA, MInn 71741, Schreiben des Pol. Leutnant u. Kommandoführer der Polizeitruppe München Abschnitt IV Hundertschaft an den Chef des Abschnittes IV und an das Staatsministerium des Innern und der Landespolizeiverwaltung (letter of pol. lieutenant and commander of the Munich Police Troop, Section IV, Group of Hundred Police, to the chief of Section IV and the State Ministry of Interior and the State Police Administration), November 13, 1920.

43. BayHStA, Generalstaatskommissar 89, Antwortschreiben des Generalkommissars an die Gemeindevertretung der Israelitischen Kultusgemeinde München (letter from the commissioner general in reply to the representative body of the Munich Israelite Religious Community), October 31, 1923.

44. Sammartino, *The Impossible Border*, 163–67.

45. Loewenfeld, *Recht und Politik*, 504.

46. Feuchtwanger, *Nur eine Frau: Jahre, Tage, Stunden*, 165.

47. BayHStA, Generalstaatskommissariat 89, Gelberger to Austrian honorary consul, January 29, 1923, cited in Hinterberger, "Unpolitische Politiker?," 415.

48. Pommerin, "Die Ausweisung von 'Ostjuden' aus Bayern 1923," 326–26.

49. Müller, *Die französische Gesandtschaft in München*, 238.

50. Ibid., 327–32. On the reaction of the Polish consular authorities, see Adelson, "The Expulsion of Jews with Polish Citizenship"; and Maurer, *Ostjuden in Deutschland, 1918–1933*, 452–55.

51. ÖStA/AdR/Konsulat München/Pol.Korr. 1919–1930, Bericht des Generalkonsuls an das Bundesministerium für Äußeres in Wien (report of Consul General to the Federal Ministry for Foreign Affairs in Vienna), October 27, 1923.

52. USNA, Records of the Department of State Relating to Internal Affairs of Germany, 1910–1929, microcopy 336, roll 19 862.00 (Political Affairs), 1923–1924, vol. 13. See "Jews Deported from Bavaria by Hundreds," Jewish Telegraphic Agency, October 29, 1923, https://www.jta.org/1923/10/29/archive/jews-deported-from-bavaria-by-hundreds.

53. Murphy, *Diplomat among Warriors*, 15–16.

54. USNA, Records of the Department of State Relating to Internal Affairs of Germany, 1910–1929, microcopy 336, roll 19 862.00 (Political Affairs), 1923–1924, vol. 13.

55. For example, the Jewish religious teacher Hermann Klugmann recounted that he no longer talked to his Protestant colleagues at Munich's Boys' Trade School (Münchner Knaben-Handelsschule) because of their antisemitic attitudes, whereas he got along well with his Catholic colleagues. See Klugmann, "Mein Leben in Deutschland vor dem 30. Januar 1933," 26.

56. Ziegler, "Kardinal Faulhaber im Meinungsstreit," 67.

57. *Allgemeine Zeitung*, September 3, 1922.

58. Dedication of the monastery school in Salzburghofen, July 12, 1922, quoted in Leugers, "'weil doch einmal Blut fliessen muss, bevor wieder Ordnung kommt,'" 97.

59. Faulhaber to Stresemann, November 6, 1923, in Volk, *Akten Michael von Faulhabers, 1917–1945*, 319, quoted in Leugers, "'weil doch einmal Blut fliessen muss, bevor wieder Ordnung kommt,'" 98.

60. *BK*, November 6, 1923.

61. Greive, *Theologie und Ideologie*, 243, note 202.

62. Faulhaber's diary entry, November 8, 1923, EAM, NL Faulhaber 10009, quoted in Leugers, "'weil doch einmal . . .,'" 98.

63. Blaschke, "Wie wird aus einem guten Katholiken ein guter Judenfeind?," 83–84.

64. Quoted in Greive, *Theologie und Ideologie*, 62–64.

65. Ibid., 64.

66. *DIZ*, May 8, 1919.

67. *MB*, August 6, 1919.

68. *VB*, June 6, 1923, 3; *VB*, June 7, 1923, 2–3; *VB*, June 8, 1923, 2.

69. Hirschberg, *Jude und Demokrat*, 237.

70. Ibid., 238.

71. Ibid., 236.

72. USHMM Washington, R 98353, Der Vertreter der Reichsregierung in München Haniel an das Auswärtige Amt, 26.1.1923. Politisches Archiv des Auswärtigen Amts (representative of

the Reich government in Munich Haniel to the Foreign Office, January 26, 1923, Political Archive of the Foreign Office) (microfilm).

73. USHMM Washington, R 98353, Bericht an das Auswärtige Amt, 2.1.1923. Politisches Archiv des Auswärtigen Amts (report to the Foreign Office, January 2, 1923, Political Archive of the Foreign Office) (microfilm).

74. USHMM Washington, R 98353, Der Vertreter der Reichsregierung in München Haniel an das Auswärtige Amt, 7.3.1923. Politisches Archiv des Auswärtigen Amts (representative of the Reich government in Munich Haniel to the Foreign Office, March 7, 1923, Political Archive of the Foreign Office) (microfilm).

75. Hürten, "Revolution und Zeit der Weimarer Republik," 484.

76. See, for example, Dornberg, *Hitlers Marsch zur Feldherrnhalle*; Gordon, *Hitler and the Beer Hall Putsch*; Mommsen, "Adolf Hitler und der 9. November 1923"; Pappert, *Der Hitlerputsch und seine Mythologisierung*. For a useful collection of source material, see Deuerlein, *Der Hitler-Putsch: Bayerische Dokumente*.

77. Hoser, *Die politischen, wirtschaftlichen und sozialen Hintergründe*, 486. The following day Gerlich, instead of printing the commentary originally planned in support of the putschists, published an article against Hitler as a traitor and supporting even greater dictatorial authority for Kahr. Ibid., 490.

78. *BK*, November 9, 1923, 1.

79. ÖStA/AdR/NPA/Liasse Bayern 2/3, Bericht des Generalkonsuls an das Bundesministerium für Äußeres in Wien (report of the Consul General to the Federal Ministry for Foreign Affairs in Vienna), November 12, 1923. Consul General Otto Günther was inclined to the view that Kahr was carrying on with his own plans for a putsch but was then surprised by Hitler. See Weigl, *Bayernbild*, 301.

80. Loewenfeld, *Recht und Politik*, 526.

81. Rothenbücher, *Der Fall Kahr*. The most detailed study of the Hitler putsch leaves it open as to what Kahr's position was. See Gordon, *Hitlerputsch 1923*, 477.

82. Hirschberg, *Jude und Demokrat*, 240.

83. Hoser, *Die politischen, wirtschaftlichen und sozialen Hintergründe*, 483–85.

84. Large, "'Out with the Ostjuden.'"

85. Loewenfeld, *Recht und Politik*, 522.

86. Kahr, "Erinnerungen" (Memoirs), BayHstA, Kahr Papers (Nachlass Kahr), 1168.

87. For a comprehensive account of the hostage-taking, see Walter, *Antisemitische Kriminalität*, 119–39.

88. Ben-Chorin, *Jugend an der Isar*, 22. See also Stadtarchiv München, *Beth ha-Knesseth: Ort der Zusammenkunft*, 110.

89. Straus, *Wir lebten in Deutschland*, 248.

90. Loewenfeld, *Recht und Politik*, 520.

91. Flemming and Schmidt, *The Diary of Karl Süßheim*, 206.

92. Ben-Chorin, *Jugend an der Isar*, 11.

93. USHMM Washington, R 98354, Der Vertreter der Reichsregierung in München Haniel an das Auswärtige Amt. Politisches Archiv des Auswärtigen Amts (representative of the Reich government in Munich Haniel to the Foreign Office, Political Archive of the Foreign Office), November 14, 1923 (microfilm).

94. ÖStA/AdR/NPA Liasse Bayern 2/3, Bericht des Generalkonsuls an das Bundesministerium für Äußeres in Wien (report of the Consul General to the Federal Ministry for Foreign Affairs in Vienna), November 12, 1923.

95. *JE*, April 4, 1924.

96. *BK*, November 13, 1923.

97. Levi, "Geschichte eines Weltbuergers," 211, memoirs in manuscript collection, LBINY.

98. These rejoinders are summarized quite comprehensively in his writing "Die Myrrhen meiner Bischofsjahre," [1st] copy, January 15, 1939, EAM, NL Faulhaber 9269/1, pages 199–208. See also the chapter "Der Kardinal und die Judenfrage," , 323–25.

99. *BK*, November 17–18, 1923.

100. Bry, *Der Hitler-Putsch*, 181–85.

101. Gritschneder, *Der Hitler-Prozeß*; Gordon, *Hitlerputsch 1923*, 423–33; Steger, "Der Hitlerprozeß und Bayerns Verhältnis zum Reich." Judge Neithardt's remarks here are translated by Jeremiah Riemer.

102. *Frankfurter Zeitung*, April 1, 1924.

103. *Frankfurter Zeitung*, April 2, 1924.

104. Walter, *Antisemitische Kriminalität*, 139–41.

105. *Die Weltbühne*, February 7, 1924.

106. Quoted in Litten, *Der Rücktritt Richard Willstätters*, 57. On the basis of the very material Litten presents, I cannot agree with his conclusion that fatigue was largely responsible for Willstätter's retirement.

107. *JE*, August 25, 1924. See also the relevant correspondence between the rector's office and faculty members in the summer of 1924, UAM, E-II-3590, including the city council's request that an effort be made to get Willstätter to stay.

108. Willstätter, "Die Geschichte meines Rücktritts," 412–15.

109. Mann, *Kampf um München als Kulturzentrum*, 8–9.

110. *Der Israelit*, January 25 and February 6, 1930; *JE*, January 24 and February 7, 1930; *BIGZ*, February 1, 1930.

111. Straus, *Wir lebten in Deutschland*, 266–67.

112. Ben-Chorin, *Jugend an der Isar*, 20.

6. A Variety of Perspectives

1. Feuchtwanger, *Success*, 717. Kutzner is the character in the novel based on Hitler.

2. Gerstenberg, *Der kurze Traum vom Frieden*, 298.

3. Klemperer, *Curriculum Vitae*, 2:619–20.

4. Gerstenberg, *Der kurze Traum vom Frieden*, 296.

5. *MNN*, June 20, 1923.

6. *NZ*, June 8, 1926.

7. The entire correspondence may be found in StdA München, Bürgermeister u. Rat 1659/3.

8. "Ernst Toller Discusses Palestine," *American Hebrew*, June 2, 1927, 178.

9. Fechenbach, *Der Puppenspieler: Ein Roman aus dem alten Würzburg*.

10. Flade, "Felix Fechenbach," 58.

11. Schueler, *Fechenbach 1894–1933*, 214; Preuss, "Im Hause der Freudlosen."

12. "Unser Felix Fechenbach," reprinted in Hartmann, "Felix Fechenbach—ein sozialistischer Zionist?," 26.

13. *Jüdisches Lexikon*, vol. 2, col. 608 (Berlin, 1927).

14. Flade, "Leben und Tod Felix Fechenbachs," 25–29.

15. MLA Monacensia L 3464, interview by Bayerischer Rundfunk with Ms. Lulu Cossmann, summer 1956, p. 4.

16. Selig, *Paul Nikolaus Cossmann*, 74–78.

17. Hirschberg, *Jude und Demokrat*, 161.

18. Arco auf Valley, *Aus fünf Jahren Festungshaft*, 13–28.

19. *VB*, July 10, 1925. As late as 1967, the fraternity newspaper *Der Rhaeten-Herold: Blätter der Katholischen Bayerischen Studentenverbindung Rhaetia* was celebrating its "dear Toni." The paper's pages extolled "forever his cheerful and open manner." See "Anton Graf Arco auf Valley," *Der Rhaeten-Herold* 295 (1967). See also the readers' letter column in *MP*, March 2, 1926.

20. StA München, Polizeidirektion 10004.

21. The only biography we have is an exhilarating but not scholarly account by Hitzer, *Anton Graf Arco*.

22. *MP*, June 5, 1927.

23. After he had converted to Buddhism, a report on Trebitsch-Lincoln's impending visit to Munich appeared in "Der Weg eines Abenteurers" (An Adventurer's Pathway), *MZ*, July 22, 1929.

24. Fraenkel, *Lebenskreise*, 52; Fraenkel, *Recollections of a Jewish Mathematician in Germany*, 34.

25. *BSZ*, October 1, 1925; see also the obituary in *MAAZ*, October 2, 1925.

26. Fraenkel, *Lebenskreise*, 31; Fraenkel, *Recollections of a Jewish Mathematician in Germany*, 17–18.

27. Flemming and Schmidt, *The Diary of Karl Süßheim*, 247, 299.

28. Chladenius, *Allgemeine Geschichtswissenschaft*, 100–101.

29. See, for example, Koselleck, "Standortbindung und Zeitlichkeit."

30. Mühsam, *Von Eisner bis Leviné*, 8.

31. See, for example, *BV*, February 23, 1929; *MP*, February 19, 1929.

32. Kriegsgeschichtliche Forschungsanstalt des Heeres, *Die Niederwerfung der Räteherrschaft*, 1.

33. Among the few exceptions were Neubauer, *München und Moskau*; Schade, *Kurt Eisner und die bayerische Sozialdemokratie*; and Speckner, "Die Ordnungszelle Bayern."

34. See Beyer, *Von der Novemberrevolution*.

35. Mitchell, *Revolution in Bavaria*, 5.

36. Bosl, *Bayern im Umbruch*.

37. See, for example, Ay, *Die Entstehung einer Revolution*; Dorst, *Die Münchner Räterepublik*; and Schmolze, *Revolution und Räterepublik in München 1918/19*.

38. *SZ*, May 13–15, 1967.

39. *Münchner Merkur*, January 15 and 16, 1969.

40. *Münchner Merkur*, January 24, 1969.

41. Ude, "Leben und Nachleben," 10.

42. On the history of the Eisner memorials, see Geschichtsverein Hadern, *Schlaglichter: Kurt Eisners Haderner Zeit*.

43. Appel, *Die letzte Nacht der Monarchie*; Höller, *Das Wintermärchen*; Schaupp, *Der kurze Frühling der Räterepublik*; Weidermann, *Träumer*.

44. *BSZ*, April 6, 2018.

45. In addition, two justice ministers, Curt Joel and Erich Koch-Weser, had Jewish ancestry but were baptized as Christians. See Pulzer, *Jews and the German State*, 272–74.

46. Cahnmann, "Die Juden in München 1918–1943," 411–12.

47. Mitchell, *Revolution in Bavaria*, 332.

48. "Anniversary of Hitler Putch As Jewish Fast Day," Jewish Telegraphic Agency, November 22, 1923, https://www.jta.org/1923/11/22/archive/anniversary-of-hitler-putch-as-jewish -fast-day.

Adelson, Józef. "The Expulsion of Jews with Polish Citizenship from Bavaria in 1923." *Polin* 5 (1990): 57–73.

Altieri, Riccardo. *Der Pazifist Kurt Eisner*. Hamburg: Kovač, 2015.

Angermair, Elisabeth. "Eine selbstbewusste Minderheit (1892–1918)." In *Jüdisches München: Vom Mittelalter bis zur Gegenwart*, edited by Richard Bauer and Michael Brenner, 110–36. Munich: Beck, 2006.

Angress, Werner T. "The German Army's 'Judenzählung' of 1916: Genesis—Consequences—Significance." *Yearbook of the Leo Baeck Institute* 23 (1978): 117–37.

———. "Juden im politischen Leben der Revolutionszeit." In *Deutsches Judentum in Krieg und Revolution*, edited by Werner E. Mosse, 137–315. Tübingen: J.C.B. Mohr, 1971.

Appel, Michael. *Die letzte Nacht der Monarchie: Wie Revolution und Räterepublik in München Adolf Hitler hervorbrachten*. Munich: DTV, 2018.

Arco auf Valley, Anton. *Aus fünf Jahren Festungshaft*. Regensburg: Verlagsanstalt vorm. G. J. Manz, 1925.

Aschheim, Steven E. *Brothers and Strangers: The East European Jew in German Jewish Consciousness, 1800–1923*. Madison: University of Wisconsin Press, 1982.

Ay, Karl-Ludwig. *Die Entstehung einer Revolution: Die Volksstimmung in Bayern während des Ersten Weltkrieges*. Berlin: Duncker & Humblot, 1968.

Bajohr, Frank. *"Unser Hotel ist judenfrei": Bäder-Antisemitismus im 19. und 20. Jahrhundert*. Frankfurt am Main: Fischer Taschenbuch Verlag, 2003.

Baron, Lawrence. "Erich Mühsam's Jewish Identity." *Yearbook of the Leo Baeck Institute* 25 (1980): 269–84.

———. "Erich Mühsams jüdische Identität." In *Erich Mühsam und das Judentum: Zwölfte Erich-Mühsam Tagung in der Gustav Heinemann Bildungsstätte Malente, 25.–27. Mai 2001*, edited by Jürgen-Wolfgang Goette et al., 157–70. Lübeck: Erich-Mühsam-Gesellschaft, 2002.

Bauer, Franz J., ed. *Die Regierung Eisner 1918/1919: Ministerratsprotokolle und Dokumente*. Düsseldorf: Droste, 1987.

Bauer, Reinhard, and Ernst Piper. *München: Die Geschichte einer Stadt*. Munich: Piper, 1993.

Bauer, Richard, and Michael Brenner, eds. *Jüdisches München: Vom Mittelalter bis zur Gegenwart*. Munich: Beck, 2006.

Bauman, Zygmunt. "Pawns in Other People's Games." *Münchner Beiträge zur jüdischen Geschichte und Kultur* 12, no. 2 (2018): 23–51.

Baur, Johannes. *Die russische Kolonie in München 1900–1945: Deutsch-russische Beziehungen im 20. Jahrhundert*. Wiesbaden: Harrassowitz, 1998.

Becker, Nikola. *Bürgerliche Lebenswelt und Politik in München: Autobiographien über das Fin de Siècle, den Ersten Weltkrieg und die Weimarer Republik.* Kallmünz/Opf.: Laßleben, 2014.

Ben-Chorin, Schalom. *Jugend an der Isar.* Gütersloh: Gütersloher Verlagshaus, 2001.

Benz, Wolfgang. "Ressentiment und Trauma: Juden und Novemberrevolution in Bayern." *Zeitschrift für Geschichtswissenschaft* 66, no. 10 (2018): 842–58.

———. *Süddeutschland in der Weimarer Republik: Ein Beitrag zur deutschen Innenpolitik 1918–1923.* Berlin: Duncker & Humblot, 1970.

Berg, Matthias. *Karl Alexander von Müller: Historiker für den Nationalsozialismus.* Göttingen, Vandenhoeck & Ruprecht, 2014.

Bernstein, Eduard. *Die Aufgaben der Juden im Weltkriege.* Berlin: Erich Reiss Verlag, 1917.

Bernstein, Michael André. *Foregone Conclusions: Against Apocalyptic History.* Berkeley: University of California Press, 1994.

Beyer, Hans. *Von der Novemberrevolution zur Räterepublik in München.* Berlin: Rütten & Loening, 1957.

Biale, David. *Gershom Scholem: Master of the Kabbalah.* New Haven, CT: Yale University Press, 2018.

Birnbaum, Immanuel. "Juden in der Münchner Räterepublik." In *Vergangene Tage: Jüdische Kultur in München,* edited by Hans Lamm, 369–71. Munich: Langen Müller, 1982.

———. "Thomas Mann und die Münchner Revolution." *Süddeutsche Zeitung,* August 20, 1955.

Bischel, Matthias. "Auf der Suche nach Stabilität in der Transformation. Gustav von Kahr. Eine teilbiographische Studie (1862–1921)." PhD dissertation, Ludwig Maximilian University of Munich, 2021.

———. "Klischeehafte Überzeichnung als Erkennungsmerkmal? Die Figur des Franz Flaucher und Gustav von Kahr." Geschichte Bayerns, March 23, 2015, https://histbav.hypotheses.org/3570.

Blaschke, Olaf. "Wie wird aus einem guten Katholiken ein guter Judenfeind? Zwölf Ursachen des katholischen Antisemitismus auf dem Prüfstand." In *Katholischer Antisemitismus im 19. Jahrhundert: Ursachen und Traditionen im internationalen Vergleich,* edited by Olaf Blaschke and Aram Mattioli, 83–84. Zürich: Orell Füssli, 2000.

Blessing, Werner. "Kirchenglocken für Eisner? Zum Weltanschauungskampf in der Revolution von 1918/19 in Bayern." *Jahrbuch für fränkische Landesforschung* 53 (1992): 403–20.

Blumenfeld, Kurt. *Erlebte Judenfrage.* Stuttgart: Deutsche Verlags-Anstalt, 1962.

Bodenheimer, Alfred. "Ernst Toller und sein Judentum." In *Deutsch-jüdische Exils- und Emigrationsliteratur im 20. Jahrhundert,* edited by Itta Shedletzky and Hans-Otto Horch, 185–93. Tübingen: Niemeyer, 1993.

Bosl, Karl, ed. *Bayern im Umbruch: Die Revolution von 1918, ihre Voraussetzungen, ihr Verlauf und ihre Folgen.* Munich: Oldenbourg, 1969.

Breines, Paul. "The Jew as Revolutionary: The Case of Gustav Landauer." *Year Book of the Leo Baeck Institute* 12 (1967): 75–84.

Brenner, Michael. "The Jüdische Volkspartei: National-Jewish Communal Politics in Weimar Germany." *Year Book of the Leo Baeck Institute* 35 (1990): 219–43.

———. "Pre–Nazi Germany Tells Us the Fight to Save American Democracy Is Just Beginning." *Washington Post,* January 9, 2021. https://www.washingtonpost.com/outlook/2021/01/09/pre-nazi-germany-tells-us-fight-save-american-democracy-is-just-beginning/ (accessed April 27, 2021).

————. "Religion, Nation oder Stamm: Zum Wandel der Selbstdefinition unter deutschen Juden." In *Nation und Religion in der deutschen Geschichte*, edited by Heinz-Gerhard Haupt and Dieter Langewiesche, 587–601. Frankfurt am Main: Campus, 2001.

————. *The Renaissance of Jewish Culture in Weimar Germany*. New Haven, CT: Yale University Press, 1996.

————. "A Tale of Two Families: Franz Rosenzweig, Gershom Scholem, and the Generational Conflict around Judaism." *Judaism* 42 (1993): 349–61.

————. "Warum München nicht zur Hauptstadt des Zionismus wurde: Jüdische Religion und Politik um die Jahrhundertwende." In *Zionistische Utopie—Israelische Realität*, edited by Michael Brenner and Yfaat Weiss, 39–52. Munich: Beck, 1999.

————. "What if the Weimar Republic Had Survived?" In *What Ifs of Jewish History*, edited by Gavriel D. Rosenfeld, 259–74. New York: Cambridge University Press, 2016.

————. "'Wir haben einander böses Blut gemacht'—Thomas Mann und die Juden." In *Thomas Mann in München IV*, edited by Dirk Heißerer, 1–35. Munich: Thomas-Mann-Förderkreis, 2008.

Brentano, Lujo. *Mein Leben im Kampf um die soziale Entwicklung Deutschlands*. Jena: E. Diederichs, 1931.

Briggs, Mitchell Pirie. *George D. Herron and the European Settlement*. Stanford, CA: Stanford University Press, 1932.

Bronner, Stephen E. "Persistent Memories of the German Revolution: The Jewish Activists of 1919." *New Politics* 5, no. 2 (1995): 83–94.

Bry, Carl Christian. *Der Hitler-Putsch: Berichte und Kommentare eines Deutschland-Korrespondenten (1922–1924) für das "Argentinische Tag- und Wochenblatt,"* edited by Martin Gregor-Dellin. Nördlingen: Greno, 1987.

Buber, Martin. *Briefwechsel aus sieben Jahrzehnten*, edited and with an introduction by Grete Schaeder, in consultation with Ernst Simon and with the participation of Rafael Buber, Margot Cohn, and Gabriel Stern. 3 vols. Heidelberg: Schneider, 1973.

————, ed. *Gustav Landauer: Sein Lebensgang in Briefen*. Frankfurt: Rütten & Loening, 1929.

————. *The Letters of Martin Buber: A Life of Dialogue*, edited by Nahum N. Glatzer and Paul Mendes-Flohr, translated by Richard and Clara Winston and Harry Zohn. New York: Schocken, 1991.

————. "Die Revolution und wir." *Der Jude* 3, nos. 8/9 (1918–1919): 345–47.

Busching, Paul. "Die Revolution in Bayern." *Süddeutsche Monatshefte* 16, no. 9 (June 1919): 17–234.

Cahnmann, Werner J. "Die Juden in München 1918–1943." *Zeitschrift für Bayerische Landesgeschichte* 42 (1979): 403–62.

————. "Die Juden in München." In *Vergangene Tage: Jüdische Kultur in München*, edited by Hans Lamm, 31–78. Munich: Langen Müller, 1982.

Chladenius, Johann Martin. *Allgemeine Geschichtswissenschaft*. Leipzig: Friedrich Lanckischens Erben, 1752.

Cornwell, John. *Hitler's Pope: The Secret History of Pius XII*. New York: Viking, 1999.

Cossmann, Paul Nikolaus. "Bolschewismus und Christentum." *Süddeutsche Monatshefte* 16 (April 1919): 75–79.

————. "Der Friede." *Süddeutsche Monatshefte* 16 (July 1919): 245–58.

———. "In der Heimat: Vom Munitionsarbeiterstreik zur Revolution." *Süddeutsche Monatshefte* 21 (May 1924): 92–94.

———. "Der Zusammenbruch." *Süddeutsche Monatshefte* 16 (December 1918): 146–66.

Darmaun, Jacques. *Thomas Mann, Deutschland und die Juden.* Tübingen: M. Niemeyer, 2003.

Déak, István. "Jews and Communism: The Hungarian Case." In *Dark Times, Dire Decisions: Jews and Communism,* edited by Dan Diner and Jonathan Frankel, 38–61. Studies in Contemporary Jewry 20. Oxford: Oxford University Press, 2004.

Delf, Hanna, ed. *Gustav Landauer—Fritz Mauthner: Briefwechsel 1890–1919.* Munich: C. H. Beck, 1994.

Deuerlein, Ernst, ed. *Der Aufstieg der NSDAP in Augenzeugenberichten.* Düsseldorf: Rauch, 1968.

———. *Der Hitler-Putsch: Bayerische Dokumente zum 8./9. November 1923.* Stuttgart: Deutsche Verlags-Anstalt, 1962.

Deutinger, Stephan, Karl-Ulrich Gelberg, and Michael Stephan. "Gustav von Kahr: Regierungspräsident von Oberbayern." In *Die Regierungspräsidenten von Oberbayern im 19. und 20. Jahrhundert,* 2nd and expanded ed., edited by Stephan Deutinger, Karl-Ulrich Gelberg, and Michael Stephan, 218–31. Munich: Regierung von Oberbayern, 2010.

———, eds. *Die Regierungspräsidenten von Oberbayern im 19. und 20. Jahrhundert,* 2nd and expanded ed. Munich: Regierung von Oberbayern, 2010.

Deutscher, Isaac. *Der nichtjüdische Jude.* Berlin: Rotbuch, 1991.

———. *The Non-Jewish Jew and Other Essays.* Oxford: Oxford University Press, 1968.

Dietrich, Christian. *Eugen Leviné: "Ich fühle russisch und denke jüdisch."* Berlin: Hentrich & Hentrich, 2017.

Diner, Dan, and Jonathan Frankel, eds. *Dark Times, Dire Decisions: Jews and Communism.* Studies in Contemporary Jewry 20. Oxford: Oxford University Press, 2004.

Dirr, Pius. "Auswärtige Politik Kurt Eisners und der Bayerischen Revolution." *Süddeutsche Monatshefte* 19 (February 1922): 241–76.

Distl, Dieter. *Ernst Toller: eine politische Biographie.* Schrobenhausen: Bickel, 1993.

Doeberl, Michael. *Sozialismus, Soziale Revolution, Sozialer Volksstaat.* Munich: Allgemeine Zeitung, 1920.

Dornberg, John. *Hitlers Marsch zur Feldherrnhalle: München, 8. und 9. November 1923.* Munich: Langen Müller, 1998.

———. *Munich 1923: The Story of Hitler's First Grab for Power.* New York: Harper & Row, 1982.

Dorst, Tankred. *Die Münchner Räterepublik: Zeugnisse und Kommentar.* Frankfurt am Main: Suhrkamp, 1968.

Dove, Richard. *Ernst Toller: Ein Leben in Deutschland.* Göttingen: Steidl, 1999.

———. *He Was a German: A Biography of Ernst Toller.* London: Libris, 1990.

Dreyer, Michael, and Oliver Lembcke. *Die deutsche Diskussion um die Kriegsschuldfrage 1918/19.* Berlin: Duncker & Humblot, 1993.

Dreyfus, Paul, and Paul Mayer. *Recht und Politik im Fall Fechenbach.* Berlin: Rowohlt, 1925.

Drößler, Stefan. "'Nathan der Weise'—ein klassisches Drama und die öffentliche Gewalt." In *Pioniere in Celluloid: Juden in der frühen Filmwelt,* edited by Irene Stratenwerth and Hermann Simon, 215–19. Berlin: Henschel, 2004.

Eckart, Dietrich. *Der Bolschewismus von Moses bis Lenin: Zwiegespräch zwischen Adolf Hitler und mir.* Munich: Hoheneichen-Verlag, 1924.

———. *Totengräber Rußlands*. Munich: Deutscher Volksverlag, Dr. E. Boepple, 1921.

Efron, John M. *Defenders of the Race*. New Haven, CT: Yale University Press, 1994.

Ehberger, Wolfgang, and Matthias Bischel, eds. *Das Kabinett Hoffmann II: Teil 1: 31. September 1919 (Die Protokolle des Bayerischen Ministerrats 1919–1945)*. Munich: Kommission für Bayerische Landesgeschichte, 2017.

Einstein, Albert. "How I Became a Zionist." *Jüdische Rundschau* (June 21, 1921): 351–52. Available in "The Berlin Years: Writings, 1918–1921" (English translation supplement), vol. 7, https:// einsteinpapers.press.princeton.edu/vol7-trans/250.

Eisner, Kurt. "Aus Tagheften 1914–18: Ein Opfer." In Eisner, *Gesammelte Schriften*, vol. 1. Berlin: P. Cassirer, 1919.

———. "Religion des Sozialismus (1908)." In Eisner, *Die halbe Macht den Räten: Ausgewählte Aufsätze und Reden*, edited by Renate and Gerhard Schmolze, 200–212. Cologne: Hegner, 1969.

———. "Revolutionsfeier." In Eisner, *Die halbe Macht den Räten: Ausgewählte Aufsätze und Reden*, edited by Renate and Gerhard Schmolze, 277–80. Cologne: Hegner, 1969.

———. "Zum 70. Geburtstag des Philosophen (4 Juli 1912)." In Eisner, *Die halbe Macht den Räten: Ausgewählte Aufsätze und Reden*, edited by Renate and Gerhard Schmolze, 122–35. Cologne: Hegner, 1969.

Eliasberg, David. "Russischer und Münchner Bolschewismus." *Süddeutsche Monatshefte* 16 (April 1919): 69–72.

Elsbach, Sebastian. "Irrwege eines Antisemiten—Ernst Niekisch in der frühen DDR." *Medaon* 15 (2021): 28. http://www.medaon.de/pdf/medaon_28_elsbach.pdf.

Engel, Amir. *Gershom Scholem: An Intellectual Biography*. Chicago: University of Chicago Press, 2017.

Fähnders, Walter. "Rubiner, Frida." *Neue Deutsche Biographie* 22 (2005): 157. https://www .deutsche-biographie.de/pnd118873245.html#ndbcontent.

Falk, Hanns. *Juden, Regierung, und Spartakus*. Berlin: Philo-Verlag, 1920.

Fattorini, Emma. *Germania e Santa Sede: Le nunziature di Pacelli fra la Grande guerra e la Repubblica di Weimar*. Bologna: Società editrice il Mulino, 1992.

Faulhaber, Michael von. *Deutsches Ehrgefühl und katholisches Gewissen*. Munich: Dr. F. A. Pfeiffer & Co., 1925.

Fechenbach, Felix. *Der Puppenspieler: Ein Roman aus dem alten Würzburg*, edited by Roland Flade and Barbara Rott. Würzburg: Königshausen & Neumann, 1988.

———. *Der Revolutionär Kurt Eisner*. Berlin: J. H.W. Dietz Nachfolger, 1929.

Feuchtwanger, Lion. *Erfolg: Drei Jahre Geschichte einer Provinz*. Berlin: Kiepenhauer Verlag, 1930; Berlin: Aufbau-Verlag, 1993.

———. "Gespräche mit dem Ewigen Juden." In *An den Wassern von Babylon: Ein fast heiteres Judenbüchlein*, edited by Hermann Sinsheimer, 51–92. Munich: G. Müller, 1920.

———. *Success: Three Years in the Life of a Province*, translated by Willa and Edwin Muir. London: Martin Secker, 1930.

———. "Vom Sinn und Unsinn des historischen Romans." *Internationale Literatur* 9 (1935): 19–23.

Feuchtwanger, Marta. *Nur eine Frau: Jahre, Tage, Stunden*. Munich: Langen Müller, 1983.

Feuchtwanger, Martin. *Zukunft ist ein blindes Spiel*. Munich: Langen Müller, 1989.

Fine, David J. *Jewish Integration in the German Army in the First World War*. Berlin: De Gruyter, 2012.

Fishman, Sterling. "The Assassination of Kurt Eisner." In *The German-Jewish Dialogue Reconsidered: A Symposium in Honor of George L. Mosse*, edited by Klaus Berghahn, 141–54. New York: Peter Lang, 1996.

Flade, Roland. "Felix Fechenbach (1894–1933)." In Flade, *Jüdische Familiengeschichten aus Unterfranken*, 53–61. Würzburg: Main-Post, 2015.

———. "Leben und Tod Felix Fechenbachs." In Felix Fechenbach, *Der Puppenspieler: Ein Roman aus dem alten Würzburg*, edited by Roland Flade and Barbara Rott. Würzburg: Königshausen & Neumann, 1988.

Flemming, Barbara, and Jan Schmidt, eds. *The Diary of Karl Süßheim (1878–1947): Orientalist between Munich and Istanbul*. Stuttgart: Franz Steiner Verlag, 2002.

Forstner, Thomas. *Priester in Zeiten des Umbruchs: Identität und Lebenswelt des katholischen Pfarrklerus in Oberbayern 1918 bis 1945*. Göttingen: Vandenhoeck & Ruprecht, 2013.

Fraenkel, Abraham Adolf. *Lebenskreise: Aus den Erinnerungen eines jüdischen Mathematikers*. Stuttgart: Deutsche Verlags-Anstalt, 1967.

———. *Recollections of a Jewish Mathematician in Germany*, edited by Jiska Cohen-Mansfield and translated by Allison Brown. Cham: Birkhäuser, 2016.

Franzos, Karl-Emil. *Halb-Asien: Land und Leute des östlichen Europa*. Stuttgart: Cotta, 1897.

Freud, Sigmund. "Ansprache an die Mitglieder des Vereins B'nai Brith (1926)." In Freud, *Gesammelte Werke*, vol. 17. Frankfurt am Main: S. Fischer, 1999.

Friedländer, Max. "Memoiren." Bundesrechtsanwaltskammer, http://www.brak.de/w/files/01_ueber_die_brak/friedlaender.pdf.

Friedländer, Saul. "Die politischen Veränderungen der Kriegszeit und ihre Auswirkungen auf die 'Judenfrage.'" In *Deutsches Judentum in Krieg und Revolution*, edited by Werner E. Mosse, 27–65. Tübingen: Mohr (Siebeck), 1971.

———. "Political Transformations during the War and Their Effect on the Jewish Question." In *Hostages of Modernization: Studies on Modern Antisemitism 1870–1933/39*, edited by Herbert A. Strauss, 150–64. Berlin and New York: De Gruyter, 1993.

———. "'Europe's Inner Demons.'" In *Demonizing the Other*, edited by Robert S. Wistrich, 215–22. London: Routledge, 1999.

Generaldirektion der Staatlichen Archive Bayerns. *Kardinal Michael von Faulhaber 1869–1952: Eine Ausstellung des Archivs des Erzbistums München und Freising, des bayerischen Hauptstaatsarchivs und des Stadtarchivs München zum 50. Todestag*. Munich: Generaldirektion der Staatlichen Archive Bayerns, 2002.

Gerrits, André W. M. "Jüdischer Kommunismus: Der Mythos, die Juden, die Partei." *Jahrbuch für Antisemitismusforschung* 14 (2005): 243–64.

Gerstenberg, Günter. *Der kurze Traum vom Frieden: Ein Beitrag zur Vorgeschichte des Umsturzes in München 1918*. Lich: Verlag Edition AV, 2018.

Geschichtsverein Hadern, ed. *Schlaglichter: Kurt Eisners Haderner Zeit: Ausstellungskatalog*. Munich: Geschichtsverein Hadern e.V, 2018.

Geyer, Martin H. *Kapitalismus und politische Moral in der Zwischenkriegszeit: oder: Wer war Julius Barnat?* Hamburg: Hamburger Edition, 2018.

———. *Verkehrte Welt: Revolution, Inflation und Moderne, München 1914–1924*. Göttingen: Vandenhoeck & Ruprecht, 1998.

Gilman, Sander L. *Jewish Self-Hatred: Anti-Semitism and the Hidden Language of the Jews*. Baltimore: Johns Hopkins University Press, 1986.

Goette, Jürgen-Wolfgang, ed. *Erich Mühsam und das Judentum: Zwölfte Erich-Mühsam Tagung in der Gustav-Heinemann Bildungsstätte in Malente, 25.–27. Mai 2001*. Lübeck: Erich-Mühsam-Gesellschaft, 2002.

Goldhagen, Daniel Jonah. *A Moral Reckoning: The Role of the Church in the Holocaust and Its Unfulfilled Duty of Repair*. New York: Alfred A. Knopf, 2002.

Gordon, Harold J. *Hitler and the Beer Hall Putsch*. Princeton, NJ: Princeton University Press, 1972.

———. *Hitlerputsch 1923: Machtkampf in Bayern 1923–1924*. Munich: Bernhard & Graefe, 1978.

Gossman, Lionel. *The Passion of Max von Oppenheim: Archaeology and Intrigue in the Middle East from Wilhelm II to Hitler*. Cambridge: Open Book Publisher, 2013.

Grady, Tim. *The German-Jewish Soldiers of the First World War in History and Memory*. Liverpool: Liverpool University Press, 2011.

Graf, Oskar Maria. *Prisoners All*, translated by Margaret Green. 1943.

———. *Wir sind Gefangene*. Berlin: Ullstein, 2010.

Grau, Bernhard. *Kurt Eisner, 1867–1919: Eine Biographie*. Munich: C. H. Beck, 2001.

———. "Revolution in Bayern: Kurt Eisner und das Ende der bayerischen Monarchie." In *Bayern und der Erste Weltkrieg*, edited by Günter Kronenbitter and Markus Pöhlmann, 203–13. Munich: Bayerische Landeszentrale für politische Bildungsarbeit, 2017.

Grebing, Helga. *Frauen in der deutschen Revolution 1918/19*. Heidelberg: Stiftung Reichspräsident-Friedrich-Ebert-Gedenkstätte, 1994.

Greive, Hermann. *Theologie und Ideologie: Katholizismus und Judentum in Deutschland und Österreich, 1918–1935*. Heidelberg: L. Schneider, 1969.

Grimpen, Albert. *Judentum und Sozialdemokratie: In ihren Beziehungen beleuchtet*. Hamburg: Self-published, 1919.

Gritschneder, Otto. *Der Hitler-Prozeß und sein Richter Georg Neithardt*. Munich: Beck, 2001.

Gruchmann, Lothar. *Justiz im Dritten Reich, 1933–1940: Anpassung und Unterwerfung in der Ära Gürtner*. Munich: Oldenbourg, 2001.

Grunberger, Richard. *Red Rising in Bavaria*. New York: St. Martin's Press, 1973.

Gumbel, Emil Julius. *Verschwörer: Zur Geschichte und Soziologie der deutschen nationalistischen Geheimbünde 1918–1924*, unabridged reissue. Frankfurt am Main: Fischer-Taschenbuch-Verlag, 1984.

———. *Vier Jahre politischer Mord*. Berlin-Fichtenau: Verlag der Neuen Gesellschaft, 1922.

———. *Zwei Jahre Mord*. Berlin: Verlag Neues Vaterland, 1921.

Gurganus, Albert Earle. *Kurt Eisner: A Modern Life*. Rochester, NY: Camden House, 2018.

———. "Sarah Sonja Lerch, née Rabinowitz: The Sonja Irene L. of Toller's 'Masse-Mensch.'" *German Studies Review* 28, no. 3 (2005): 607–20.

Guttkuhn, Peter. "Jüdische Neo-Orthodoxie 1870 bis 1919 in Lübeck." In *Erich Mühsam und das Judentum*, edited by Jürgen-Wolfgang Goette, 30–35. Lübeck: Erich-Mühsam-Gesellschaft, 2002.

Haberer, Erich E. *Jews and Revolution in Nineteenth-Century Russia*. Cambridge: Cambridge University Press, 1995.

Hackeschmidt, Jörg. "Die hebräischen Propheten und die Ethik Kants: Hermann Cohen in kultur- und sozialhistorischer Perspektive." *Aschkenas* 5 (1995): 121–29.

Haffner, Sebastian. *Die verratene Revolution*. Bern, Munich: Scherz, 1969.

———. *Failure of a Revolution: Germany 1918–1919*, translated by Georg Rapp, with a foreword and afterword by Richard Bruch. Chicago: Banner Press, 1986.

Hamann, Brigitte. *Hitler's Vienna*. New York: Oxford University Press, 1999.

———. *Hitlers Wien*. Munich: Piper, 2001.

Harris, James F. *The People Speak! Anti-Semitism and Emancipation in Nineteenth-Century Bavaria*. Ann Arbor: University of Michigan Press, 1994.

Hartmann, Jürgen. "Felix Fechenbach—ein sozialistischer Zionist?" *Rosenland: Zeitschrift für lippische Geschichte* 6 (2008): 25–28.

Haug, Wolfgang. *Erich Mühsam: Schriftsteller der Revolution*. Reutlingen: Trotzdem-Verlag, 1979.

Hausberger, Brigitte. "My Father, Gustav Landauer." In *Gustav Landauer: Anarchist and Jew*, edited by Paul Mendes-Flohr, Anya Mali, and Hanna Delf von Wolzogen, 233–37. Berlin: De Gruyter Oldenbourg, 2015.

Hennig, Diethard. *Johannes Hoffmann: Sozialdemokrat und Bayerischer Ministerpräsident*. Munich: Saur, 1992.

Heißerer, Dirk. "Bruder Hitler? Thomas Manns Entlarvung des Nationalsozialismus." In Heißerer, *Bruder Hitler? Thomas Mann und der Nationalsozialismus: Texte und Vorträge*, 65–101. Munich: NS-Dokumentationszentrum München, 2018.

Herbeck, Ulrich. *Das Feindbild vom "jüdischen Bolschewiken": Zur Geschichte des russischen Antisemitismus vor und während der Russischen Revolution*. Berlin: Metropol 2009.

Hermann, Angela. "Im Visier der Diplomaten: Nuntiatur- und Gesandtschaftsberichte zur Münchner Revolutions- und Rätezeit." *theologie.geschichte Beihefte* 7 (2013): 31–58.

Herz, Rudolf and Dirk Halfbrodt, *Revolution und Fotografie: München 1918/1919*. Berlin: Nishen, 1988.

Heusler, Andreas. *Das Braune Haus: Wie München zur "Hauptstadt der Bewegung" wurde*. Munich: Deutsche Verlags-Anstalt, 2008.

———. "Hauptstadt der Bewegung." Historisches Lexikon Bayern, January 23, 2018. https://www.historisches-lexikon-bayerns.de/Lexikon/Hauptstadt_der_Bewegung,_München (accessed January 1, 2021).

———. *Lion Feuchtwanger: Münchner—Emigrant—Weltbürger*. St. Pölten, Salzburg, Vienna: Residenz-Verlag, 2014.

Heusler, Andreas, and Andrea Sinn, eds. *Die Erfahrung des Exils: Vertreibung, Emigration, und Neuanfang: Ein Münchner Lesebuch*. Munich: DeGruyter Oldenbourg, 2015.

Heydorn, Heinz-Joachim. "Vorwort." In Gustav Landauer, *Aufruf zum Sozialismus*, edited by Heinz-Joachim Heydorn, 5–46. Frankfurt am Main: Europäische Verlagsanstalt, 1967.

Hillmayr, Heinrich. *Roter und Weißer Terror in Bayern nach 1918: Ursachen, Erscheinungsformen und Folgen der Gewalttätigkeiten im Verlauf der revolutionären Ereignisse nach dem Ende des Ersten Weltkrieges*. Munich: Nusser, 1974.

Hinterberger, Hans. "Unpolitische Politiker? Die bayerischen 'Beamtenministerpräsidenten' 1920–1924 und ihre Mitverantwortung am Hitlerputsch." PhD dissertation, University of Regensburg, 2016.

Hirschberg, Max. *Bolschewismus: Eine kritische Untersuchung über die amtlichen Veröffentlichungen der russischen Sowjet-Republik*. Munich and Leipzig: Duncker & Humblot, 1919.

———. "The Communist Terror in Munich." *The Nation*, July 19, 1919.

———. *Der Fall Fechenbach vor dem Münchner Volksgericht: Eine Darstellung nach den Akten.* Berlin: Verlag für Sozialwissenschaft GmbH, 1922.

———. *Der Fall Fechenbach: Juristische Gutachten.* Tübingen: J.C.B. Mohr, 1924.

———. *Jude und Demokrat: Erinnerungen eines Münchner Rechtsanwalts 1883–1939,* edited by Reinhard Weber. Munich: Oldenbourg, 1998.

Hirte, Chris. *Erich Mühsam—Eine Biographie.* Freiburg: Ahriman-Verlag, 2009.

———. "Erich Mühsam und das Judentum." In *Erich Mühsam und das Judentum,* edited by Jürgen-Wolfgang Goette, 52–70. Lübeck: Erich-Mühsam-Gesellschaft, 2002.

Hitler, Adolf. *Mein Kampf: Eine kritische Edition,* vol. 1, edited by Christian Hartmann, Thomas Vordermayer, Othmar Plöckinger, and Roman Töppel. Munich and Berlin: Institut für Zeitgeschichte, 2016.

———. *Mein Kampf,* translated by Ralph Manheim. Boston: Houghton Mifflin, 1971.

———. *Mein Kampf,* translated by James Murphy. London: Hurst and Blackett, 1939.

———. "Rede auf NSDAP-Führertagung in Plauen i.V. am 12.6.1925" (speech at the NSDAP Leader Conference in Plauen i.V., June 12, 1925), in Hitler, *Reden Schriften Anordnungen,* 99. See Andreas Heusler, "Hauptstadt der Bewegung," Historisches Lexikon Bayern, January 23, 2018, https://www.historisches-lexikon-bayerns.de/Lexikon/Hauptstadt_der_Bewegung, _München (accessed January 1, 2021).

Hitzer, Friedrich. *Anton Graf Arco: Das Attentat auf Kurt Eisner und die Schüsse im Landtag.* Munich: Knesebeck u. Schuler, 1988.

———. *Der Mord im Hofbräuhaus: Unbekanntes und Vergessenes aus der Baierischen Räterepublik.* Frankfurt am Main: Röderberg-Verlag, 1981.

Hofmiller, Josef. "Nietzsche und der Bolschewismus." *Süddeutsche Monatshefte* 16 (January 1919): 290–92.

———. *Revolutionstagebuch 1918/1919: Aus den Tagen der Münchner Revolution.* Leipzig: K. Rauch, 1939.

Holländer, Ludwig. *Der Antisemitismus in der Gegenwart.* Berlin: Riesser, 1919.

Höller, Ralf. *Das Wintermärchen: Schriftsteller erzählen die Bayerische Revolution und die Münchner Räterepublik 1918–1919.* Berlin: Edition TIAMAT, 2017.

Hoser, Paul. "Münchner Neueste Nachrichten." Historisches Lexikon Bayerns, July 3, 2006. http://www.historisches-lexikon-bayerns.de/Lexikon/Münchner Neueste Nachrichten (accessed August 5, 2018).

———. *Die politischen, wirtschaftlichen und sozialen Hintergründe der Münchner Tagespresse zwischen 1914 und 1934: Methoden der Pressebeeinflussung.* Frankfurt am Main: P. Lang, 1990.

———, ed. *Die Revolution 1918/19 in der Provinz.* Konstanz: Universitätsverlag, 1996.

———. "Die Rosenbaumkrawalle von 1921 in Memmingen." In *Geschichte und Kultur der Juden in Schwaben,* vol. 3 of *Zwischen Nähe, Distanz und Fremdheit,* edited by Peter Fassl, 95–109. Augsburg: Wissner, 2007.

Hübner, Christoph. *Die Rechtskatholiken, die Zentrumspartei und die katholische Kirche in Deutschland bis zum Reichskonkordat von 1933: Ein Beitrag zur Geschichte des Scheiterns der Weimarer Republik.* Münster: Lit, 2014.

Huch, Ricarda. "Kurt Eisners Todestag: Eine Münchner Erinnerung." In Huch, *Erinnerungen an das eigene Leben,* 435–41. Cologne: Kiepenheuer & Witsch, 1980.

Hug, Heinz. *Erich Mühsam: Untersuchungen zu Leben und Werk*. Glashütten im Taunus: D. Auvermann, 1974.

Hürten, Heinz. "Revolution und Zeit der Weimarer Republik." In *Handbuch der bayerischen Geschichte*, vol. 4, edited by Alois Schmid, 440–99. Munich: C. H. Beck, 2002.

Hurwicz, E(lias). "Die Weltexpansion des Bolschewismus: Versuch einer Prognose." *Süddeutsche Monatshefte* 16 (April 1919): 9–12.

Jacob, Frank. "Kurt Eisner, der unvollendete Revolutionär." *Zeitschrift für Geschichtswissenschaft* 66, no. 10 (2018): 826–41.

Jelavich, Peter. *Munich and Theatrical Modernism: Politics, Playwriting, and Performance, 1890–1914*. Cambridge, MA: Harvard University Press, 1985.

Joachimsthaler, Anton. *Hitlers Weg begann in München 1913–1923*. Munich: Herbig, 2000.

Jochmann, Werner, ed. *Adolf Hitler: Monologe im Führerhauptquartier: Die Aufzeichnungen Heinrich Heims*. Hamburg: A. Knaus, 1980.

Jones, Mark. *Founding Weimar: Violence and the German Revolution of 1918–1919*. Cambridge: Cambridge University Press, 2016.

Jüdisches Kulturmuseum Augsburg-Schwaben, ed. *"... zäh, genial, unbedenklich ..." Die Schriftstellerin Paula Buber (1877–1958)*. Exhibit catalog. Augsburg: Jüdisches Kulturmuseum Augsburg-Schwaben, 2017. https://www.jkmas.de/online-ausstellungen/ (accessed January 17, 2021.

Jungblut, Gerd W., ed. *Erich Mühsam: Briefe an Zeitgenossen*, vol. 1. Berlin: Guhl, 1978.

Kafka, Franz. *Briefe 1902–1924*. Frankfurt am Main: Fischer, 1966.

———. *Letter to His Father (Brief an den Vater)*, translated by Ernst Kaiser and Eithne Wilkin. New York: Schocken, 1966.

———. *Letters to Friends, Family, and Editors*, translated by Richard and Clara Winston. New York: Schocken, 1977.

Kahr, Gustav von. "Erinnerungen" (Memoirs). Unpublished manuscript, Kahr Papers (Nachlass Kahr), Bayerisches Hauptstaatsarchiv.

———. "Lebenserinnerungen." Unpublished manuscript, Kahr Papers (Nachlass Kahr), Bayerisches Hauptstaatsarchiv.

Kalmar, Ivan. *Early Orientalism: Imagined Islam and the Notion of Sublime Power*. London and New York: Routledge, 2012.

Kampf, Andrea. "Frauenpolitik und politisches Handeln von Frauen während der Bayerischen Revolution 1918/19." PhD dissertation, FernUniversität Hagen, 2016.

Karl, Josef. *Die Schreckensherrschaft in München und Spartakus im bayr. Oberland: Tagebuchblätter und Ereignisse aus der Zeit der "bayr. Räterepublik" und der Münchner Kommune im Frühjahr 1919*. Munich: Hochschulverlag, 1919.

Karo, Georg. "Deutsche Schuld und deutsches Gewissen." *Süddeutsche Monatshefte* 18 (May 1921): 99–100.

Kauffeldt, Rolf. *Erich Mühsam: Literatur und Anarchie*. Munich: W. Fink, 1983.

———. "Zur jüdischen Tradition im romantisch-anarchistischen Denken Erich Mühsams und Gustav Landauers." *Bulletin des Leo Baeck Instituts* 69 (1984): 3–28.

Kayser, Rudolf. "Der jüdische Revolutionär." *Neue Jüdische Monatshefte* 5 (1919): 96–98.

Kellogg, Michael. *The Russian Roots of Nazism: White Emigrés and the Making of National Social-ism, 1917–1943*. Cambridge: Cambridge University Press, 2005.

Kerekes, Lajos. "Die 'Weiße Allianz'—bayrisch-österreichisch-ungarische Projekte gegen die Regierung Renner im Jahre 1920." *Österreichische Osthefte* 7 (1965): 353–66.

Kershaw, Ian. *Hitler, 1889–1936: Hubris*. New York: W. W. Norton, 1999.

Kiiskinen, Elina. *Die Deutschnationale Volkspartei (Bayerische Mittelpartei) in der Regierungspoli-tik des Freistaats während der Weimarer Zeit*. Munich: Beck, 2005.

Kirschner, Emanuel. "Erinnerungen aus meinem Leben: Memoiren." Unpublished manuscript in the memoirs collection of the *Year Book of the Leo Baeck Institute*.

Kistenmacher, Olaf. *Arbeit und "jüdisches Kapital": Antisemitische Aussagen in der KPD-Tageszeitung "Die Rote Fahne" während der Weimarer Republik*. Bremen: Edition Lumiere, 2016.

Kitzinger, Heinrich. "Der Fall Fechenbach." *Zeitschrift für die gesamte Strafrechtswissenschaft* 44 (January 1924): 136–44.

Klatt, Ingaburgh. "Siegfried Mühsam und seine Erzählungen zum jüdischen Leben um die Mitte des 20. Jahrhunderts." In *Erich Mühsam und das Judentum*, edited by Jürgen-Wolfgang Goette, 38–51. Lübeck: Erich-Mühsam-Gesellschaft, 2002.

Klemperer, Victor. *Curriculum Vitae: Erinnerungen 1891–1918*. 2 vols. Berlin: Aufbau Taschen-buch Verlag, 1996.

———. *I Will Bear Witness*. New York: Random House, 2000.

———. *Man möchte immer weinen und lachen in einem: Revolutionstagebuch 1919*. Berlin: Aufbau, 2015.

———. *Munich 1919: Diary of a Revolution*, translated by Jessica Spengler. Cambridge: Polity Press, 2017.

Klugmann, Hermann. "Mein Leben in Deutschland vor dem 30. Januar 1933." In *Die Erfahrung des Exils: Vertreibung, Emigration, und Neuanfang: Ein Münchner Lesebuch*, edited by Andreas Heusler and Andrea Sinn, 24–35. Munich: DeGruyter Oldenbourg, 2015.

Knütter, Hans-Helmut. *Die Juden und die deutsche Linke in der Weimarer Republik 1918–1933*. Düsseldorf: Droste, 1971.

Köglmeier, Georg. *Die zentralen Rätegremien in Bayern 1918/19*. Munich: Beck 2001.

Koktanek, Anton N., ed. *Oswald Spengler: Briefe 1913–1936*. Munich: Beck, 1963.

Kornacker, Susanne. "Regierung von Jehovas Zorn, 1918." Historisches Lexikon Bayerns. August 7, 2006. https://www.historisches-lexikon-bayerns.de/Lexikon/Regierung_von_Jehovas_Zorn,_1918 (accessed February 10, 2021).

Koselleck, Reinhart. "Standortbindung und Zeitlichkeit: Ein Beitrag zur historiographischen Erschließung der geschichtlichen Welt." In *Objektivität und Parteilichkeit*, edited by Reinhart Koselleck et al., 17–46. Munich: Deutscher Taschenbuch-Verlag, 1977.

Kraepelin, Emil. "Persönliches." In *Selbstzeugnisse*, edited by Wolfgang Burgmair, Eric J. Eng-strom, and Matthias M. Weber. Munich: Belleville, 2000.

———. "Psychiatrische Randbemerkungen zur Zeitgeschichte." *Süddeutsche Monatshefte* 16 (June 1919): 171–83.

Kraftzick, Anna-Maria. "Das Sammellager Fort Prinz Karl bei Ingolstadt 1920–1924." *Sammel-blatt des Historischen Vereins Ingolstadt* 124 (2015): 329–42.

Kramer, Ferdinand. "Bayerischer Ministerpräsident." Historisches Lexikon Bayerns, November 24, 2016. https://www.historisches-lexikon-bayerns.de/Lexikon/Bayerischer_Ministerpräsident (accessed February 8, 2021).

———. "Kirchen und Religion in den 'Lebenserinnerungen' von Gustav von Kahr." Zeitschrift für bayerische Landesgeschichte 80 (2017): 213–44.

Kreiler, Kurt. Die Schriftstellerrepublik: Zum Verhältnis von Literatur und Politik in der Münchner Räterepublik: Ein systematisches Kapitel politischer Literaturgeschichte. Berlin: Guhl, 1978.

Kriegsgeschichtliche Forschungsanstalt des Heeres, ed. Die Niederwerfung der Räteherrschaft in Bayern 1919, vol. 4 of Darstellungen aus den Nachkriegskämpfen deutscher Truppen und Freikorps. Berlin: Mittler, 1939.

Kritzer, Peter. "Die SPD in der bayerischen Revolution von 1918." In Bayern im Umbruch: Die Revolution von 1918, ihre Voraussetzungen, ihr Verlauf und ihre Folgen, edited by Karl Bosl, 427–52. Munich: Oldenbourg, 1969.

Krull, Germaine. La Vie mène la danse. Paris: Éditions Textuel, 2015.

Krumeich, Gerd, and M. Rainer Lepsius, eds. Max Weber Gesamtausgabe, vol. II/10.1 of Briefe von 1918–1920. Tübingen: J.C.B. Mohr (P. Siebeck), 2012.

Kurz, Isolde. "Aus den Tagen der Münchener Räterepublik." Neue Freie Presse, July 12, 1919; Morgenblatt, no. 19713.

Lamm, Hans, ed. Vergangene Tage: Jüdische Kultur in München. Munich: Langen Müller, 1982.

Landauer, Carl. "The Bavarian Problem in the Weimar Republic, 1918–1923: Part I." Journal of Modern History 16, no. 2 (1944): 93–115. www.jstor.org/stable/1871341 (accessed February 21, 2021).

———. "The Bavarian Problem in the Weimar Republic: Part II." Journal of Modern History 16, no. 3 (1944): 205–23. http://www.jstor.org/stable/1871460 (accessed February 21, 2021).

——— "Erinnerungen an die Münchner Sozialdemokratie 1921–1923." In Vergangene Tage: Jüdische Kultur in München, edited by Hans Lamm, 380–86. Munich: Langen Müller, 1982.

Landauer, Gustav. Aufruf zum Sozialismus. Berlin: Cassirer, 1919.

———. "Die Legende des Baal Schem." Das literarische Echo 13, no. 2 (1910): column 148.

———. "Martin Buber." Neue Blätter (Hellerau) 3, nos. 1/2 (1913): 90–107; reprinted in Gustav Landauer: Dichter. Ketzer. Außenseiter: Essays und Reden zu Literatur, Philosophie, Judentum, vol. 3 of Werkausgabe, edited by Hanna Delf, 162–70. Berlin: Akademie Verlag, 1997.

———. "Ostjuden und Deutsches Reich." Der Jude 1 (1916–1917): 433–34.

———. Rechenschaft. Berlin: P. Cassierer, 1919.

———. Sein Lebensgang in Briefen, unter Mitwirkung von Ina Britschgi-Schimmer herausgegeben von Martin Buber, vol. 2. Frankfurt am Main: Rütten & Loening, 1929.

———. "Sind das Ketzergedanken?" In Landauer, Werkausgabe, vol. 3, edited by Gert Mattenklott und Hanna Delf, 170–74. Berlin: Akademie Verlag, 1997.

Laor, Dan. "Agnon in Germany, 1912–1924: A Chapter of a Biography." AJS Review 18, no. 1 (1993): 75–93.

Large, David Clay. "'Out with the Ostjuden': The Scheunenviertel Riots in Berlin, November 1923." In Exclusionary Violence: Antisemitic Riots in Modern German History, edited by Christhard Hoffmann, Werner Bergmann, and Helmut Walser Smith, 123–40. Ann Arbor: University of Michigan Press, 2002.

———. *The Politics of Law and Order: A History of the Bavarian Einwohnerwehr, 1918–1921. Trans-actions of the American Philosophical Society* 70, part 2. Philadelphia: American Philosophical Society, 1980.

———. *Where Ghosts Walked: Munich's Road to the Third Reich.* New York: W. W. Norton, 1997.

Lenhard, Philipp. *Friedrich Pollock: Die graue Eminenz der Frankfurter Schule.* Berlin: Jüdischer Verlag im Suhrkamp Verlag, 2019.

Lerner, Robert. *Ernst Kantorowicz: A Life.* Princeton 2017.

Lessing, Theodor. *Der jüdische Selbsthaß.* Berlin: Jüdischer Verlag, 1930.

Leugers, Antonia: "'Weil doch einmal Blut fliessen muss, bevor wieder Ordnung kommt': Erzbischof Faulhabers Krisendeutung in seinem Tagebuch 1918/19." *theologie.geschichte Bei-hefte* 7 (2013): 61–114.

Leviné, Eugen. "Rede vor Gericht." In *Die Münchner Räterepublik: Zeugnisse und Kommentar,* edited by Tankred Dorst, 157–67. Frankfurt am Main: Suhrkamp, 1968.

Linse, Ulrich. *Gustav Landauer und die Revolutionszeit 1918/19.* Berlin: Kramer, 1974.

———. "'Poetic Anarchism' versus 'Party Anarchism': Gustav Landauer and the Anarchist Movement in Wilhelminian Germany." In *Gustav Landauer: Anarchist and Jew,* edited by Paul Mendes-Flohr, Anya Mali, and Hanna Delf von Wolzogen, 45–63. Berlin: De Gruyter Oldenbourg, 2015.

Litten, Freddy. *Der Rücktritt Richard Willstätters und seine Hintergründe: Ein Münchner Univer-sitätsskandal?* Munich: Institut für Geschichte der Naturwissenschaften, 1999.

Lixl, Andreas. *Ernst Toller und die Weimarer Republik 1918–1933.* Heidelberg: Winter, 1986.

Loewenfeld, Philipp. *Recht und Politik in Bayern zwischen Prinzregentenzeit und Nationalsozial-ismus: Die Erinnerung von Philipp Löwenfeld,* edited by Peter Landau and Rolf Rieß. Ebels-bach: Aktiv Druck & Verlag, 2004.

Löffelmeier, Anton. "Besaß Kurt Eisner die bayerische Staatsangehörigkeit? Zum Quellenwert erhaltener Gemeindeakten." *Archive in Bayern* 6 (2010): 393–411.

Löwenthal, Leo. "Ein unveröffentlichter Brief aus dem Jahr 1920." *Sans Phrase: Zeitschrift für Ideologiekritik* 12 (2018): 69–71.

Loiperdinger, Martin. "Nathan der Weise: Faschistische Filmzensur, Antisemitismus, und Ge-walt anno 1923." *Lessing Yearbook* 14 (1982): 61–69.

Longerich, Peter. *Hitler: A Biography.* Oxford: Oxford University Press, 2019.

Löwy, Michael. *Redemption and Utopia: Jewish Libertarian Thought in Central Europe: A Study in Elective Affinity.* London: Athlone, 1992.

———. "Romantic Prophets of Utopia: Gustav Landauer and Martin Buber." In *Gustav Lan-dauer: Anarchist and Jew,* edited by Paul Mendes-Flohr, Anya Mali, and Hanna Delf von Wolzogen, 64–81. Berlin: De Gruyter Oldenbourg, 2015.

Lunn, Eugene. *Prophet of Community: Romantic Socialism of Gustav Landauer.* Berkeley: Uni-versity of California Press, 1973.

Luxemburg, Rosa. *Das Menschliche entscheidet: Briefe an Freunde.* Munich: Paul List, 1958.

Mann, Golo. *Geschichte und Geschichten.* Frankfurt am Main: S. Fischer, 1961.

Mann, Heinrich. "Kurt Eisner." In Mann, *Macht und Mensch,* 170–75. Munich: Kurt Wolff, 1919. Reprinted in *Revolution und Räterepublik,* edited by Gerhard Schmolze. Munich: Deutscher Taschenbuch-Verlag, 1978.

Mann, Thomas. *Diaries 1918–1939*, selection and foreword by Hermann Kesten, translated from the German by Richard and Clara Winston. New York: H. N. Abrams, 1982.

———. "German Letter." *Dial* 75, no. 4 (October 1923): 369–75.

———. *Doctor Faustus*, translated from the German by John E. Woods. New York: A.A. Knopf, 1997.

———. *Essays II, 1914–1926, Kommentar*, edited by Hermann Kurzke, vol. 15 of *GKFA*. Frankfurt am Main: S. Fischer, 2002.

———. *Tagebücher 1918–1921*, edited by Peter de Mendelssohn. Frankfurt am Main: S. Fischer, 1979.

———. (untitled). In *Kampf um München als Kulturzentrum: Sechs Vorträge*, 7–12. Munich: R. Pflaum, 1926.

Martynkewicz, Wolfgang. *Salon Deutschland: Geist und Macht 1900–1945*. Berlin: Aufbau, 2007.

Maurer, Trude. *Ostjuden in Deutschland, 1918–1933*. Hamburg: Christians, 1986.

Meinecke, Friedrich. *Die deutsche Katastrophe: Betrachtungen und Erinnerungen*, 3rd ed. Wiesbaden: E. Brockhaus, 1947.

Meining, Stefan. "Ein erster Ansturm der Antisemiten: 1919–1923." In *Versagte Heimat: Jüdisches Leben in Münchens Isarvorstadt 1914–1945*, edited by Douglas Bokovoy and Stefan Meining, 53–74. Munich: P. Glas, 1994.

Mendelsohn, Ezra, ed. *Essential Papers on Jews and the Left*. New York: New York University Press, 1997.

Mendes, Philip. *Jews and the Left: The Rise and Fall of a Political Alliance*. New York: Palgrave Macmillan, 2014.

Merz, Johannes. "Auf dem Weg zur Räterepublik: Staatskrise und Regierungsbildung in Bayern nach dem Tode Eisners (Februar/März 1919)." *Zeitschrift für bayerische Landesgeschichte* 66 (2003): 541–64.

Metz, Markus, and Georg Seeßlen. "Erich Wagowski und seine 'Filmhaus Bavaria GmbH': Eine jüdische Kinogeschichte (BR Hörbild und Feature 'Land und Leute')." Bayerischer Rundfunk, radio broadcast on Hörfunk Bayern 2, October 2, 2010.

Meyer, Michael A. "Great Debate on Antisemitism: Jewish Reaction to New Hostility in Germany 1879–1881." *Year Book of the Leo Baeck Institute* 2 (1966): 137–70.

Meyer-Frank, Julie. "Erinnerungen an meine Studienzeit." In *Vergangene Tage: Jüdische Kultur in München*, edited by Hans Lamm, 212–17. Munich: Langen Müller, 1982.

Meyer-Leviné, Rosa. *Leviné: Leben und Tod eines Revolutionärs: Erinnerungen*. Frankfurt am Main: Fischer-Taschenbuch-Verlag, 1974.

———. *Leviné: The Life of a Revolutionary*. Farnborough: Saxon House, 1973.

Mitchell, Allan. *Revolution in Bavaria 1918–1919*. Princeton, NJ: Princeton University Press, 1965.

———. *Revolution in Bayern 1918/1919*. Munich: Beck, 1967.

Mommsen, Hans. "Adolf Hitler und der 9. November 1923." In *Der 9. November: Fünf Essays zur deutschen Geschichte*, edited by Johannes Willms. Munich: Beck, 1995.

Monacensis. "Und immer wieder Fechenbach." *Die Weltbühne*, March 1, 1923.

Morris, Douglas G. *Justice Imperiled: The Anti-Nazi Lawyer Max Hirschberg in Weimar Germany*. Ann Arbor: University of Michigan Press, 2005.

Mosse, George L. *German Jews beyond Judaism*. Bloomington and Cincinnati: Indiana University Press and Hebrew Union College Press, 1985.

Mosse, Werner E., ed. *Deutsches Judentum in Krieg und Revolution 1916–1923: Ein Sammelband*. Tübingen: J.C.B. Mohr, 1971.

———, ed. *Die Juden im Wilhelminischen Deutschland 1890–1914: Ein Sammelband*. Tübingen: J.C.B. Mohr, 1976.

Mühsam, Erich. *Gedichte. Prosa. Stücke*, vol. 1 of *Ausgewählte Werke*. Berlin: Verlag Volk und Welt, 1978.

———. *Das Standrecht in Bayern*. Berlin: Vereinigung Internationally Verlagsanstalten, 1923.

———. *Der Krater*. Berlin: K. Guhl, 1977.

———. *Erich Mühsam: Diaries*. http://www.muehsam-tagebuch.de/tb/diaries.php#d_1919_07_06.

———. *Die Jagd auf Harden*. Berlin: Neuer biographischer Verlag, 1908.

———. *Tagebücher 1910–1924*. Munich: Deutscher Taschenbuch-Verlag, 1995.

———. *Von Eisner bis Leviné: Die Entstehung der bayerischen Räterepublik*. Berlin: Fanal-Verlag E. Mühsam, 1929.

———. "Zur Judenfrage." *Die Weltbühne* 16, no. 49 (December 2, 1920): 643–47.

———. "Durch Absonderung zur Gemeinschaft." In Gustav Landauer, *Revolution and Other Writings: A Political Reader*, edited and translated by Gabriel Kuhn. Oakland, CA: PM Press, 2010.

Mühsam, Paul. *Mein Weg zu mir: Aus Tagebüchern*. Konstanz: Rosgarten-Verlag, 1978.

Mühsam, Siegfried: *Die Killeberger: Nach der Natur aufgenommen von Onkel Siegfried*, 3rd ed. Leipzig: Kaufmann, 1910.

———. *Neu-Killeberg: Der "Killeberger" zweiter Teil*. Leipzig: Kaufmann, 1913.

Müller, Andrea. *Die französische Gesandtschaft in München in den Jahren der Weimarer Republik*. Munich: Utz, 2010.

Müller-Meiningen, Ernst. *Aus Bayerns schwersten Tagen: Erinnerungen und Betrachtungen aus der Revolutionszeit*. Berlin: W. de Gruyter, 1923.

Müller, Karl Alexander von. *1919–1932*, vol. 3 of *Im Wandel einer Welt: Erinnerungen*, edited by Otto Alexander Müller. Munich: Süddeutscher Verlag, 1966.

———. *Mars und Venus: Erinnerungen 1914–1919*. Stuttgart: Kilpper, 1954.

———. "Neue Urkunden." *Süddeutsche Monatshefte* (July 1921): 52.

Murphy, Robert. *Diplomat among Warriors*. Garden City, NY: Doubleday, 1964.

Nagorski, Andrew. *Hitlerland: American Eyewitnesses to the Nazi Rise of Power*. New York: Simon & Schuster, 2012.

Naumann, Cornelia. *Der Abend kommt so schnell: Sonja Lerch—Münchens vergessene Revolutionärin*. Meßkirch: Gmeiner-Verlag, 2018.

———. "Exkurs über die Gießener Jahre von Sarah Sonja Rabinowitz." In Günter Gerstenberg, *Der kurze Traum vom Frieden: Ein Beitrag zur Vorgeschichte des Umsturzes in München 1918*, 279–88. Lich: Verlag Edition AV, 2018.

Neliba, Günter. *Wilhelm Frick: Der Legalist des Unrechtsstaates: eine politische Biographie*. Paderborn: Schöningh, 1992.

Neubauer, Helmut. *München und Moskau 1918/1919: Zur Geschichte der Rätebewegung in Bayern*. Munich: Isar Verlag, 1958.

Neumeyer, Alfred. *Lichter und Schatten: Eine Jugend in Deutschland*. Munich: Prestel-Verlag, 1967.

Nickmann, Walter, and Joachim Schröder. "Revolution und 'Ordnungszelle Bayern.'" In *Die Münchner Polizei und der Nationalsozialismus*, edited by Joachim Schröder, 17–25. Essen: Klartext, 2013.

Niehuss, Merith. "Parteien, Wahlen, Arbeiterbewegung." In *München—Musenstadt mit Hinterhöfen: Die Prinzregentenzeit (1886–1912)*, edited by Friedrich Prinz and Marita Kraus, 44–53. Munich: Beck, 1988.

Niekisch, Ernst. *Gewagtes Leben: Begegnungen und Begebnisse*. Cologne: Kiepenheuer & Witsch, 1958.

Noske, Gustav. *Erlebtes aus Aufstieg und Niedergang einer Demokratie*. Offenbach: Bollwerk-Verlag K. Drott, 1947.

Oppenheimer, Karl, and Klara Oppenheimer. "Der Antisemitismus." *Süddeutsche Monatshefte* 16, no. 10 (July 1919): 124–29.

Pacelli, Eugenio. "Kritische Online-Edition der Nuntiaturberichte Eugenio Pacellis (1917–1929)." http://www.pacelli-edition.de/index.html.

Pappert, Lars. *Der Hitlerputsch und seine Mythologisierung im Dritten Reich*. Neuried: Ars Una, 2001.

Penslar, Derek J. *Jews and the Military: A History*. Princeton, NJ: Princeton University Press, 2013.

Pfoser, Alfred, Kristina Pfoser-Schewig, and Gerhard Renner, eds. *Der Skandal*, vol. 1 of *Schnitzlers "Reigen."* Frankfurt am Main: Fischer, 1933.

Piper, Ernst. *Alfred Rosenberg: Hitlers Chefideologe*. Munich: Blessing, 2005.

Plöckinger, Othmar. *Unter Soldaten und Agitatoren: Hitlers prägende Jahre im deutschen Militär*. Paderborn: Schöningh, 2013.

Pommerin, Reiner. "Die Ausweisung von 'Ostjuden' aus Bayern 1923: Ein Beitrag zum Krisenjahr der Weimarer Republik." *Vierteljahrshefte für Zeitgeschichte* 34, no. 3 (1986): 311–40.

Pranckh, Hans Freiherr von, ed. *Der Prozeß gegen den Grafen Anton Arco-Valley*. Munich: J. F. Lehmann, 1920.

Prater. *Thomas Mann: A Life*. Oxford: Oxford University Press, 1995.

Preuss, Walter. "Im Hause der Freudlosen: Erinnerungen an Felix Fechenbach." *Mitteilungsblatt der Hitachduth Olej Germania* (Vereinigung der Juden aus Mitteleuropa), March 21, 1969.

Pringsheim, Hedwig. *Meine Manns: Briefe an Maximilian Harden*, edited by Helga and Manfred Neumann. Berlin: Aufbau-Verlag, 2006.

Pulzer, Peter. "Die jüdische Beteiligung an der Politik." In *Die Juden im wilhelminischen Deutschland 1890–1914: Ein Sammelband*, edited by Werner E. Mosse, 143–240. Tübingen: J.C.B. Mohr, 1976.

———. *Jews and the German State: The Political History of a Minority, 1848–1933*. Detroit: Wayne State University Press, 2003.

Pyta, Wolfram. *Hitler: der Künstler als Politiker und Feldherr: eine Herrschaftsanalyse*. Munich: Siedler, 2015.

Rappaport, Moriz. *Sozialismus, Revolution, und Judenfrage*. Leipzig and Vienna: Tal, 1919.

Rees, David A. "Ein Dichter, ein Mädchen und die jüdischen Speisegesetze: Gershom Scholems Entscheidung für München und die Kabbala." *Münchner Beiträge zur jüdischen Geschichte und Kultur* 2 (2007): 19–29.

Reich, Jakob. "Eine Episode aus der Geschichte der Ostjuden Münchens." In *Vergangene Tage: Jüdische Kultur in München*, edited by Hans Lamm, 400–404. Munich: Langen Müller, 1982.

Reuth, Ralf Georg. *Hitlers Judenhass: Klischee und Wirklichkeit*. Munich: Piper, 2009.

Rilke, Rainer Maria. *Briefe zur Politik*, edited by Joachim W. Storck. Frankfurt am Main: Insel, 1992.

———. *Letters of Rainer Maria Rilke 1910–1926*, vol. 2, *1910–1926*, translated by Jane Bannard Greene and M. D. Herter. New York: W. W. Norton: 1948.

Ritter, Gerhard. *Staatskunst und Kriegshandwerk*, vol. 4. Munich: Oldenbourg, 1968.

Rogalla von Bieberstein, Johannes. *Jüdischer Bolschewismus: Mythos und Realität*. Dresden: Edition Antaios, 2002.

Rohrbacher, Stefan. *Gewalt im Biedermeier: Antijüdische Ausschreitungen in Vormärz und Revolution (1815–1848/49)*. Frankfurt am Main: Campus-Verlag, 1993.

Rosenberg, Alfred. "Die russisch-jüdische Revolution." *Auf gut deutsch*, February 21, 1919.

Rosenthal, Jacob. *Die Ehre des jüdischen Soldaten: Die Judenzählung im Ersten Weltkrieg und ihre Folgen*. Frankfurt am Main: Campus-Verlag, 2007.

Roth, Guenther. "Edgar Jaffé and Else von Richthofen in the Mirror of Newly Found Letters." *Max Weber Studies* 10, no. 2 (July 2010): 151–88.

Rothenbücher, Karl. *Der Fall Kahr*. Tübingen: Mohr, 1924.

Ruppert, Andreas. "Felix Fechenbach als Soldat—Feldpostbriefe 1914 bis 1918." *Rosenland: Zeitschrift für lippische Geschichte* 13 (2015): 4–24.

Sabrow, Martin. *Die verdrängte Verschwörung: Der Rathenau-Mord und die deutsche Gegenrevolution*. Frankfurt am Main: Fischer-Taschenbuch-Verlag, 1999.

Sammartino, Annemarie. *The Impossible Border: Germany and the East, 1914–1922*. Ithaca, NY: Cornell University Press, 2010.

Schade, Franz. *Kurt Eisner und die bayerische Sozialdemokratie*. Hanover: Verlag für Literatur und Zeitgeschehen, 1961.

Schaeder, Grete, ed. *1897–1918*, vol. 1 of *Martin Buber: Briefwechsel aus sieben Jahrzehnten*. Heidelberg: Schneider, 1972.

Schäfer, Ingrid. *Irma Fechenbach-Fey: Jüdin, Sozialistin, Emigrantin 1895–1973*. Lemgo: Institut für Lippische Landeskunde, 2003.

Schaupp, Simon. *Der kurze Frühling der Räterepublik: Ein Tagebuch der bayerischen Revolution*. Münster: UNRAST, 2017.

Schmalzl, Markus. *Erhard Auer: Wegbereiter der parlamentarischen Demokratie in Bayern*. Kallmünz: Laßleben, 2013.

Schmolze, Gerhard, ed. *Revolution und Räterepublik in München 1918/19 in Augenzeugenberichten*. Düsseldorf: Rauch, 1969.

Schmolze, Renate, and Gerhard Schmolze, eds. *Die halbe Macht den Räten: Ausgewählte Aufsätze und Reden*. Cologne: Hegner, 1969.

Scholem, Betty, and Gershom Scholem. *Mutter und Sohn im Briefwechsel, 1917–1946*, edited by Itta Shedletzky in association with Thomas Sparr. Munich: C. H. Beck, 1989.

Scholem, Gershom. *From Berlin to Jerusalem: Memories of My Youth*, translated from the German by Harry Zohn, foreword by Moshe Idel. Philadelphia: Paul Dry Books, 2012.

———. *The Messianic Idea in Judaism*. New York: Schocken, 1971.

————. *Von Berlin nach Jerusalem: Jugenderinnerungen*, expanded edition, translated from Hebrew by Michael Brocke and Andrea Schatz. Frankfurt am Main: Jüdischer Verlag, 1994.

————. "Zum Verständnis der messianischen Idee im Judentum." In Scholem, *Judaica 1*. Frankfurt am Main: Suhrkamp, 1963.

Schönhärl, Korinna. *Wissen und Visionen: Theorie und Politik der Ökonomen im Stefan George-Kreis*. Berlin: Akademie Verlag, 2009.

Schopf, Wolfgang. "Blende auf! Josef Breitenbach." In *Fractured Biographies*, edited by Ian Wallace, 17–54. Amsterdam. Rodopi, 2003.

Schricker, Rudolf. *Rotmord über München*. Berlin: Zeitgeschichte, 1934.

Schröder, Joachim. "Der Erste Weltkrieg und der 'jüdische Bolschewismus.'" In *Nationalsozialismus und Erster Weltkrieg*, edited by Gerd Krumeich, 77–96. Essen: Klartext, 2010.

Schueler, Hermann Kurt. *Auf der Flucht erschossen: Felix Fechenbach 1894–1933: Eine Biographie*. Cologne: Kiepenheur & Witsch, 1981.

————. "Fechenbach 1894–1933: Die Entwicklung eines republikanischen Journalisten." PhD dissertation, University of Bonn, 1980.

Schwend, Karl. *Bayern zwischen Monarchie und Diktatur*. Munich: Pflaum, 1954.

Sebottendorff, Rudolf von. *Bevor Hitler kam*. Munich: Deukula-Grassinger, 1933.

Seemann, Birgit. *Hedwig Lachmann-Landauer: Dichterin, Antimilitaristin, deutsche Jüdin*. Frankfurt am Main: Campus-Verlag, 1998.

Selig, Wolfram. *Paul Nikolaus Cossmann und die Süddeutschen Monatshefte von 1914–1918: Ein Beitrag zur Geschichte der nationalen Publizistik im Ersten Weltkrieg*. Osnabrück: Fromm, 1967.

Seligmann, Michael. *Aufstand der Räte: Die erste bayerische Räterepublik vom 7. April 1919*. Grafenau: Trotzdem-Verlag, 1989.

Sieg, Ulrich. "Bekenntnis zu nationalen und universalen Werten: Jüdische Philosophen im Deutschen Kaiserreich." *Historische Zeitschrift* 263 (1996): 609–39.

————. "'Der Wissenschaft und dem Leben tut dasselbe not: Ehrfurcht vor der Wahrheit': Hermann Cohens Gutachten im Marburger Antisemitismusprozeß 1888." In *Philosophisches Denken—Politisches Wirken: Hermann-Cohen-Kolloquium Marburg 1992*, edited by Reinhard Brandt and Franz Orlik, 222–49. Hildesheim: Olms, 1993.

————. *Jüdische Intellektuelle im Ersten Weltkrieg: Kriegserfahrungen, weltanschauliche Debatten und kulturelle Neuentwürfe*. Berlin: Akademie Verlag, 2001.

Sinn, Andrea. *"Und ich lebe wieder an der Isar": Exil und Rückkehr des Münchner Juden Hans Lamm*. Munich: Oldenbourg, 2008.

Sippl, Carmen. "Der 'Bote von außen': Alexander Eliasberg und Thomas Mann." *Münchner Beiträge für Jüdische Geschichte und Kultur* 1 (2017): 40–57.

Small, William. "In Buddha's Footsteps: Feuchtwanger's Jud Süß, Walther Rathenau, and the Path to the Soul." *German Studies Review* 12 (1989): 469–85.

Specht, Heike. *Die Feuchtwangers: Familie, Tradition, und jüdisches Selbstverständnis*. Göttingen: Wallstein, 2006.

————. "Zerbrechlicher Erfolg." In *Jüdisches München: Vom Mittelalter bis zur Gegenwart*, edited by Richard Bauer and Michael Brenner, 137–156. Munich: Beck, 2006

Speckner, Herbert. "Die Ordnungszelle Bayern: Studien zur Politik des bayerischen Bürgertums, insbesondere der Bayerischen Volkspartei, von der Revolution bis zum Ende des Kabinetts Dr. von Kahr." PhD dissertation, Erlangen, 1955.

Spengler, Oswald. *Preußentum und Sozialismus*. Munich: C. H. Beck, 1921.

Sperans [Kurt Eisner]. "Ein Fäulnisprozeß (1893)." In Kurt Eisner, *Taggeist: Culturglossen*, 44–55. Berlin: Edelheim, 1901.

———. "Sporen." In Kurt Eisner, *Taggeist: Culturglossen*, 22–29. Berlin: Edelheim, 1901.

Stadtarchiv München, ed. *Beth ha-Knesseth: Ort der Zusammenkunft: Zur Geschichte der Münchner Synagogen, ihrer Rabbiner und Kantoren*. Munich: Buchendorfer, 1999.

———, ed. *"Ich lebe! Das ist ein Wunder": Schicksal einer Münchner Familie während des Holocaust*. Munich: Buchendorfer Verlag, 2001.

Steger, Bernd. "Der Hitlerprozeß und Bayerns Verhältnis zum Reich 1923/24." *Vierteljahrshefte für Zeitgeschichte* 25 (1977): 441–66.

Sternsdorf-Hauck, Christiane. *Brotmarken und rote Fahnen: Frauen in der bayerischen Revolution und Räterepublik*. Frankfurt am Main: isp-Verlag, 1989.

Straus, Rahel. *Wir lebten in Deutschland: Erinnerungen einer deutschen Jüdin 1880–1933*. Stuttgart: Deutscher-Verlags-Anstalt, 1962.

Stürmer, Michael, Gabriele Teichmann, and Wilhelm Treue. *Wägen und Wagen: Sal. Oppenheim jr. & Cie: Geschichte einer Bank und einer Familie*. Munich: Piper, 1994.

Terpitz, Olaf. "Simon Dubnow und seine Übersetzer." In *Transit und Transformation: Osteuropäisch-jüdische Migranten in Berlin 1918–1939*, edited by Verena Dohrn and Gertrud Pickhan, 114–35. Göttingen: Wallstein-Verlag, 2010.

Tharaud, Jerome, and Jean Tharaud. *Die Herrschaft Israels*. Vienna: Amalthea, 1927.

Thoß, Bruno. *Der Ludendorff-Kreis 1919–1923: München als Zentrum der mitteleuropäischen Gegenrevolution zwischen Revolution und Hitler-Putsch*. Munich: Wölfle, 1978.

———. "Weißer Terror, 1919." Historisches Lexikon Bayerns, September 11, 2012. https://www.historisches-lexikon-bayerns.de/Lexikon/Weißer_Terror,_1919 (accessed September 19, 2018).

Tiedemann, Eva Maria. "Erscheinungsformen des Antisemitismus in Bayern am Beispiel der Bayerischen Antisemitischen Volkspartei und ihrer Nachfolgeorganisationen." In *Geschichte und Kultur der Juden in Bayern: Aufsätze*, edited by Manfred Treml and Josef Kirmeier, 387–96. Munich: Haus der Bayerischen Geschichte, 1988.

Toller, Ernst. "Die Wandlung." In Toller, *Gesammelte Werke*, vol. 2, edited by John M. Spalek and Wolfgang Frühwald. Munich: Hanser 1978.

———. *Eine Jugend in Deutschland*. In Toller, *Gesammelte Werke*, vol. 2, edited by Wolfgang Frühwald and John M. Spalek. Munich: Hanser, 1978.

———. *I Was a German*, translated by Edward Crankshaw. London: John Lane/Bodley Head, 1934.

———. *Seven Plays*, translated by Edward Crankshaw. London: John Lane, 1935.

Toury, Jacob, *Die politischen Orientierungen der Juden*. Tübingen: Mohr Siebeck, 1966.

Trebitsch-Lincoln, Ignaz. *Der größte Abenteurer des XX. Jahrhunderts!? Die Wahrheit über mein Leben*. Leipzig: Amalthea-Verlag, 1931.

———. *The Autobiography of an Adventurer*, translated by Emile Burns. New York: H. Holt & Co., 1932.

Treitschke, Heinrich von. "Unsere Aussichten." *Preußische Jahrbücher* 44 (1879): 559–76.

Ude, Christian. "Leben und Nachleben des bayerischen Ministerpräsidenten Kurt Eisner." *Münchner Beiträge zur Jüdischen Geschichte und Kultur* 1 (2008): 9–29.

Ullrich, Volker. *Ascent: 1889–1939*, vol. 1 of *Adolf Hitler*. New York: Alfred A. Knopf, 2016.

Vatlin, Alexander. "Weltrevolutionär im Abseits: Der Kommissar der bayerischen Räterepublik Tobias Axelrod." *Vierteljahrshefte für Zeitgeschichte* 62 (April 2014): 515–36.

Veidlinger, Jeffrey. *In the Midst of Civilized Europe: The Pogroms of 1918–1921 and the Onset of the Holocaust*. New York: Metropolitan Books, 2021.

Verein jüdischer Hochschüler Bar Kochba in Prag, ed. *Vom Judentum: Ein Sammelbuch*. Leipzig: K. Wolff, 1913.

Volk, Ludwig. *Akten Kardinal Michael von Faulhabers, 1917–1945*, vol 1. Mainz: Matthias-Grünewald-Verlag, 1975.

Volkert, Wilhelm, ed. *Ludwig Thoma: Sämtliche Beiträge aus dem "Miesbacher Anzeiger" 1920/21*. Munich: Piper, 1989.

Wachsmann, Alfred. "Hitler wurde in Bayern nicht allzu ernst genommen." In *Vergangene Tage: Jüdische Kultur in München*, edited by Hans Lamm, 387–91. Munich: Langen Müller, 1982.

Wadler, Arnold. *Der Turm von Babel: Urgemeinschaft der Sprachen*. Basel: Geering, 1935.

Walser Smith, Helmut. *Die Geschichte des Schlachters: Mord und Antisemitismus in einer deutschen Kleinstadt*. Göttingen: Wallstein-Verlag, 2002.

———. "When Was Adolf Hitler? Deconstructing Hitler's Narratives of Autobiographical Authenticity." *German Yearbook of Contemporary History* 3 (2018): 59–70.

Walter, Dirk. *Antisemitische Kriminalität und Gewalt: Judenfeindschaft in der Weimarer Republik*. Bonn: Dietz, 1999.

Wassermann, Jakob. *Mein Weg als Deutscher und Jude*. Berlin: S. Fischer, 1921.

———. *My Life as German and Jew*, translated by S. N. Brainin. New York: Coward-McCann, 1933.

Wasserstein, Bernard. *The Secret Lives of Trebitsch Lincoln*. New Haven, CT: Yale University Press, 1988.

Weber, Thomas. *Becoming Hitler*. Oxford: Oxford University Press, 2017.

———. *Wie Adolf Hitler zum Nazi wurde: Vom unpolitischen Soldaten zum Autor von "Mein Kampf."* Berlin: Propyläen Verlag, 2016.

Weidermann, Volker. *Träumer: Als die Dichter die Macht übernahmen*. Cologne: Kiepenheuer & Witsch, 2017.

Weigand, Katharina, ed. *Münchner Historiker zwischen Politik und Wissenschaft: 150 Jahre Historisches Seminar der Ludwig-Maximilians-Universität*. Munich: Utz, 2010.

Weigl, Michael. *Das Bayernbild der Repräsentanten Österreichs in München 1918–1938: Die diplomatische und konsularische Berichterstattung vor dem Hintergrund der bayerisch-österreichischen Beziehungen*. Frankfurt am Main: Lang, 2005.

Weil, Martin. *A Pretty Good Club: The Founding Fathers of the US Foreign Service*. New York: W. W. Norton, 1978.

Weisz, Christoph. "Die Revolution von 1918 im historischen und politischen Denken Münchener Historiker." In *Bayern im Umbruch: Die Revolution von 1918, ihre Voraussetzungen, ihr Verlauf und ihre Folgen*, edited by Karl Bosl, 535–78. Munich: Oldenbourg, 1969.

Wertheimer, Jack. *Unwelcome Strangers: East European Jews in Imperial Germany*. New York: Oxford University Press, 1987.

Weyl, Gerda. "Eisner, Kurt." In *Encyclopedia Judaica*, vol. 6, column 378. Berlin: Eshkol, 1930.

Willstätter, Richard. "Die Geschichte meines Rücktritts." In *Vergangene Tage: Jüdische Kultur in München*, edited by Hans Lamm, 412–19. Munich: Langen Müller, 1982.

Winkler, Heinrich August. *Age of Catastrophe*, translated by Stewart Spencer. New Haven, CT: Yale University Press, 2015.

———. *1933–1990*, vol. 2 of *Germany: The Long Road West*. Oxford: Oxford University Press, 2006.

Wirsching, Andreas. "Hitlers Authentizität: Eine funktionalistische Deutung." *Vierteljahrshefte für Zeitgeschichte* 64, no. 3 (2016): 387–417.

Wistrich, Robert S. *Demonizing the Other*. London: Routledge, 1999.

———. *Revolutionary Jews from Marx to Trotsky*. London: Harrap, 1976.

Wolf, Hubert. *Pope and Devil: The Vatican's Archives and the Third Reich*. Cambridge, MA: Harvard University Press, 2010.

Wolf, Siegbert: "'. . . der Geist ist die Gemeinschaft, die Idee ist der Bund': Gustav Landauers Judentum." *Schriften der Erich-Mühsam-Gesellschaft* 21 (2002): 85ff.

Wolin, Richard. "Reflections on Jewish Secular Messianism." In Wolin, *Labyrinths: Explorations in the Critical History of Ideas*, 43–54. Amherst: University of Massachusetts Press, 1995.

Yerushalmi, Yosef Hayim. *Freuds Moses: Endliches und unendliches Judentum*. Frankfurt am Main: Fischer-Taschenbuch-Verlag, 1999.

———. *Freud's Moses: Judaism Terminable and Interminable*. New Haven, CT: Yale University Press, 1991.

Zadoff, Mirjam. *Der rote Hiob: Das Leben des Werner Scholem*. Munich: Hanser, 2014.

———. "Shades of Red: Biografik auf den Barrikaden." *Jahrbuch des Simon-Dubnow-Instituts* 16 (2017): 273–98.

Zadoff, Noam. *Gershom Scholem: From Berlin to Jerusalem and Back*. Waltham: Brandeis University Press, 2018.

Ziegler, Walter. "Kardinal Faulhaber im Meinungsstreit: Vorwürfe, Kritik, Verehrung, Bewunderung." In *Kardinal Michael von Faulhaber 1869–1952: Eine Ausstellung des Archivs des Erzbistums München und Freising, des Bayerischen Hauptstaatsarchivs und des Stadtarchivs München zum 50. Todestag, 6. Juni bis 28. Juli 2002*, 64–93. Munich: Generaldirektion der Staatlichen Archive Bayerns; Archiv des Erzbistums München und Freising, 2002.

Zuber, Brigitte. "Im Netz bayerischer Eliten: Schaltstellen zwischen Wirtschaft, Staat, Kirche, und Paramilitär 1916 bis 1933." In *Wegbereiter des Nationalsozialismus: Personen, Organisationen, und Netzwerke der extremen Rechten zwischen 1918 und 1933*, edited by Daniel Schmidt et al., 143–60. Essen: Klartext, 2015.

INDEX